TRAVEL
&LEISURE

London

by Erika Lederman

Macmillan • USA

MACMILLAN TRAVEL
A Simon & Schuster Macmillan Company
1633 Broadway
New York, NY 10019

Find us online at **http://www.mgr.com/travel** or on
America Online at Keyword: **Frommer's**

ISBN: 0-02-860694-9
ISSN: 1086-4040

Editor: Cheryl Farr
Production Editor: Trudy Brown
Digital Cartography by Ortelius Design
Design by Amy Peppler-Adams, designLab—Seattle
All illustrations by Ray Skibinski

SPECIAL SALES
Bulk purchases (10+ copies) of Frommer's and selected
Macmillan travel guides are available to corporations,
organizations, institutions, and charities at special discounts,
and can be customized to suit individual needs. For more
information write to: Special Sales, Macmillan General
Reference, 1633 Broadway, New York, NY 10019.

Manufactured in Singapore

CONTENTS

List of Maps

About the Author
Erika Lederman was born in New York City. In 1991, after 6 years in the contemporary art market (watching it go from boom to bust), she left New York for Tokyo. What a surprise it was to learn that there were other places to live in this world—even if they didn't have a 24-hour Korean deli and a nail salon on every corner—that she could love just as much as she adored New York City! Erika worked for two years in Japan covering the contemporary art and culture scene for *Conde Nast Traveler* and Tokyo-based publications, then spent the next two in London, where she worked as London Correspondent for *Travel & Leisure*. She currently lives in Hong Kong.

Acknowledgments
The author would like to thank Emma Harding, who provided invaluable help in researching this project. Other researchers include Christina Jeager and Sarah Hamilton. The British Tourist Association was helpful with advice and information, and I am grateful for the opinionated views of Craig Markham of the Firmdale Hotels.

An Additional Note
Please be advised that travel information is subject to change at any time—and this is especially true of prices. We therefore suggest that you write or call ahead for confirmation when making your travel plans. The author, editor, and publisher cannot be held responsible for the experiences of readers while traveling. Your safety is important to us, however, so we encourage you to stay alert and be aware of your surroundings. Keep a close eye on cameras, purses, and wallets, all favorite targets of thieves and pickpockets.

INTRODUCING
LONDON

To the visitor from the New World, London is a jumble of antiquities, a labyrinthine junk store with finds at every corner. When I first arrived, I found myself exploring every mews and alleyway I happened upon. And I remember being quite smug about my first apartment. "It's pre-war," I proclaimed to all who would listen. "Which war?" was the regular amused reply. Years later, I continue to be awed; it seems that every house is the birthplace of someone famous or the scene of an invention, each corner the site of an important speech, a battle, or an especially vile crime.

Londoners' attitudes toward their own city can be puzzling. There is a defiant defensiveness in the proclamation "I love New York." Londoners are cooler and more detached; but when provoked, they reveal how deeply and unalterably in love they are with their city—even if it is a love sustained by a rosy view of the past.

The city grew from the river. The Thames was its first thoroughfare, its lifeline and its means of social irrigation. Because the first route to London was up the river, successive waves of immigrants—Italians, Jews, Huguenots, Bangladeshi, and many others—settled in what became known as the "East End," a series of waterside working-class communities that has nurtured its own culture, patois, and social mores (as well as inspiring a television soap opera). They settled in the east because, being foreigners, they had been barred in times past from entering the City itself. Yet there were immigrants in London from the beginning; Romans founded a settlement here nearly 2,000 years ago.

When Londoners talk about "the City," they mean the area that the Romans originally walled (it still vestigially is) and called "Londinium," and which covers no more than one square mile between Tower Bridge and Blackfriars Bridge. The Lord Mayor of London

Tower Bridge

represents only this square mile, and its streets are patrolled by the separate City Police. The City is the Wall Street of Britain; it does not include the famous shopping streets or theater district. It's an entity unto itself, parochial yet worldly, with its own rituals and customs, and a preoccupation with bulls and bears and commodity prices.

The larger, sprawling city we call London is governed not from the City but from the town halls of its more than 30 boroughs. Britain is governed not from the City but from Westminster, a mile upriver. Westminster, once a small city, too, now takes in Covent Garden, Soho, the theater district, and the main shopping streets of central London. Because of its geographical relationship with the original walled City, the modern city center is known as the "West End."

While the City remained fiercely independent and introspective, Westminster was the royal seat; for that, London has good reason to be grateful. The royal residences of Westminster (St. James's, Buckingham Palace, and Clarence House) are joined to that of Kensington (Kensington Palace) by a long swathe of royal parks. You can walk miles across the city—through St. James's Park, Green Park, Hyde Park, and Kensington Gardens—and be surrounded by greenery at all times. With Holland Park, Regent's Park, and the Georgian and Victorian squares of Bloomsbury, Chelsea, and Kensington, London has a remarkably green inner city.

Born from two separate cities on the river, modern London is, not surprisingly, a complex patchwork of villages. To anyone from outside, Chelsea is probably the most familiar district name in the capital. It's also a neighborhood that perfectly demonstrates London's enigmatic charm, contriving to be grand and, at the same time, a pristine village. It has been smart, then bohemian; it's now both, and richer than ever. It has London's most discreet streets, yet its main thorough-fare, King's Road—if no longer quite as outré as it was in the 1960s, its hippie heyday—remains bereft of cau-tion. The district is always unmistakably Chelsea, yet, like London itself, it has many moods.

The changes of mood can be sudden. South Ken-sington has some of the trendiest boutiques and wealthi-est streets in Britain, North Kensington some of the poorest. Yet deprivation has not bred dullness, nor iso-lation. Take Brixton, south of the river. Less than a ghetto (despite occasional tensions), it has an amazing market brimming with yams, saltfish, West Indian bread, and, for some strange reason, wigs. And why not?

In recent decades, the underground railway lines, rather than the river, have influenced where people settled. Parts of South London became places of cheap housing when they were ignored by the underground systems; but when the new Victoria line went south in 1969, these neighborhoods suddenly became attractive to a new generation of young, professional people who no longer wished to live out in the suburbs. The con-temporary equivalent was the 1980s boom in London's Docklands (which, a decade later, is only beginning to take off). Gentrification has also taken place in several districts that were originally enclaves for a flood of im-migrants. Notting Hill is a good example: Here the Portuguese, Spanish, and Caribbean communities exist side by side with media trendies. Microwavable Chicken Tikka is now one of the best sellers in the terribly middle-class Marks & Spencer food market. The social classes are as identifiable in London as they are any-where else in Britain, but nowhere else do they so readily live side by side.

Strangers get lost in London. So do Londoners (who, I am convinced, have not the slightest idea of direc-tion—try asking whether a landmark is north or south!)—unless, of course, they are taxi drivers. This is a city where it is truly a delight to lose oneself; indeed, that's the best way to see the city. This is not a city for people who are afraid of getting lost, who believe that every city should be built as a piece, at a single stroke, to a well-ordered plan. London, bless its heart, was not built for efficiency. Explore and enjoy.

London Today

Whether you're hanging out in chi-chi Chelsea, trendy Notting Hill, or leafy Hampstead, every village of the sprawling metropolis that is London has its "high street" and its own individual flavor. This is a city of contrasts, where office blocks throw shadows on the daily milk truck that still makes its rounds.

Here's the good news: London has a transport system that covers most corners of the city (and now offers direct access to the continent via the Channel Tunnel). By the end of the century, three new tube lines are set to be completed. While it can be insufferably hot and crowded, and very often delayed (or on strike), the Tube invariably gets you where you are going.

Eating in London is no longer a compromising experience. With it's trio of Michelin-rated 3-star restaurants, gastronomic London has made a name for itself on the world dining stage. And "Swinging London" is here again—there's a renewed interest in London's young designers. Liz Tilberis of the U.S. fashion bible *Harpers Bazaar* was at the front of the American press pack last year when it arrived en masse to cover London's Fashion Week. The contemporary art scene is also drawing international attention. Whether or not you go for Damien Hirst's lamb in formaldehyde, the massive media coverage that accompanies his shows and draws attention to the scene can't be denied. And Goldsmith's College and the Royal College of Art are churning out graduates whose works are increasingly adorning the walls of international galleries.

Everyone here gets healthcare under the NHS (National Health Service); the majority of Londoners see their local general practitioner without spending a penny. Even if it does take years on a waiting list to treat that gangrened foot, a Londoner can expect some of the best healthcare in Europe. And, if indeed you do get into Oxford or Cambridge, there's no need for your parents to take out a 2nd mortgage on the house—grants cover tuition and most expenses.

The London "bobby" continues to prowl the streets without regularly carrying firearms. And then of course there's the Royal Mail—any American would be impressed. First-class post mailed from within the United Kingdom arrives the next day, and the early morning mail is followed by an afternoon delivery.

But London is plagued by bomb scares, labor strife, terrible traffic, racism, and political scandal. In 1986, losing her patience with a Labour-dominated Greater London Council, Margaret Thatcher had it abolished. There's now no citywide governing body overseeing London (think of NYC without its Mayor); as a result, many public services have fallen victim to a bureaucratic tangle of borough councils and committees with no central governing body. Lack of centralization has meant that most building development projects are dominated by economically motivated private interests. The Docklands, conceived in the early 1980s, is a testament to improper planning and rampant greed. Once the largest inner-city building projects in Europe, inadequate transportation access and empty office blocks forced many of the developers to seek relief in the bankruptcy courts. Only now, a decade later, is the project finally achieving some degree of solvency.

London struggles to shelter its homeless, and there are long waiting lists for public housing. Beggars, a recent development, are a now daily reality. The arts suffer badly from cuts in public subsidies and there have been no contemporary grand cultural monuments comparable to Paris's Glass Pyramid or National Library; London has been preoccupied dismantling its governing body and Prince Charles is too busy criticizing contemporary architecture.

But change is afoot. In 1995, the National Lottery was inaugurated, and its funds are being funneled into the arts and charities. It's estimated that two-thirds of the adult population participates weekly; as a result, the art world is set to benefit generously. Already, institutions are clamoring for priority. The Royal Opera House in Covent Garden (with plans for an extensive renovation and expansion) and the Tate Gallery's Bankside project (a new contemporary art museum on the South Bank in a former power station) are looking for handouts; even the Church has joined the queue. All is not rosy, though; the British tabloids, quick to seize upon the "life-is-unfair" element of any story, are stirring up controversy by suggesting that it is "working men and women" who spend their hard-earned pennies on lottery tickets, only the "rich toffs" benefit (presumably only "rich toffs" attend opera and art exhibitions). Meanwhile, West End theater and cinema owners are lobbying to move the Saturday draw to Sunday, citing dramatic audience drainage as the hopeful stay home to watch the lottery results on the telly.

While London remains part of the powerful financial world trinity that includes New York and Tokyo, a spate of foreign buyouts of some of the oldest and most revered English firms has taken control away from the City and placed it into the hands of European and American institutions. Barings, the Queen's bank, was sent asunder by a rogue trader (as all the world knows) and is now under Dutch ownership. S. G. Warburg, Kleinwort Benson, and Smith New Court have been the most recent victims. The Lloyd's names, once the most prestigious group of investors in Britain, are now in settlement negotiations with underwriting syndicates after loosing millions of pounds in recent years. Suddenly, some of London's oldest families are covering their losses by selling the family silver and titles. The market for an ancient lordship of the manor has plummeted by 40%.

Political scandals—most of which revolve around issues of sex—continue to flourish, perhaps because Victorian standards of morality are still pushed by a cynical press. Each year promises a fresh batch of salacious stories and proffered resignations; 1994 was a banner year. In addition to the usual affairs and illegitimate offspring, one Conservative MP was found dead in his home in London, having "died from asphyxiation while engaging in a form of sexual gratification involving self-strangulation and the inhalation of stimulants." Hmmm.

Even outside the bedroom, politics in London are never dull. The Tory Party has recently emerged from the brink of crisis. Prime Minister John Major, plagued by attacks within his own party—the most ferocious coming from Margaret Thatcher—challenged his colleagues to "put up or shut up." A party leadership contest was staged, which Major won, but the seeds of dissent have been planted. The main issues have been fought between the "Euro-sceptics" and the more moderate European Community factions, with the debate over a common European Currency getting particularly heated. Meanwhile, the Labour Party's Tony Blair continues to charm the Liberals, making the Conservative infighting extremely untimely—for the conservatives.

An Overview of London

While Central London doesn't formally define itself, most Londoners today would probably accept the

Underground's Circle line as a fair boundary. The city center is customarily divided into two areas, the City and the West End. These are surrounded first by Inner London, and then by the sprawling hinterland of Outer London.

You'll find the greatest number of hotels in the west, in inner districts such as Kensington, Chelsea, and Victoria, and in the West End—the area that most Londoners regard as the real city center by virtue of its shops, restaurants, and theaters. Even though the City is jeweled with historic sights, the original 1-square-mile area is primarily a business district.

In much the way that the City is a buffer to the east, so is the river to the south. The Barbican Centre in the City and the South Bank Arts Centre across the river were both conscious attempts to extend the geographical spread of Central London's nocturnal life, but it really fades in the City and only half-heartedly crosses the Thames. Many Londoners are disinclined to cross the river, much like New Yorkers who never go to Brooklyn.

In the past, many "south-of-the-river" districts closer to London have had little to recommend themselves to visitors, but some now fashionable residential enclaves have spawned a number of excellent restaurants in recent years, and gentrification is accelerating. The Millennium project includes plans for a new Tate Gallery Bankside Museum of Contemporary Art that should rival Paris's Pompidou; for the construction of a footbridge that will connect St. Paul to the South Bank and the recently completed Shakespeare's Globe Theatre; and for the development of a green walkway that will link these projects to the already developed Butler's Wharf area. Nevertheless, there's only one recommended tourist hotel at present south of the river, and not many more east of Tower Bridge. So visitors generally stick to the center, the north, or the west.

This brief rundown of London districts should help you orient yourself:

The Main Areas
The City
London began here, with the fortified Roman settlement founded in the 1stC AD. **St. Paul's Cathedral** is the centerpiece of a 1-square-mile area rich in historical, architectural, and social interest that retains its identity, influence, and unique form of self-government.

Today, "the City" is shorthand for money; this is where the great banking, insurance, and commodity trading concerns are based. During the day, more than 300,000 people work here, but at night and on weekends it can be a concrete and glass desert. It may be best to visit the City on a weekend, when it's easier to enjoy the hidden, almost secret places that give the area its appeal. Be warned, though: It can be hard to find an open pub or restaurant. Even the famous Wren churches are often closed on Sunday—the best time to visit them is weekday lunch times.

The City doesn't easily yield up its past. The Great Fire of 1666, the bombs of 1940, the IRA bombs of the early 1990s, and the zeal of modern developers have swept away much of the old. In its place is what seems a haphazard collection of office buildings, for the most part demonstrating the poverty of modern architecture. The City does have its own unique geography, though, with fascinating nooks and crannies.

To an astonishing extent, the City retains elements of its medieval character. Within the area bounded by the old walls (the gates were at Ludgate, Newgate, Aldersgate, Cripplegate, Bishopsgate, and Aldgate), you can easily work out what was where. Cheapside, for example, with the surrounding Milk, Poultry, and Bread streets, marks the site of the main market.

The Guildhall is still the City's parliament, and **Mansion House** the palace of its head, the Lord Mayor. He's selected annually by a complex system based on ancient privileges rather than mere residence. City livery companies, descended from medieval trade guilds, have an important part to play in choosing and providing the aldermen and sheriffs from whom the Lord Mayor must come. The liveries still have their own halls, their own constitutions, and their own regalia, even though they're hardly connected with their original trades. The City still has its own police force (look at the badges on the helmets—they're different from those elsewhere in London), and on royal ceremonial occasions the monarch won't enter the City unless greeted on its borders by the Lord Mayor.

In 1993, in response to a wave of terrorism, a series of stringent measures were taken to ensure security: Many City streets have been closed to traffic, and buildings which were once open to the public viewing now strictly control entry. Livery company halls don't have regular opening hours and will admit visitors only on open days. For information, contact the **City**

of London Information Centre, St Paul's Churchyard, EC4 (☎ 0171/332-1456).

The West End

Unlike the City, the West End has no precise borders,
but is divided by its main thoroughfares into clearly
defined neighborhoods. Simply by crossing the street
it's possible to leave behind a neighborhood of one quite
distinct character and enter what seems to be another
world.

Mayfair is the neighborhood of exclusive hotels,
expense-account restaurants, embassies, haute couture
houses, and casinos. Its "high" shopping street is Bond
Street, which is currently going through a very stylish
revival.

Soho is seductive not for its sex stores—which are
no more or less inviting than those in other cities—but
for its delicatessens, patisseries, moderately priced restaurants, and outdoor cafés as well as its gossipy
confluence of Italian waiters, Cockney editors, lengthy
lunchers, and other miscreants. Its trendiness has long
attracted media folk. Across Shaftesbury Avenue,
Soho's cosmopolitanism hardens into Chinatown.

Covent Garden, despite the misgivings of purists,
has proved to be one of the most successful examples
anywhere of the regeneration of a discarded facility. This
wholesale fruit-and-vegetable market has been turned
into a great area for entertainment, strolling, eating,
and shopping, albeit one mostly geared to tourists.
The most fiercely community-conscious of all the
inner city areas, it has come to stand for everything
opposed to big business and development.

Bloomsbury, with its bookish dignity, is home to
the British Museum and the nucleus of London University, whose visitors and students find peace in its many
green squares.

Belgravia is the most elegant part of the West End,
with its early 19thC houses and the beautiful gardens
of Belgrave Square (from which the neighborhood takes
its name). The area today is dominated by embassies as
well as the homes of the very wealthy. Belgravia's "neighborhood shop" is Harrod's. Just around the corner is
Knightsbridge.

St. James's is gentlemen's clubland, with Jermyn
Street as its shopping thoroughfare. The name is broadly
applied to the neighborhood around St. James's Street
and St. James's Square, on the hill running down from
Piccadilly to St. James's Palace, constituting an area that

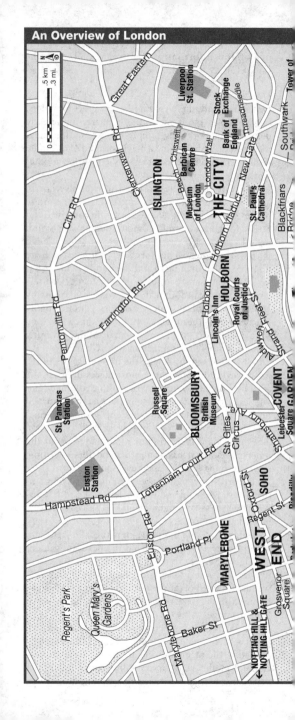

An Overview of London

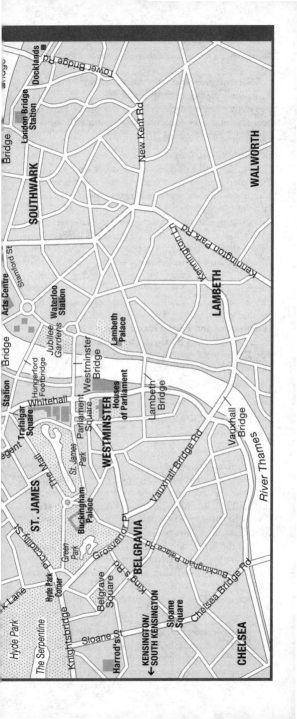

has perhaps changed less than any other over the last 50 years.

Westminster is media shorthand for Parliament. Apart from Westminster Abbey, all the dominant buildings in this area are dedicated to government. There are no shops and very few residents—just a rich seam of pomp and circumstance.

Beyond the West End

Beyond Central London, several inner districts make their own unique contributions to metropolitan life. The most obvious are **Kensington,** with its famous museums, which extends to Notting Hill and Portobello Road, eventually giving way to Hammersmith, which has a few respected theaters; and elegant and fashionable **Chelsea,** with its boutiques and restaurants, which spills over into Fulham.

In the north, **Islington** has emerged as the outstanding example of the arty rejuvenation of London's old working-class inner boroughs; **Primrose Hill** is another quaint village. Also in the north is intellectual **Hampstead** and **Highgate.** Maritime **Greenwich** is to the east, villagey **Dulwich** to the south, and riverside **Richmond** to the west. All of these are, to varying degrees, outer districts, although London stretches even further beyond them, in an exhausting sprawl of 1930s-era suburbs.

London's Districts A to Z

Battersea

British Rail from Waterloo or Victoria.

Little remains of the old Thameside village of Battersea, now part industrial sprawl and part gentrified residential area. The dominant—and increasingly admired—landmark is Sir Giles Gilbert Scott's vast **Battersea Power Station,** brick-built in the modern, monumental style of the 1930s. Sir Nikolaus Pevsner thought it "one of the first examples in England of a frankly contemporary industrial architecture." Any baby-boomer approaching from Chelsea will immediately recognize the 4 chimneys, deified on the cover of Pink Floyd's *Animals* in 1977. It's a sad but still proud shell.

Belgravia

Tube: Hyde Park Corner, Knightsbridge, Sloane Sq., Victoria.

London's most magnificent terraces make up the great squares of Belgravia, developed in a frenzy of activity following the establishment of nearby Buckingham Palace as the royal residence in the 1820s. **Belgrave Square** is the centerpiece of the fairly regular plan, with its massive, classically decorated blocks and grand corner houses surrounding private sunken gardens. **Eaton Square,** to the south, is a long rectangle, with the King's Road running through the middle of its stuccoed terraces. To the south is **Chester Square;** some find it the most appealing of the three.

Blackheath
British Rail from Charing Cross.

As its name suggests, Blackheath was a grim place before it became a fashionable country address in the 18thC. This refreshingly open, high clearing southeast of Greenwich, near the royal residences of **Greenwich** and **Eltham Palace,** is now surrounded by the fine, elegantly unadorned classical houses of the age.

Bloomsbury
Tube: Euston, Russell Sq., Holborn.

Bloomsbury was an inconspicuous residential area when Virginia and Leonard Woolf, Roger Fry, Lytton Strachey, and Maynard Keynes made it their fortress from 1904–39. Before long, the likes of T.S. Eliot, Bertrand Russell, and D.H. Lawrence were drawn to the center of the action, even if they didn't agree with "The Group."

Now world-famous as the literary heartland of London, Bloomsbury boasts some of the city's most beautiful squares. It's also home to a host of publishing companies, **London University,** and the **British Museum.**

The University has buildings throughout Bloomsbury, the best of which is the original **University College** in Gower Street, a splendid classical building (1827–29). The **Senate House** in Malet Street is an essay in 1930s classicism. Also here is the **Percival David Foundation of Chinese Art.** Looming over Bloomsbury, the **British Telecom Tower** (1964) in Cleveland Street is a familiar landmark.

Chelsea
Tube: South Kensington, Sloane Sq.

Many hold Chelsea to be London's quintessential "village," and it has long been the most fashionable district in the capital. On the one hand, the pretty, well-maintained houses in its quiet streets retain the feel of an elegant country village; by contrast, the King's Road is outré, noisy, and bohemian in a way no other place can imitate.

Only in the later 18thC did this quiet village at the river's edge become a part of London. But apart from the Charles II–commissioned **Royal Hospital** and the **Chelsea Physic Garden** (a delightful place to take a stroll and tea), little remains of old Chelsea. The area around **Cheyne Walk** includes the few remaining old houses, such as **Lindsey House** and **Carlyle's House.** Most of Chelsea's housing dates from the 19thC; some of it is very grand, and some mere artisans' cottages (now quite sought after).

In the late 1800s, Chelsea became known as an artists' colony. Pre-Raphaelites such as Rossetti, Burne-Jones, and Morris lived here; Whistler settled here, quarreling with Oscar Wilde, who lived in Tite Street; Americans Henry James and Jack London were attracted to the area. Everywhere you look, blue plaques mark the former abodes of the famous. After World War II, the avant-garde again made this their home. Angry young men like John Osborne grabbed attention at the **Royal Court Theatre** in 1956, artists crowded into **Finch's** pub on Fulham Road, and Mary Quant began selling clothes in King's Road, which became a major center for cult fashion.

On the Chelsea/Fulham border is **Chelsea Harbour,** a luxury development of apartments and restaurants with a private marina. Driving by the Chelsea Harbour Club, you'll often see paparazzi perched on ladders, trying to get a shot of Di entering or exiting the exclusive gym.

Chiswick

Tube: Turnham Green.

Along the main western routes out of the capital, parts of the old riverside village of Chiswick survive. You'll find a still and dreamy quarter by turning sharp left onto Church Street at the monster Hogarth Roundabout, where the Great West Road traffic is forced to pause. Whistler and Hogarth are buried in the churchyard at **St. Nicholas.** The mall along the Thames has some beautiful riverside homes and charming pubs that offer some of the best river views in the area—if you can get a seat. On Great West Road are **Hogarth's House** and **Chiswick House.**

The City: East

Tube: Monument, Tower Hill.

The City to the east of an invisible line running from **London Bridge** to Liverpool Street Station is dominated by the great maritime trading interests. Until the

19thC, almost all trade goods were brought ashore here. A number of fine Wren–designed churches (and a few surviving older ones) are also here. The Richard Rogers–designed **Lloyd's** building (1986) at 1 Lime St. continues to rank as London's most controversial and innovative building. In the southeast corner is the **Tower of London.** Just to the north is **Trinity Square,** with a well-preserved portion of Roman wall. Over Lower Thames Street is Wren's **Monument,** commemorating the Great Fire of London.

The City: North
Tube: Liverpool St., Barbican, Bank.

The northern part of the City contains a number of important institutions and a great many lesser offices. As a result, it's less suited for strolling than other parts of the City. In the north are the spectacularly redeveloped **Liverpool Street Station,** with its Victorian hotel, and the postwar developments of **Broadgate, London Wall,** and the **Barbican.**

To the south, forming the real center of the City, are the financial and administrative institutions, the **Guildhall,** the **Bank of England,** the **Stock Exchange** (now closed to the public), and the **Royal Exchange.** Next to the Bank of England, look for Wren's **St. Margaret's Lothbury** and **no. 7 Lothbury:** Victorian architecture at its imaginative best. Lothbury leads into Throgmorton Street (the Stock Exchange is on the right), which then becomes Old Broad Street. Here stands the tallest, perhaps most exciting and dramatic of the City's contemporary office buildings, the **National Westminster Bank** tower.

The City: South
Tube: St. Paul's, Mansion House, Cannon St.

This is the central area between **St. Paul's Cathedral** and **London Bridge,** south of Cheapside, Poultry, and Cornhill. Just beyond Queen Street, around Mansion House tube station, are some smaller and older streets, home to some fine Wren churches and livery halls. Facing Upper Thames Street is **Vintners' Hall,** one of the best of the livery halls, built in 1671. Between Cannon Street Station and King William Street (which leads onto **London Bridge**) is yet another fascinating maze of small streets, with several historic pubs and wine bars. Next to London Bridge is the **Fishmongers' Hall** (1831–4), the best-sited and grandest livery company hall, with an imposing Classical facade overlooking the river.

Butler's Wharf   Just across Tower Bridge, on the south side of the river at **Surrey Docks,** the Victorian warehouses of **Butler's Wharf** have been refurbished by Sir Terence Conran to provide offices, workshops, houses, shops, and restaurants. The centerpiece is Conran's Gastrodome; it's also home to the **Design Museum.**

The City: West
Tube: St. Paul's.

Most of the western part of the modern City falls outside the old Roman walled town. Of prime interest are **Fleet Street,** the Inner and Middle **Temple,** and **St. Paul's Cathedral.**

The stretch of riverside to the south of St Paul's is disfigured by the traffic of Upper Thames Street, although **St. Benet's** (1677–83) remains as one of the most delightful and best preserved of Wren's churches. **Ludgate Hill,** site of the medieval "Lud Gate" until 1769, offers the best view of the portico of St. Paul's.

Another of the old roads out of the City passed through Newgate, site of the notorious jail and now the **Old Bailey.** To the north of Holborn Viaduct is **Smithfield,** long the site of the famous medieval St. Bartholomew's Fair, about which Ben Jonson wrote his play in 1614, and the place where Wat Tyler and his rebel peasants confronted Richard II in 1381; Lord Mayor Walworth showed the City's customary independence by simply drawing his sword and killing Tyler.

Covent Garden
Tube: Covent Garden.

London's historic fresh fruit and vegetable market has found new life as a delightful area for wandering, shopping, and eating. Although over recent years new buildings have eaten away at the old and the population of the area has fallen, the best buildings remain, and although the trendy shops and bars have brought a huge influx of mainly young tourists, the district retains the earthy feel of old London, with some tasteful modern patronage.

The present market buildings appeared in 1828–32, with the fine iron and glass canopies added later. In its restored state, the marriage of severe classicism to the more ornate roof creates a stunning effect. Other later market buildings surround the piazza. The best, **Floral Hall** (1858), is a superb example of the iron-and-glass architecture that sprang up after the 1851 Crystal Palace.

The market itself is at its liveliest at lunchtime. To the east of the piazza, Russell Street is lined with fashionable wine bars thick with young ad execs and publishers—not so different from those who congregated in the famous 18thC coffeehouses.

Covent Garden is traditionally London's theater area, and **St. Paul's, Covent Garden** is the actors' church. Russell Street crosses Bow Street; next to Floral Hall is the **Royal Opera House** (1857–58). Russell Street will take you to the **Theatre Royal,** founded in 1663 by Charles II, whose Nell Gwynne was an orange-seller in Covent Garden. The present building (1810–12) is London's most beautiful theater. Covent Garden is also bordered by 2 of London's main theatrical streets; to the south is the **Strand** and, to the west, **St. Martin's Lane.** The northern continuation of St. Martin's Lane is drab Monmouth Street, which leads to **Neal's Yard** and **Neal Street,** with craft stores, vegetarian restaurants, and health-food stores. Housed in a glass-domed building, **Endell Street Place** has craft workshops, a shop, and special exhibitions.

Docklands

Tube: Tower Hill, then Docklands Light Railway.

In 1981, the London Docklands Development Corporation (LDDC) was formed to redevelop Wapping, the Isle of Dogs, the Royal Docks, and Surrey Docks in the largest, the most ambitious scheme of its kind in Europe. Since then, many businesses have moved to the area, including most of the **Fleet Street** newspapers. This 21stC river city in the making has been criticized for being an architectural mishmash that's difficult to live and work in, and it fell into receivership in the early 1990s, but things have started looking up— occupancy is up and a consortium has bought back the site from the banks.

On the Isle of Dogs, the grand and extraordinarily ambitious **Canary Wharf** is intended to be the heart of Docklands. This huge 71-acre site is dominated by a 800-foot-high tower, the tallest building in the United Kingdom, designed by Cesar Pelli. The observation deck is strictly off limits to the public, but there are lots of shops and restaurants in the **Piazza.** The country's largest and best-equipped sports complex, **London Arena**, has opened nearby in Limeharbour. Opposite is the **Docklands Visitor Centre** (☎ 0171/512-3000).

The best way to see Docklands is from the **Docklands Light Railway** (☎ 0171/538-0311).

Suspended 20 feet above the ground for much of its route, it affords panoramic views of the area. The red, white, and blue computer-driven trains look even more like toys than the buildings below.

The LDDC arranges guided tours by bus for groups (☎ 0171/512-3000, ext. 3513), and **Dockland Tours** (☎ 0171/252-0742) offers walking and bus tours with local guides.

Dulwich
British Rail from Victoria to West Dulwich.

Although considerably south of the city center, the village of Dulwich is well worth the short train ride. The charming village, with wooden signposts, broad open spaces, and historic buildings, is a preserved jewel. The unique **Dulwich College** is here.

Greenwich
British Rail from Charing Cross.

It's no longer regarded as the center of the world, despite the continuing primacy of the Greenwich Meridian (0° longitude) and Greenwich Mean Time (GMT), and yet the sheer self-confidence of this easternmost community suggests otherwise. Bold and grand in every way, the city's most spectacular architectural ensemble sweeps down to the river through fine parkland, unifying its splendid buildings in an elegant classicism.

It owes its prominence to its historic position as the capital port of a great seafaring nation; its maritime character will strike you immediately. Dominating the river is the magnificent Baroque **Royal Naval College.** Farther back from the river is the **National Maritime Museum,** in the Queen's House. After the Queen's House, you pass into **Greenwich Park,** where one hill is topped by a Henry Moore statue, others by the **Royal Observatory.** Greenwich has an attractive town center, with wine bars, antique stores, and an excellent weekend market (see "Shopping").

Greenwich is best approached by riverboat; you can also arrive via British Rail or by taking the Docklands Light Railway through the Island of Dogs to the Island Gardens terminus, then walking through the Victorian-tiled Greenwich Footway Tunnel under the Thames.

Hampstead
Tube: Hampstead.

Hampstead Heath's high and hilly grassland, scattered ponds, and dense woodland make this village seem much farther than 4 miles from city center. The village itself still follows the street patterns of an earlier time: Around the hills wind convoluted lanes lined with attractive 19thC and earlier houses, now favored by successful academics, artists, and media folk, who give Hampstead its arty reputation.

The Heath itself stretches across to **Highgate,** some parts wild and open, others enclosed and wooded. To the south is **Parliament Hill,** festooned with kites on weekends and offering a fine view across the dense housing of Kentish Town to the City beyond.

Highgate
Tube: Highgate, Archway.

North of Central London, this twin village of **Hampstead** lies across the Heath and enjoys spectacular views across the city. It takes its name from a tollgate that used to be near its center, and its dizzying height, which is best appreciated by approaching steep **Highgate Hill** or **Highgate West Hill.** The High Street has good 18thC terraced houses, and South Grove on the left leads to the intersection with West Hill and The Grove, with an attractive terrace built around 1700. A plaque commemorates Coleridge, who lived in one of the houses; his tomb is in the aisle of the nearby church of **St. Michael,** an imposing 19thC Gothic edifice with **Highgate Cemetery** behind it.

Kensington & South Kensington
Tube: South Kensington, High Street Kensington.

Pleasant and prosperous, **Kensington** has a few enclaves of ostentatious wealth. The predominant pattern is of good 19thC terraces and villas, large late-Victorian and Edwardian apartment buildings, major shopping streets that include the better department stores, and little roads of classy boutiques and antique stores. Good taste abounds.

In the 17thC, two great houses emerged from the manors scattered among the fields: **Holland House and Park** and **Kensington Palace.** West of the palace is Kensington Palace Road, known as "Millionaires' Row," consisting of grand mansions now largely occupied by embassies; you can explore this private road on foot. Kensington High Street is a busy shopping street. Kensington Church Street runs north from Kensington High Street to Notting Hill Gate; it's lined with many good antique stores and clothes boutiques.

The central part of Kensington, thought of as **South Kensington** (the name of the tube station serving it), is dominated by a complex of museums and colleges set up on land bought with the proceeds from Prince Albert's Great Exhibition, held in Hyde Park in 1851. He's commemorated by the **Albert Memorial** and **Royal Albert Hall.**

The eastern part of Kensington is predominantly residential. Beyond the **Victoria & Albert Museum** is the **Brompton Oratory,** with the shopping center of the Brompton Road beyond, and the incomparable **Harrods** department store. **Walton Street,** just off Draycott Avenue, is lined with wonderful boutiques and shops catering to rich trendies.

Kew
Tube: Kew Gardens; British Rail to Kew Bridge from Waterloo; or riverboat from Westminster pier.

The village, grouped around Kew Green, is the archetype of an English country village—it's about as close to the ideal as you can get. The main reason for coming here, however, is the **Royal Botanic Gardens,** more popularly known simply as Kew Gardens. The greatest scientific institution of its kind in the world, it's also a garden of matchless beauty.

Marylebone
Tube: Baker St., Great Portland St.

During the 18thC, the fashionable West End expanded north to surround the village of St. Marylebone. The streets form a near-perfect grid, with the major ones running north-south from **Regent's Park** toward Oxford Street. Somewhat anonymous in character, it now consists largely of smart houses and apartment blocks, with some busy shopping streets.

Mayfair
Tube: Bond St., Green Park.

The most exclusive of London's "villages," Mayfair smells of wealth, sometimes conspicuous, at other times (this is England, after all) discreet. Nowhere in London will you see more Rolls Royces or diamonds. Mayfair is a roughly square-shaped section of the West End, bordered by Oxford Street, Regent Street, Piccadilly, and Park Lane; within you'll find expensive shops, luxurious hotels, casinos, and homes of the rich.

The development of this area began in about 1700; by 1800 it was filled with squares and terraces. **Grosvenor Square** is the largest, with the **United States Embassy** at its western end; the original houses are gone. **Hanover Square** is the oldest (c. 1715). **Berkeley Square** is best known, thanks to its mythical nightingale.

The shopping streets scattered throughout Mayfair best preserve its reputation for high living. Around **Bond Street** (New and Old) are the best art and antique dealers, and more recently, trendy boutiques; South Molton Street for the younger—and less monied—folks; and North and South Audley streets for the extra-extravagant. Along hilly, elegant Brook, Mount, and Curzon streets are smaller, well established, conspicuously exclusive shops. **Savile Row** has the world's finest gentleman's tailors. Nineteenth century **Shepherd Market** is an enclave of alleyways lined with smart shops and cafes.

Notting Hill & Notting Hill Gate
Tube: Notting Hill Gate, High Street Kensington.

Notting Hill has been a enclave of multi-cultural London ever since the immigrant wave of Caribbeans in the 1950s. These days, it's very hip. The high street is marred by an unfortunate string of 1960s concrete and glass monstrosities, but once north of this busy shopping area, the posh Victorian villas reveal themselves. The hub of Notting Hill action is found along Westbourne Grove. Check out the **Westbourne Grove Public Lavatories,** a blue-tiled public "loo" designed by CZWG Architects in 1993, also housing one of the most over-priced florists in London. Every August, the area hosts the famous **Notting Hill Carnival,** the largest street fair in Europe, featuring Caribbean bands and food stalls.

The spine of **Notting Hill** is **Portobello Road,** lined with antiques stalls every Saturday. The overhead highway acts as an unofficial barrier between the well-heeled yuppies and the immigrant communities, but the continuing demand for a W11 postal code is blurring the boundary.

Just to the south of **Notting Hill Gate** is the tiny enclave of **Hillgate Village,** with mews-style houses painted in candy colors, and quite a few nice restaurants and pubs.

Richmond & Richmond Park
Tube: Richmond.

To the west of London, south of the Thames, this beautiful riverside town is famed for its royal connections. The Palace of Sheen, first occupied by Henry I in 1125, began the royal connection; Henry VII rebuilt it as **Richmond Palace.** Henry died in the palace, as did Elizabeth I in 1603. Charles I was the last king to live there. Very little remains of the great Tudor palace; what's left can be seen on the western side of Richmond Green.

Richmond Hill, to the south, offers one of London's most remarkable views. Preserving this un-spoiled vista over **Marble Hill House** and **Ham House** across the wooded expanse of the Thames Val-ley was a rare triumph of planning control. The view has been painted by Reynolds, Turner, Constable, and other great artists.

Richmond Park is the most telling reminder of Richmond's royal connection; its 2,000 acres comprise the most natural stretch of green land in London. Its rough heath and woodland contain a great variety of native plants, birds, and animals, even protected herds of red and fallow deer. The highest points offer excel-lent views.

St James's

Tube: Piccadilly Circus, Green Park.

Despite being unprotected by conservationists, that strange species known as the English Gentleman sur-vives. Come to St. James's, the most upper class of London's neighborhoods, the area between **St James's Park** and **Piccadilly,** and you'd never know they were a rare breed—for this is their district.

The centerpiece is **St. James's Square,** with a large central garden, and an equestrian statue of William III from 1807 at its center. To the south, running parallel to the park, is **Pall Mall,** a splendid road lined with gentlemen's clubs. **St. James's Palace** is at the west-ern end, with St. James's Street stretching north to Piccadilly, lined with more gentlemen's clubs. St. James's Place leads off to the west toward **Green Park;** mag-nificent **Spencer House** (1756–66) overlooks the park.

St James's is justly famed for its shops, with the most traditional approach to service and quality in London.

Soho

Tube: Piccadilly Circus, Tottenham Court Rd., Leicester Sq.

Every city has its low-life area, of course, but in few are the red lights woven into a texture of such richness and variety as in London's Soho. These densely packed streets in the heart of the West End, bounded by Oxford Street, Regent Street, Shaftesbury Avenue, and Charing Cross Road, are famous for their gloriously cosmopolitan mix of people and trades.

A decade ago, the thriving sex industry threatened to engulf Soho; even the pub where Dylan Thomas used to drink himself into oblivion became a sex cinema. That destruction has now largely been halted: Respectable businesses have returned, and fashionable restaurants and shops prosper; it's also the heart of London's recently expanding cafe society. But Soho wouldn't be Soho without a few sex parlors.

Across Shaftesbury Avenue, a busy street lined with theaters, is London's **Chinatown,** centered on Gerrard Street: small, authentic, and packed with excellent restaurants. But Soho's heart—with marvelous French and Italian delicatessens, together with fine butchers, fish stores, and wine merchants—is farther north, on Brewer, Old Compton, and Berwick streets; the latter is also an excellent open-air fresh food market, becoming more expensive and exotic in Rupert Street, south through Walker Court. To the north of Old Compton Street, Dean, Frith, and Greek streets have fine little restaurants, pubs, and clubs. The British movie industry has its center in Wardour Street. Throughout, blue plaques mark apparently run-down buildings with famous associations: Blake was born in Marshall Street; Chopin gave recitals in Meard Street; and in Frith Street, Marx worked, Baird first demonstrated TV, and Hazlitt died. The northwestern part of Soho has less character: **Carnaby Street** was the mecca of the Swinging Sixties, but now only tourists abound.

Westminster
Tube: Westminster.

Like the City, London's most stately district has remained almost free from residential invasion and is devoted to business—in this case, government. It's dominated by the mother of parliaments at the **Palace of Westminster,** attended by the officialdom of **Whitehall.** Next to Parliament is **Westminster Abbey.**

Parliament Square, an open space created at the time of the building of the Palace of Westminster, is appropriately studded with statues of great statesmen: Disraeli, Palmerston, Abraham Lincoln, Winston Churchill. In front of the abbey is **St. Margaret,** the parish church of the Houses of Parliament, and always a fashionable place for weddings (Pepys, Milton, and Churchill were all married here). In Victoria Street, two important landmarks are **Westminster Cathedral** and **New Scotland Yard,** the Metropolitan Police's modern headquarters.

DINING

Dining Out in London

Formerly the butt of gastronomic jokes, London is no longer a foodie wasteland. Over-boiled vegetables and sticky-sweet rice pudding, once the highlights of the English dining tradition, are still around, but with a little effort you can avoid such fare and eat really well.

Last year, Michelin awarded 3 sets of 3 stars to London restaurants (**La Tante Claire, Chez Nico at Ninety Park Lane,** and **Marco Pierre White: The Restaurant** were the winners), bringing the city in close running with Paris, which boasts 5 3-star eateries (London now actually boasts 4, if you include the **Waterside Inn** in nearby Bray). Dining establishments now open with the same fanfare and expectations that accompany New York openings. Local chefs like Marco Pierre White and Nico Ladenis have achieved celebrity (and attitude) on par with the royals. "Masterchef," a weekly TV cooking competition, is one of Britain's most-watched programs, with championship contestants achieving cult status (one former winner just opened a restaurant). And design has overtaken the restaurant world: Newcomers like **Coast, Mezzo,** and the **Atlantic Bar & Grill** serve up good food in stunning spaces.

In terms of variety, London has some of the best Indian food outside of India, as well as top-notch Chinese. London's wine lists are also offering incredible variety, with a wide choice of Continental bottles, and some from the more interesting vineyards in Australia, New Zealand, South Africa, and America.

Recent years have also seen something of a revival of traditional British cooking. Just as nouvelle cuisine brought French cooking up-to-date, so is British cooking now being reworked, and sausages and faggots are once again fashionable. The omnipresent punk-shorn Gary Rhodes, with his own BBC food series, leads the neotraditionalist pack, performing miracles in the kitchen of the **Greenhouse,** where his stocks simmer for days. Even lowly fish-and-chip stands and pie-and-mash shops, where jellied eel is the stock-in-trade, are experiencing something of a renaissance.

Under the vague rubric of "Modern British," a whole new generation of chefs are incorporating influences from farther afield—particularly Italy, California, and Asia—and creating a contemporary idiom. **Alastair Little** (of his namesake restaurant), Sally Clarke (**Clarke's**), and Stephen Bull (**Fulham Road**) are overseeing serious eateries that won't fail to impress the discriminating foodie.

These days, London seems to be on an offal binge. Some of the trendiest menus in town feature marrow and various innards, with **St. John** in Smithfield being the leader in this department. And while the English are traditionally eager carnivores, oyster bars, seafood menus, and caviarterias are flourishing. Another recent trend has been the conversion of pubs from emporiums of false Victoriana serving suspicious-looking sausage into food-conscious environments where you might actually want to spend some time. **The Eagle** in Farringdon, where farmhouse tables and fresh Mediterranean-style food has replaced the standard decor and pub grub, was the first of these conversions; **The Cow** and **The Engineer** followed in suit.

The fashion of dinner as theater, with huge restaurants seating over 200, continues, with brand leader Sir Terence Conran (**Quaglino's, Le Pont de la Tour,** and **Mezzo**) joined by **Belgo Centraal** and Bruno Loubet's **L'Odeon.** These new giants dramatically alter the character of dinner on the town—table hopping and loud banter are the modus operandi, and the vibe is certainly one of "see and be seen."

The most encouraging trend is London's slowly developing cafe society. Stroll down Frith Street in Soho and you'll see Londoners doing the Paris thing *en plein air.* This has riled up the Westminster City Council, which has been known to pull chairs out from under unsuspecting diners. A compromise is sure to be reached.

Finally, be sure to check out one or two of London's in-store eateries. Trendy shopping outlets are opening up dining emporiums at a fast rate. Some of the better ones are **Nicole's** at Nicole Fahri,

Emporio Armani, L'Express, and **Joe's Cafe** in Joseph.

Choosing a Restaurant

Since central London has at least 7,000 restaurants, you'd think there'd be enough tables to go around. But the top restaurants are often booked days in advance, so it's advisable to make reservations. Lunch is usually served from 12 to 2:30pm and dinner from 7 to 10:30pm, though some restaurants, such as **Le Caprice,** the **Atlantic,** and **Quaglino's,** serve after 11:30pm. Many restaurants around the theater district have special pre- and post-theater menus; **Four Seasons** even promises to feed you from their 2- or 3-course menu and get you on your way within an hour.

The bad news is that dinner at London's better restaurants will rarely cost you less than £30 a head, out-pricing the equivalent meal in New York by almost 30%. That said, there are bargains to be had, especially if you opt for better pub fare or an ethnic meal. In addition, many of the big names are now offering set price meals, predominately at lunch time. **Marco Pierre White: The Restaurant,** Nico's establishments, **Auburgine,** and **La Tante Claire** offer such deals—a good way to try some of London's best at a price that's easy on the wallet.

Finally, a note about service: In general, you'll find the staff at London eateries to be perfectly pleasant, especially at the top-rated restaurants. Things start to get patchy at the smaller, cheaper eateries and cafes. I'm continually amazed that certain establishments re- main open; perhaps due, at least in part, to the British reticence to complain. If you do experience bad service, let it be known, and don't tip if you feel it hasn't been earned.

Price Chart

Our price categories are based on the approximate cost of a three course meal for one, with service and Value Added Tax (VAT), but no wine.

Symbol	Category	Current Prices
$$$$	Very Expensive	more than £40
$$$	Expensive	£25–£40
$$	Moderate	£15–£25
$	Inexpensive	less than £15

Restaurants by Neighborhood

Bayswater
The Cow. **$$**

Belgravia/Knightsbridge
The Fifth Floor Restaurant.
$$$
The Halkin. **$$$**
★Marco Pierre White: The
Restaurant. **$$$$**
Pizza on the Park. **$**

Bloomsbury
Chiaroscuro. **$$**
Museum Street Cafe. **$$**
★Wagamama. **$**

*Chelsea/South
Kensington*
Albero & Grana. **$$$**
★★Aubergine. **$$$**
Bar Central. **$$**
★★Bibendum Restaurant and
Oyster Bar. **$$$$** or **$$**
Bombay Brasserie. **$$$**
★Chez Max. **$$$**
Daphne's. **$$$**
Enterprise. **$$**
Establishment. **$$**
★★Fulham Road. **$$$**
Nam Long. **$$**
Nippon Tuk. **$$**
★★La Tante Claire. **$$$$**
Wodka. **$$**

Covent Garden
Belgo Centraal. **$$**
Christopher's American Grill.
$$$
Crank's Covent Garden. **$**
The Ivy. **$$$**
Neal's Yard Dining Rooms. **$**
Orso. **$$$**
Simpson's-in-the-Strand.
$$$

East End & City
The Eagle. **$**
F. Cooke & Sons. **$**
M Fish. **$**
Moshi Moshi Sushi. **$**

*Fulham/Hammersmith/
Chiswick*
★The Brackenbury. **$$**
★The Chiswick. **$$$**

Chutney Mary. **$$$**
Riva. **$$**
★River Cafe. **$$$**

Islington/King's Cross
★Granita. **$$**

*Kensington/Notting Hill/
Maida Vale*
The Belvedere. **$$$**
Books for Cooks. **$**
★★Clarke's. **$$$**
Geale's. **$**
Jimmy Beez. **$$**
Kensington Place. **$$$**
Leith's. **$$$$**
Malabar. **$$**
★192. **$$**
Osteria Basilico. **$$**
★Sugar Club. **$$**
W11. **$$**

Mayfair
★★Chez Nico at Ninety Park
Lane. **$$$$**
Claridge's—The Causerie.
$$$
★★Coast. **$$$**
The Connaught. **$$$$**
★Criterion Brasserie. **$$$**
The Dorchester. **$$$$**
Four Seasons. **$$$$**
Le Gavroche. **$$$$**
Goode's. **$$$**
Greenhouse. **$$$**
Langan's Brasserie. **$$$**
Nicole's. **$$$**
L'Odeon. **$$$$**
Sofra Restaurant. **$$**
Tamarind. **$$$**

Primrose Hill
The Engineer. **$$**

St. James's
★Le Caprice. **$$$**
★Quaglino's. **$$$**
The Square. **$$$**
33 St. James's Street. **$$$**

Soho
★Alastair Little. **$$$$**
Alfred. **$$**
Atlantic Bar & Grill. **$$$**

Bahn Thai. **$$$**
Bistrot Bruno. **$$$** or **$$**
The French House Dining
    Room. **$$**
Fung Shing. **$$**
Gay Hussar. **$$$**
Interlude de Chavot.
    $$$$
★Mezzo. **$$$**
New World. **$**

South Bank
Blue Print Cafe. **$$**
People's Palace. **$$**
★Le Pont de la Tour. **$$$$**

Westminster/Victoria
Atrium. **$$**
Jenny Lo's Tea House. **$**
Tate Gallery Restaurant. **$$$**

Restaurants by Cuisine

American
Christopher's American Grill.
$$$

Anglo-Irish
Atrium. **$$**

Belgian
Belgo Centraal. **$$**

British
Alfred. **$$**
Claridge's—The Causerie.
    $$$
The Connaught. **$$$$**
The Dorchester. **$$$$**
F. Cooke & Sons. **$**
Geale's. **$**
Goode's. **$$$**
Greenhouse. **$$$**
M Fish. **$**
Simpson's-in-the-Strand. **$$$**
Tate Gallery Restaurant. **$$$**

Chinese
The Dorchester. **$$$$**
Fung Shing. **$$**
Jenny Lo's Tea House. **$**
New World. **$**

French
★★Aubergine. **$$$**
Bistrot Bruno. **$$$** or **$$**
★Chez Max. **$$$**
★★Chez Nico at Ninety Park
    Lane. **$$$$**
Le Gavroche. **$$$$**
Interlude de Chavot. **$$$$**
L'Odeon. **$$$$**
★★La Tante Claire. **$$$$**

Hungarian
Gay Hussar. **$$$**

Indian
Bombay Brasserie. **$$$**
Chutney Mary. **$$$**
Malabar. **$$**
Tamarind. **$$$**

International
Books for Cooks. **$**

Italian
The Dorchester. **$$$$**
The Halkin. **$$$**
Orso. **$$$**
Osteria Basilico. **$$**
Pizza on the Park. **$**
Riva. **$$**
★River Cafe. **$$$**

Japanese
Moshi Moshi Sushi. **$**
Nippon Tuk. **$$**
★Wagamama. **$**

Modern British
★Alastair Little. **$$$$**
Atlantic Bar & Grill. **$$$**
Bar Central. **$$**
The Belvedere. **$$$**
★★Bibendum Restaurant and
    Oyster Bar. **$$$$** or **$$**
Blue Print Cafe. **$$**
★The Brackenbury. **$$**
★Le Caprice. **$$$**
Chiaroscuro. **$$**
★The Chiswick. **$$$**
★★Clarke's. **$$$**
★★Coast. **$$$**
★Criterion Brasserie. **$$$**
Daphne's. **$$$**
Enterprise. **$$**
Establishment. **$$**
The Fifth Floor Restaurant.
    $$$
Four Seasons. **$$$$**

The French House Dining Room. **$$**
★★Fulham Road. **$$$**
★Granita. **$$**
The Ivy. **$$$**
Jimmy Beez. **$$**
Kensington Place. **$$$**
Langan's Brasserie. **$$$**
Leith's. **$$$$**
★Marco Pierre White: The Restaurant. **$$$$**
★Mezzo. **$$$**
Museum Street Cafe. **$$**
Nicole's. **$$$**
★192. **$$**
People's Palace. **$$**
★Le Pont de la Tour. **$$$$**
★Quaglino's. **$$$**
The Square. **$$$**
33 St. James's Street. **$$$**
W11. **$$**

New Zealand
★Sugar Club. **$$**

Polish
Wodka. **$$**

Pub
The Cow. **$$**
The Eagle. **$**
The Engineer. **$$**

Spanish
Albero & Grana. **$$$**

Thai
Bahn Thai. **$$$**

Turkish
Sofra Restaurant. **$$**

Vegetarian
Crank's Covent Garden. **$**
Neal's Yard Dining Rooms. **$**

Vietnamese
Nam Long. **$$**

Critic's Choice

For pure glamour, my all-time favorite continues to be **Le Caprice.** When I can't book a table, I ask if there are any seats at the bar—it has a great atmosphere and you're in the heart of the action—and survey the buzzy scene in the mirror behind the bar. All customers are treated equally, so the linen is out and the full menu is available. **Bibendum,** where the tubby stained-glass Michelin man is offset by sparkling cutlery (and the sparkling diners), also scores high on the glamour meter. For more understated sophistication, **Fulham Road** has an elegance that attracts upscale diners who demand good food and good design.

These days, when black-clothed hipsters feel like stepping out, they head for **Coast,** the newest restaurant from the **Atlantic Bar & Grill** team. Every detail, down to the ashtrays and staff uniforms, have the mark of good design. Not far from the club set's headquarters in All Saints Road is the new **Sugar Club,** where they come for the New Zealand–inspired menu and the easy access to the **Mas Cafe,** the local watering hole across the street. Practically an institution, **192** is always packed with more of this breed; during summer months, the sidewalk tables are prime for seeing and being seen.

continues

The perennially jet-lagged, and night owls in general, prefer **Quaglino's** (but only during the late hours, when the tourists have returned to their hotels) and **The Ivy,** where they can order up a full meal well past most restaurants' regular closing hours. Marco Pierre White's newest venture, the **Criterion Brasserie,** also keeps late hours, serving up classy brasserie-style cuisine in a drop-dead gorgeous room late into the evening. For cheaper eats, there's always **La Brasserie,** very French and perennially stylish; the seriously budget conscious should try the **Brick Lane Beigel Bake,** open 24 hours (see "Cafes and Patisseries" below for details on both).

When the weather turns warm, Londoners head for the street and turn their noses up to the sun. The terrace at **The Belvedere** in Holland Park is divine, but for sheer drama, the **Blue Print Cafe,** with the most stunning views over Tower Bridge, is a picture-postcard experience.

I am a devotee of **Jimmy Beez** for Saturday or Sunday brunch. The chef, who trained at Arizona 206 in New York, has put together an inspired menu of brunch classics and Asian-flavored specialties; located at the top end of Portobello Road, it's a natural stop after trawling the market. If you're hankering for a real American-style brunch, **Christopher's** is your spot. On Sundays, the ground floor bar serves a cafe menu—a kid-friendly choice. The kids will be treated like stars at **Chiaroscuro,** near the British Museum, where on Saturdays the upper floor is turned into a crèche and the owner's under-12 experts decide on the day's menu. And **Nicole's** now serves breakfast; situated in the heart of Mayfair near the auction houses and most of the better hotels, it's convenient for a power breakfast or a pre-auction fill-up.

If you're dining solo, the bars at some of the more stylish restaurants encourage conversation. Try **Kensington Place,** a stylish and lively neighborhood stalwart, or **Albero & Grana,** a trendy tapas bar.

At this writing, three notable openings had just taken place: **Mezzo, L'Odeon,** and a new outpost **Alistair Little,** all which are discussed below. Since opening, all three have received rave reviews; any foodie obsessed with what's new and hot should check them out.

London's Restaurants A to Z

★Alastair Little

49 Frith St., W1. ☎ 0171/
734-5183. No credit cards.
Reservations advised. Closed:
Sun, Christmas, bank holidays.
Tube: Leicester Sq., Tottenham
Court Rd. MODERN BRITISH.
$$$$.

You'd never think that this was
the domain of the chef that
many claim to be the best in
London. But the tired, stark
interior serves to keep your
mind on the exquisite cuisine.
Some critics have complained
that Little spends too much of
his time in Italy teaching his
craft, but I've yet to find the
simple Mediterranean-style
cuisine lacking. The menu
changes twice daily; on my last
visit, the roast fillet of sea bass
with parsley sauce was bursting
with fresh, clean flavor. But
the prices are quite steep,
considering the environment;
check out the tiny basement
dining area under the air-
conditioning unit for lunch,
which offers a great deal on a
3-course meal.

Little has just opened a
Notting Hill outpost (136A
Lancaster Rd., W11; ☎ 0171/
243-2220) that's also garnering
raves for its classic Mediterranean-style dishes and avant-
garde restraint.

Albero & Grana

Chelsea Cloisters, 89 Sloane
Ave., SW3. ☎ 0171/225-1048.
AE, D, DC, MC, V. Reservations
advised. Closed: Sun lunch,
some bank holidays. Tube: South
Kensington, Sloane Sq. SPANISH.
$$$.

Sloane Ranger meets City
Slicker at this top-notch
Spanish restaurant, where
Flamenco colors and music set
the mood for the city's best
Spanish cuisine. In the kitchen
is a Michelin-starred chef,
whose reworkings of
traditional dishes are
consistently fine. Try the
lasagna de morcilla starter (a
lasagna of black pudding with
a green pepper sauce), a house
specialty. The wine list, once
lacking, has been updated to
capitalize on Spain's diverse
wine culture. The front of the
restaurant is devoted to a very
happening tapas bar where you
can graze on tempting plates
of mixed paella or Spanish
sausage with chickpeas. This
is a good place to watch the
suited after-work crowd
exchange phone numbers.
It's great for a light Sunday
evening meal, too.

Alfred

245 Shaftesbury Ave., W1.
☎ 0171/240-2566. AE, D, DC,
MC, V. Reservations advised.
Closed: Sun, Christmas, Boxing
Day, New Year's Day, Mon bank
holidays. Tube: Tottenham Court
Rd. BRITISH. **$$**.

Fred Taylor, formerly of Fred's
Drinking Club in Soho, has
moved on to bigger and better
things. This busy, buzzy
designer cafe has a slightly
retro feel to it; one critic
compared the colors—yellow
Formica tables, glossy blue
walls, drab brown paneling—
to an Edward Hopper
tableaux. It's one of London's
better dining values: Bring a
big appetite—the portions of
traditional British fare are
daunting. Rabbit in beer-and-
sage sauce and steak with
Stilton butter are lavished with
care and flair, as are the good
puddings and fine English
cheeses. The beer list has a
good sampling of local brews,
and this is one of the few
places where you can try
Anglo wines. Downstairs is a
large bar serving more

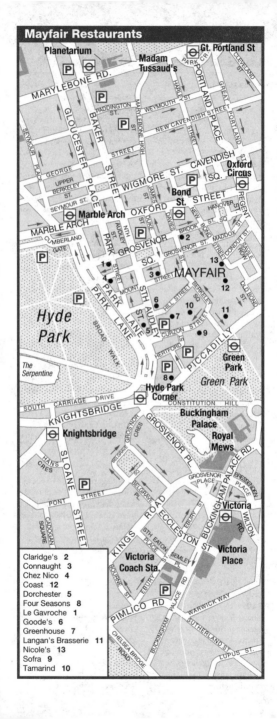

Mayfair Restaurants

Planetarium

Madam Tussaud's

Gt. Portland St

MARYLEBONE RD.

PADDINGTON ST.

WEYMOUTH ST.

NEW CAVENDISH STREET

BAKER STREET

GLOUCESTER PLACE

MARYLEBONE HIGH STREET

HARLEY ST.

PORTLAND PLACE

GREAT PORTLAND STREET

CLEVELAND ST.

PARK CR.

WIGMORE ST.

CAVENDISH

Oxford Circus

GEORGE ST.

UPPER BERKELEY ST.

SEYMOUR PLACE

JAMES ST.

Bond St.

SQ.

REGENT ST.

HANOVER SQ.

Marble Arch

OXFORD STREET

DUKE ST.

DAVIES ST.

NEW BOND ST.

CONDUIT ST.

MARBLE ARCH

MADDOX ST.

BROOK 2

MAYFAIR

13

CUMBERLAND GATE

GROSVENOR ST.

GROSVENOR

SQ.

NTH AUDLEY ST.

STH AUDLEY ST.

MOUNT ST.

BERKELEY STREET

OLD BOND ST.

SAVILE ROW

1

4

3

12

6

HILL STREET

10

11

Hyde Park

PARK LANE

7

5

CURZON STREET

9

BROAD WALK

HERTFORD ST.

PICCADILLY

Green Park

The Serpentine

8

Hyde Park Corner

Green Park

SOUTH CARRIAGE DRIVE

CONSTITUTION HILL

KNIGHTSBRIDGE

Buckingham Palace

Knightsbridge

GROSVENOR CRES

GROSVENOR PL.

Royal Mews

HANS CRES

SLOANE STREET

BEDFORD

BELGRAVE PL.

GROSVENOR PLACE

BRESSENDEN PLACE

PONT STREET

CADOGAN SQUARE

Victoria

WILTON RD.

KINGS ROAD

ECCLESTON ST.

BUCKINGHAM PALACE RD.

EBURY ST.

STH EATON PLACE

SEMLEY PL.

Victoria Place

Victoria Coach Sta.

BOURNE ST.

EBURY ST.

PIMLICO RD.

BUCKINGHAM PALACE RD.

WARWICK WAY

CHELSEA BRIDGE ROAD

SUTHERLAND ST.

LUPUS ST.

Claridge's	2
Connaught	3
Chez Nico	4
Coast	12
Dorchester	5
Four Seasons	8
Le Gavroche	1
Goode's	6
Greenhouse	7
Langan's Brasserie	11
Nicole's	13
Sofra	9
Tamarind	10

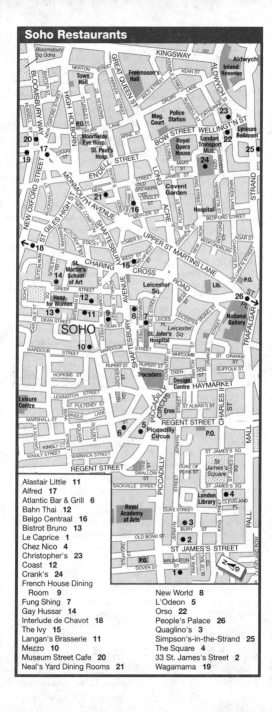

Soho Restaurants

traditional drinks. Alfresco
tables are available.

Atlantic Bar & Grill

20 Glasshouse St., W1.
☎ 0171/734-4888. AE, D, DC,
MC, V. Reservations required.
Tube: Piccadilly Circus. MODERN
BRITISH. **$$$**.

The hot venue of 1994, the
Atlantic has been overshad-
owed since by the spate of
large-scale openings. Situated
in a former art-deco ballroom,
the space is impressive and
cutting-edge. If the '80s-style
yuppie dares show his face
again, he'll be seen here; over-
30s might feel out of place.
There's a good selection of
mixed platters with a
Mediterranean bent (good for
sharing) as well as more serious
food, such as seared, pan-fried
foie gras; everything is done
exceedingly well.

Atrium

4 Millbank, SW1. ☎ 0171/
233-0032. AE, D, DC, MC, V.
Reservations advised. Closed:
Sat lunch, Sun, Christmas, bank
holidays. Wheelchair accessible.
Tube: Westminster. ANGLO-
IRISH. **$$**.

Restaurateur Antony Worrall
Thompson continues his
impressive list of successes with
this one, in a soaring 6-story
atrium a stone's throw from
Westminster. Don't be
surprised to see some scandal-
stricken MP enjoying a pint
and a hearty sandwich at
lunch. I'm partial to the
lunchtime fare, too: generous
servings of fresh soups and
salads, plus an exquisite
selection of sandwiches that all
taste as if they're cut straight
off the bone. And the treacle
pudding's a winner.

★★Aubergine

11 Park Walk, SW10. ☎ 0171/
352-3449. AE, D, DC, MC, V.

Reservations required. Closed:
Sat lunch, Sun, bank holidays, 2
weeks in Aug. Tube: South
Kensington. FRENCH. **$$$**.

If things keep going as they
have, you might want to book
before you leave home in
order to secure a table for
dinner here. The interior is a
peaceful environment with
pastel landscapes and primrose
walls—a cool veneer that
serves to hide the fireworks
going off in the kitchen, where
chef Gordon Ramsey, a
protégé of Marco Pierre White
who also trained with Joel
Robuchon in Paris, performs
culinary miracles. De Niro has
been spotted here, as have
members of the royal family,
probably all lured by the starter
cappuccino of haricots blancs
with truffle oil—a heavenly
soup. The menu changes
seasonally; a wonderful lamb
and an awesome fig tart are
available in winter. Service is
French in tone (that is to say, a
bit condescending), but it's
worth putting up with. The
fixed-price lunch is an
economical way to go.

Bahn Thai

21a Frith St., W1. ☎ 0171/
437-8504. AE, DC, D, MC, V.
Reservations advised. Closed:
Christmas, Easter, bank holidays.
Tube: Leicester Sq., Tottenham
Court Rd. THAI. **$$$**.

This was one of London's first
Thai restaurants, and it's still
one of the best. The downstairs area opens up in summer,
leaving little division between
diners and crawlers along
rockin' Frith Street. It will take
you some time to get through
the book-sized menu, but take
care and you'll be rewarded
with authentic and inspired
Thai cuisine. The crispy fried
pomfret served with a seriously
spicy sauce is perfectly done.
There are also some offbeat

choices, such as frog's legs and wild boar. The wine list has been well chosen to complement the food; Thai beer is also available. The pace is relaxed (sometimes too much—service can be slow) and portions are sometimes meager for the price.

Bar Central

316 King's Rd., SW 3. ☎ 0171/352-0025. AE, V, MC. Reservations advised. Closed: Christmas. Tube: Sloane Sq. MODERN BRITISH. **$$**.

This noisy, see-and-be-seen spot on King's Road has a discriminating Chelsea clientele and a vaguely French/Italian menu (there's even a pizza oven) with lots of salads and pastas. The mussels with tomato, basil, and white wine are terrific; the Caesar salad is already a fixture. The food is served against a backdrop of indigo blue and buttermilk-yellow walls with pared-down Conran-style furnishings. The bar is a nice place for a beer (try the locally brewed Freedom) and a pizza. In summer, tables spill out onto the sidewalk, expanding the people-watching pool.

Belgo Centraal

50 Earlham St., WC2. ☎ 0171/813-2233. AE, DC, D, MC, V. Reservations advised in one dining room; no reservations taken in second. Closed: Christmas. Wheelchair accessible. Tube: Covent Garden. BELGIAN. **$$**.

This newest member of the Belgo family keeps the crowds coming with its Covent Garden location and drop-dead *Bladerunner*-gone-medieval interior. There are two food halls: one for those on the move (no reservations, long tables, fast service), another for more serious eaters; both are

reached via a large metal elevator that gives you a view of the open kitchen. Mussels are done every which way and served by the ton, all accompanied by frites—the house specialty. Soups, roasts, sandwiches, and salads round out the menu, but it's best to stick to the mussels. The beer is Belgian, of course—more than 100 brands are available.

The Belvedere

Holland Park, off Abbotsbury Rd., W8. ☎ 0171/602-1238. AE, D, DC, MC, V. Reservations required. Closed: Sun dinner, Christmas, Boxing Day. Tube: Holland Park. MODERN BRITISH. **$$$**.

To be honest, nobody goes to this restaurant for the food—it's the promise of a terrace table overlooking lovely flower gardens and fountains on a perfectly sunny summer evening that draws the crowds. The food isn't terrible; it's just uninspired and nothing revolutionary (except for the Grand Marnier mousse on a Florentine base with a white-chocolate sauce—truly delicious). But if the weather forecast doesn't follow through on its promises, all isn't lost; the 2-story inside dining room is dominated by large arched windows that fill the space with light, and some of the upstairs tables have a nice view of Holland Park.

★★Bibendum Restaurant and Oyster Bar

Michelin House, 81 Fulham Rd., SW3. Restaurant: ☎ 0171/581-5817; Oyster Bar: ☎ 0171/589-1480. AE, MC, V. Reservations required. Closed: Dec 25–28. Tube: South Kensington. MODERN BRITISH. Restaurant **$$$$**; Oyster Bar **$$**. Save your pennies for this special treat. Sir Terence

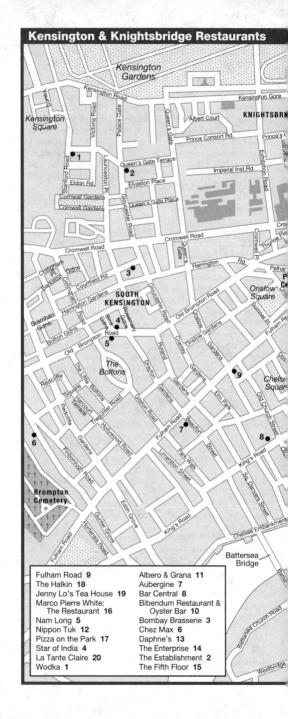

Kensington & Knightsbridge Restaurants

Kensington Gardens

Kensington Gore

KNIGHTSBRI

Albert Court

Prince Consort Rd.

Kensington Road

Yeomans

Kensington Square

Victoria Road

Palace Gate

Queen's Gate

Prince's C

Exhibition Road

Launceston Pl.

Queen's Gate Terrace

Stanford Road

Eldon Rd.

Elvaston Place

Imperial Inst.Rd.

Gloucester Road

Cornwall Gardens

Cornwall Gardens

Queen's Gate Place

Cro

Cromwell Road

Queen's Gate

Cromwell Pl

Thurloe Pla

Cromwell Road

Harrington Rd.

Pelham

P

Collingham Pl. Gdns

Barkston

Courtfield Rd.

Gloucester Road

Onslow Square

Onslow C

Harrington Gardens

Old Brompton Road

Sumner Pl.

Fulham Re

Bramham Gdns.

Rosemary

Onslow Gardens

Bolton Gdns.

Chary

Old Brompton

Roland

Crawley

Dov

Redcliffe

Drayton Gardens

Onslow Gardens

Elm Park

Chelsea Squar

SOUTH KENSINGTON

The Boltons

The Little Boltons

Harcourt Terrace

Gilston Road

Fulham Road

Park Walk

Beaufort Street

Old Church Street

Tregunter Road

Hollywood Road

Limerston Street

King's Road

Sq. Danvers Street

Redcliffe Gardens

Finborough Road

Edith Grove

Chelsea Embankment

Gunter Grove

Hortensia Road

King's Road

Brompton Cemetery

Fulham Road

Battersea Bridge

Battea

Battersea Church Road

Westbridge

Fulham Road **9**	Albero & Grana **11**
The Halkin **18**	Aubergine **7**
Jenny Lo's Tea House **19**	Bar Central **8**
Marco Pierre White: The Restaurant **16**	Bibendum Restaurant & Oyster Bar **10**
Nam Long **5**	Bombay Brasserie **3**
Nippon Tuk **12**	Chez Max **6**
Pizza on the Park **17**	Daphne's **13**
Star of India **4**	The Enterprise **14**
La Tante Claire **20**	The Establishment **2**
Wodka **1**	The Fifth Floor **15**

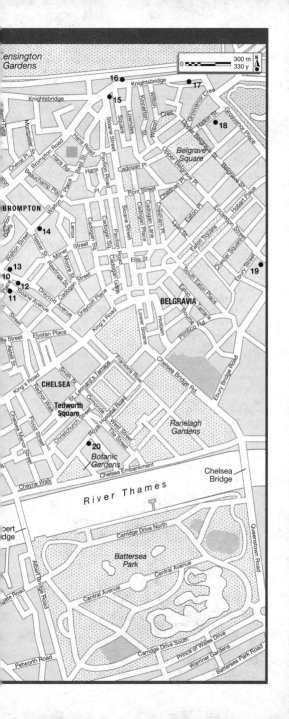

Conran's Bibendum is a foodies' paradise, with the original Michelin man rendered in stained glass, huge windows letting in enough light to make the glassware and cutlery sparkle, and talented Matthew Harris in the kitchen. The fantastic food is prepared with strong flavors and minimal frill—and served at fantastic prices. While the menu might sound simple, everything is done just right; even the fish-and-chips are lavished with TLC. And the wine list is arguably the best in town. The oyster bar, adjacent to the housewares emporium, offers a selection of salads and crustacea perfect for a light Sunday evening dinner; a glass of bubbly rounds off a shoppers' snack just fine.

Bistrot Bruno

63 Frith St., W1. ☎ 0171/ 734-4545. AE, D, DC, MC, V. Reservations advised. Closed: Sat lunch, Sun, Christmas–New Year's Day. Tube: Leicester Sq., Tottenham Court Rd. FRENCH. Bistrot **$$$**; Cafe **$$**.

Bruno Loubet, who just opened the mega L'Odeon, continues to garner rave reviews at this Soho brasserie. A media crowd fills the austere interior, which is offset by an eclectic menu of excellent French fare. The flavor couplings might seem a bit out there on paper, but 90% of the time Loubet gets it right. The duck livers on sweetcorn pancakes with garlic sauce coalesce beautifully. While it might be a bit much for the skeptics, the poached strawberries with green peppercorn ice cream is a winner. For cheaper eats, the adjacent **Cafe Bruno** serves up a lighter, simpler menu at lighter prices.

Blue Print Cafe

Design Museum, Butler's Wharf, SE1. ☎ 0171/378-7031. AE, D, DC, MC, V. Reservations advised. Closed: Sun eves, Christmas. Wheelchair accessible. Tube: Tower Hill. MODERN BRITISH. **$$**.

This is another of Sir Terence Conran's successful eateries, and it has all the hallmarks:

Blue Print Cafe

good clean design, an interesting crowd, and the kind of food people want to eat. The restaurant, inside the Design Museum, is cheaper than Conran's other Gastrodome joint, Pont de la Tour, and the execution is a notch above nearby Cantina del Ponte and the Chop House. During the summer months, be sure to reserve a table on the terrace—you'll have the best views in town of the gloriously illuminated Tower Bridge. The food is Mediterranean in flavor; the Caesar salad and pasta dishes are good bets—the gnocchi is light and beautifully presented. If you've got room, try one of the terrific desserts, the cara-melized banana and cinnamon ice cream is homemade and divine.

Bombay Brasserie

Courtfield Close, Courtfield Rd., SW7. ☎ 0171/370-4040. D, DC, V. Reservations advised. Closed: Christmas, Boxing Day. Tube: Gloucester Rd. INDIAN. **$$$**.

Bombay Brasserie ranked for years as one of London's most impressive Indian restaurants, featuring specialties from all over India (Goa, Bombay, Punjab). Today, both the colonial decor and the regional home cooking seem frayed at the edges: Criticism has been leveled at tired, overcooked dishes. It's generally expensive for an Indian restaurant, but the fixed-price buffet lunch is a good value. Despite critics' reservations, this remains a good choice for entertaining. The staff is cosmopolitan and friendly, and the restaurant serves every day until midnight.

Books for Cooks

4 Blenheim Crescent, W11. ☎ 0171/221-1992. No credit cards. Reservations required. Closed: eves, Sun, holidays. Tube: Notting Hill Gate. INTERNATIONAL. **$**.

This bookstore, crammed to the rafters with every cookbook ever published, has a small kitchen in the back where guest chefs test recipes from the stock. With only 12 seats and 5 tables, reservations are necessary, especially on weekends. The staff is friendly and knowledgeable, and meals have the atmosphere of a small luncheon gathering. This is not for the picky eater since there's no choice, but you're sure to be well fed.

★ The Brackenbury

129-131 Brackenbury Rd., W6. ☎ 0181/748-0107. AE, D, DC, MC, V. Reservations advised. Closed: Mon and Sat lunch, Sun dinner, bank holidays, 10 days at Christmas. Tube: Hammersmith. MODERN BRITISH. **$$**.

Hammersmith locals have been reluctant to spread the word about this unpretentious neighborhood restaurant. The decor is simple and unpretentious, somewhat wine-barish, with diners spilling out onto the sidewalk when the weather permits. Chef Adam Robinson, a former protégé of Alastair Little, capitalizes on what's available seasonally. The menu changes twice daily and ranges from a superbly done burger and fries to steamed saffron-infused turbot and mussels. Desserts are equally simple and delicious. A confident wine list offers lots of selections by the glass.

★ Le Caprice

Arlington House, Arlington St., SW1. ☎ 0171/629-2239. AE, D, DC, MC, V. Reservations required. Tube: Green Park. MODERN BRITISH. **$$$**.

Many consider this to be the most glam spot in town; it's certainly my favorite—very art deco, with lots of mirrors, glass, and black-and-white photos everywhere. Its late-night hours make this place popular among the jet-set. But go even if you're a mere mortal; service is discreet and everyone is made to feel special. Le Caprice always gets it right; just when you're starting to feel jaded about dining in London, a visit here will restore your faith. I love the risotto Nero and salmon fishcakes—comfort food that never fails to soothe the soul. For dessert, tuck into a pear Tatin. There's a great Sunday brunch from noon to 3:30pm, where you can experience Le Caprice at a more digestible price tag. It can be hard to book a table here; if you can't get one, try to get a seat at the bar, where dinner is still served on white linen, and you can survey the crowd in the mirror behind the bar.

★ Chez Max

168 Ifield Rd., SW10. ☎ 0171/ 835-0874. V. Reservations advised. Closed: Christmas, Easter, bank holidays. Tube: Earl's Court. FRENCH. **$$$**.

This place is hard to find, but well worth the trip. Max himself will elucidate the menu for you upon request; it's poetry to the ears as he describes the classic French dishes, which are simply and expertly prepared. The dining room is in the basement of a traditional Chelsea townhouse, very unpompous and relaxed; there's also a small all-weather patio. Area residents treat this as their local, but word has spread, and many are making the trip from farther afield. The crème brûlée "aux saveurs d'orange" is orgasmic. Serious

Francophiles will be well satisfied.

★★Chez Nico at Ninety Park Lane

Grosvenor House, 90 Park Lane, W1. ☎ 0171/409-1290. AE, D, DC, MC, V. Reservations required. Closed: Sat lunch, Sun. Wheelchair accessible. Tube: Hyde Park Corner, Marble Arch. FRENCH. **$$$$**.

Now the holder of three Michelin stars, Nico Ladenis continues to perform culinary miracles. Many consider him the best French chef in the capital, and serious foodies flock here. The dining room, which has its own street entrance, is comfortable but nothing remarkable—elegant and unfussy, plenty of space, lots of mirrors and windows. The food, though, is remarkable, and consistently so. Foie gras with artichoke slices and haricot verts, duck confit with plum sauce—not for the calorie counter, but sinfully good. If you've gone this far, you might as well try the poire Hélène, a poached pear with chocolate sauce, mint sorbet, and little biscuits, dense with almonds and cream. To accompany such fare is an excellent (though very expensive) wine list. Dinner doesn't come cheap, but the fixed-price lunch is a fair value.

If Chez Nico is too rich for your wallet, try **Nico Central** (35 Great Portland St., W1; ☎ 0171/436-8846) or **Simply Nico** in Victoria (48A Rochester Row, SW1; ☎ 0171/630-8061), where Ladenis oversees kitchens entrusted to his protégés. Both locations offer one of the best deals in town: a 3-course prix-fixe for £26, including VAT and service.

Chiaroscuro

24 Coptic St., WC1. ☎ 0171/
636-2731. AE, MC, V.
Reservations advised. Closed:
Sat lunch, Sun dinner. Tube:
Tottenham Court Rd. MODERN
BRITISH. **$$**.

During the week, a Covent
Garden expense-account
advertising crowd settles into
this predominately white
room, with suspended wire
lights, glass roof, and closely
packed cherry-wood tables, a
stone's throw from the British
Museum. On Sundays,
however, it's a completely
different story: lured by the
kid-friendly atmosphere,
mommies drop in with the
little ones. The upstairs dining
room is turned into a toy and
fun room, and kids eat free
from a menu of such yummy
fare as grilled chicken, sweet
endives with a bowl of chips,
and homemade desserts. But
you don't need to be a kid to
appreciate the food: An
artichoke galette with an herb
mayonnaise and saffron risotto
is equally delicious.

★ The Chiswick

131 Chiswick High Rd., W4.
☎ 0181/994-6887. AE, MC, V.
Reservations required. Closed:
Sat lunch, Sun dinner, Christmas,
bank holidays. Wheelchair
access. Tube: Turnham Green.
MODERN BRITISH. **$$$**.

This new sister restaurant to
the Brackenbury, the very local
Shephard's Bush hangout,
recently won the 1995 *Time
Out* award for best Modern
British restaurant in London.
While it might seem to be out
of the way for most tourists
(Chiswick is on the western
borders of the city), it's well
worth a detour for the
excellent food and value. Lilac
walls, beechwood tables, tile
floors, and Jacobsen chairs give
the room a very cool, no-frills

feel. The crowd is made up of
the well-heeled locals, who
were in desperate need of an
outstanding restaurant; you'll
spot the occasional celebrity
here as well. Inventive food is
the draw; I had a sublime
chicken liver salad, and the
pear sorbet was perfect. There's
also a wide-ranging wine list
that offers lots of options by
the half-litre. Make the trip
and you won't be disap-
pointed.

Christopher's American Grill

18 Wellington St., WC2.
☎ 0171/240-4222. AE, D, DC,
MC, V. Reservations advised.
Closed: Sun dinner, bank
holidays. Tube: Covent Garden.
AMERICAN. **$$$**.

If you're hankering for a bit of
home, this is the place to dine.
Well known for their Sunday
brunch, this grand restaurant
does all the classic American
dishes well, including excellent
steaks (portions are Fred
Flintstone–sized), Caesar
salads, and crab cakes. The
dining room, with a soaring
Italianate stone staircase
winding from the downstairs
bar, has a very relaxed
atmosphere. The bar is perfect
for pre- or post-theater meals.
The staff all look like they
stepped out of the pages of
Vogue, but are surprisingly
pleasant.

Chutney Mary

535 Kings Rd., SW10. ☎ 0171/
351-3113. AE, DC, D, MC, V.
Reservations advised. Closed:
Boxing Day. Tube: Fulham
Broadway. INDIAN. **$$$**.

The scene is pure British
Raj—wicker armchairs, palms,
a lovely conservatory—and the
food is prepared by chefs
brought directly from India,
who specialize in the hybrid
cuisine of the Raj years. The

kitchen is keenly watched over by co-owner Namita Panjabi, who has spent much time researching the menu in order to ensure authenticity. Order a wide selection of starters—the calamari fried with chili and served with rocket is excellent—and move on to the Masala roast lamb or crab vindaloo; the choices are mouthwatering. All the chutneys are made on the premises from house recipes, and chilis are liberally used. You're likely to dine among lots of suits on expense accounts.

Claridge's—The Causerie

Brook St., W1. ☎ 0171/629-8860. AE, D, DC, MC, V. Reservations required. Wheelchair accessible. Tube: Bond St. BRITISH. **$$$**.

This art-deco dining room is often packed with aristocratic ladies and their nephews at lunchtime, when there's a sumptuous smorgasbord of over 20 dishes, including many with fish and smoked meats. You can have more of the same at dinner or opt for the hot dish of the day, followed by cheese or dessert—perfect for pre- or post-theater. Seating is on small sofas for two, arranged with enough privacy for an intimate téte-à-téte.

★★ Clarke's

124 Kensington Church St., W8. ☎ 0171/221-9225. V. Reservations required. Closed: Sat, Sun, 2 weeks in Aug, Christmas, Easter. Tube: Notting Hill Gate. MODERN BRITISH. **$$$**.

Some people are put off by the fixed dinner menu, but others love the fact that the choices are made for them—you could do worse than put your palate in the hands of Sally Clarke.

One of the top female chefs in London, Clarke's simple and unfussy restaurant, with brasserie-style chairs and white walls, attracts a loyal following. The ingredients are fresh as can be, and the dishes deceptively hearty and elegant.

The food is inspired by the best California chefs (Clarke trained at Chez Panisse) and the excellent wine list is purely West Coast. The menus are set and posted in the window at the start of each week. Regulars rave about the delights of the char-grill, which produces most of the main dishes, such as skewered lamb and grilled scallops with lentils baked in cumin, coriander, and cream. And the fresh-baked bread is legendary.

★★Coast

26b Albermarle St., W1. ☎ 0171/495-5999. AE, MC, V. Reservations advised. Closed:Christmas. Tube: Piccadilly Circus. MODERN BRITISH. **$$$**.

Billed as one of the "next generation of restaurants to cater for *our* generation," this sister restaurant to the very successful Atlantic Bar & Grill is a dramatic space with an imposing glass front, parquet wood floors, mint walls with sci-fi pod lighting, and a 5-meter work by artist Angela Bulloch described as a "drawing machine" that plots lines directly onto the walls based on the movement in the room. Every detail, from the uniforms to the menus, was designed by London's hottest names, and the kitchen is home to one of London's brightest stars, serving up international cooking with an emphasis on light and seasonal dishes. Start with a goat cheese mousse with rocket and roasted pepper and move on to a lovely seared tuna with fennel and yogurt sauce; you might want to finish off with "Something Chocolate," 4 different versions of truffles with a raspberry coulis.

Downstairs is a private salon encased in a glass conservatory, where the trendies gather to stare each other down. Excellent Bloody Marys.

The Connaught

Carlos Place, W1. ☎ 0171/499-7070. AE, D, DC, MC, V. Reservations required. Jacket and tie required. Wheelchair accessible. Tube: Bond St. BRITISH/FRENCH. **$$$$**.

A veritable institution, the Connaught continues to serve up classic English fare with a liberal sprinkling of French classics under the direction of chef Michel Bourdin, who's been in the kitchen for more than 20 years. There are actually two restaurants, the Grill and the larger, more clubby Restaurant, both offering the same menu. The word stuffy doesn't begin to describe the pompousness that permeates these walls—even the mineral water is served in gold-rimmed glasses. Americans flock here to soak up some original English pretension (and pay much too much for the experience). Classics include Irish stew and salmon quenelles in a pink champagne sauce. Fixed-price menus are available for lunch and dinner (the dinner deal is only available in the Grill). Children under six should be left at home.

The Cow

89 Westbourne Park Rd., W2. ☎ 0171/221-0021. MC, V. Reservations advised. Closed: Mon lunch. Wheelchair access to bar only. Tube: Westbourne Grove. PUB/BRITISH. **$$**.

Tom Conran, son of Sir Terence, has made his own name in food. After cutting his teeth at the Oyster bar of dad's Bibendum and opening a small prepared-foods shop in Notting Hill, his most recent project is a converted local pub that now ranks as the hippest hangout for the trustafarians that populate the area. The feel is a cross between French cafe and Irish pub. Simple, well-prepared meals are served upstairs; downstairs is a hearty drink and raw bar. The best value is The Cow Special—six rocks and a pint of Guinness for £7.

Crank's Covent Garden

1 The Market, Covent Garden, WC2. ☎ 0171/379-6508. AE, MC, V. Reservations not necessary. Closed: Christmas. Tube: Covent Garden. VEGETARIAN. **$**.

All outlets of Crank's are packed with office workers at lunch. The food is strictly vegetarian, well-prepared, reasonably priced and fresh, and presented cafeteria style. The menu has been recently revitalized under the direction of a new chef that has catered for an A-list of celebrity veggies. This newest outlet, billed as the "biggest vegetarian food emporium in the U.K.," has outside tables overlooking buzzy Covent Garden and wait service at dinner. Try the fired aubergine slices with a fromage frais and sundried-tomato mousse; even if you're a staunch carnivore, you'll find the flavors vibrant. Serious vegans can rest assured: the fruit and vegetables are all organic, and the eggs are free-range. Full à la carte service, available at dinner, is an excellent value.

★Criterion Brasserie

224 Piccadilly, W1. ☎ 0171/930-0488. AE, D, DC, MC, V. Reservations required. Tube: Piccadilly Circus. MODERN BRITISH. **$$$**.

This is arguably the most beautiful dining room in London. But the Criterion has long served mediocre food—until now, that is. Finally, it's offering cuisine fit to be served in such a splendid Byzantine setting. Marco Pierre White (in association with hotelier extraordinaire Rocco Forte) has taken over this glittery prize, bringing with him the two head chefs from The Canteen (where White held court before his falling out with owner Michael Caine).

The menu consists of timeless French classics, prepared with a modern touch. Soups (the mussel soup with saffron is delicious), risottos (all are spot on), pastas, and frisee salads make up the 1st-course choices. For a main, the poached, smoked haddock with egg is a perfect brasserie dish; blackleg chicken with bacon-and-bread sauce and juices is classy comfort food. The desserts are inspired, especially the baked apple and fruits in champagne jelly. Service is very French (read: very formal and slightly pompous). While the prices are a bit beyond everyday brasserie levels, it's worth it to dine in such grand surroundings.

Daphne's

112 Draycott Ave., SW3. ☎ 0171/589-4257. AE, D, DC, V. Reservations required. Closed: 10 days at Christmastime. Tube: South Kensington. MODERN BRITISH. **$$$**.

This chic hang-out, where the local Eurotrash gather to trash each other, is a big-time ladies who (don't eat) lunch scene during the day (Princess Di, Ivana, and the rest of them). In deference to the clientele, the menu is a dieter's dream, with a wide choice of salads; nondieters can choose from Mediterranean-inspired risottos and hearty grills and roasts. The desserts are excellent, with a range of soufflés including chocolate, Grand Marnier, or lemon. The garden room in the back is quite pretty, but the place to be seen is definitely the glitzy front room.

The Dorchester

53 Park Lane, W1. ☎ 0171/629-8888. AE, D, DC, MC. Reservations advised. Oriental: closed Sat lunch, Sun; Terrace: open Fri and Sat eves only. Tube: Hyde Park Corner, Marble Arch. VARIOUS CUISINES. **$$$$**.

The Dorchester has four restaurants: the **Dorchester Bar**, serving antipasti and light Italian dishes; **The Terrace**, for Friday and Saturday dinner and dancing; **The Grill Room**, for traditional English fare; and **The Oriental**, serving classic Cantonese dishes. All are independent, with separate kitchens and chefs. The most interesting of the four is The Oriental, with a varied dim sum menu served at lunchtime and a wide choice of traditional Hong Kong–style dishes, such as shark's fin, abalone, and pigeon. If you're strapped for cash, however, you're better off venturing into Chinatown.

The Eagle

159 Farringdon Rd., EC1. ☎ 0171/837-1353. No credit cards. Closed: Sat, Sun, 3 weeks at Christmastime, bank holidays. Tube: Farringdon. PUB. **$**.

This was the first in the spate of trendy pub renovations serving seriously good food.

Bare wood floors and cozy sofas set the tone, luring patrons from the nearby offices of the left-wing daily Guardian.

An open-plan kitchen is on view behind the bar, where you order and pay before being served at a table—if you can get one. Great soups, salads, and pastas are all prepared with strong flavors and hearty odors (the pastas with a heavy dose of olive oil). The Eagle is very busy, but it's worth the wait for the excellent value. But be forewarned: No reservations and no credit cards are taken.

The Engineer

65 Gloucester Ave., NW1.
☎ 0171/722-0950. AE, D, DC, MC, V. Closed: Tues lunch, Christmas, Boxing Day. Wheelchair accessible. Tube: Chalk Farm. MODERN BRITISH. **$$**.
If you're spending the afternoon exploring Primrose Hill or Camden, this is the place to stop. Another one of the new spruced-up pubs, The Engineer is both a friendly bar and a local restaurant serving up good, fresh food. The simple, reasonably priced menu, filled with delectables like squid rings with black olives, coriander, and sesame, is also notable for its nice selection of vegetarian dishes.

Enterprise

35 Walton St., SW3. ☎ 0171/584-3148. AE, MC, V. Reservations advised. Closed: Christmas, Boxing Day, New Year's Day, Jan 2. Tube: Knightsbridge. MODERN BRITISH. **$$**.
If you're in Knightsbridge, this clubby restaurant, with banquettes and bare floors, is a good place to stop on trendy Walton Street. The shopping

ladies love this place for lunch; in the evening it becomes a bit of a pick-up scene. The menu revolves around grilled meats and fish; there are also plenty of salads, which can be ordered as either main courses or starters. Sundried tomatoes and goat cheese abound. While certainly not worth a special trip, this well-located place is perfectly pleasing.

Establishment

1 Gloucester Rd., SW7.
☎ 0171/589-7969. AE, MC, V. Reservations advised. Closed: Sat, Sun. Tube: Gloucester Rd. MODERN BRITISH. **$$**.
I like this place. A 2-story restaurant that somehow manages to achieve a slightly Southwestern feel despite the African artifacts that line the walls, it's the kind of place that you'd find yourself visiting regularly if you lived in the neighborhood. The Kemps, who are also behind 3 of my favorite London hotels and consistently get it right, have done it again, creating a lively, casual space serving the kind of food people like to eat. The menu mainly consists of grills, salads, and pastas—nothing revolutionary, just good food at good prices.

F. Cooke & Sons

41 Kingsland High St., E8.
☎ 0171/254-2878. No credit cards. No reservations. Closed: Sun, Christmas, Boxing Day, New Year's Day. Wheelchair accessible. British Rail: Dalston Junction. BRITISH. **$**.
For the true East End experience, stop into this most famous of eel-and-pie shops. The turn-of-the-century interior is all tiles and steel. Eels-and-mash in liquor is very much an acquired taste; if you can't bare the thought of it, try the steak and kidney pie. You

can buy live eels just outside the shop.

The Fifth Floor Restaurant

Harvey Nichols, Knightsbridge, SW1. ☎ 0171/235-5250. AE, D, DC, MC, V. Reservations advised. Closed: Sun dinner, Christmas. Wheelchair accessible. Tube: Knightsbridge. MODERN BRITISH. **$$$**.

This swanky rooftop dinner spot is on the top floor of London's trendiest department store. A big ladies-who-lunch crowd gives way to a dinner scene where movers and shakers meet to make deals. A great view of Knightsbridge is available to windowside patrons. The Modern British menu even successfully manages to take a few risks: carrot-and-coconut soup, native oysters with spicy sausages, langoustine frittata with crème fraîche and caviar. Finish off with the chocolate macadamia-nut tarte—it's flawless. The daytime wine list is abbreviated, but there's a massive selection at dinnertime. Don't be surprised by the range of champagnes—this is Knightsbridge, after all.

Four Seasons (formerly Inn on the Park)

Hamilton Place, Park Lane, W1. ☎ 0171/499-0888. AE, D, DC, MC, V. Reservations required. Jacket and tie required. Wheelchair accessible. Tube: Hyde Park Corner, Green Park. FRENCH. **$$$$**.

In contrast to the pompous Edwardian decor, the food being served at this luxury hotel takes risks. Chef Jean-Christophe Novelli, who recently replaced Bruno Loubet (now of Bistrot Bruno), offers up a seasonally changing menu that, when

translated into English, defies the imagination. The French cooking is fabulously rich and daring, but the presentation is sometimes a bit over the top. The goat cheese ravioli with artichokes is a winner, as is the poached turbot in coconut milk on a bed of almond and cauliflower puree. There's a wide choice of offals and a few healthy dishes, marked on the menu with an asterisk—but I suspect this is a trick to get you to splurge on dessert. The wine list ranks as one of the best in town; you name it, it's most likely in the cellar. Many half-bottles are also available, and there's a page of mineral waters. You'll have a fine view of the park.

The French House Dining Room

49 Dean St., W1. ☎ 0171/437-2477. AE, D, DC, MC, V. Reservations advised. Closed: Sun, Christmas, Easter, bank holidays. Tube: Piccadilly Circus, Leicester Sq. MODERN BRITISH. **$$**.

A young, very trendy New York writer I know makes a pilgrimage to The French House Dining Room whenever he's in London. Situated above a pub, the decor is slightly seedy, with just the right edge to it: we call it "Soho bohemian." The menu, which changes twice daily, is best described as British bistro fare, with such homespun dishes as roast belly of pork with red cabbage, meatballs with mash, and homemade soup. Starter servings can be parsimonious, but the main courses more than make up for it. Breads are baked fresh daily, and the cheeses are British. Always a buzzy feeling here.

★★Fulham Road

257-259 Fulham Rd., SW10.
☎ 0171/351-7823. AE, MC, V.
Reservations advised. Closed:
Sat lunch, Sun, Christmas, Good
Friday, bank holidays. Tube: South
Kensington. MODERN BRITISH.
$$$.

Time Out's Best New
Restaurant of 1995 has
Stephen Bull, one of London's
most respected restaurateurs,
behind the scenes. Inside is a
soothing environment of pale
yellow walls and Diego
Giacommetti–print cushions.
The menu is packed with
interesting combinations such
as hot buttered oysters with
sevruga caviar and tartare of
veal, lemon, and garlic, as well
as offal dishes like mixed grill
of pork loin, belly, black
pudding, and pig's trotter. It all
sounds heavy, but it's really
surprisingly light and delicate.
The high prices reflect the
excellent service and the
consistent quality, but dinner
here might demand a special
occasion.

Fung Shing

15 Lisle St., WC2. ☎ 0171/
437-1539. AE, D, DC, MC, V.
Reservations advised. Closed:
Christmas Eve, Christmas, Boxing
Day. Tube: Leicester Sq.
CHINESE. **$$**.

Chinatown presents a
bewildering choice of
restaurants. Most are perfectly
reasonable, but for excellent
Cantonese food Fung Shing
stands out. It's small and rather
cramped, but its Cantonese is
the very best. Avoid the set
menus and order from those
dishes listed under the heading
"Chef Special."

Le Gavroche

43 Upper Brook St., W1.
☎ 0171/408-0881. AE, D, DC,
MC, V. Reservations required.

Jacket and tie required. Closed:
Sat, Sun, Dec 23–Jan 2. Tube:
Bond St. FRENCH. **$$$$**.

For the money you spend here
you could fly to Paris—but
there you won't get the
wonderful creations of Michel
Roux, son of Albert and
nephew of Michel, Sr., the
famous brothers from
Burgundy who created Le
Gavroche. Theirs is widely
regarded as one of the 2 or 3
best French restaurants in
London. The menu is
sufficiently varied to meet
most requirements, and it does
list a few popular classics
among the heavenly sauces and
soufflés, mousses and
mousselines. Although Le
Gavroche doesn't specialize in
fish, its mousseline of lobster
and turbotin in Chardonnay
are notable delights.
Burgundian the Roux family
may be, but the lengthy wine
list pays equal homage to
Bordeaux. Service is attentive,
courteous, and helpful, and the
ambiance formal but unstuffy.
The fixed-price lunch is almost
a bargain.

Gay Hussar

2 Greek St., W1. ☎ 0171/
437-0973. AE, D, DC, MC, V.
Reservations advised. Closed:
Sun, bank holidays. Tube:
Tottenham Court Rd.
HUNGARIAN. **$$$**.

The name predates any sexual
connotation, and persuasions
are more obviously political in
this famous plotting place: It's
an irony that a Hungarian
émigré establishment should
be so well patronized by
leading socialist politicians, but
they obviously enjoy such
Central European sustainers as
cherry soup, pressed boar's
head, goose, mallard,
dumplings, and lemon cheese
pancakes. The lunch menu

offers a considerable selection of dishes, all at modest prices. Although it has changed hands, care has been taken to keep the restaurant exactly as it was in 1953—clubby, with paneled walls and velvet seats—in the famous Mr. Sassie's day.

Geale's

2 Farmer St., W8. ☎ 0171/ 727-7969. MC, V. No reservations. Closed: Mon, Sun, 10 days at Easter, 2 weeks in July, 2 weeks at Christmastime. Wheelchair accessible. Tube: Notting Hill Gate. BRITISH. **$**.

Fish-and-chips should be eaten out of a newspaper held hotly in the hand, in the course of a winter's evening stroll; every true Briton knows that, in much the way that all Americans prefer their franks served up at a ball game. The notion of a fish-and-chip restaurant is heresy enough to the purist, and a fashionable one defies the logic of the world's greatest take-out food. But Geale's has done it. Success hasn't spoiled the place, though; it remains very basic, with excellent fish, despite such nonsense as a wine list. Be prepared to stand in line to get in.

Goode's

Thomas Goode, 19 South Audley St., W1. ☎ 0171/409-7242. AE, D, DC, MC, V. Reservations advised. Closed: Sun. Wheelchair accessible. Tube: Green Park. MODERN BRITISH. **$$$**.

Breakfast, lunch, and dinner are now being served in this formal dining room attached to Thomas Goode's china emporium. Gold wallpaper, heavy silk brocade curtains, sparkling white marble floors, and lots of tassels attract the rail-thin and well-heeled. The china, of course, is the best. Go ahead—don't be

embarrassed—lift up the tea cup and check the mark; if you like it, you can buy it in the adjacent shop. The kitchen is overseen by the well-known catering firm Mustard, on whose canapés many of the diners have noshed at some of London's smartest addresses. The salad of artichoke hearts, crisp asparagus, poached quail's egg, and saffron dressing is light and fresh. To follow, you might try the salmon lasagna with courgette strips and pimento puree. A waitstaff sporting gold waistcoats is overly conscientious. You get the picture.

★Granita

127 Upper St., N1. ☎ 0171/ 226-3222. AE, MC, V. Reservations advised. Closed: Mon, Tues lunch, 10 days at Christmastime, 5 days at Easter, last 2 weeks of Aug. Tube: Highbury and Islington, Angel. MODERN BRITISH. **$$**.

Once Labour Party Leader Tony Blair was spotted here, the word was out; all of a sudden, people from as far away as SW3 were spied dining here, on stunningly simple food at reasonable prices. The menu changes seasonally and states exactly what's available without any hyperbole or fancy talk. The bruschetta slathered with aubergine and tahini paste followed by sweet duck breast sauced with orange and Grand Marnier are mighty pleasing. If you haven't filled up on the delicious homemade bread, indulge in a dessert— how about a pear and almond tart? As the Almeida Theatre is just around the corner, you're sure to get settled in before last orders.

Greenhouse

27a Hays Mews, W1. ☎ 0171/ 499-3331. AE, D, DC, MC, V.

Reservations essential. Closed: Sat, Christmas, bank holidays. Tube: Green Park. BRITISH. **$$$**.

Chef Gary Rhodes, with his Bart Simpson hairdo, BBC series *Rhodes Around Britain,* and volumes of cookbooks, is certainly no wallflower. As such, he has no trouble pulling in the crowds at this unfussy country-style Mayfair restaurant. Rhodes has a revolutionary talent for transforming solid, traditional British favorites, such as Lancashire hotpot, oxtail, sponge, and bread and butter puddings into refined, melt-in-the-mouth specialties with subtly combined flavors. While his name is often associated with the classics, Rhodes is not afraid to borrow, combine, and transform to make them work, and his success rate is enviable. Starters in particular—smoked haddock with Welsh rarebit on a tomato and chive salad, for example—reveal a Continental influence.

The Halkin

5 Halkin St., SW1. ☎ 0171/ 333-1234. AE, D, DC, MC, V. Reservations advised. Closed: Sat-Sun lunch, bank holidays. Wheelchair accessible. Tube: Hyde Park Corner, Victoria. ITALIAN. **$$$**.

Minimalist elegance best describes the dining room of this cool, Italian-style Belgravia hotel. Armani-clad waiters silently scurry about well-spaced tables, and the artfully prepared food looks too slick to be as good as it is. This is mouthwatering fare that doesn't get enough attention. Recently awarded a Michelin star, The Halkin has all the hallmarks of haute cuisine: amuse-gueules, petits fours, and excellent execution. Chef Stefano Cavallini keeps flavors bright and strong; false notes

are rare. The risottos are very fine, the pastas flawless, and the desserts. . . . You walk away feeling well-fed without the lethargy that often accompanies a grand meal. The set lunch menu is a good way to sample this clever, delicious fare.

Interlude de Chavot

5 Charlotte St., W1. ☎ 0171/ 637-0222. AE, D, DC, MC, V. Reservations essential. Closed: Sat lunch, Sun, bank holidays. Tube: Goodge St., Tottenham Court Rd. FRENCH. **$$$$**.

With Marco Pierre White pulling his Godfather act once again, Interlude has quickly made a name for itself since opening in late '95. With the Master's protégé, Eric Crouillere-Chavot, in the kitchen, expect serious food—at serious prices. The sophisticated French cooking is derivative of MPW's idiom: strong flavors and unfussy presentation. Try the chargrilled tuna carpaccio with tomato sorbet, or the stuffed rabbit's legs with squid on a pearl barley risotto with marscopone. Well-spaced tables are elegantly set with fine linens and glassware, and such grown-up decor is complemented by grown-up service.

The Ivy

1 West St. ☎ 0171/836-4751. AE, D, DC, V. Reservations required. Closed: bank holiday lunches. Tube: Leicester Sq. MODERN BRITISH. **$$$**.

You'll see many famous faces at this London institution. Perfect for a special meal before or after theater, it's also a good spot for entertaining clients. Service is smooth and discreet—mere mortals suffer not a bit. And wood paneling, leaded glass, and cozy banquettes make it one of

London's most romantic eating spots. The menu is a nice mix of comfort food—hamburgers, oysters, scrambled eggs—and haute fare, such as sevruga caviar with buckwheat blinis. Last orders at midnight can accommodate the terminally jet-lagged.

Jenny Lo's Tea House

14 Eccleston St., SW1. ☎ 0171/ 259-0399. No credit cards. Reservations not necessary. Closed: Sun bank holidays. Wheelchair accessible. Tube: Victoria. CHINESE. **$**.

Run by the daughter of the legendary Ken Lo, who is often credited with introducing authentic Chinese food to London, this Pimlico noodle shop does a swift business in cheap, tasty spring rolls, dumplings, and steaming hot bowls of soup noodles. The alcohol is strictly BYO, with a £1 cover charge; better to opt for one of the therapeutic teas, blended by house herbalist Dr. Xu. With communal-style seat-ing at 4 long black tables, it's not a place to linger, anyway.

Jimmy Beez

303 Portobello Rd., W10. ☎ 0181/964-9100. AE, MC, V. Reservations advised. Closed: Christmas–Jan 3, Notting Hill Carnival. MODERN BRITISH. Tube: Ladbroke Grove. **$$**.

This is casual eating in a funky environment. The menu is a diverse choice of Asian/ Californian/Mediterranean cuisine (the chef trained at New York's Arizona 206); the Peking Duck salad is a favorite. The crowd is very cool and disaffected. The music is often a bit too loud, but when we requested that it be turned down, we were accommo-dated (albeit begrudgingly). To escape the din, you might try

for an outside table in the warmer months (though the street scene during Portobello market hours can be equally unnerving). The quality of the food and cheap prices make putting up with the noise level worth it. Perfect for lunch after a morning cruise down Portobello Rd.

Kensington Place

201-207 Kensington Church St., W8. ☎ 0171/727-3184. MC, V. Reservations required. Closed: Christmas Eve, Christmas, Boxing Day, New Year's Day. Wheelchair accessible. Tube: Notting Hill Gate. MODERN BRITISH. **$$$**.

Everyone complains about the noise level here—but it doesn't keep away the crowds of mostly media folks, who jostle nightly for a window table. Kensington Place can claim many firsts: The Mediterranean angle was adopted here way before it hit the rest of London's menus, and the loft-like space, featuring gobs of plate glass, was London's first "dinner as theater" experience. The simple, innovative cuisine sometimes misses, but mostly hits. When I was last there, I was so-so about a couscous with rabbit, merguez, and harissa, but my dining companion was ecstatic about the grilled sea bass with lentils and salsa verde. They made it up to me, though—the lemon tart was perfection. The menu changes often and your options can be a bit limited.

Under the same manage-ment on the other side of the Royal Borough is Launceston Place (1A Launceston Place, W8; ☎ 0171/937-6912) has a cozier feel, more like a private dining room than a restaurant. Here, accomplished chef Charles Mumford produces fine Modern British cuisine (salt cod fishcakes with aioli, warm chicken liver with chives), but doesn't exclude stalwart favorites like beef sirloin for Sunday lunch.

Langan's Brasserie

Stratton St., W1. ☎ 0171/493-6437. AE, D, DC, MC, V. Reservations required. Closed: Sun, bank holidays. Tube: Green Park. MODERN BRITISH. **$$$**.

Michael Caine, the archetypal knowing Cockney, was one of the founding members of this place, headquarters of London's cafe society, where the famous are not only sketched on the menu but also seated at the tables. Despite Peter Langan's sad death, his buzzing brasserie has retained its pizzazz, even if more tourists and soccer stars than moguls and movie stars have crept in of late. The food, under the control of roving chef Richard Shepherd, has lost a little of its edge, but remains surprisingly superior; try the spinach soufflé, croustade d'oeufs de caille, profiteroles with chocolate sauce. Langan's may not be at its zenith, but this is still an exciting dining room: a wonderfully lit huge space, filled with white-covered tables, black-aproned waiters, beautiful modern paintings, and above all, people.

Leith's

92 Kensington Park Rd., W11. ☎ 0171/229-4481. AE, D, DC, MC, V. Reservations advised. Closed: Mon and Sat lunch, Sun, Christmas, Aug Bank Holiday. Tube: Notting Hill Gate. MODERN BRITISH. **$$$$**.

Leith's was founded by Prue Leith, an impressive food writer and the Leith behind Leith's School of Food and Wine. Leith's has always been a temple of the very best English food with an especially inventive style, served from a very short menu. The new owners, who have run the restaurant for the past 8 years, claim that the quality of food remains unmistakably "Leith's" and in keeping with its Michelin star status. The restaurant is well known for its trolley of cold starters, on which a typical item might be smoked trout pâté parcels wrapped in smoked salmon. Dishes from the kitchen are usually even better: Stilton soup is a favorite, perhaps followed by traditional roast duckling served with a light orange jus. There's a varied menu of delectable vegetarian dishes; an excellent, if expensive, wine list (with many available by the glass); and superb vegetables, cheeses, and delicious desserts served from a groaning trolley. You'll enjoy it all in a soothing, elegant interior featuring leather chairs, banquettes, and a waitstaff with Noël Coward aspirations.

M Fish

12 Ivory House, St. Katherine's Dock, E1. ☎ 0171/680-0990. MC, V. Reservations not necessary. Tube: Tower Hill, DLR Tower Gateway. ENGLISH. **$**.

This place is a funky turn on the trad fish-and-chip restaurant: The Swiss chef serves up this English staple with a Japanese twist. There's haddock fillet in oriental batter seasoned with spring onion, sesame seeds, soy sauce, and shrimp paste. Cod comes fried in sundried tomato and saffron batter. Dips, which include tartar sauce as well as sweet-and-sour, chili-and-tomato, and cumin-and-coriander mayonnaise, give a lift to the fillet. The chips are well-seasoned, ungreasy skin-on

wedges. Japanese tea, beer, and
a few wines are available.
Design is sleek and modern:
The pale wood tables are laid
with chopsticks and large
white napkins, and the staff is
in clingy black.

Malabar

27 Uxbridge St., W8. ☎ 0171/
727-8800. MC, V. Reservations
advised. Closed: Christmas, last
week in Aug. Tube: Notting Hill
Gate. INDIAN. **$$**.

This friendly Indian restaurant
with attractive European decor
is in a quaint area of Notting
Hill Gate known as Hillgate
Village. Popadom with a nice
trio of chutneys greets diners
upon arrival. The menu is
quite short but the fare is
inspired, with spices and herbs
used quite distinctively in such
tempting specialties as shashlik
kebab, venison marinated in
tamarind, and chicken with
cloves and ginger, all served
authentically on stainless-steel
plates. Main course portions
often seem a bit stingy,
though.

★ Marco Pierre White: The Restaurant

Hyde Park Hotel, 66
Knightsbridge, SW1. ☎ 0171/
259-5380. AE, D, DC, V.
Reservations required. Closed:
Sat lunch, Sun, Christmas.
Wheelchair accessible. Tube:
Knightsbridge. MODERN
BRITISH. **$$$$**.

Marco Pierre White, London's
most talked-about chef,
(known for both his fiery
temperament and his award-
winning food) won his 3rd star
from Michelin in 1995;
concurrently (coincidentally?),
his name increased in size on
the awning outside the
restaurant. Some of the best
chefs in London have trained
with MPW, though many have
been reluctant to admit it

recently; these days, it's almost
a badge of honor to have had
words with the Great One.
That said, the food is excellent
and very grown up; choices
include soup of red mullet;
salad of potatoes and lobsters
with truffles; roast Bresse
pigeon on cabbage cooked
with goose fat; and Pierre
Kaufmann's braised pig
trotters. While the dining
room leaves some cold, (we're
told it's about to be refur-
bished), the food is top-notch
and elegantly presented. If
you're wallet is thin, try the
fixed-price lunch—the
blackberry soufflé is to die for.
And the service is the best in
the city—as long as you don't
upset the chef.

★ Mezzo

100 Wardour St., W1. ☎0171/
403-4455. AE, D, DC, MC, V.
Reservations required.
Restaurant: closed Sat lunch.
Tube: Tottenham Court Rd.
MODERN BRITISH. Restaurant
$$$**; cafe **$$.

This brand-new restaurant from
Sir Terence Conran is the
hottest dining venue in town.
Housed in the former Marquee
Club, where Jimi Hendrix and
Eric Clapton once played,
Mezzo delivers good design and
good food, with an open
kitchen boasting more than 100
chefs and seating for more than
750 diners. Set on 2 floors, it
houses the Mezzonine, with
an Asian-influenced menu;
Mezzo, serving up classic grills
and crustacea; a bakery;
patisserie; and Cafe Mezzo,
offering sandwiches, snacks,
and drinks. There'll be live jazz,
funk, and soul on the
weekends.

Moshi Moshi Sushi

Unit 24, Liverpool St. Station,
EC2. ☎0171/247-3227. MC, V.
Reservations not accepted.
Closed: Sat, Sun, bank holidays,

Christmas. Tube: Liverpool St. JAPANESE. **$**.

If you've been to Tokyo, you'll know the drill at this conveyor-belt sushi joint situated above the tracks at Liverpool Station. Plates of top-quality sushi snake around the counter atop the bar; diners grab what they want and pay according to the number and color of plates taken. At lunch, it's 3-deep at the bar with hordes of Japanese businessmen.

Museum Street Cafe

47 Museum St., WC1. ☎ 0171/405-3211. AE, MC, V. Closed: Sat, Sun, Christmas, last week in Aug. Wheelchair accessible. Tube: Tottenham Court Rd. MODERN BRITISH. **$$**.

Some of the best Modern British cuisine in the least pretentious of surroundings, a stone's throw from the British Museum. Chefs Gail Koerber and Mark Nathan have combined their talents to produce some exquisite dishes, using the freshest ingredients, simply cooked and artistically presented. The recently expanded dining room has white walls and simple furniture, and the menu is short and to the point. A meal might start with a light leek and saffron tart, a more robust black bean soup, or porcini risotto, accompanied by deliciously crusty homebaked bread. Most of the main courses are wonderfully succulent chargrilled fish or meats, served with a crisp, fragrantly dressed salad. Try to save space for one of the mouthwatering desserts.

Nam Long

159 Old Brompton Rd., SW5. ☎ 0171/373-1926. AE, D, DC, MC, V. Reservations advised.

Closed: Sat lunch, Sun. Tube: Gloucester Rd. FRANCO-VIETNAMESE. **$$**.

The front of this joint is a Sloanie bar that also attracts a big American expat crowd. In the restaurant, you'll find an authentic Franco-Vietnamese menu that is better than you'd expect. Excellent choices include crystal spring rolls with prawns, pork, and vermicelli with fresh mint and coriander in rice paper, served cold; grilled sole with lemongrass; and braised prawns with ginger and onions. The flavors are clear and strong.

Neal's Yard Dining Rooms

First floor, 14 Neal's Yard, WC2. ☎ 0171/379-0298. No credit cards. No reservations. Closed: Sat–Mon eves, Christmas, Boxing Day. Tube: Covent Garden. VEGETARIAN. **$**.

Located upstairs overlooking the Yard, this is a good spot for a tasty, inexpensive meal. The menu basically consists of vegetarian street food from around the globe. There's an Indian thali, a Mexican ensemble, a West African stew, and a Turkish meze, plus a few smaller dishes like hummus and falafel. The kitchen is open plan; diners can either seat themselves around the bar or share a communal table. In summer, the large windows open on the buzzy scene below.

New World

1 Gerrard Place, W1. ☎ 0171/734-0677. AE, D, DC, MC, V. Reservations not necessary. Closed: Christmas, Boxing Day. Tube: Leicester Sq. CHINESE. **$**.

This is a dead ringer for a Hong Kong dining hall where hundreds of people can be accommodated at lunch, when

dim-sum trolleys ply 3
ornately decorated floors. The
cuisine is authentic Cantonese.
Evening meals are dominated
by stir-frys and all the obscure
ingredients you'd expect, like
shark's fin and jellyfish.

Nicole's

Nicole Fahri, 8 New Bond St.,
W1. ☎ 0171/499-8408. AE, D,
DC, MC, V. Reservations advised.
Closed: Sun. Tube: Green Park.
MODERN BRITISH. **$$$**.
It seems to be a trend these
days: swanky retailers opening
swanky restaurants. Nicole's is
the latest, with a former
Clarke's protégé in the kitchen
delivering beautifully prepared
cuisine with a hint of a
California influence. The
dining room is light and casual,
dotted with convex gilded
mirrors, so most of the
decoration is provided by the
diners themselves. When the
ladies who lunch dominate the
crowd, you can choose from
the main menu or a lighter bar
menu of salads and pastas. The
duck confit, the flavor of the
moment at many London
restaurants, has a nice crisp
skin and is served with a white
bean puree. Breakfast is now
served as well.

Nippon Tuk

165 Draycott Ave., SW3.
☎ 0171/589-8464. AE, MC, V.
Reservations advised. Closed:
Sun. Tube: South Kensington.
JAPANESE/SCANDINAVIAN. **$$**.
A little gem with only 10 seats
tucked away from the street in
the heart of retail Knight-
bridge, this might well be the
smallest restaurant in town. A
great lunch spot with a mix of
sushi and smorgasbord.

★192

192 Kensington Park Rd., W11.
☎ 0171/229-0482. AE, D, DC,
V. Reservations advised. Closed:

Christmas, Boxing Day, bank
holidays, Notting Hill Carnival.
Tube: Ladbroke Grove. MODERN
BRITISH. **$$**.
This is still one of the trendiest
places in town. It continues to
be the local canteen for
Notting Hill's media crowd;
and the food and wine
continue to be pretty good
value. The style is self-
conscious postmodern with a
1950s edge to it. For the best
view of the groovy crowd, go
for a table upstairs, or, better
yet, a sidewalk table, which
provides maximum exposure.
In the Modern European
manner, the menu features
warm salads, grilled fish, goat
cheese, and lentils. The wine
list is excellent.

L'Odeon

65 Regent St., W1. ☎ 0171/
287-1400. AE, D, DC, MC, V.
Reservations advised. Closed:
Christmas, New Year's Day.
Wheelchair accessible. Tube:
Piccadilly Circus. FRENCH.
$$$$.
This brand-new Bruno Loubet
(of Bistrot Bruno) establish-
ment is the newest of the
flashy, megasized eateries
sprouting up all over London,
L'Odeon is situated on the 1st
floor of a Regent Street terrace
designed by John Nash in
1810. Inside is a glamorous
1930s atmosphere, with
dramatic sweeping staircase,
hammered pewter bar, and 9
large windows overlooking
Piccadilly Circus. The menu
promises French-style cooking
combining classic and
contemporary methods: foie
gras terrine spiked with roast
spicy pears; grilled asparagus,
soft-boiled egg sauce,
parmesan crackling; lobster,
spring onion, and mangetout
risotto, with orange and
cardammom oil. Promising to
seat more than 200 diners, this

Notting Hill Restaurants

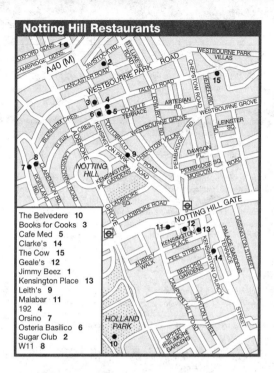

The Belvedere **10**
Books for Cooks **3**
Cafe Med **5**
Clarke's **14**
The Cow **15**
Geale's **12**
Jimmy Beez **1**
Kensington Place **13**
Leith's **9**
Malabar **11**
192 **4**
Orsino **7**
Osteria Basilico **6**
Sugar Club **2**
W11 **8**

is sure to be a buzzy dining spot.

Orso

27 Wellington St., WC2. ☎0171/240-5269. No credit cards. Reservations advised. Closed: Christmas, Boxing Day. Tube: Covent Garden. ITALIAN. **$$$**. This fashionable (but somewhat loud) restaurant was the first of the new breed of Italian restaurants in which the cooking is truly praiseworthy, rather than merely passable. The shortish menu features good meat and offal dishes and excellent vegetables, as well as crispy pizzas and the usual crop of homemade pastas. The wine list has been thoughtfully chosen and priced. Open from noon to midnight, and with 2 evening sittings and crisp service, this is an excellent spot either for a pre- or post theater supper.

Osteria Basilico

29 Kensington Park Rd., W11. ☎ 0171/727-9957. MC, V. Reservations advised. Tube: Ladbroke Grove. ITALIAN. **$$**. Another Notting Hill hangout that's always packed. The crowds gather for well-priced pasta, offered at 2 sittings. Bare scrubbed tables and thick glass tumblers enforce the rustic Italian atmosphere. Service can be brusque in order to get you out before the next wave. Avoid the basement, especially in summer, when it gets unbearably stuffy; alfresco tables are available then.

People's Palace

Royal Festival Hall, South Bank, SE1. ☎0171/928-9999. AE, D, DC, MC, V, all foreign currencies. Reservations advised. Closed: Christmas day. Wheelchair accessible. Tube: Waterloo. MODERN BRITISH. **$$**.

The jury is still out on the newest restaurant from Gary Rhodes, punk champion of British Cuisine. One thing's for sure: This place fills a gaping hole in the South Bank dining repertoire. Situated in the Royal Festival Hall, this is the place to fill up before or after the show. It's an open, airy room (it does lack charm, however—some have compared it to an airport hanger), good prices, and views over the Thames. Those looking for Rhodes' classic English fare will be disappointed, though. Tired of being pigeonholed as the savior of classic British cuisine, I suspect, Rhodes has spread his wings, offering a selection of dishes influenced by a wide range of cuisines.

Pizza on the Park ✓

11 Knightsbridge, SW1. ☎0171/ 235-5550. AE, D, DC, MC, V. Reservations taken for music room only. Closed: Christmas. Wheelchair accessible. Tube: Hyde Park Corner. ITALIAN. **$**.
This is the grandest of all the PizzaExpresses, a very reliable and high quality chain of stylish pizzerias; even Greenhouse chef Gary Rhodes has sung the praises of this rapidly expanding empire. I must admit, I find myself here often—it's easy and the food's really good. Individual pizzas are made fresh and come with a variety of toppings; there's also a selection of salads and light pastas. Other popular locations include 30 Coptic St., WC1 (near the British Museum); 29 Wardour St., W1; 10 Dean St., W1; and 137 Notting Hill Gate, W11. There's live jazz here and at Dean Street.

★Le Pont de la Tour

Butler's Wharf, Shad Thames, SE1. ☎ 0171/403-8403. AE, D, DC, V. Reservations required. Closed: Sat lunch, Christmas, Good Friday. Wheelchair accessible. Tube: Tower Hill, London Bridge. MODERN BRITISH. **$$$$**.
Sir Terence Conran has a sure touch when it comes to restaurants—which isn't surprising, since his 2 great passions are good food and good design. At Bibendum, Quaglino's, and the Blue Print Cafe, and now at Le Pont de la Tour, he has created the kind of restaurants that people love to be in and the sort of food they love to eat. This one is part of his converted warehouse complex, Butler's Wharf, and has exceptional views of Tower Bridge and the Thames. The long, glossy dining room, with mirrors, pillars, partitions, and black-framed picture windows, is especially stylish at night. The food is in Bibendum-style, but it's not as accomplished. A typical meal might be fish soup with rouille, tete de veau, sauce ravigote, and crème brûlée, or beef consommé with Madeira, followed by lemon sole and chips. The long wine list is strong on Burgundy and dessert wines.

For cheaper fare, drop into **Cantina del Ponte** next door. Outside seats have an equally pleasing view, and the Mediterranean-inspired menu features tasty salads, grills, and pizzas.

★Quaglino's

16 Bury St., SW1. ☎ 0171/ 930-6767. AE, D, DC, MC, V. Reservations required. Closed: Christmas, New Year's Day. Wheelchair accessible. Tube: Green Park. MODERN BRITISH. **$$$**.
Making your entrance down the MGM Grand–style staircase sets the tone for

Conran's megasized temple to the Paris Brasserie. Try as you like to disparage this instant success—it continues to please. The wonderful international menu includes such treats as sesame noodles, oysters from the crustacea bar, crab with mirin and soy, and a wide range of grills. Out-of-towners tend to dominate during pretheater hours, but locals come by in the later hours for a glass of bubbly and a light meal. The puddings are sublime. Another feather in Sir Terence's cap.

Riva

169 Church Rd., SW13. ☎ 0181/748-0434. AE, MC, V. Reservations advised. Closed: Sat lunch, Christmas, Easter, bank holidays. British Rail: Barnes. ITALIAN. **$$**.

After a day of antiquing in charming Barnes, treat yourself to a fine meal at Riva. The frequently changing menu offers a wide range of mouth-watering options; it might take you awhile to make up your mind. Sapore di mare, a platter of home-smoked scallops served in the shells with brown lentils, can satisfy 2. The pastas are served in 1st and main course sizes; I adored a farfalle sauced with buffalo ricotta, pine kernels, and basil. If you go for only one dessert (though you'll be tempted for more) it must be the sbrisolona, a maize and almond crumble soaked in vin santo and served with marscopone. The long, elegant dining room is filled with locals who, cheered by the consistently good food, display a clubby camaraderie.

★River Cafe

Thames Wharf, Rainville Rd., W6. ☎ 0171/381-8824. AE, MC, V. Reservations required. Closed: Sun dinner, Christmas, bank holidays. Wheelchair accessible. Tube: Hammersmith. ITALIAN. **$$$**.

The River Cafe is very much copied, but still without peer. The Thames-side space, in a hard-to-navigate side street of Hammersmith, was designed by Richard Rogers, one of London's biggest architectural names (he did the Pompidou Center in Paris) and husband of one the chefs. The front of the recently renovated bar is of highly polished steel, reflecting diners and the view outside— so keep your legs crossed. The clientele tends to be those sympathetic to the contemporary design industry and willing to pay quite a lot for outstanding Northern Italian fare. The menu changes daily, but might include grilled fresh sardines with mint, chili, and lemon; pan-fried venison marinated with juniper berries and Barolo; and wood-roasted Dover sole with bay leaves, fennel, and spinach. Relying on the best ingredients, the kitchen doesn't get between the natural flavors of the food and the customer. During summer, try to reserve a table outside.

Simpson's-in-the-Strand

100 Strand, WC2. ☎ 0171/836-9112. AE, D, DC, MC, V. Reservations required. Closed: Christmas, Boxing Day, New Year's Day, Good Friday. Wheelchair accessible. Tube: Temple. BRITISH. **$$$**.

This is unquestionably the most famous home of roast beef and nursery puddings (spotted dick, treacle roll)—very male, very British. Simpson's now offers a hearty traditional English breakfast and late night jazz throughout the week.

Sofra Restaurant

18 Shepherd St., W1. ☎ 0171/
493-3320. AE, D, DC, MC, V.
Reservations advised. Tube:
Green Park, Hyde Park Corner.
TURKISH. **$$**.

This long established and
stylish restaurant remains one
of the city's best spots for
Turkish fare. You'll be
greeted with a mixed platter
of olives, chilis, cucumber,
and carrots and a warm basket
of bread. After settling in, you
can choose between a
"healthy" fixed menu of
Middle Eastern meze or the
lengthy à la carte menu with
such classics as lamb guvec
(stew). Finish off with a
Kazandibi (milk pudding
topped with cinnamon).
Downstairs is much more
spacious than the cramped
upper dining room. Service
is impeccable.

The Square

32 King St., SW1. ☎ 0171/
839-8787. AE, D, DC, MC, V.
Reservations advised. Closed:
Sat–Sun lunch, Dec 24–Jan 4
(except New Year's Eve), bank
holidays. Tube: Piccadilly Circus,
Green Park. MODERN BRITISH.
$$$

Despite the boisterous interior,
with geometric bursts of color,
white walls, and dangling
window ornaments, the prices
ensure that the clientele is
well-behaved. The inventive
menu changes twice daily,
with the fish dishes deserving
special attention. Choices
might include seared tuna with
tartare of vegetables and soy-
wilted greens, or fillet of
turbot with pea risotto and
Parmesan. There's a lengthy
and complex wine list that
soars into the stratospheric
price range of £245. Rumor
has it that the Square will be
moving locations; call before
you go.

★ Sugar Club

33a All Saints Rd., W11.
☎ 0171/221-3844. MC, V.
Reservations advised. Closed:
Christmas, New Year's Day,
Notting Hill Carnival weekend.
Tube: Westbourne Park. NEW
ZEALAND. **$$**.

This is the newest addition to
the Notting Hill eating scene,
and it's been receiving rave
reviews. New Zealand chef
Peter Gordon cooks with
flair, adding his homeland
influences to European ideas.
Hopefully, Gordon can
maintain the excitement
necessary in order to attract
the perpetually bored Notting
Hill trendies who have been
migrating here from the Mas
Cafe, their drinking hangout
across the street. You'll be
immediately enticed by the
wonderful ciabatta roles with
chives and sweet butter.
Moving on, grilled scallops
with Thai spices and crème
fraîche, and grilled salmon
with blackened sweet potato
are some of the goodies you'll
find on the menu. The 2-story
space is easy on the eyes—pale
walls, dim lights. There's a cozy
garden outside.

Tamarind

20 Queen St., W1. ☎ 0171/
629-3561. AE, D, DC, MC, V.
Reservations advised. Closed:
Sat lunch, Dec 25–28. Tube:
Green Park. INDIAN. **$$$**.

This very smart, new,
"designer" Indian restaurant is
as far away from a local curry
house as you can get. Blond
wood, gold leaf, slate, and
stone abounds, with a dash
of color provided by saris
displayed in glass cases. The
chef, flown in from the
Oberoi in Delhi, has created a
menu built around 2 gigantic
Tandoor ovens; from these
come breads, free-range
chickens, meat, game, fish,

and shellfish, all freshly prepared in the North Indian style. The murge tandoor (marinated chicken on the bone with traditional spices) was excellent, but some of the other dishes were a bit disappointing, considering the hype. Still, Tamarind ranks as the hot Indian restaurant of the moment.

★★La Tante Claire

68-69 Royal Hospital Rd., SW3. ☎ 0171/352-6045. AE, D, DC, MC, V. Reservations required weeks in advance. Closed: Sat–Sun. Tube: Sloane Sq. FRENCH. **$$$$**.

One of London's 3-star restaurants (it was the only establishment to hold the honor until 1995), this is the place to go if you feel like showing off. Surprisingly, the tone isn't stuffy in this light and airy environment, with generously spaced tables—enjoyment of the food is the primary concern. The kitchen is ruled with an iron fist by Pierre Koffman; rarely leaving the kitchen, he oversees every detail, ensuring a consistency that's legendary. Signature dishes include tranche de foie gras et pain grille and pied de cochon aux morilles (pig's trotter). A predominantly classical wine list complements the exquisite and complex sauces. Try the fixed-price lunch for a more economical experience—it's one of the best deals in town.

Tate Gallery Restaurant

Tate Gallery, Millbank, SW1. ☎ 0171/834-6754. MC, V. Reservations advised. Closed: eves, Sun, Christmas, New Year's Day, Good Friday, May Day. Wheelchair accessible. Tube: Pimlico. BRITISH. **$$$**.

This isn't a museum snack bar—it's a full-scale restaurant, whose reputation was founded on its excellent and well-priced wine list as well as the beauty and wit of its Rex Whistler mural. The food, once dull, is at last catching up with the wine; the menu always includes tempting vegetarian dishes. Try to leave room for one of the excellent puddings. Open for lunch only.

33 St. James's Street

33 St. James's St., SW1. ☎ 0171/930-4272. AE, MC, V. Reservations required. Closed: Sat lunch, Sun. Tube: Green Park. MODERN BRITISH. **$$$**.

Yet another restaurant that's known by its address only. While many in the art world are familiar with the owner, the formidable Old Masters dealer Derek Johns, very few were aware of his passion for food. Johns is a former *Masterchef* champion, and he has very clear ideas about how a restaurant should be run and the quality of food served in it. This place attracts the clubby St. James's crowd and serves as the art-world canteen, especially during auction time. High ceilings, soothing yellow walls, and beautiful paintings on food themes done in the styles of the Old Masters set the stage for very grown-up fare prepared by an accomplished chef in a state-of-the-art kitchen. Start with the warm asparagus and caramelized calves sweetbreads with raspberry dressing, then move on to the poached Dover sole with fresh pasta, crisp bacon, and chervil sauce. Or try one of the grills; a different spit-roasted choice is featured each day of the week. Dessert, if you have room, will not disappoint. Plans are afoot for breakfast openings.

★Wagamama

4 Streatham St., WC1. ☎ 0171/
580-9365. No credit cards.
Reservations not taken. Closed:
Christmas, bank holidays.
Tube: Tottenham Court Rd.
JAPANESE. **$**.

This simple, stylish, and
inexpensive Japanese noodle
shop is very popular; expect a
fast-moving queue. Seating is
communal-style, and orders are
taken by staff outfitted with
hand-held computers that
transmit your choice directly
to the open kitchen. Diners
are on the young side and at
the height of the lunch hour,
the din is deafening. Main
courses are based around
ramen, usually stir-fried or in
soup with a wide range of tasty
morsels added. Veggies will like
the wide selection of raw
juices. When you become
hooked, buy yourself a
Wagamama T-shirt or shopping
bag. Set to open soon is a
Lexington Street branch—
hopefully, this will alleviate the
waiting.

W11

123a Clarendon Rd., W11.
☎ 0171/229-8889. AE, MC, V.
Reservations advised. Closed:
Aug Bank Holiday. Tube: Holland
Park. MODERN BRITISH. **$$**.

This is my local hangout, and
I'm always surprised at how
little recognition it gets in the
press. But then again, I guess
that's good for the natives,
who most nights can be
assured of securing a table. The
interior is best described as
quasi-Mediterranean: terra-
cotta walls, wrought iron, and
dripping candles. Try to
reserve a table on the ground
floor, where things are a bit
more buzzy. The daily menu
offers a good selection of grills
and pastas. The roast chicken is
always a winner, especially on
a cold winter night. The
service can be a bit slow, but
it's a friendly place and nobody
seems to be in much of a hurry.

Wodka

12 St. Albans Grove, W8.
☎ 0171/937-6513. AE, D, DC,
MC, V. Reservations advised.
Closed: Sat and Sun lunch,
Christmas, bank holidays. Tube:
High Street Kensington. POLISH.
$$.

Most famous for the wide
range of vodkas on offer,
Wodka specializes in Polish
cuisine with a contemporary
edge. Servings are generous
and the fare, not surprisingly,
tends to revolve around meat.
Expect lots of blinis filled with
yummy treats like caviar, herring,
and smoked salmon. The interior
is a slightly stark, nothing fussy,
but it attracts a buzzy local
crowd. The owner is a real live
Polish prince.

Cafes & Patisseries

London is sufficiently cosmopolitan to have a number
of good patisseries and cafes. Check out what the people
in black are doing at **Lisboa Patisserie** (57 Goldborne
Rd., W10; Tube: Ladbroke Grove), where you'll find
not only excellent coffee but wonderful custard cakes.
The trendsters are also hanging out at the **Living Room**
(3 Bateman St., W1; Tube: Tottenham Court Rd.); last
time I was there, a very serious fellow was busy sipping
cappuccino while devouring a volume of Anais Nin's
erotica. Also in Soho is **Bar Italia** (22 Frith St., W1;

Tube: Tottenham Court Rd.), open practically all hours, a social center for the early-hours demimonde.

Cyberia (39 Whitfield St., W1; Tube: Goodge St.), the internet cafe, is a magnet for on-line junkies. For an hourly fee, patrons can feed on pastries and coffees while they surf the net—perfect for e-mail addicts.

The **Jerusalem Coffee House** (55 Britton St., EC1; Tube: Farringdon) has a welcoming fireplace in the front room that lures a steady stream of locals, who sit for hours over a cup. While many people are familiar with Tom Conran's food emporium, **Tom's** (226 Westbourne Grove; Tube: Notting Hill Gate), few people are aware of the 3 small tables out back. This place is strictly self-service; grab one of his awesome sandwiches, like goat cheese, basil, and sundried tomato on focaccia, and a cappuccino and head for the garden. Also in Notting Hill is **Fat Rascals** (52 Ledbury Rd., W11; Tube: Notting Hill Gate), a great stop for a light breakfast or a cup of tea with a generous-sized croissant.

You can't miss the glossy hi-tech **Pret-a-Manger** (main branch 54–58 Oxford St., W1; Tube: Oxford Circus) outlets that are thankfully popping up all over London. Excellent coffee, fresh sandwiches, sushi, and desserts are beautifully prepared at reasonable prices—finally a decent sandwich shop in London!

Very funky and a bit out of the way is the **Delfina Studio Cafe** (50 Bermondsey St., SE1; Tube: London Bridge). This former Bermondsey chocolate factory has been converted into studio space for young artists, and the cafe serves up Mediterranean fare at starving-artist prices. For a break from shopping along Kensington Church Street, stop into **&Clarke's** (124a Kensington Church St., W8; Tube: Notting Hill Gate), attached to the legendary Clarke's restaurant, for a heavenly slice of quiche and a cappuccino. The service can be frosty, but the leek-and-goat-cheese quiche is so good that I keep coming back for the abuse. For gossipy ambiance, try **Patisserie Valerie** (44 Old Compton St., Soho, W1; Tube: Tottenham Court Rd.); for privacy and good pastries, visit nearby **Maison Bertaux** (28 Greek St., W1; Tube: Leicester Sq.); for sheer elegance and delicious brioches, the 70-year-old **Maison Sagne** (105 Marylebone High St., W1; Tube: Baker St.); for excellent pastries, **Maison Bouquillon** (41 Moscow Rd., W2; Tube: Bayswater).

Some of the museums have nice cafes/restaurants. Top spots include **The ICA Cafe** (ICA, The Mall, SW1;

Tube: Green Park), which offers imaginative salads; and the **Whitechapel Cafe** (Whitechapel High St., E1; Tube: Aldgate East). One of my favorites is the **Patisserie Valerie** that recently opened at the **Royal Institute for British Architects** (66 Portland Place, W1; Tube: Great Portland St.). Not only is the setting on the mezzanine of this listed building divine, but coming here is a great excuse to pop into the awesome architecture bookstore downstairs; excellent pastries as well as light lunches are served.

If you're in the East End, don't miss the **Brick Lane Beigel Bake** (159 Brick Lane, E1; Tube: Liverpool St.), open 24 hours and serving the best bagels in town. For meals any hour of the day, **La Brasserie** (272 Brompton Rd., SW3; Tube: South Kensington) is smack in the middle of shopper's Knightsbridge. A wonderful stylish setting and excellent steak frites.

The Dome (354 King's Rd., SW3; Tube: Sloane Sq.) is a posers paradise, located on a major scoping corner of the King's Road. A short selection of light meals and cappuccinos is available throughout the day; doors open onto the street on warm summer days. And there's always **Picasso** (127 King's Rd., SW3; Tube: Sloane Sq.). There's nothing special about this tired local cafe, but it's been the place to hang out for so many years now, it's practically an institution.

Cafes have suddenly sprouted up in chic shopping venues around town; it's an interesting trend that makes great sense. Most serve light meals but some are quite serious (see Nicole's, p.54), serving a full range of food. A good place for breakfast and light meals throughout the day is the stylish cafe/restaurant in **Emporio Armani** (191 Brompton Rd., SW3; Tube: Knightsbridge), serving superior Italian food, now much in vogue: a good lunch stop during a day of Knightsbridge shopping. Equally chic and convenient for lunch is **The King's Road Cafe,** located in Habitat (208 King's Rd., SW3; Tube: Sloane Sq.), serving Mediterranean-inspired food to match the furniture. **DKNY** (27 Old Bond St., W1; Tube: Green Park) has a soaring space on Bond Street, where homesick New Yorkers can peruse the *New York Times* and order up a brownie or "salt-beef" (that's corned beef for us) on rye. (Be forewarned: The last time I stopped by it was served with cream cheese!) **Space NK,** (41 Earlham St., Thomas Neal's Centre, WC2; Tube: Covent Garden) the trendy fashion outlet in Covent Garden, has a handsome bar with a short menu of light snacks and coffees. **L'Express** will be found at most branches of the stylish designerwear emporium Joseph; centrally located branches include 16 Sloane St. (Tube: Knightsbridge) or the branch at Simpson's, Piccadilly (Tube: Piccadilly Circus). **Selfridge's** (Oxford St.,W1;Tube: Bond St.) has teamed up with Terence Conran to create a slick cafe, **Premier,** behind the grand clock of the landmark store; tuck into a tasty menu of pastries and light meals. If you find yourself at **Harrod's** (Knightsbridge, SW1; Tube: Knightsbridge), stop by the oyster bar in the ground-floor food hall. A great range of white wines and champagne complement a selection of the best on a half shell. For more healthy fare, there's also a great one-man juice bar (go for the Booster, a refreshing mix of carrot, spinach, and beetroot).

The best shop-and-dine spot is still the cafe at **Harvey Nichols** (109–125 Knightsbridge, SW1;Tube: Knightsbridge). This buzzy 5th-floor aerie is located smack in the middle of the glorious food hall.

Afternoon Tea

Most of the better hotels offer a traditional afternoon tea, usually between 3:30 and 5:30pm. Taking tea is a uniquely metropolitan experience. A choice of India or China blends, Earl Grey, camomile, or even tilleul (linden or lime-blossom), if you care to ask, is offered at the **Ritz Hotel;** it's essential to reserve in advance. For those seeking a bit of English stuffiness, the **Palm Court** at the **Waldorf,** WC2, stages tea dances on weekends; take a 3-course tea and a spin around the dance floor. Those who enjoy the full gastronomic delights favor **Brown's Hotel** and the Park Room at the **Hyde Park Hotel;** those more concerned with the drink itself tend to prefer the **Ritz** and the Savoy group (which includes **Claridge's,** the **Connaught,** and the **Berkeley**), which has its own blend. For sheer drama, the **Landmark** serves tea in the soaring Winter Garden Atrium. (For exact locations, see "Accommodations.")

One of the most stylish places to take afternoon tea is **Fortnum & Mason** (181 Piccadilly, W1; ☎ 0171/734-8040; Tube: Piccadilly Circus), either in the St. James's room or Fountain restaurant, which serve sandwiches and cakes as well as salads and high-tea specialties such as Welsh rarebit. Of the other department stores that offer afternoon tea, **The Terrace Bar** in **Harrod's** (Knightsbridge, SW1; ☎ 0171/730-1234; Tube: Knightsbridge), with an attractive conservatory, has a fairly expensive fixed-price menu, but you can eat as much as you like. Tea is also served in the more formal Georgian Restaurant. **Thomas Goode** (19 South Audley St., W1; ☎ 0171/409-7242; Tube: Green Park) does a nice tea in their formal silk-swathed dining room; it's served on fine china that you can purchase in the shop on your way out.

A more funky place for tea is the small, cluttered tearoom **Still Too Few** (300 Westbourne Grove, W11; ☎ 0171/727-7752; Tube: Notting Hill Gate), open only Saturdays when the Portobello market is in full swing. There are always homemade cakes, savory sandwiches, and a cream tea. Another atmospheric spot is the **Original Maid's of Honour Tearooms** (Kew Rd.; ☎ 0181/940-1171; Tube: Kew), adjacent to Kew Gardens (just outside the gates), an inviting, crowded salon that feels of another era. The specialty is the "Maid of Honour," a pastry specially created for King Henry VII.

But my all-time favorite has to be the tearoom in the **Chelsea Physic Garden** (Royal Hospital Rd., SW3; ☎ 0171/352-5646; Tube: Sloane Sq.), open Wednesday afternoons from April until October. After a wander through the extraordinary fauna, stop in the tea room for creamy cakes. A close 2nd is the **Orangery** (Kensington Gardens, W8; ☎ 0171/937-9561; Tube: High Street Kensington) in Kensington Gardens. Built in 1704 for Queen Anne, this elegant glassed-in conservatory is in the shadow of Kensington Palace. Who knows—you might even spot Princess Di.

Pubs

In most countries, it's difficult for even the experienced traveler to visit a strange town and immediately spot a place where it'll be possible to relax and, with luck, meet a few friendly natives. British pubs, however, are rooted in their local communities, and each painted sign outside a pub heralds a singular identity that is its quintessential charm.

Pubs can vary considerably, from temples of false Victoriana to the truly inspired, retaining original details and charm. London has pubs that grew out of every period of England's history, and their names reveal their backgrounds: A pub that stands on the site of a colonial Roman taverna may be called The Vines or The Grapes; a hostel for workers on some medieval construction project might be The Builders or The Bridge; a monastery hospice for pilgrims, The Angel or The Salutation. Although the term "public house" wasn't used until the mid-1880s, that's what they all are, whether they were built as coaching inns, Georgian coffeehouses, or gin palaces for the new city-dwellers of the Victorian age.

The pub's most important function is to provide an informal setting for conversation. Increasing numbers of pubs serve meals, too (some are even now better known as restaurants than as pubs; the noteworthy ones are listed in "London's Restaurants A to Z"), but a good many still employ the impenetrable pork pie as a defense against would-be diners, thus freeing themselves to concentrate on the serving of drink.

What to Drink

The true stock-in-trade of the pub is beer. Because London is so close to the hop gardens of Kent, it has long had a tradition of especially "hoppy" beers. Two London breweries, **Whitbread** and **Watneys,** are national giants; the truly local breweries are small firms like **Fuller's** (London Pride) and **Young's.** Young's, in particular, has championed the unique British tradition of having their beer conditioned at the pub, in the cask, and drawn by a hand pump (or "beer engine") at a natural cellar temperature. An ale should never be cold, but served like a red wine, a fact that surprises many tourists.

Another puzzler for foreigners is the lack of waiter service, although you may find it in some lounge-type bars. The purist likes to stand up while he enjoys his pint, and to drink it from a straight, handleless glass.

Pub Hours

Britain's inconvenient drinking laws, devised during World War I to curb drunkenness, were finally relaxed in 1988, and again in 1995. Pubs may now stay open from 11am to 11pm Monday to Saturday, and Sunday from noon to 10:30pm. Within these limits, the exact opening hours are at the discretion of the landlord. Opening hours tend to be longer in and around tourist attractions. In the City, pubs may close early and remain shuttered on weekends.

Ten minutes before closing, the barman sings out "last orders." Closing time is announced as "time gentlemen please," and customers are given up to 20 minutes to drink up.

Neighborhood Pubs
Central London
The busy **Black Friar** (174 Queen Victoria St., EC4; Closed: Sat–Sun; Tube: Black Friars) is handy for

Fleet Street and the City. The astonishing interior is an outstanding manifestation of the later Arts and Crafts movement. Don't miss the tiny nook at the back of the main bar. A good range of real ale is served.

Bunch of Grapes (207 Brompton Rd., SW3; Tube: Knightsbridge), west of Harrod's, has a beautiful Victorian interior. It's pleasantly dark, with an intimate little bar at the back. Country beers from Everard's and Wells are served, as are substantial hot snacks. Popular with tourists.

Discreetly tucked away in a leafy street, **The Clifton** (96 Clifton Hill, NW8; Tube: St. John's Wood) is a real gem, with 3 drinking areas served by an impressive oak bar. Open fireplaces and a delightful outdoor patio forecourt makes this a favorite with the St. John's Wood crowd. Nearby is the Saatchi Collection. Decent pub food.

The tiny **Dog & Duck** (Frith St., W1; Tube: Tottenham Court Rd.) serves superb Guinness in a tiled, mirrored genuine Victorian bar. The crowd tends to be made up of trendies and sensibly dressed young couples.

The few remaining Fleet Street scribes still favor Dr. Johnson's old pub, **Ye Olde Cheshire Cheese** (Wine Office Court, EC4; Tube: St. Paul's), for its low-ceilinged friendliness and Marston's beer, despite it now being a tourist haunt. There are salads and sandwiches in the pub, and the adjoining restaurant offers its famous steak, kidney, and mushroom pudding.

Even the bar staff fits the image at Soho's definitively picturesque **French House** (49 Dean St., W1; Tube: Leicester Sq.). Visitors either adore "The French" or wholly fail to be engaged by its perverse charm, but true Soho lovers have been loyal for decades. Indifferent beer and unexciting wine: try the champagne instead.

The type of inn that is the **George Inn** (77 Borough High St., SE1; Tube: London Bridge), with galleries from which patrons could watch shows presented by strolling players in the courtyard, inspired the layout of the first theaters, including Shakespeare's Globe. The George is the last galleried inn in London, and only part of it still stands. It's attractive and comfortable, with 4 small bars (one serving bar food) and an expensive, oak-beamed restaurant. Wethered's Bitter is dispensed from a recently restored 150-year-old beer engine.

At Hyde Park Corner, down a tiny, unpromising mews called Old Barrack Yard, is the **Grenadier** (18 Wilton Row, SW1; Tube: Hyde Park Corner), said to have been the Duke of Wellington's local. You can drink outside this pretty pub, and eat full meals inside at reasonable prices. Ruddle's County is on tap.

The tiny, basic **Guinea** (30 Bruton Place, W1; Tube: Green Park) in the heart of London, would pass for a village local if it weren't full of ad execs and book editors. Hard to find (it's down a mews), but worth the effort. The adjoining restaurant serves excellent beef and good Bordeaux, but is very expensive. This is a Mayfair outpost for Young's brewery.

In lovely Cheyne Walk overlooking the river, you'll find the more-than-400-year-old **King's Head and Eight Bells** (50 Cheyne Walk, SW3; Tube: Sloane Sq.), with its 18thC decor and prints of old Chelsea on the walls. There's a permanent buffet, and Wethered's, Flowers, and Marston's Pedigree on tap.

Dryden dubbed the **Lamb and Flag** (Rose St., WC2; Tube: Covent Garden) "The Bucket of Blood" after being mugged in the adjoining alley. It's as dark and poky as ever, but you'll meet none more intimidating than the graphic-design crowd that spreads itself almost into Garrick Street.

Behind Simpson's shop and gentlemanly Jermyn Street is the **Red Lion** (2 Duke of York St., SW1; Tube: Piccadilly Circus), said to be the best example of a small Victorian gin palace. Burton's beer is on tap, and hot snacks are available.

Art Nouveau bronze nymphs and an equally decorative, predominantly male clientele inhabit theaterland's

George Inn

spectacular **Salisbury** (90 St. Martin's Lane, WC2; Tube: Leicester Sq.). Guinness is on tap, and a cold buffet and hot snacks are available.

The **Sun Inn** (63 Lamb's Conduit St., WC1; Tube: Holborn) is a specialty beer pub offering never fewer than a dozen out-of-town brews, usually ranging from Boddington's to Old Peculier. The manager will proudly show you his cellars (reserve in advance) when he's not too busy slaking the thirsts of medics from Great Ormond Street Hospital, or feeding them tasty hot snacks.

An open-plan kitchen, mix-and-match chairs, wood floors, and excellent Mediterranean-inspired food makes **The Westbourne** (101 Westbourne Park Villas, W2; Tube: Westbourne Park) popular with the hip Notting Hill crowd. If you don't go for Guinness, there's an impressive wine list.

Windsor Castle (114 Campden Hill Rd., W8; Tube: Notting Hill Gate) is another popular Notting Hill pub, with an open fire in the oak-beamed bar for winter and a large walled garden for summer. Charrington's IPA and Bass are served, as is good British fare like roast beef and Yorkshire pudding and fish-and-chips.

North London

Hampstead   The picturesque **Holly Bush** (22 Holly Mount, NW3; Tube: Hampstead) dates back to 1796. Edwardian gas lamps and a sagging ceiling add atmosphere to this local watering hole. A light menu of British basics is served.

Among the well-known Hampstead pubs, the **Flask** (14 Flask Walk, NW1; Tube: Hampstead) is the best-liked locally. It's a genuine neighborhood pub, with interesting tiling inside and out, a lively regular clientele, and Young's on tap. It's in a pretty alleyway, near a couple of bookstores, just around the corner from Hampstead tube station.

South London

Greenwich   Named after the famous tea clipper that's permanently berthed nearby, the Georgian **Cutty Sark** (Ballast Quay, Lassell St., SE10; British Rail: Maze Hill), dating from the early 1800s, has Bass on tap.

Southwark   The beer is brewed in the cellar at the **Goose and Firkin** (47 Borough Rd., SE1; Tube: Elephant and Castle), where bitters with names such as Goose, Borough, Dogbolter, and Earthstopper bring in a young, enthusiastic clientele.

The well-restored **Mayflower** (117 Rotherhithe St.,
SE16; Tube: Rotherhithe), with a verandah over the
river and a restaurant, serves Charrington's IPA and Bass.
In the same docklands area is one of Pepys' favorite
pubs, the **Angel** (101 Bermondsey Wall East, SE16),
serving Courage's beer.

West London

Barnes   The village pond, alive with ducks and fringed
with weeping willows and oak trees, lies opposite the
Sun Inn (7 Church Rd., SW13; British Rail: Barnes).
There are seats by the pond, but you could just as well
sit outside the pub with a pint of Taylor Walker's beer.
Remarkably rural for a place that's a double-decker bus
ride (no. 9) from Piccadilly. Inside, it's low-ceilinged
and cozy.

Barnes has lots of interesting pubs: Just down High
Street are the **Bull's Head** for jazz, and the **White
Hart** for its riverside verandah. Both sell Young's beer.

Hammersmith   This riverside **Dove** (19 Upper Mall,
W6; Tube: Hammersmith), with its own terrace and
just upstream from the splendid Hammersmith Bridge,
is rich in historical and literary associations: Part of the
pub was built by George III's son, Prince Augustus
Frederick. Fuller's beer is on tap.

Closer to the bridge is the **Blue Anchor** (13 Lower
Mall, W6), with a fine pewter bar and enormous beer
engine serving Courage's.

Richmond   The Victorian **Orange Tree** (1 Clarence
St.; Tube: Richmond; for show details, call 0181/
940-0140), a theater pub, is large and rambling, yet
somehow intimate. Young's beer and a good range of
bar meals are available. Also especially recommended is
the **Old Ship** (3 King St.), facing the main George
Street, known for its cheering, open fires in winter and
Young's on tap.

ACCOMMODATIONS

Choosing the Accommodation That's Right for You

London's large luxury hotels have had to work hard to weather the recession of past years. They're still outrageously expensive, but they have improved their facilities, installing business centers, cordless phones, fax machines, and PCs as well as fitness centers, saunas, and swimming pools. I am, however, still partial to the city's smaller, more intimate hotels. More often than not, their personal touches and charm far outweigh any lack of services.

London is rife with seedy lodging houses (none of which are included here), but there continues to be a serious dearth of well-maintained, medium-priced hotels. If that's what you're looking for, you might instead consider booking a room at a bed-and-breakfast. It's best to have a recommendation, as standards do vary; but if you're successful, you may end up with more than a comfortable, reasonably priced accommodation—you might also make some new friends.

If you've been to London before, you might try a hotel outside of the hotel ghetto of the West End. Notting Hill and Holland Park are beautiful, leafy residential sections that also offer great dining options.

Your Options

Luxury Hotels   At the most expensive end of the spectrum, the grand old hotels of London—the Savoy, Claridge's, the Ritz, Dorchester, Connaught, Brown's, and the like—bear witness to the English notion of style as something that murmurs rather than shouts. They assume that quality is timeless, so the decor can seem old-fashioned to some. They were built for people with ancient country estates who needed a home-away-from-home in town. Others may prefer something less English.

Most of the international chains, such as Hyatt, Sheraton, and Hilton, have at least one establishment in London, offering the style and service to which their regular patrons are accustomed. Since most of these hotels offer conference facilities and are popular with business travelers, advance reservations are essential. Of the British chains, Trust House Forte is the largest, with the Grosvenor House as its flagship. Inter-Continental has a stronghold in London, with several top hotels, including the Inter-Continental and May Fair, under its aegis. The deluxe Savoy group includes the Savoy, Berkeley, Connaught, and Claridge's.

House Hotels   In the mid-price range (beware—these rates are slowly creeping up), "house hotels" are becoming increasingly popular. These attractive converted-terrace-houses usually only have a few rooms. They range from the designer-decorated, such as Dorset Square, The Sloane, The Cranley, and L'Hotel, to the quaint and more budget oriented, like Ebury Court.

Executive Accommodations   Business travelers have a wealth of choices. Some of the hotels that are largely oriented to the business traveler, with several floors dedicated to executive accommodations, are the Halkin, the Hyatt Carlton Tower, and Inter-Continental, the latter 2 with fully equipped business centers as well; the superb Howard, near the City; and 2 luxurious options, 47 Park Street and the Dorchester. Many of the larger hotels have conference facilities.

Bed-and-Breakfasts   A less expensive type of British accommodation is a boarding house, or bed-and-breakfast (B&B). At their best—Aster House and Collin House are good examples—they're clean, comfortable, and friendly. Currently, however, good B&Bs are in short supply; don't reserve a room at one without a recommendation you can trust. The following services will arrange a B&B room for you: **Bed & Breakfast,** P.O. Box 66, Bell Street, Henley-on-Thames, Oxfordshire RG9 1XS (☎ 01491/578-803, fax 01491/410806; in the U.S., 800/367-4668); and **Worldwide Bed & Breakfast Association** (☎ 0181/742-9123, fax 0181/749-7084; in the U.S., 800/852-2632).

Home Stays   The British Tourist Authority is promoting a pleasant alternative: staying with a British family. *Stay in a British Home* is available from British Tourist Authority offices in the United States (see

"The Basics," p. 256). There are also a few recommended booking agencies; the best is the **Bulldog Club,** run by Anna Cryer, 15 Roland Gardens, SW7 3PE (☎ 0171/341-9495, fax 0171/341-9496; in the U.S., 905/737-2798, fax 905/737-3179). For an annual membership fee of £25, they'll arrange accommodations for you in some of London's poshest homes in Knightsbridge, South Kensington, Chelsea, and beyond. Rates are £95 per night, breakfast included.

Apartments   Staying in a serviced apartment is a great alternative to a hotel, especially if you wish to entertain or are bringing your family. Business travelers, perhaps seeking complete privacy, can also find them preferable to the glare of a large hotel. One of the newest apartment hotels, located in the heart of Mayfair, is the art-deco furnished **Ascott** (49 Hill St., W1; ☎ 0171/499-6868; fax 0171/499-0705). The trendiest, attracting film folk on location is the ultramodern **Fountains** (1 Lancaster Terrace, W2; ☎ 0171/221-1400; fax 0171/229-3917). The **Athenaeum** (p. 75) and **Grosvenor House** (p. 90) also have large numbers of 1-, 2-, and 3-bedroom apartments.

If the idea of a self-catering (efficiency) apartment appeals to you, look for the list in the booklet *Self-Catering Apartments and Accommodation Agencies in London,* available from British Tourist Authority offices or from the London Tourist Board. Most estate agents in London that handle rentals also have a number of short-term lets available.

Making Reservations

Book your hotel room well in advance and directly with the hotel; avoid using an agency, which may add exorbitant commissions, as well as calling the "800" number—you usually can't negotiate with the reservations agents that take your call. I don't suggest arriving without a reservation, especially during the peak season (i.e., summer), when rooms are scarce. And be sure to state your preferences—a quiet or nonsmoking room, one with a view, one with a separate shower, etc.—when booking. Most hotels are continually updating their accommodations; inquire into the availability of newly refurbished rooms. Upon arrival, if the room you're assigned is not to your liking, don't be shy; if it smells of stale smoke or the sound of drilling in the street will keep you from a good night's sleep, ask to be shown another room.

You can make advance reservations at a wide range of hotels by calling the **London Tourist Board Accommodation Booking Line** (☎ 0171/824-8844, fax 0171/259-9056); they'll hold your room with a Visa or MasterCard. If you do arrive in London without a room, try booking through the **London Tourist Board Information Centres** at Heathrow, Greenwich, Islington, Richmond, and Victoria Station.

Rates

Where rates are concerned, be aggressive. When booking, ask about weekend or corporate rates, any special deals that might be available, or, even more brazenly, if the rate quoted is the best they can do. Make sure to ascertain whether the rates quoted include breakfast and value-added tax (VAT). London hotels usually charge by the person, rather than by the room, and sometimes include breakfast in the price—increasingly only a Continental breakfast of toast or croissants and coffee, with a supplement charged for the full fried English breakfast. Prices will, of course, be cheaper for rooms without ensuite bathrooms. Service is usually included. If you are very pleased with the service, give a small tip to the chambermaid or receptionist.

Price Chart

Our price categories are based on the approximate cost of a double room with private bath (unless otherwise noted), including VAT. Single rooms are somewhat cheaper. The category assigned to each hotel is based on actual costs quoted across these price categories in mid-1995. Naturally, actual prices tend to rise, but, in general, hotels stay in the same price category.

Symbol	Category	Current Prices
$$$$$	Very Expensive	more than £190
$$$$	Expensive	£141–£190
$$$	Moderate	£101–£140
$$	Inexpensive	£70–£100
$	Budget	less than £70

Hotels by Neighborhood

Bayswater
★★ Hempel's. **$$$$**

Bloomsbury
★ Morgan Hotel. **$**

Covent Garden/Soho/Strand
★★ Covent Garden Hotel. **$$$$**
★★ Hazlitt's. **$$$**

★ Savoy. **$$$$$**
Waldorf. **$$$$$**

Knightsbridge/Belgravia
★ Basil Street Hotel. **$$$$**
★ Beaufort. **$$$$**
★ Berkeley. **$$$$$**
★ Capital. **$$$$$**
Diplomat. **$$$**
★ Durley House. **$$$$$**
★ Halkin. **$$$$$**
L'Hotel. **$$$$**
Hyatt Carlton Tower. **$$$$$**
Hyde Park. **$$$$$**
Lanesborough. **$$$$$**
★ Lowndes. **$$$$$**

Marylebone/West End
★ Dorset Square Hotel. **$$$**
Durrants Hotel. **$$$**
Landmark. **$$$$$**

South Kensington/ Chelsea
★ Aster House Hotel. **$$**
Conrad. **$$$$$**
Cranley. **$$$**
Cranley Gardens Hotel. **$$**
★★ Draycott. **$$$$**
★ Egerton. **$$$$**
★★ Eleven Cadogan Gardens. **$$$$**
★ Franklin. **$$$$**
Number 16. **$$$**
★★ Pelham. **$$$$**
★ Sloane Hotel. **$$$**
Sydney House. **$$$$**
Wilbraham. **$$**

City
Great Eastern. **$$**
Howard. **$$$$$**

Kensington/Holland Park/Notting Hill
★ Blake's. **$$$$$**
★ Gore. **$$$$**
★ Halcyon. **$$$$$**
Hotel 167. **$$**
Pembridge Court. **$$$$**
★ Portobello. **$$$**

Blackheath
Bardon Lodge. **$$**

Mayfair/Piccadilly
Athenaeum. **$$$$$**
★ Brown's. **$$$$$**
★★ Claridge's. **$$$$$**
★★ Connaught. **$$$$$**
★★ Dorchester. **$$$$$**
Four Seasons. **$$$$$**
★★ 47 Park Street. **$$$$$**
Grosvenor House. **$$$$$**
Inter-Continental. **$$$$$**
May Fair. **$$$$$**
Le Meridien London. **$$$$$**
Ritz. **$$$$$**.

St. James's
★ Dukes Hotel. **$$$$**
St. James's Club. **$$$$$**
Stafford. **$$$$$**
★ 22 Jermyn Street. **$$$$**

Victoria
Collin House. **$**
Ebury Court. **$$$**
★ Goring. **$$$$**

Critic's Choice

I admit it, I'm not partial to the big hotels, but there are a few that manage to impart a more personal touch. Two outstanding ones in this category are the highly gilded **Dorchester** and the grand **Lanesborough**.

For romance, it's got to be **Blake's**—but only if you can book one of the deluxe rooms. If you end up with one of the minuscule standard doubles, you'll feel anything but romantic—you'll be too busy itching for some personal space. Of the small boutique hotels, I adore the **Draycott** and **11 Cadogan Gardens.** These special places are perfect for a romantic weekend; both have rooms overlooking the gardens (some have garden access).

If you're looking for a traditional English touch, any of the Kemps' beautifully appointed hotels, such as the chintz- and flower-filled **Pelham,** will fit the bill. They manage to do it well without it feeling contrived or stale. A bit toned down, but equally English, are **Dukes** and the **Egerton.** Both were recently renovated, and the modern facilities are now cleverly hidden beneath a veneer of traditional decor.

The club crowd is staying at the **Portobello Hotel.** The cabin-sized singles are cheap and cheerful, and the location, in the heart of their stomping ground, Notting Hill, is ideal.

Many of the hotels have been upgrading their health clubs, but the most comprehensive continues to be the one at **Le Meridien.** With squash courts, a swimming pool, billiard tables, and a central location, it's the choice for many fitness-minded business travelers.

Everybody's attention is turning to two brand-new hotels on the scene: The Kemps' **Covent Garden Hotel** is simply stunning, and is centrally located to the theater district and Soho; Anouska Hempel's newest venture in Bayswater, **Hempel's** (set to open any minute now), promises to be ultra–design conscious.

London's Hotels A to Z

★ Aster House Hotel
3 Sumner Place, London SW7 3EE. ☎ 0171/581-5888; fax: 0171/584-4924. 14 rooms. Tube: South Kensington. MC, V. **$$**. At the end of an early Victorian terrace lies this affordable B&B. Guests get their own front door key and access to the prize-winning gardens in the rear. They tryhard here to approximate traditional English style, but, for the price, don't expect miracles. The special rooms with 4-poster beds are quite spacious. All bathrooms are ensuite, but they're quite cramped. The buffet breakfast, included in the price, is served in a lovely conservatory; the variety of dishes is broader than you'd expect, with an emphasis on the healthy. All rooms are nonsmoking, but guests are free to smoke in the garden.

Athenaeum
116 Piccadilly, London W1V 0BJ. ☎ 0171/499-3464; 800/ 335-3300; fax: 0171/493-0644

Dukes Hotel

or 800/335-3200. 133 rooms, 34 self-catering apartments. Tube: Green Park. AE, D, DC, MC, V. **$$$$$**.

This smallish 1940s-era hotel is pristine, impeccably run, and full of good ideas. Attention to detail is the keynote: You'll be warmly welcomed by the genial head porter, Alex; if you decide to take a jog in the park, they'll lend you a track suit; if you take an afternoon nap, your sheets will be changed again before bedtime. The hotel has gone through a complete overhaul recently, and the updated furnishings, while still very chintzy, are fresh and pleasing. And the new health club is gorgeous— lots of marble, a plunge pool, and all the expected fittings. Unlike so many of today's hotels, the Athenaeum doesn't skimp on towels—there aremounds of them in the luxurious bathrooms. The relatively new restaurant, Bulloch's, feels like a private library. *Amenities:* Small health club, access to tennis courts, conference facilities, VCR, 24-hour room service, A/C, 8 suites wheelchair accessible.

Bardon Lodge

15-17 Stratheden Rd., Blackheath, SE3 7TH. ☎ 0181/853-4051; fax: 0181/858-7387. 67 rooms, 61 with bath. British Rail from Waterloo. AE, MC, V. **$$**.

Good inexpensive hotels are hard to come by in London; it may be necessary to look farther afield for a fair deal. Blackheath is an impressive place near Greenwich with a vast common and fine Georgian houses. Bardon Lodge, owned and run with some pride by Donald Nott, is a beautifully kept hotel with spacious rooms (most have only a shower cubicle, though) and a pleasant dining room. *Amenities*: Conference facilities, restaurant.

★ Basil Street Hotel

8 Basil St., London SW3 1AH. ☎ 0171/581-3311; 800/448-8355; fax: 0171/581-3693. 92 rooms, 72 with bathroom. Tube: Knightsbridge. AE, D, DC, MC, V. **$$$$**.

Many frequent visitors to London won't stay anywhere else but at this centrally located hotel—Harrod's,

Harvey Nichols, and all of Knightsbridge are right outside your door. Terribly old-fashioned and still privately owned, the dowdy but well-loved Basil Street is housed in an Edwardian building that still has many of its original nooks and crannies. A magnificent staircase leads to a lounge bar with comfy sofas and a dining room that features traditional English fare. The restaurant and hallways are filled with rich carpets, fine paintings, and British and Oriental antiques. Furnishings in the bedrooms, each unique, are traditional without too much fuss; room sizes vary considerably. For excellent value, try the rooms without ensuite facilities. The Parrot Club is one of the few ladies' social clubs; female guests get automatic membership. *Amenities:* Conference facilities, restaurant, VCR on request, 24-hour room service, partial A/C.

★ Beaufort

33 Beaufort Gardens, London SW3 1PP. ☎ 0171/584-5252; fax: 0171/589-2834 or 800/584-7764. 28 rooms. Tube: Knightsbridge. AE, D, DC, MC, V. **$$$$**.

The Beaufort, run by an all-women team, does its best to make guests feel at home in its 2 renovated Victorian town houses, tucked away in a cul-de-sac steps from Harrod's. Upon arrival, you're given a front door key and told to help yourself at the drinks cabinet—on the house. The high-ceilinged rooms are large and elegantly appointed with stylish fabrics and fresh flowers. While the rates seem high, the level of service and the added perks more than compensate. Harry, the resident cat, keeps watch over

all who enter. *Amenities:* Access to health club with pool and tennis courts, VCR, A/C, 4 rooms wheelchair accessible.

★ Berkeley

Wilton Place, London SW1X 7RL. ☎ 0171/235-6000; 800/63-SAVOY; fax: 0171/235-4330. 160 rooms. Tube: Knightsbridge, Hyde Park Corner. AE, D, DC, MC, V. **$$$$$**.

Noël Coward's old Berkeley is gone, but much of its character has re-emerged in the new one, built by the same management in 1972. Overlooking Hyde Park and Knightsbridge, the hotel successfully mixes old and new, largely through its renowned emphasis on service. The rooms are spacious and well-appointed, all with sitting rooms and big, tiled bathrooms —nothing daring, just classic British style with a touch of opulence. The stunning rooftop pool is modeled after a Roman temple. And inside you'll find one of London's better French restaurants, a tiered bar, and a Mediterranean-inspired dining room. At my last visit, the Berkeley was about to undergo a massive 2-year refurbishment that will extend not only to the decor, but will bring the hotel up-to-date with computer jacks, audio-visual tools in conference rooms, and expanded fitness facilities. *Amenities:* Large health club with indoor pool, sauna, access to tennis courts, 3 restaurants, conference facilities, VCR, 24-hour room service, A/C, movie theater, beauty parlor.

★ Blake's

33 Roland Gardens, London SW7 3PF. ☎ 0171/370-6701; 800/926-3173; fax: 0171/373-0442. 51 rooms. Tube: South Kensington. AE, D, DC, MC, V. **$$$$$**.

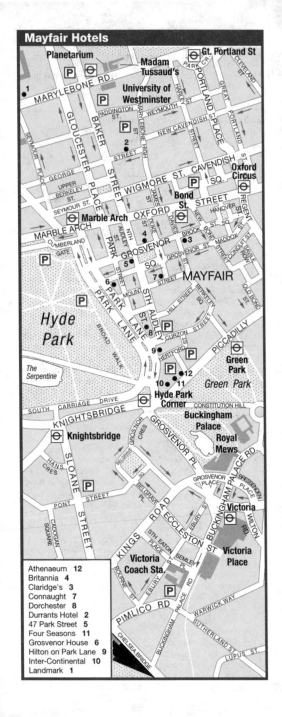

Mayfair Hotels

Planetarium
Madam Tussaud's
Gt. Portland St
University of Westminster
MARYLEBONE RD.
1
PARK CR.
PORTLAND
CLEVELAND
SEYMOUR
PLACE
GLOUCESTER
PLACE
BAKER STREET
PADDINGTON ST.
WEYMOUTH
HARLEY ST.
GREAT PORTLAND ST.
NEW CAVENDISH ST.
PORTLAND PLACE
GEORGE
UPPER BERKELEY ST.
SEYMOUR ST.
WIGMORE ST.
JAMES
CAVENDISH SQ.
Oxford Circus
Bond St.
2
STREET
MARBLE ARCH
OXFORD
NTH AUDLEY ST.
DUKE ST.
STREET
DAVIES
HANOVER SQ.
REGENT ST.
4
GROSVENOR
3
BROOK
MADDOX ST.
CONDUIT ST.
SAVILE ROW
CUMBERLAND GATE
PARK LANE
5
SQ.
GROSVENOR ST.
NEW BOND ST.
MAYFAIR
7
STREET
BERKELEY SQ.
OLD BOND ST.
Hyde Park
PARK LANE
STH AUDLEY ST.
MOUNT ST.
HILL STREET
BROAD WALK
6
8
CURZON STREET
PICCADILLY
9
HERTFORD ST.
Green Park
The Serpentine
12
10   11
Green Park
Hyde Park Corner
CONSTITUTION HILL
SOUTH CARRIAGE DRIVE
KNIGHTSBRIDGE
Buckingham Palace
GROSVENOR PL.
GROSVENOR ROAD
Royal Mews
Knightsbridge
HANS CRES
SLOANE STREET
BELGRAVE PL.
GROSVENOR CRES
BELGRAVE SQ.
PONT STREET
CADOGAN SQUARE
GROSVENOR PLACE
BRESSENDEN PLACE
KINGS ROAD
ECCLESTON
SOUTH EATON PLACE
EBURY ST.
BUCKINGHAM PALACE RD.
WILTON RD.
Victoria
Victoria Place
Victoria Coach Sta.
SEMLEY PL.
BOURNE ST.
PIMLICO RD.
EBURY
BUCKINGHAM PALACE RD.
WARWICK WAY
SUTHERLAND ST.
CHELSEA BRIDGE
LUPUS ST.

Athenaeum   12
Britannia   4
Claridge's   3
Connaught   7
Dorchester   8
Durrants Hotel   2
47 Park Street   5
Four Seasons
Grosvenor House 6
Hilton on Park Lane 9
Inter-Continental 10
Landmark   1

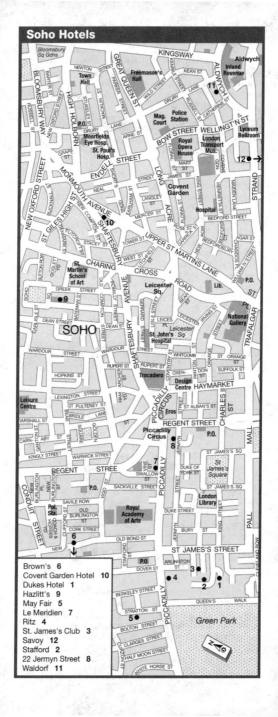

Soho Hotels

Brown's **6**
Covent Garden Hotel **10**
Dukes Hotel **1**
Hazlitt's **9**
May Fair **5**
Le Meridien **7**
Ritz **4**
St. James's Club **3**
Savoy **12**
Stafford **2**
22 Jermyn Street **8**
Waldorf **11**

This is the mandatory hostelry for media folk and celebrities, who are suitably at home in a hotel owned by designer Anouska Hempel. It doesn't get any better than this—over the top without being garish. From the black-and-white dining room and the plush, pristine bathrooms to the magnificent birdcage and the beautifully maintained gardens, every detail has been attended to—and it shows. The standard doubles and singles are tiny, but you wouldn't come here to stay in one anyway, this is the kind of place where you splurge on the special suite with the sunken bed. Downstairs is one of the better hotel restaurants in town; it's open until midnight and rates high in the romance department. Service is impeccable. Amenities: Access to nearby health club, restaurant, VCR on request, 24-hour room-service, partial A/C.

★ Brown's

Albermarle St., London W1X 4BP. ☎ 0171/493-6020; 800/ 225-5843; fax: 0171/493-9381. 116 rooms. Tube: Green Park. AE, D, DC, MC, V. **$$$$$**.
This terribly British hotel, part of the Forte empire, hasrecently refurbished the public areas and many of the guest rooms, which has meant an upgrade in facilities, but not a change in atmosphere—the place still drips in warm oak and mahogany and classic English style (this is still one of the best places in town to have afternoon tea). The four largest double rooms now have 4-poster beds, and all rooms have an extra line for fax or modem use (which is fitting, as Brown's was the originating point of Britain's first successful telephone call—Mr.

Bell himself was the caller). The updated rooms have a lighter and more Continental feel than the floral schemes that dominate some of the older ones. The theater district is nearby, as is Bond Street. Amenities: Access to health club with pool, 2 restaurants, conference facilities, VCRs on request, 24-hour room service, A/C.

★ Capital

22 Basil St., London SW3 1AT. ☎ 0171/589-5171; 800/926-3199; fax: 0171/225-0011. 48 rooms. Tube: Knightsbridge. AE, D, DC, MC, V. **$$$$$**.
You can't beat this location—situated right behind Harrod's. While the building itself is fairly new, the exterior and common rooms have been completely refurbished, bringing the facade more in line with the rest of the Victorians on the street. The beautiful lounges, decorated with swags of sumptuous silks, cozy chairs, and fine antiques, are the work of none other than designer extraordinaire, Nina Campbell. Margaret Levin, the owner, is no slouch when it comes to style, and she has personally overseen the furnishing of the guest rooms; the Ralph Lauren blue room is a favorite. The excellent formal dining room has a Michelin star. Be sure to try their own wine, grown at their vineyard in France—it's a winner. *Amenities:* Access to health club with pool, restaurant, conference facilities, VCR on request, 24-hour room service, A/C.

★★ Claridge's

Brook St., London W1A 2JQ. ☎ 0171/629-8860; 800-SAVOY; fax: 0171/499-2210. 190 rooms. Tube: Bond St. AE, D, DC, MC, V. **$$$$$**.

Visiting royals and statesmen are inclined to choose Claridge's, which, despite its fame, is imperturbably discreet. Service is the hotel's hallmark: A guest who has been shopping returns with a brace of pheasants; without batting an eyelid, the porter carries them for her as if they were Gucci suitcases. There's no bar—such trappings don't fit a country house, even if it is in the middle of London. You can cozy up with a drink in the living room, where a small orchestra plays at lunchtime and in the evening. Art-deco styling abounds, but the tone is better set by the log fires in the suites. The Penthouse suites have stunning views of Westminster Cathedral and Big Ben. A recent renovation has added 7 deluxe double rooms and a much-needed health club. The Causerie offers an excellent value-for-the-money smorgasbord lunch. Amenities: Small health club, access to indoor pool and tennis courts, 2 restaurants, conference facilities, VCR on request, 24-hour room service, A/C, 25 rooms wheelchair accessible.

Conrad

Chelsea Harbour, London SW10 OXG. ☎ 0171/823-3000; 800/ HILTONS; fax: 0171/351-6525. 160 suites. Tube: Fulham Broadway. AE, D, DC, MC, AE. **$$$$$**.

Many people bypass the Conrad, claiming its location in the new Chelsea Harbour development is too inconvenient and too "modern" for London. If you want traditional English charm, this is not the place for you. But if you want a top-notch business hotel, the Conrad is a good choice. They make it as easy as possible for you to get into the

city center with such extras as Jaguar service to Harrod's. The suites are done in English style and have all the electronic gizmos you'll need; penthouse suites have balconies over the harbor. The health club is one of the better in town, the conference facilities are top-notch, and the harborside lounges and restaurants offer some of London's best alfresco dining. Amenities: Large health club, indoor pool, conference facilities, 24-hour room service, VCR, 2 restaurants, A/C, 2 suites wheelchair accessible.

★★ Covent Garden Hotel

8 Monmouth St., London WC2. ☎ 0171/806-1000; fax: 0171/ 806-1100. 50 rooms. Tube: Covent Garden, Leicester Sq. AE, D, DC, MC, V. **$$$$**.

I must admit it—I'm biased toward all the hotels in the Firmdale Group, run by Tim and Kit Kemp. They do hotels so well it's hard not to be. This is the newest in their empire, and it's a gem. The Kemps have taken over a large Victorian building in the heart of Covent Garden, just across from the famous Neal's Yard. They've completely gutted it to ensure that all the amenities will be the most up-to-date of London's boutique hotels. Rooms are large, seriously soundproofed, and have 2-line phones, marble baths with double vanities and separate showers, large desks, built-in wardrobes, comfy chairs, and separate entries, so no one ever walks directly into a bedroom. And the decor—Oriental carpets, lush fabrics, antiques; many of the bedspreads have Asian crewel work. Some rooms retain the original beams; others have reading nooks. This is very much a city hotel, with rooftops visible from every window. Suite 410 has a wonderful terrace, and Room 303 is a 2-story loft-like space. Downstairs is a small cafe-style lounge that spills onto the street and a traditional barber shop. *Amenities:* Small health club, restaurant, conference facilities, 24-hour room service, VCR, A/C, 42 rooms wheelchair accessible.

Collin House

104 Ebury St., London SW1W 9QD. ☎ and fax: 0171/730-8031. 13 rooms, 8 with bath. Tube: Victoria. No credit cards. **$**. Basic is the word for this B&B. It feels like a small ski-chalet, with blond wood, crisp, clean sheets, and minimal decor. The walls are lined with photos of the Welsh countryside taken by the owner. The breakfast room, while spartan, is clean and comfortable. Some rooms do have bathrooms, but those that don't have facilities only a few steps away. Two rooms in the back can be sectioned off to form their own suite with bath—perfect for families.

★★ Connaught

16 Carlos Place, London W1Y 6AL. ☎ 0171/499-7070; 800/63-SAVOY; fax: 0171/495-3262. 90 rooms. Tube: Green Park. AE, D, DC, MC, V. **$$$$$**. This is one of the finest of London's grand old hotels; time seems to stand still here. Service is impeccable, and discretion has been elevated to an art form; the staff even keeps detailed records of regular patrons' habits and preferences. No false glamour or airs here. A wide, ornate staircase dominates the reception hall, which is appointed like an English gentleman's club.

Air-conditioning has made its way into most of the rooms, but don't expect the high-tech gadgets found in the chains—the Connaught likes to keep the modern world at bay. The high staff-to-room ratio, however, assures that all your needs will be met. Bedside is a 3-button call system that will bring maid, valet, or room service immediately to your side. Formality is encouraged; coats and ties are required at all times in the famous dining rooms—even for breakfast. *Amenities:* Access to health club with pool, 2 restaurants, conference facilities, A/C, 24-hour room service.

Cranley

10-12 Bina Gardens, London SW5 0LA. ☎ 0171/373-0123; 800/553-2582; fax: 0171/373-9497. 36 rooms. Tube: Gloucester Rd. AE, D, DC, MC, V. **$$$**. Three Georgian town houses have been expertly restored by American Bonnie DeLoof. Original details, including several fireplaces, have been kept intact. The textbook English Country Home decor—chintz and traditional antiques—is matched with modern facilities and excellent service. The bedrooms have kitchenettes if you're not up to going out, and the 2 ground-floor suites have private terraces and Jacuzzis. *Amenities:* Access to health club, VCR on request, A/C.

Cranley Gardens Hotel

8 Cranley Gardens, London SW7 3DB. ☎ 0171/373-3232; 800/44-UTELL; fax: 0171/373-7944. 85 rooms. Tube: Gloucester Rd, South Kensington. AE, D, MC, V. **$$**. The low rates and location are the big draws of this Victorian townhouse hotel. Nothing

fancy here—clean, simple rooms done in pastels and a nicely appointed breakfast room make this hotel a very good value for the money. They try hard in the reception area, which, in terms of decor, misses the mark by a mile—much too frilly, even bordering on the garish. *Amenities:* Restaurant, conference facilities, VCR on request, 24-hour room service.

Diplomat

2 Chesham St., London SW1X 8DT. ☎ 0171/235-1544; fax: 0171/259-6153. 27 rooms. Tube: Knightsbridge, Sloane Sq. AE, D, DC, MC, V. **$$$**.

Affordable rates in one of London's most posh neighborhoods make the Diplomat, in an 1822 historic building, a find. Steps from Harrod's, the hotel has well appointed rooms with tiled baths, most accessed via a lovely glass-domed stairwell with a gilded circular staircase. Go for the Cromwell Room; while partially below street level, it has a separate dressing room with plenty of space. *Amenities:* Restaurant, partial A/C.

★★ Dorchester

Park Lane, London W1A 2HJ. ☎ 0171/629-8888; 800/727-9820; fax: 0171/409-0114. 244 rooms. Tube: Hyde Park Corner. AE, D, DC, MC, V. **$$$$$**.

With its stately terraces, the Dorchester looks like an ocean liner that has somehow been moored on Park Lane. The hotel, now owned by the Sultan of Brunei, is dripping with cornices, swags, and expensive fabrics. A gold-gilt entrance and columned lounge, where guests take tea, will not fail to awe new arrivals. The rooms are individually decorated in a style vaguely referred to as "Georgian Country House." The Oliver Messel suite (Messel was a famous theatrical designer), has been restored to its original grandeur—even the TV is draped with silk swags. All the rooms were updated during a massive 1989 renovation with air, 2-line phones, cable TV, and magnifying mirrors in the bathrooms. The spa is an art-deco masterpiece, a soothing oasis for the stressed-out or jet-lagged. Of the 3 restaurants, the Oriental is the most exciting, offering a choice of Far Eastern cuisines. With a very high staff-to-room ratio, the Dorchester excels in service; the General Manager is often noted as one of the best in London. *Amenities:* large health club, 2 restaurants, conference facilities, VCR on request, A/C, 24-hour room service, 2 rooms wheelchair accessible.

★ Dorset Square Hotel

39/40 Dorset Sq., London NW1 6QN. ☎ 0171/723-7874; fax: 0171/724-3328. 37 rooms. Tube: Baker St. AE, MC, V. **$$$**.

Situated in a lovely Regency square, this is one of London's best and most stylish "house hotels." It's run by the Kemps' Firmdale Group, which includes the stunning new Covent Garden Hotel. You'll be immediately struck by the decor, a contrived but nevertheless charming evocation of the country house style almost alarming in its perfection. The 1st-floor balconied rooms have grand pianos, making this a popular choice with classical musicians. All the bedrooms are impressive and come with marble baths. Service is intelligent and efficient. If

Kensington & Knightsbridge Hotels

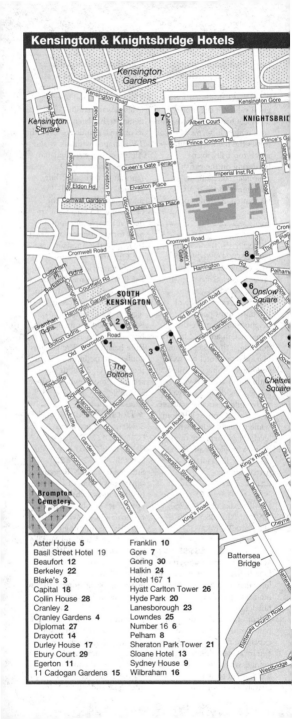

Aster House **5**	Franklin **10**
Basil Street Hotel **19**	Gore **7**
Beaufort **12**	Goring **30**
Berkeley **22**	Halkin **24**
Blake's **3**	Hotel 167 **1**
Capital **18**	Hyatt Carlton Tower **26**
Collin House **28**	Hyde Park **20**
Cranley **2**	Lanesborough **23**
Cranley Gardens **4**	Lowndes **25**
Diplomat **27**	Number 16 **6**
Draycott **14**	Pelham **8**
Durley House **17**	Sheraton Park Tower **21**
Ebury Court **29**	Sloane Hotel **13**
Egerton **11**	Sydney House **9**
11 Cadogan Gardens **15**	Wilbraham **16**

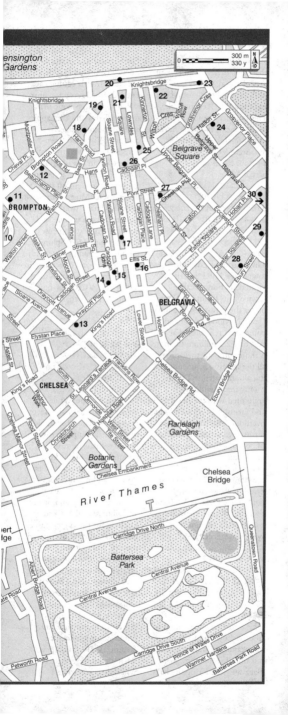

reserved in advance, a chauffeur-driven Bentley is at your disposal. Guests have use of the central garden, and steps away is lovely Regent Park. This is a nice choice off the beaten track. *Amenities:* Access to health club with pool, restaurant, VCR on request, 24-hour room service, partial A/C.

★ Dukes Hotel

35 St. James's Place, London SW1A 1NY. ☎ 0171/491-4840; 800/381-4702; fax: 0171/493-1264. 66 rooms. Tube: Green Park. AE, D, DC, MC, V. **$$$$**.

This charming Edwardian townhouse hotel is perfectly located, and impeccable service is its hallmark. Now under the private ownership of David Naylor-Leyland and completely refurbished at a cost of £2.5 million, the hotel is thoroughly up-to-date with all the necessities, including full air and satellite TV. The rooms are individually appointed with the best fabrics and furnishings without being overdone. The bar is famous for its dry martinis and range of cognacs; the dining room is one of the most pleasant spots in London for a leisurely breakfast. *Amenities:* Access to health club, restaurant, conference facilities, VCR on request, 24-hour room service, partial A/C, 66 rooms wheelchair accessible.

★★ Draycott

24-26 Cadogan Gardens, London SW3. ☎ 0171/730-6466; fax: 0171/730-0236. 25 rooms. Tube: Sloane Sq. AE, D, DC, MC, V. **$$$$**.

This beautifully appointed and discreet hotel attracts a big entertainment industry crowd; last time I stopped by, Joan Baez was wandering the halls. The friendly staff of this Chelsea gem look as if they've just come from a casting call. The balconied reception area, which has a large stone urn always filled with green apples, leads to rooms in the 2 converted Victorian town houses, where even the staff can get lost in the labyrinthine layout. Guests have access to the private gardens off the sitting room. Most rooms have fireplaces; many overlook the gardens. All are unique, and even the smallest single is lovingly appointed. Splurge for Room 11, a junior suite with a 4-poster bed and direct garden access. *Amenities:* Access to health club, VCRs, 24-hour room service, partial A/C.

★ Durley House

115 Sloane St., London SW1X 9PJ. ☎ 0171/235-5537; 800/553-6674; fax: 0171/259-6977. 11 suites. Tube: Sloane Sq. AE, MC, V. **$$$$$**.

If you don't like hotels, Durley House is for you. While it verges on the frilly, the decor is so tasteful and of such high quality that you really can't fault it—these are real antiques. Lots of quirky oil-paintings, big bunches of fresh flowers, and oriental rugs fill every room. Many have fireplaces, some grand pianos, and all have well-stocked kitchens for those who just can't bear another overpriced meal. If you're feeling like a couch potato, 24-hour room service will serve you at your own dining table. The service is top-notch and discreet, as you would expect from a Firmdale Hotel. *Amenities:* Access to health club and tennis court, conference facilities, VCR on request, 24-hour room service, 1 suite wheelchair accessible.

Durrants Hotel

George St., London W1H 6BJ.
☎ 0171/935-8131; fax: 0171/
487-3510. 92 rooms. Tube: Bond
St., Baker St. **$$$**.

This attractive small hotel is
perennially popular, even
though the rooms are rather
small. A portrait of a Durrant
patriarch from 1782 hangs
among the delightful
collection of oils and prints.
There are leather chairs and
pretty desks in the writing
room, antiques for sale, a
fireplace in the bar, Ruddles
beer in the bottle, and
pheasant for dinner when it's
in season. The rooms are
uninspired, verging on the
drab, but some have brass
bedsteads. A recent refurbish-
ment has converted all rooms
into ensuite facilities.
Amenities: Restaurant,
conference facilities, VCR on
request, 24-hour room service,
partial A/C.

Ebury Court

26 Ebury St., SW1W 0LU.
☎ 0171/730-8147; fax: 0171/
823-5966. 42 rooms, 22 with
bath. Tube: Victoria. AE, D, DC,
MC, V. **$$$**.

Even though it's slightly worn
and frayed at the edges, this is
one of the few reliable hotels
on Ebury Street, a ghetto of
low-priced hotels near
Buckingham Palace and the
Tate. The hotel, actually 5
joined Victorian town houses,
has been run by the same
family for over 50 years.
Claiming to evoke the charm
of an English country house,
the furnishings are really a
mish-mash of found antiques
and knickknacks. On my last
visit, some of the bedspreads
were in need of replacement,
but you might consider that all
part of the charm. Not all
rooms have bathrooms—the

shared bathrooms are clean and
quite basic—and not all
bathrooms have showers. If
you don't go ensuite, you'll be
loaned a white terry robe so
you don't have to show off
your sleepwear to your fellow
guests. The most recently
refurbished rooms are on the
lower ground floor; the views
suffer, but the decor is much
more up to date. The staff is
friendly and helpful. Rates
include an excellent full
English breakfast of haddock
and kippers. *Amenities:*
Restaurant, conference
facilities.

★★ Eleven Cadogan Gardens

11 Cadogan Gardens, London
SW3 2RJ. ☎ 0171/730-3426;
800/359-8361; fax: 0171/730-
5217. 60 rooms. Tube: Sloane
Sq. AE, D, DC, MC, V. **$$$$**.

This is one of my favorite
hotels in London. It's so
discreet that there's no sign,
even on the door, which is
kept locked (no wonder this
place is favored by diplomats!).
An ongoing refurbishment of
the common areas and rooms
ensures that this perfect hotel
remains fresh and up to date.
William Morris wallpaper and
wood paneling adorn the
reception area, and oil portraits
of someone's ancestors line the
stairway. Every room is unique
and is done up with the best—
Sanderson and Canovas fabrics
and wallpapers, Victorian
antiques. Ask for a room
overlooking the gardens; the
Garden Suite is a 2-story
paradise with its own private
entrance. A chauffeured
Mercedes is available at your
bidding. A dining room is in
the works, and the final
touches have just been made
on the new gym. *Amenities:*
Small health club, restaurant,

conference facilities, VCR on request, 24-hour room service, partial A/C.

Four Seasons (formerly Inn on the Park)

Hamilton Place, Park Lane, London W1A 1AZ. ☎ 0171/ 499-0888; 800/223-6800; fax: 0171/493-6629. 228 rooms. Tube: Hyde Park Corner. AE, D, DC, MC, V. **$$$$$**.

The only European hotel in the Four Seasons group is kept in superb condition. Favored by business travelers, it is best known as the home of Howard Hughes during one of his most demanding years. Despite being built in 1970, the architecture has the look of the 1950s, and some of its suites are in a '30s style. The hotel is lavishly furnished with antiques, and each room is individually decorated. In the Queen Anne–style lounge, 10 different variations on the theme of tea are offered to the soothing accompaniment of a pianist or harpist. Service in the hotel is outstanding, and it boasts 2 superb restaurants. *Amenities:* Health club, 2 restaurants, conference facilities, VCRs, 24-hour room service, A/C, 228 rooms wheelchair accessible.

★★ 47 Park Street

47 Park St., London W1Y 4EB. ☎ 0171/491-7282; 800/ 451-5536; fax: 0171/491-7281. 52 suites. Tube: Marble Arch. AE, D, DC, MC, V. **$$$$$**.

This luxury hotel has much to recommend it, but I'd stay here even if it were dump solely on account of its world-renowned restaurant, Le Gavroche, which also provides 24-hour room service. Why did they bother to put kitchenettes into every room when such culinary treasures can be had at any hour? Each

suite, decorated in a tasteful mix of French and English styles, has the ambiance of an aristocratic Edwardian pied-à-terre. The common rooms are clubby but formal; the jacket-and-tie requirement is enforced, even at the bar. Service is discreet and attentive. This is a very nice alternative to the larger neighboring Park Lane establishments. *Amenities:* Access to health club with pool, restaurant, conference facilities, VCR on request, 24-hour room service, A/C, 3 suites wheelchair accessible.

★ Franklin

28 Egerton Gardens, London SW3 2DB. ☎ 0171/584-5533; 800/473-9487; fax: 0171/ 584-5449 or 800/473-9489. 40 rooms. Tube: South Kensington. AE, D, DC, MC, V. **$$$$**.

★ Egerton

17-19 Egerton Terrace, London W3 2BX. ☎ 0171/589-2412; 800/473-9492; fax: 0171/584-6540. 28 Rooms. Tube: South Kensington. AE, MC, D, DC, V. **$$$$**.

These new Victorian town-house hotels, both owned by David Naylor-Leyland (who also owns Dukes), are across the garden from one another. Both offer the same top-notch service, with the Egerton having a larger percentage of singles than the Franklin, which has access to a lovely communal garden. Each unique room is outfitted with traditional English fabrics (many from Colefax and Fowler), oils, and lovely antique and reproduction furnishings. Spring for a garden room in the Franklin; most have 4-poster beds, and all have French windows that open directly onto the private grounds. Both impeccably maintained hotels are without the wear and tear that often plagues smaller hotels. There's an honor system in the lounges, which are spacious and inviting, much like the drawing room of a country estate. *Amenities:* Access to health club with pool, each with 1 restaurant, conference facilities, VCR on request, 24-hour room service, A/C.

★ Gore

189 Queen's Gate, London SW7 5EX. ☎ 0171/584-6601; fax: 0171/589-8127. 54 rooms. Tube: Gloucester Rd. AE, D, DC, MC, V. **$$$$**

The recent sale of the Gore to the owners of Hazlitt's has given this already warm and welcoming hotel an extra fillip. They decorated where necessary, piled up the potted plants, and put 5,000 pictures on the walls. They also invited Anthony Worrall-Thompson, owner of the adjoining One Ninety Queen's Gate, to take over the hotel's existing restaurant; it's now the popular Bistro 190. Bedrooms are individually and prettily decorated, but some are on the smallish side. Of the honeymoonish deluxe rooms, one, done in Italian style, has a bed that belonged to Judy Garland, stained-glass windows, and a magnificent tiled bathroom. This is a happy hotel (save the rear lounge, which has a sobering effect) with some illustrious names (particularly of musicians) often appearing in its register. *Amenities:* Access to health club with pool, conference facilities, 2 restaurants, VCR on request.

★ Goring

15 Beeston Place, Grosvenor Gardens, London SW1W 0JW. ☎ 0171/396-9000; fax: 0171/834-4393. 77 rooms. Tube:

Victoria. AE, D, DC, MC, V. **$$$$**.

Opened in 1910 as the first hotel in the world with central heating and private bathrooms, the Goring is still privately run, now by the grandson of the original Mr. Goring. This is a beautiful hotel, with wide hallways, a clubby lounge over-looking lovely gardens, and a formal dining room. Most rooms have been recently refurbished, but try to book a garden room—number 38 if you can, which has a large balcony. Bright fabrics, gorgeous original cornices, and wood paneling abound. All rooms have marble baths; deluxe rooms have separate showers. The current Mr. Goring has a fondness for fluffy stuffed rams, which at first can be alarming—I thought a small animal had found its way into my room. Over the years, because of the proximity of Buckingham Palace, the hotel has lodged many dignitaries. Service at the Goring is top-notch, and the owner is always in attendance. *Amenities:* Access to health club with plunge pool, restaurant, conference facilities, VCR on request, 24-hour room service, partial A/C.

Great Eastern

Liverpool St., London EC2M 7QN. ☎ 0171/283-4363; fax: 0171/283-4897. 161 rooms, 126 with bath. Tube: Liverpool St. AE, D, DC, MC, V. **$$**.

This hotel is away from the West End (which is only a few stops on the tube), in the heart of old London—handy for those wishing to travel to the eastern counties or to the continent. There's a genuine quality about traditional railway hotels like this one, with its spacious,

high-ceilinged bedrooms—
although more have twin beds
than doubles—and simple
fittings. Some rooms have just
wash basins, but the majority
have baths, usually with big,
deep tubs (but often without
showers). A magnificent
stained-glass dome hangs over
Bowlers, 1 of 2 restaurants.
Amenities: Conference
facilities, 2 restaurants, 24-hour
room service, 10 rooms
wheelchair accessible.

Grosvenor House

Park Lane, London W1A 3AA. ☎
0171/499-6363; 800/225-5843;
fax: 0171/493-3341. 454 rooms,
141 apartments. Tube: Marble
Arch. AE, D, DC, MC, V. **$$$$$**.
The first luxury hotel on Park
Lane, Grosvenor House is now
the flagship hotel of the Forte
empire. Built on the site of a
former residence of the Duke
of Wellington, the 2 current
Luytens structures are
connected by the lobby, a
cavernous tasseled and
upholstered affair. The unique
rooms are quite large by
London standards and done in
Mulberry colors, not too
flouncy or frilly. What the
newer 1960s-era rooms lack in
views, they make up for in
peace and quiet. All bathrooms
have bidets and what must be

the fluffiest bath mats in
London. The hotel's Chez
Nico at Ninety Park Lane, one
of London's best restaurants,
was recently endowed with 3
Michelin stars. The north side
of the structure is devoted to
apartments—self-contained
flats with all the perks of a
luxury hotel. The famous
Grosvenor House annual
antiques fair is held in June
(see "Calendar of Events" in
"The Basics" chapter).
Amenities: Large health club,
indoor pool, 3 restaurants,
conference facilities, VCR on
request, 24-hour room service,
A/C (in hotel only), executive
floor, 2 rooms wheelchair
accessible.

★ Halcyon

81 Holland Park, London W11
3RZ. ☎ 0171/727-7288; fax:
0171/229-8516. 44 rooms. Tube:
Holland Park. AE, D, DC, MC, V.
$$$$$.
Located in one of London's
poshest areas, the Halcyon is
very expensive and very à la
mode. It's ideally situated, away
from the hubbub but just a
short taxi ride from the city
center, which makes it very
popular with media folk
seeking a calm oasis from
prying eyes and paparazzi. The
interior is a kind of modern

Suite at the Halcyon

rendition of the belle époque style, luxurious and very soothing. Some of the individually decorated rooms are quite spacious—the Halcyon suite has its own conservatory. Many have 4-poster beds. There's a very fine restaurant, which opens onto a small garden for drinks in the summer; the well-heeled area residents treat this as their local "pub." *Amenities:* Access to health club with pool and tennis courts, conference facilities, restaurant, VCR on request, 24-hour room service, A/C.

★ Halkin

5 Halkin St., London SW1X 7DJ. ☎ 0171/333-1000; 800/637-7200; fax: 0171/333-1100. 41 rooms. Tube: Hyde Park Corner. AE, D, DC, MC, V. **$$$$$**. Conceived and built in the height of the 1980s boom, the Halkin has all the amenities that go with 1980s style—1 room even gives its inhabitant direct access to the FT financial lines! This is a chintz-free zone with spare, hi-tech rooms that reek of unencumbered taste. Despite the blond wood and stripped-down furnishings, the feeling is not at all cold—rather, it oozes cool, modern Italian style, with crisp sheets, clever lighting, and plush bathrooms. All rooms have personal faxes and cable TV. The restaurant just won its 1st Michelin Star, and many consider it the best nouveau Italian in town. The Halkin also gets the vote for best dressed staff, all of whom sport Armani. *Amenities:* Access to health club, restaurant, conference facilities, VCRs, 24-hour room service, A/C.

★★ Hazlitt's

6 Frith St., London W1V 5T2. ☎ 0171/434-1771; fax: 0171/439-1524. 23 rooms. Tube:

Tottenham Court Rd. AE, D, DC, MC, V. **$$$**.
Hazlitt's is named after the essayist William Hazlitt, who lived and died here in 1830. These days, his former residence is situated in the heart of rockin' Soho, steps away from some of the best restaurants in town. On a sunny day, it might seem as if all of 20-something London is dining on your doorstep; if you crave peace and quiet, it might be wise to book a back room. I like this place; the floors are uneven, the Georgian decor spare—one might even say puritanical—but it's appealing, with antiques gathered by the owner, who scours estate auctions and sales. It's popular with artists and writers; in the lounge are signed copies of books written by former guests. The sitting room is tired and shabby, but the service is friendly and the rooms are quirky. There's only 1 bathroom outfitted with a shower; the others have freestanding tubs with spray attachments. Crisp white linens adorn the beds, many of which are either half- or 4-posters. The ambiance and professional young staff make up for the lack of luxury and extras. *Amenities:* VCR on request.

★★ Hempel's

Hempel Sq., 31-35 Craven Hill Gardens, London W2 3EA. ☎ 0171/298-9000; fax: 0171/402-4666. 50 rooms. Tube: Lancaster Gate. AE, D, DC, MC, V. **$$$$**.
This place was not yet open at press time, but if it's anything like Anouska Hempel's other over-the-top joint, Blake's, it's sure to be a stunner. Advance press promises that Hempel's will "set the standard for . . . a very modern, innovative way

of life." A tall order, but if anyone can do it, Anouska can. Facilities include 6 suites, 6 serviced apartments, a private garden, library, and video conferencing facilities. All rooms have a bevy of high-tech gadgets, such as fax machines and computer ports. Watch this one. *Amenities:* Small health club, conference facilities, restaurant, VCR, 24-hour room service, A/C, 3 rooms wheelchair accessible.

L'Hotel

28 Basil St., London SW3 1AT. ☎ 0171/589-6286; fax: 0171/225-0011. 12 rooms. Tube: Knightsbridge. AE, D DC, MC, V. **$$$$**.

The well-heeled clientele of this up-market version of a B&B come here to get away from the relentless pace of a large, bustling full-service hotel. Rooms are fairly small, and attractive without being glamorous. Breakfast, both full English and Continental, is served in the smart basement Metro wine bar, which is also open to nonguests for light French lunches and dinners. As befits a sister establishment of the Capital, next door, the staff is professional and courteous. You'll find lots of charm here, but you'll pay for it. *Amenities:* Restaurant.

Hotel 167

167 Old Brompton Rd., London SW5V 0AN. ☎ 0171/373-0672; fax: 0171/373-3360. 19 rooms. Tube: Gloucester Rd. AE, D, DC, MC, V. **$$**.

This Victorian town-house B&B attracts a mix of Generation-Xers and young 30-somethings. Every room is uniquely designed in a variety of motifs—art deco, Japanese, or modern. Bathrooms are small, but functional. The hotel

is on busy Brompton Road, but double glazing ensures that the noise is kept to a low hum. Continental breakfast is served in the lobby. *Amenities:* VCR on request.

Howard

Temple Place, London WC2R 2PR. ☎ 0171/836-3555; 800/221-1074; fax: 0171/379-4547. 137 rooms. Tube: Temple. AE, D, DC, MC, V. **$$$$$**.

This is one of the few hotels in the City, which, until recently, was short of hotels—rather inconvenient for business travelers with little time on their hands. The ostentatious decor in the public rooms goes over the top, but the bedrooms are more understated and luxurious. There's a multitude of business facilities, and service is appropriately smooth. *Amenities:* Restaurant, conference facilities, 24-hour room service, A/C, 5 rooms wheelchair accessible.

Hyatt Carlton Tower

2 Cadogan Place, London SW1X 9PX. ☎ 0171/235-1234; fax: 0171/245-6570. 224 rooms. Tube: Knightsbridge. AE, D, DC, MC, V. **$$$$$**.

Whether you require an enormous breakfast or a kosher dinner, American-cut beef or contemporary French cuisine, the Carlton Tower can satisfy your wishes. And such demands are made: Guests here range from rock stars to foreign politicians. The hotel lobby has about as much charm as an airport lounge, and there always seems to be a lot of activity around the safety deposit room. That said, this is a recently renovated, perfectly inoffensive hotel with large rooms and predictable furnishings. Now with a well-equipped business center, it's one of London's better business hotels, and the gym is one of the best in town and has awesome views. The location, in a quiet square, has a character of its own. *Amenities:* Large health club, 3 restaurants, VCR on request, conference facilities, 24-hour room service, A/C, 5 rooms wheelchair accessible.

Hyde Park

66 Knightsbridge, London SW1Y 7LA. ☎ 0171/235-2000; 800/ 225-5843; fax: 0171/235-4552. 185 rooms. Tube: Knightsbridge. AE, D, DC, MC, V. **$$$$$**.
The Hyde Park has always been one of the top hotels in London, attracting all kinds of big names, from exiled royalty to Luciano Pavarotti. Currently, however, it's best known for Marco-Pierre White's 3-star restaurant, modestly called "Marco Pierre White: The Restaurant." Another member of the Forte Hotel empire, the hotel has been recently refurbished with fine antiques and paintings. The guest rooms are spacious and understated; those on the higher floors offer views over Knightsbridge. The new fitness center is glaringly white. *Amenities:* Health club with plunge pool, conference facilities, 2 restaurants, VCR on request, 24-hour room service, A/C, 2 rooms wheelchair accessible.

Inter-Continental

One Hamilton Place, Hyde Park Corner, London W1V 0QY. ☎ 0171/409-3131; 800/327-0200; fax: 0171/409-7460. 460 rooms. Tube: Hyde Park Corner. AE, D, DC, MC, V. **$$$$$**.
This is an American-style luxury hotel, with spacious rooms outfitted with hi-tech gadgets—voice-mail, movies, satellite TV, dual-voltage power

points, and phones in the bathrooms. It's an anonymous 1970s structure, but the hotel tries hard to make the rooms unique; each one is individually decorated with plants and inspired artwork. The 7 new luxury suites are filled with plants, books, a personal stereo, and a video system. Most rooms have excellent views of Hyde Park; to ensure a nice view, try for as high a floor as possible. And while Hyde Park Corner might rank as one of the busiest intersections in Europe, the triple-glazed windows keep noise to a discreet hum. The lobby is a nondescript affair with a casual coffee house, a bar, and the excellent Soufflé restaurant. This is very much the business traveler's hotel, with excellent conferencing facilities (including one of London's few video-conferencing centers), a health club with Jacuzzis and treatment rooms, and a business center right off the lobby. *Amenities:* Small health club with plunge pool, conference facilities, 2 restaurants, VCR on request, 24-hour room service, A/C, 2 rooms wheelchair accessible.

Landmark (formerly the Regent)

222 Marylebone Rd., London NW1 6JQ. ☎ 0171/631-8000; 800/457-4000; fax: 0171/ 631-8033. 305 rooms. Tube: Marylebone. AE, D, DC, MC, V. **$$$$$**.
Millions of dollars have been poured into the renovation of this hotel, and it shows. Many are put off by its location outside of Mayfair, but you shouldn't be; while the neighborhood doesn't have the charm of Chelsea or Knightsbridge, it's thoroughly convenient to all of London's

sights and attractions. The centerpiece of this former Victorian railway hotel is the Winter Garden atrium, a soaring conservatory where you can take advantage of one of the best teas in town. The rooms are some of London's largest, and while they're all similarly styled, they're decorated well, with lots of blond wood, marble baths, and an impressive collection of contemporary art. Regent's Park is steps away, where you can play tennis or enjoy a specially packed picnic. *Amenities:* Large health club, indoor pool, access to tennis courts, 2 restaurants, conference facilities, VCR on request, A/C, 4 rooms wheelchair accessible.

Lanesborough

I Lanesborough Place, London SW1X 7TA. ☎ 0171/259-5599; fax: 0171/259-5606. 95 rooms. Tube: Hyde Park Corner. AE, D, DC, MC, V. **$$$$$**.
Thanks to triple glazing, a rather somber hush pervades this recent addition to London's deluxe hotels. The Lanesborough occupies the entirely rebuilt former St. George's Hospital, a landmark building designed by William Wilkins in 1829. The quasi-Regency style decor is a bit much—this place screams money. You'll find 24-hour butler service, computer-controlled lighting, state-of-the-art audio and video equipment, personal fax and phone lines, and personalized stationery in every room; but each one is a mirror of the next, down to the same pink-and-blue striped wallpaper. *Amenities:* Small health club, conference facilities, restaurant, VCR on request, 24-hour room service, A/C, 1 room wheelchair accessible.

★ Lowndes

Lowndes St., London SW1X 9ES. ☎ 0171/823-1234; 800/233-1234; fax: 0171/235-1154. 78 rooms. Tube: Knightsbridge. AE, D, DC, MC, V. **$$$$$**.
Part of the Hyatt chain, the Lowndes' small size and chi-chi location, around the corner from Harvey Nichols and Harrod's, make it perfect for those wanting big chain service on a small scale. The modern building is perfectly inoffensive; it even manages to exude charm thanks to the lovely street-level restaurant. Each room is individually decorated, but they tend to revolve around the same chintzy theme. The standard doubles are a bit small, but all have the facilities you would expect from a Hyatt, including satellite TV and minibars. Try to book one of the rooms with a terrace overlooking the garden. The Brasserie is perfect for late night snacks and light meals; during the summer months, the open terrace almost makes you feel like you're in Paris. Guests tend to be well-heeled Europeans and business travelers seeking an intimate hotel with consistent service. Amenities: Access to health club with pool and tennis courts, restaurant, conference facilities, VCR on request, 24-hour room service, A/C, 9 rooms wheelchair accessible.

May Fair

Stratton St., London W1A 2AN. ☎ 0171/629-7777; 800/327-0800; fax: 0171/629-1459. 285 rooms. Tube: Green Park. AE, D, DC, MC V. **$$$$$**.
Part of the Inter-Continental hotel group, the May Fair, an Edwardian edifice originally opened in 1927, feels like a small hotel but actually houses more than 280 rooms. The

location couldn't be better, just off Piccadilly and smack in between the theater district and West London. The hotel caters to the business traveler and members of the entertainment industry. The rooms are uniquely decorated in traditional, predictable English style. Photos of some of the more famous guests are mounted on the walls bedside, as if they were close relatives. Recently, 4 luxury suites have been refurbished, each one done up around a cultural theme, with the Monte Carlo Suite being the most opulent. The lobby features a grand floating staircase and a small lounge where afternoon tea is served, accompanied by a harpist. There are 2 bars and 2 restaurants, a formal and a casual version of each. The health club has a small pool equipped with a current machine; it's just like swimming in the Atlantic. *Amenities:* Large health club, indoor pool, 2 restaurants, conference facilities, VCR on request, 24-hour room service, A/C, 3 rooms wheelchair accessible.

Le Meridien London

21 Piccadilly, London W1V 0BH. ☎ 0171/734-8000; fax: 0171/437-3574. 309 rooms. Tube: Piccadilly Circus. AE, D, DC, MC, V. **$$$$$**.
The once-famous Piccadilly hotel was transformed in 1985 into Le Meridien, a hotel very much in the modern idiom but retaining all the Piccadilly's architectural glories. The Edwardian extravagance of the interior—protected by preservation orders—has been restored, with the Oak Room as its superb pièce de résistance. The pillared roof terrace has been glassed-in to create a stunning

conservatory-style brasserie. The rooms range dramatically in size; a few have balconies overlooking Piccadilly, and a few have been enlarged to studio-style suites. Try to book a room far from the elevator, as past guests have complained about the hall noise. Executives in particular will be lured by the extensive conference facilities and the luxurious basement health club, which includes a pool, a gym, squash courts, and Turkish baths. *Amenities:* Large health club, conference facilities, 2 restaurants, VCR on request, 24-hour room service, A/C, 1 room wheelchair accessible.

★ Morgan Hotel

24 Bloomsbury St., London WC1B 3QJ. ☎ 0171/636-3735. 17 rooms, 4 apartments. Tube: Tottenham Court Rd. No credit cards. **$**.
It's not surprising that the Morgan instills the loyalty that it does. This marvelous B&B spares no effort in guaranteeing the comfort of its guests. The blooming flower boxes that greet you upon arrival announce an attention to detail that's consistent throughout. If you're staying in one of the guest rooms, you'll find deep red carpets and batik bedspreads; the apartments are outfitted with polished furniture and English prints. Room rates include English breakfast; apartment rates include daily maid service. *Amenities:* A/C.

Number 16

16 Sumner Place, London SW7 3EG. ☎ 0171/589-5232; fax: 0171/584-8615. 36 rooms, 32 with bath. Tube: South Kensington. AE, D, DC, MC, V. **$$$**.
This place is more B&B than full-service hotel, but the

accommodating staff can meet most needs. What sets this group of 4 Victorian town houses apart are the awesome gardens—reserve one of the rooms that opens directly onto its own private patio. The interior is outfitted in typical, slightly worn English country-house style (even the floors creak). In keeping with Victorian tradition, the drawing room, which was for the ladies, is light and flowery; the men's haven, the library, is dark and masculine. The sexes now mix freely at the honor bar. Breakfast is served in the conservatory or alfresco, while the fountain bubbles into a fish pond. Some rooms are a little tired, but the hotel is well maintained and terribly charming. Not all rooms have tubs. *Amenities:* Access to health club with pool, VCR on request, room service until 11pm.

★★ Pelham

15 Cromwell Place, London SW7 2LA. ☎ 0171/589-8288; fax: 0171/584-8444. 37 rooms. Tube: South Kensington. AE, MC, V. **$$$$**.

Just minutes from the Victoria and Albert Museum, Harrod's, and Hyde Park, this hotel is discreetly housed in an early 19thC white stuccoed terrace house. Again, the Kemps get it right—the Pelham is close to perfect. Each room is individually appointed with the most tasteful antiques and paintings available—even the knickknacks are exquisite. They all retain some original architectural details and are outfitted with eiderdown duvets, Oriental carpets, and unique oils; even the smallest room will have a handsome desk. The lounges are dripping with sumptuous fabrics, wood paneling, and heaps of fresh

flowers; there's a marvelous old 3-seater conversation chair in the hall. You'll feel as if you're staying with very established, well-off friends, who are terribly British but not stuffy. *Amenities:* Conference facilities, restaurant, VCR on request, 24-hour room service, A/C.

Pembridge Court

34 Pembridge Gardens, London W2 5DX. ☎ 0171/229-9977; 800/709-9882; fax: 0171/727-4982. 20 rooms. Tube: Notting Hill Gate. AE, D, DC, MC, V. **$$$$**.

This cozy Victorian town-house hotel is wonderfully situated, a few steps from the tube stop and smack in the heart of Notting Hill Gate—perfect for the Portobello Road trawlers. The sitting room is pleasant and informal, accented by an interesting collection of framed antique textiles. Some accommodations, such as the Lancaster and the Holland rooms, are very spacious. Service is friendly and efficient, and Churchill and Spencer, the famous resident cats, guard the door against undesirables. Rates include service and a full English breakfast. *Amenities:* Access to health club with pool, VCR, 24-hour room service, partial A/C.

★ Portobello

22 Stanley Gardens, London W11 2NG. ☎ 0171/727-2777; fax: 0171/792-9641. 24 rooms. Tube: Notting Hill Gate. AE, D, DC, MC, V. **$$$**.

I list this hotel in the "moderate" price category, but room sizes vary dramatically—from the minuscule "cabin rooms" to spacious "special rooms"—and the larger doubles are definitely in the expensive category. This is where I put my parents up when they come to town. They love the Notting Hill location and the idiosyncratic room decor; it's looking a bit tired, but it's all part of the charm. Room 13, with its 4-poster bed and nice lounge area, is my favorite. Only suites and "special rooms" have full baths (all others have showers); these are spacious and fun—a good choice for a romantic weekend. Service can be erratic; I spied many breakfast trays lying in wait on a recent late afternoon visit. Breakfast and light meals are served in the small, pleasant restaurant. *Amenities:* Access to health club with pool, restaurant, VCR on request, 24-hour room service, partial A/C.

Ritz

150 Piccadilly, London W1V 9BG. ☎ 0171/493-8181; 800/526-6566; fax: 0171/493-2687. 130 rooms. AE, D, DC, MC, V. Tube: Green Park. **$$$$$**.

Many people assume that the Ritz, now part of the Mandarin Hotel Group, is a large impersonal hotel, but it really isn't. The style, quite unique for London, recalls Belle Époque France with gold swags, brightly lit rooms, and delicate furnishings. All the guest rooms have fireplaces, and the larger ones have large walk-in closets; some of the marble bathrooms can accommodate a small party. The Piccadilly side is a bit noisy, but double glazing keeps the roar to a minimum. The spectacular Palm Court is *the* place for tea—reservations must be made weeks in advance; guests get top priority. A jazz band plays on weekend evenings; it's a nice break from the Muzak that dominates most grand hotel lobbies. The stunning

restaurant opens up onto a private dining terrace. For a more intimate experience, there's the Rivoli Room, a small, clubby lounge where guests gather for drinks or small meetings. *Amenities:* Access to health club with pool, 2 restaurants, VCR on request, 24-hour room service, partial A/C, 130 wheelchair accessible.

St. James's Club

7 Park Place, London SW1A 1LP. ☎ 0171/629-7688; 800/877-0447; fax: 0171/491-0987. 59 rooms. Tube: Green Park. AE, D, DC, MC, V. **$$$$$**.

This prestigious, exclusive club now offers "temporary memberships," so mere mortals can now stay here. For the past year, the St. James's Club has been undergoing a serious $4-million refurbishment: The Victorian townhouse exterior has been completely restored, and it positively sparkles; inside, an up-to-date infrastructure is hidden underneath a Modern English veneer. While some lament the demise of the clubby, quirky atmosphere and the restaurant (there's now only a 10-seat "dining area"), others welcome the stripped-down modern surroundings. The reception area is an elegant marble-clad affair, and the inviting lounge is outfitted with velvet sofas and Oriental carpets. The rooms have all been redone in 1 of 2 color schemes: blue or burgundy, with mahogany furnishings; fabric-covered headboards in Mulberry textiles, and bathrooms (all with phones) sporting lots of Italian marble. Many of the suites have private terraces or patios. A minuscule fitness area has both a steam room and sauna. The location is a winner—near the theater district, some of London's best restaurants, and Bond Street. Members of clubs with reciprocal relationships get reduced rates. *Amenities:* Small health club, restaurant, conference facilities, VCR on request, 24-hour room service, A/C.

★ Savoy

The Strand, London WC2R 0EU. ☎ 0171/836-4343; 800-SAVOY; fax: 0171/240-6040. 220 rooms. Tube: Charing Cross. AE, D, DC, MC, V. **$$$$$**.

On your approach, you'll notice that the taxis making their way to the hotel drive on the right rather than the left; the Strand is the only street in Britain where traffic conforms to the rest of Europe. From its tucked-away front entrance to its gardens facing the Thames in the back, the Savoy is full of extravagant treats. An open fire greets guests; afternoon tea, with piano accompaniment, is served in a garden setting with a gazebo; and recent renovation has uncovered more 1920s-era features. The emphasis is on impeccable hotel-keeping and thorough comfort, with Irish linen sheets, and mattresses made by the Savoy's own workshop. Most bathrooms have marble floors and satisfyingly deep tubs. Even though they're ridiculously expensive, the river-view suites are booked months in advance—there are probably no better views in London. There are 3 restaurants to choose from: the famous Savoy Grill, where the rich and powerful do much of their business; the River Restaurant; and a recent addition, the beautifully decorated "chablis and seafood" bar, where you can have anything from a cup of coffee (the hotel has its own

blend) to a full meal. In the past, service from waiters has been criticized for being patchy, but I failed to notice any flaws on my most recent visit. *Amenities:* Large health club, heated rooftop pool, access to tennis courts, 3 restaurants, conference facilities, 24-hour room service, A/C, VCR on request, 14 rooms wheelchair accessible.

★ Sloane Hotel

29 Draycott Place, London SW3 2SH. ☎ 0171/581-5757; 800/324-9960; fax: 0171/584-1348. 12 rooms. Tube: Sloane Sq. AE, D, DC, MC, V. **$$$**.

Another perfectly appointed Victorian terrace-house hotel in chic Chelsea, the Sloane is owned by a serious antique fanatic who is often spotted at the weekly furniture auctions around town. The standard doubles are tight but lovingly appointed; up a notch, you'll find the rooms more spacious, with the best being the galleried suites. All are individually decorated and ooze with expensive silks and tapestries; the Nina Campbell room is done in swags of luscious floral fabrics, while the Designer's Guild room is a 2-story canopied paradise. Many regulars come back to their favorite rooms again and again. The hallways are covered with beautifully framed prints and paintings, and the whole place smells delicious. Guests take breakfast in the cozy rooftop lounge or, when the weather permits, on the terrace. I was particularly impressed with the high level of security— a high-tech monitoring system oversees all who enter and leave. *Amenities:* VCR, 24-hour room service, A/C.

Stafford

St. James's Place, London SW1A
1NJ. ☎ 0171/493-0111; 800-
525-4800; fax: 0171/493-7121.
73 rooms. Tube: Green Park. AE,
D, DC, MC, V. **$$$$**.
Serious wine lovers won't be
disappointed by the Stafford, at
the end of a cul-de-sac in
clubby St. James's, which has
underground cellars dating
back 300 years. The cellars
now house an atmospheric
subterranean dining room and,
of course, an extensive
selection of wines. During the
war, American and Canadian
forces used the cellars as a club;
a range of memorabilia from
that time is on display. The
hotel stands on the site of the
former residence of
Christopher Wren; the present
building, constructed in the
18thC, blends well with the
Gentlemen's clubs that dot the
area. The rooms are decorated
in the classic British style,
without too much frill. The
back rooms are bright and
sunny, and the cul-de-sac
assures that all are quiet. The
Stafford has recently renovated
a series of carriage houses
adjacent to the courtyard. All
of these suites have beamed
ceilings, fireplaces, and stereos
with CD players; many have 4-
poster beds and Jacuzzis. The
lounge is a nice place for tea,
and there's the clubby
American Bar where, over the
years, barman Charles has been
collecting ties and caps of
former guests. It's a nice spot
for lunch during summer,
when the bar opens up onto
the courtyard. *Amenities:*
Restaurant, conference
facilities, VCR on request, 24-
hour room service, A/C, 20
rooms wheelchair accessible.

Sydney House

9-11 Sydney St., London SW3
6PU. ☎ 0171/376-7711; fax:
0171/376-4233. 21 rooms. Tube:
South Kensington. AE, D, DC,
MC, V. **$$$$**.
This Victorian town house in
Chelsea is a real charmer, with
a bold and unusual mix of
fabrics and furnishings. The
Paris Room is a rich, playful
affair done in a symphony of
reds and Toile de Jouy; the
Chinese Leopard Room
features Biedermeier furniture
and animal-print furnishings.
For honeymooners, the Royale
Room boasts a 4-poster bed
tented in white silk and
brocade. The sunny restaurant
is open to guests only;
attentive to the many
businesswomen who tend to
favor Sydney House, it offers
light and healthy meals.
Amenities: Conference
facilities, restaurant, 24-hour
room service, VCR on request.

★ 22 Jermyn Street

22 Jermyn St., London SW1Y
6HL. ☎ 0171/734-2353; 800/
682-7807; fax: 0171/734-7808.
17 rooms. Tube: Piccadilly Circus.
AE, D, DC, MC, V. **$$$$**.
Ideally located for sightseeing
and steps from fashionable
Jermyn Street shops, this
Edwardian townhouse hotel is
a real jewel. Discretion is the
keynote here—you might pass
right by the entrance on first
try. There are no common
spaces, but the rooms have all
that you would expect from a
5-star hotel, including CNN,
fax lines, and voice mail. Many
of the traditionally decorated
suites can be connected with
other rooms, and all the sofas
pull out into beds; the
majority can accommodate a
small meeting. Henry Togna,
the owner, whose family has
run the hotel for 80 years, has
membership privileges at some
of the best clubs in town and
would be happy to escort you
as his guest. Very traditional,

very St. James's. *Amenities:* Access to health club with pool and tennis courts, conference facilities, VCR, 24-hour room service, partial A/C, 1 room wheelchair accessible.

Waldorf

Aldwych, London WC2B 4DD. ☎ 0171/836-2400; fax: 0171/836-7244. 292 rooms. Tube: Covent Garden. AE, D, DC, MC, V. **$$$$$**.

Exemplifying the Edwardian era with its crystal chandeliers, marble floors, potted plants, and cozy period-bedrooms, this comfortable hotel offers both old-world charm and excellent service and facilities. It's ideally located for the serious theater-goer. The famous Waldorf tea dances are still going strong every weekend. *Amenities:* Access to health club with pool, conference facilities, 2 restaurants, 24-hour room service, A/C.

Wilbraham

Wilbraham Place, Sloane St., London SW1X 9AE. ☎ 0171/730-8296; fax: 0171/730-6815. 52 rooms, 48 with bath. Tube: Sloane Sq. No credit cards. **$$**.

This is how you'd imagine your English grandmother's house to look. This genteel, slightly faded Victorian town house between Chelsea and Knightsbridge offers rooms with such details as wood paneling, fireplaces, and leaded windows. If you need a large room, try to reserve one of the 4 suites or a deluxe twin—No. 1, deluxe twin with a large bathroom, is a good choice. *Amenities:* Restaurant, 24-hour room service.

Also Worth a Mention

Travelers looking for familiar comforts might also like these amenity-packed, business-oriented hotels: the **Hilton on Park Lane** (☎ 0171/493-8000 or 800/HILTONS; **$$$$$**), which would be right at home in midtown Manhattan; the adjacent town house–like **London Mews Hilton** (☎ 0171/493-7222 or 800/HILTONS; **$$$$$**), where you'll still have access to all the facilities next door; the Georgian-style **Britannia** (☎ 0171/629-9400 or 800/327-0200; **$$$$$**), in the heart of Mayfair on Grosvenor Square; and the **Sheraton Park Tower** (☎ 0171/235-8050 or 800/325-3535; **$$$$$**), an unattractive modern edifice with an interior that's slightly more grand than you'd expect.

Sights &
Attractions

L ONDON ISN'T AN EASY CITY TO GRASP IN THE ABSTRACT.
It lacks the clearly defined historic core that, in cities such as Paris or Rome, clusters so many visitor
attractions and historic highlights within a walkable
radius. And, where the island of Manhattan gives New
York a defined area to hold in the mind's eye, London
seems to sprawl formlessly. This city isn't only large—
it's also largely unplanned.

Many of the city's most important sights lie within
the area generally recognized as Central London—the
original City and the West End. But a great many more,
from Hampton Court Palace and the Royal Botanic
Gardens in Kew to the William Morris Gallery in
Walthamstow, lie well away from the center. So, the
first challenge awaiting you is to form a mental map of
the city and a realistic idea of its scale; once you've
done that, you can plot out a reasonable sightseeing
plan for yourself.

For First-Time Visitors

British Museum

Buckingham
Palace

Butler's Wharf

Greenwich and the
Royal Observatory
(including a boat
ride there)

National Gallery

Portobello Market
(see "Shopping")

Royal Botanic
Gardens at Kew

Sir John Soane
Museum

Victoria and Albert
Museum

Westminster Abbey

Orientation Tours

Coach Tours

All the tours listed below can be reserved through the London Tourist Board Centres at Victoria Station, Harrods or Selfridges:

Original London Sightseeing Tour (☎ 0181/877-1722) will take you all around the city in an open-top double-decker. Buses depart Marble Arch (and many other locations) every 15 minutes (more often during the summer) from 10am to 5pm; commentary is available in 8 languages. **The Big Bus Company** (☎ 0181/944-7810) has open-top bus tours, accompanied by live commentary, departing from Marble Arch, Green Park, and Victoria every 10 to 15 minutes. **Discovery Tours** (☎ 0171/828-1400) offers air-conditioned coach tours of London. **Harrod's** (☎ 0171/581-3603) very luxurious 2-hour tours depart from door no. 8 of the department store at 10:30am, 1:30pm, and 4pm; commentary is available in 8 languages. **Frames Rickards** (☎ 0171/837-3111) and **Evan Evans** (☎ 0171/930-2377) offer various coach sightseeing tours led by qualified "blue badge" guides; call for details.

Boat Tours

Since the demise of the London Riverbus shuttle service, transport on the Thames is limited to the various pleasure crafts that cruise the river. Despite the sometimes annoying commentary, the cruises do allow you to catch a glimpse of the city from a different point of view. Most leave from **Westminster Pier** (☎ 0171/930-4097), **Charing Cross Pier** (Victoria Embankment, ☎ 0171/987-1185), and **Tower Pier** (☎ 0171/488-0344). The routes are divided into "downstream" (toward the Tower of London and Greenwich to the Thames Barrier) and "upstream" (toward Kew, Richmond, and Hampton Court). Special cruises are also scheduled, including the "Afternoon Tea Cruise" (Bateaux London; ☎ 0171/925-2215) and the "Elvis the Cruiser Diner" dinner cruise with live show (City Cruises; ☎ 0171/237-5134). Or call the London Tourist Bureau's **Rivertrip Line** (☎ 0839/123 432).

Another alternative view of the city can be had aboard the narrowboats that ply the canals between Little Venice in the West and Camden Lock in the north. **Jason's Trip** (☎ 0171/286-3428) offers one-way and round-trip services, along with a very inoffensive running commentary that allows time for pondering

the passing scenery. **London Waterbus Co**. (☎ 0171/
482-2550) does the same route, but without the commentary, and offers a special London Zoo admission/
waterbus ticket fare; call to inquire.

Walking Tours

Despite its size, London is a marvelous city for taking a
walk. The following companies organize walking tours:

The very enthusiastic guides of **Original London
Walks** (☎ 0171/624-3978) will talk you through the
streets of London. The "Jack The Ripper" walk is a
favorite.

Citisights of London's (☎ 0181/806-4325) most
popular walk is the "London Story," which starts at the
Museum of London.

Historical Tours (☎ 0181/668-4019) walks
include a "Historic Pub Walk" in Mayfair and Chelsea,
and the "London of Dickens and Shakespeare."

Bicycle Tours

London Bicycle Tour Company (☎ 0171/
928-6838) offers 3-hour tours on Sundays that circle
the city and get you up close to landmarks including Shakespeare's Globe and St. Paul's Cathedral.
Both bike-hire and guides are provided.

Private Tours

If you'd like to go sightseeing in the company of a qualified Blue Badge Guide (many of them driver-guides),
you should contact **Tour Guides Ltd.** (☎ 0171/
495-5504), **Take a Guide** (☎ 0181/960-0459), or
British Tours (☎ 0171/629-5267).

Special-Interest Tours

Architectural Dialogue (☎ 0181/341-1371) offers
architectural tours, each with a distinct theme, such as
"Georgian London" or "Modern and Beyond." Guides
are enthusiastic and very knowledgeable. Private tours
of areas outside of London are also offered. Destinations and themes include Lutyens houses, "Arts and
Crafts" tours, and Cambridge and Bath.

The Jewish Museum (☎ 0171/284-1997) offers
a range of guided tours covering Jewish London.

Gastro-Soho Tours (☎ 0181/348-7767) guide
visitors around Soho's diverse food shops. The tours,
which are run by Jenny Linford, author of the *Food
Lover's Guide to London,* start in Chinatown and
proceed to Soho.

The 18thC listed ★★ **Dennis Severs House** (18 Folgate St., E1; ☎ 0171/247-4013) has been restored to its original condition by owner Dennis Severs. Severs gives candlelit tours, conjuring up the life of a master weaver in Georgian London and giving visitors a sense of what life must have been like here 200 years ago.

Towpath Treks (☎ 01296/395 566) organizes tours along the canals that crisscross London; you'll see the city from a very different point of view. They also do a "Grand Union Canal Walk," a 12-day trip covering 145 miles, from London to Birmingham.

Country Walks (☎ 01306/884-886) hosts wonderful walking tours around the countryside in Sussex, a short train ride from London. The tours are run by the Zafts, a husband-and-wife team, and other serious walkers who have trod most of the hills and downs in the area and have an encyclopedic knowledge of the countryside. The walks vary from 3 to 7 miles and always include a lunch in a funky pub or charming tearoom.

Gentle Journeys (☎ 0171/720 4891) organizes a series of 1-day tours throughout the summer to England's notable houses and gardens.

Special Moments

London is best discovered off the beaten track, away from the museums and monuments and in little bits that are usually beyond the parameters of a tourist's visit. Below are some of the experiences that make London one of my very favorite places to be:

I still get a thrill when riding on the **Number 11 bus**—front seat, upper deck, of course. You'll make your way past many of the major sights, including Trafalgar Square and Westminster Abbey, before ending up on the King's Road. Once there, you might want to get off around Flood Street; from there, it's a quick walk to one of my all time favorite teas at the **Chelsea Physic Garden,** one of Europe's oldest botanic gardens. On Wednesday afternoons from April to October, tea is served in a lovely cafe; afterward, you can explore the grounds or relax in one of the secluded corners.

Even if you've been to London many times before, a boat along the canal from Little Venice to Camden Lock is always a good bet. Of all the boat operators listed above, I prefer **Jason's Trip.** The commentary is knowledgable but there's not too much of it, so you're able to just sit

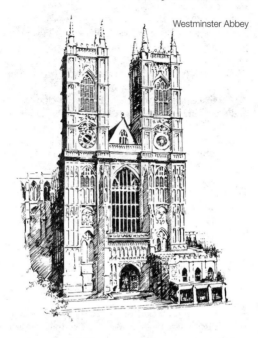

Westminster Abbey

back and soak in the sights and atmosphere—fishermen, idyllic back gardens, and historic sights.

Secret bits of London that even most insiders don't know about include the **Kensington Roof Gardens,** above Barker's department store on Kensington High Street. These are private gardens, but you can gain access if they're not being used for a private function. This is a real treat—flamingos, fountains, and green lawns spread over $1^1/_2$ acres above the city. Enter at 99 Derry St., sign in, and take the elevator to the top floor. Bring a lunch along.

Another hidden gem is the **garden at Westminster Abbey.** Surprisingly, this space is under-subscribed— it's one of the city's loveliest green spots, right in the center of town. Only open on Tuesdays and Thursdays, it's a quiet haven with the spires of Westminster Palace in the background. **Fenton House** in Hampstead also has a lovely walled garden; the hidden nooks and crannies make it a perfect spot for a picnic.

My favorite cut-through from Notting Hill Gate to Kensington is along the road that passes behind Kensington Palace. **Kensington Palace Gardens** is lined with opulent mansions, now mostly used by

embassies. Don't be put off by the police barricade at
either end—it's there for cars; pedestrians are free to
pass. Also brimming with atmosphere are the courtyards of the famous **Inns of Court. Lincoln's Inn** is
the best preserved, and the immaculate lawns of Lincoln's
Inn Fields catapults me into another time.

Culinary delights unique to London include lunch
in the test kitchen at **Books for Cooks.** Open middays
only, the kitchen in the back of the bookstore tries out
recipes from its endless stock of international cookbooks.
Since there are only 5 tables, booking is a must.

Another little known fact are the 3 small tables in
the back garden of **Tom's** in Notting Hill. This pre-
pared-food shop makes some of the best sandwiches in
town and the small garden is a nice place to read the
paper. And if you're hankering for a bit of news from
home, stop by the cappuccino bar at **DKNY** on Bond
Street, where you'll find current copies of the *New York
Times* and *The New Yorker.*

The annual open-air production of *A Midsummer's
Night Dream* in Regent's Park is a yearly pilgrimage
for me—it's great fun under the stars. Impoverished
opera lovers should take advantage of the **Royal Opera House's** staging of a series of live transmissions.
Pavarotti and his friends, performing live, are beamed
into the piazza on a large screen. It's opera for the
people—pack a picnic of wine and cheese, and get there
early to claim your piece of concrete.

Oh, yes—and I love the history-of-dress installa-
tion in the **Victoria and Albert Museum;** the corsetry
display is always good for a sigh or two of disbelief.

Sights & Attractions by Category

★ Holland House and Park
Horse Guards Parade
Houses of Parliament. *See*
    Palace of Westminster
Kensington Palace
★ Kenwood House
Lambeth Palace
★ Leighton House
★★ Lincoln's Inn
Mansion House
Marble Hill House
Osterley Park
★ Palace of Westminster
★ Royal Academy of Arts
Royal Courts of Justice
Royal Hospital, Chelsea
★ Royal Institute of British
    Architects
St. James's Palace
★ Spencer House
Staple Inn
Syon House
★ Temple
★ Tower of London
William Morris Gallery

Monuments

Albert Memorial and Royal
    Albert Hall
Charing Cross
Cleopatra's Needle
★ Highgate Cemetery
Marble Arch
The Monument
Nelson's Column, Trafalgar
    Square

Museums & Galleries

★ Apsley House, the
    Wellington Museum
Bethnal Green Museum of
    Childhood
★★ British Museum and
    Library
Carlyle's House
★★ Courtauld Institute
    Galleries
Design Museum
Dickens's House
Dr. Johnson's House
★ Dulwich College and
    Picture Gallery
Florence Nightingale Museum
Freud Museum
HMS *Belfast*

Hogarth's House
Imperial War Museum
Keats's House
★ Kenwood House
Jewish Museum
London Toy and Model
    Museum
Museum of London
London Transport Museum
Madame Tussaud's
Museum of Mankind
★ Museum of the Moving
    Image
National Army Museum
★★ National Gallery
★ National Maritime
    Museum and Queen's
    House
National Portrait Gallery
Natural History Museum
The Percival David Founda-
    tion of Chinese Art
Planetarium
Public Record Office Museum
★ Royal Academy of Arts
★ Royal Observatory
★ Saatchi Gallery
Science Museum
Serpentine Gallery
★ Shakespeare Globe Centre
Sherlock Holmes Museum
★★ Sir John Soane Museum
★ Tate Gallery
Theatre Museum
★★ Victoria and Albert
    Museum
★ Wallace Collection.
★ Whitechapel Art Gallery
William Morris Gallery

Of General Interest

Albert Memorial and Royal
    Albert Hall
Barbican
★ Burlington Arcade
    (Piccadilly Circus)
Horse Guards Parade
London Bridge
London Dungeon
Old Bailey
Rock Circus
St. Pancras Station
South Bank Arts Centre
Tower Bridge
Tower Hill Pageant
Trocadero (Piccadilly Circus)

Parks & Gardens

★★ Chelsea Physic Garden
Greenwich Park
Hampstead Heath
★ Holland House and
   Park
★ Hyde Park
★ Kensington Gardens
★★ Regent's Park
Richmond Park
★★ Royal Botanic Gardens
   (Kew Gardens)
★ St. James's Park
The Zoo

Squares & Streets

Downing Street
Fleet Street
The Mall
Pall Mall
Piazza and Central Market
Piccadilly Circus
Strand
Trafalgar Square
Whitehall

Sights & Attractions by Neighborhood

Bayswater
London Toy and Model
   Museum

Bloomsbury
★★ British Museum and
   Library
Dickens's House
The Percival David Founda-
   tion of Chinese Art
St. George's
St. Pancras Station

Chelsea/South
Kensington
Albert Memorial and Royal
   Albert Hall
★ Brompton Oratory
Carlyle's House
★★ Chelsea Physic Garden
National Army Museum
Natural History Museum
Royal Hospital, Chelsea
   Science Museum
★★ Victoria and Albert
   Museum

Chiswick/Hammersmith
★ Chiswick House
Hogarth's House

City
Barbican
College of Arms
Guildhall
London Bridge
Mansion House
The Monument
Museum of London
Old Bailey

St. Bartholomew-the-Great
St. Mary Abchurch
St. Mary-le-Bow
★★ St. Paul's Cathedral
★ St. Stephen Walbrook
Tower Bridge
Tower Hill Pageant
★ Tower of London
★★ Dennis Severs House

Covent Garden
Cleopatra's Needle
★★ Courtauld Institute
   Galleries
London Transport Museum
Piazza and Central Market
★ St. Mary-le-Strand
★ St. Paul's, Covent Garden
Theatre Museum

East End
Bethnal Green Museum of
   Childhood
★ Whitechapel Art Gallery

Greenwich
Greenwich Park
★ National Maritime
   Museum and Queen's
   House
★ Royal Observatory

Hampstead/Highgate
★ Fenton House
Freud Museum
Hampstead Heath
★ Highgate Cemetery
Keats's House
★ Kenwood House

Holborn
Fleet Street
★ Gray's Inn
Dr. Johnson's House
★★ Lincoln's Inn
Public Record Office
  Museum
Royal Courts of Justice
★★ Sir John Soane
  Museum
Staple Inn
Strand
★ Temple

Islington/Finsbury/ Camden
Jewish Museum

Kensington/Notting Hill
★ Holland House and Park
★ Hyde Park
★ Kensington Gardens
Kensington Palace
★ Leighton House
Serpentine Gallery

Knightsbridge/Belgravia
★ Apsley House, the
  Wellington Museum
★ Buckingham Palace

Marylebone
Madame Tussaud's
Planetarium
★★ Regent's Park
★ Royal Institute of British
  Architects
Sherlock Holmes Museum
★ Wallace Collection
The Zoo

Mayfair
★ Burlington Arcade
  (Piccadilly Circus)
Marble Arch
Museum of Mankind

Piccadilly/St. James's
The Mall
Pall Mall
Piccadilly Circus
★ Royal Academy of Arts
St. James's, Piccadilly
St. James's Palace
★ St. James's Park

★ Spencer House
Trocadero (Piccadilly Circus)

Soho/Trafalgar Square
Charing Cross
★★ National Gallery
National Portrait Gallery
Rock Circus
★★ St. Martin-in-the-Fields
Trafalgar Square

South Bank
HMS *Belfast*
Design Museum
Florence Nightingale Museum
Imperial War Museum
Lambeth Palace
London Bridge
London Dungeon
★ Museum of the Moving
  Image.
Royal National Theatre
★ Shakespeare Globe Centre
South Bank Arts Centre
★ Southwark Cathedral

Westminster/Whitehall
★ Banqueting House
Cabinet War Rooms
Downing Street
Horse Guards Parade
Houses of Parliament. *See*
  Palace of Westminster
★ Palace of Westminster
★ Tate Gallery
★★ Westminster Abbey
★ Westminster Cathedral
Whitehall

To the North
★ Saatchi Gallery
William Morris Gallery

To the South
★ Dulwich College and
  Picture Gallery
Eltham Palace

To the West
★ Ham House
★★ Hampton Court Palace
Marble Hill House
Osterley Park
Richmond Park
★★ Royal Botanic Gardens
  (Kew Gardens)
Syon House

London's Sights A to Z

Albert Memorial and Royal Albert Hall

Kensington Gore, SW7. ☎ 0171/589-8212. Visitors are allowed in when the hall is not in use. Free admission. Tube: Knightsbridge, South Kensington, High Street Kensington.

These fine examples of Victoriana are dedicated to Victoria's consort, who encouraged the institutionalization of arts and sciences that give this corner of Kensington its character. The **Albert Hall** was erected in 1867–71. The huge amphitheater is used for everything from boxing to concerts, notably during the summer "Prom" season (see "The Arts").

All you can currently see of the **Albert Memorial** is the world's tallest freestanding piece of scaffolding, as the memorial is in the midst of a massive conservation program. When not covered in tubing, the statue of Albert himself is utterly uninspired, but there are endless details to admire in the inventive mélange of granite, marble, bronze, and semiprecious stones that makes up the base and surrounding structure.

★ Apsley House, the Wellington Museum

141 Piccadilly, W1. ☎ 0171/499-5676. Open 11–4:30pm Tues–Sun and bank holiday Mon. Admission charged. Tube: Hyde Park Corner.

Once the first of a row of artisocratic houses a traveler from the west would encounter when approaching the city (and hence known as "No. 1, London"), Apsley House still puts on a brave show—despite now being surrounded on 3 sides by London's busiest roads. This is especially true since its massive and thoughtful refurbishment. Calm pervades the majestic rooms once occupied by the Duke of Wellington, Britain's greatest soldier.

The duke purchased the brick-fronted mansion, built by Robert Adam in 1771–78, from his elder brother in 1817. Wellington transformed the elegant house into a palace with the help of architect Benjamin Wyatt. The house was clearly intended to impress at a time when the Duke's political career was at its height (he was prime minister from 1828–1830). And impress it did—during the Reform crisis of 1832, a mob stoned the house, and iron shutters replaced the windows.

Because of the transformation, you'll find 2 complementary styles within. Adam's work has a delicate elegance, whereas Wyatt's changes and additions are on a grander scale. This contrast is not too obvious on the

ground floor, where the duke's fine collection of porcelain and dinner services are displayed in rooms that
retain some air of domesticity; but it strikes you forc-
ibly on reaching the stairwell, where the graceful curve
of Adam's design is offset by Wyatt's heavy, ornate ban-
ister. The stair now houses Antonio Canova's massive
neoclassical statue of the nude Napoleon as a Roman
Emperor, whose privates are covered by one of the
largest fig-leafs ever carved.

The best example of Adam's interior work is the
Piccadilly Drawing Room at the top of the stairs. Wyatt's
work is best seen in the splendid Waterloo Gallery; the
8 large windows have shutters that slide out to reveal
mirrors, turning the room into a glittering hall of light
in the evening.

The fine paintings at Apsley House are largely those
of the first duke, with a few additions and loans.
Velázquez dominates the Spanish collections. Murillo
and Ribera are also represented, as are many Dutch and
Flemish artists. There are many portraits of Wellington's illustrious contemporaries, including an equestrian
study of the duke himself, painted by Goya.

The Basement Gallery is a changing display of plate
and china, costume orders and decorations, and other
personal effects of Wellington's. Look for the Duke's
Death Mask, taken 3 days after his death.

★ Banqueting House

Whitehall, SW1. ☎ 0171/930-4179. Open Mon–Sat 10am–5pm; last
admission at 4:30. Closed sometimes on short notice. Admission
charged. Tube: Westminster, Charing Cross.

A superb Palladian building, Banqueting House was
originally the focal point of the great royal palace of
Whitehall. The single hall to survive a fire of 1688, it's
today in a very different setting, across busy Whitehall
from Horse Guards Parade and dominated by large government offices. Designed by Inigo Jones in 1619–22,
it has a flamboyance of design—but also a classical so-
lemnity and clarity—based on a double cube, which
was entirely novel in its day. On the ceiling are giant
canvases Charles I commissioned from Rubens of the
apotheosis of his father, James I. Installed in 1635, their
incredible scale and vigorous movement are entirely
baroque in feeling, contrasting strongly with Jones's
classicism. Rubens ultimately received a knighthood and
a pension; Charles I, ironically, was led to his execution
in 1649 from the window of this hall.

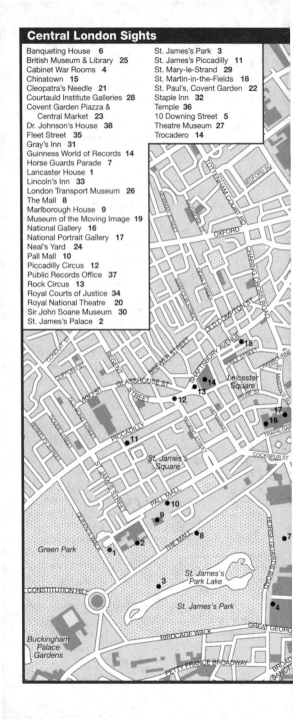

Central London Sights

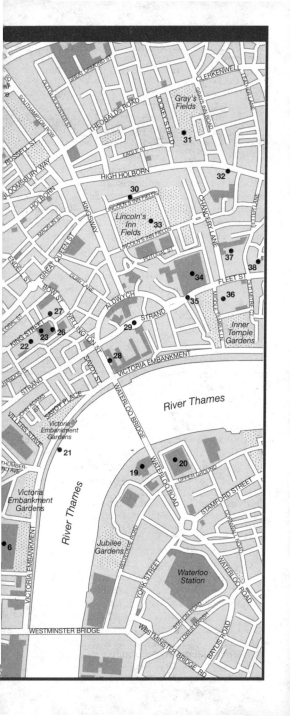

Barbican

Silk St., EC2. Box office ☎ 0171/638-8891; information ☎ 0171/
638-4141. Open daily 9am–11:30pm. Free admission to complex;
tickets can be purchased for events and productions. Tube: Barbican,
Moorgate.

This former bomb site now rises as London's boldest
piece of Utopian planning. Opened in 1982, the
Barbican's complex design and sumptuous interior con-
stitute the largest social and arts center in Europe. On a
bad day, it can seem grim and forbidding, a monument
to the failed dreams of modern architecture, but it does
have a certain excitement, with angular towers soaring
upward and walkways sweeping across. And sometimes
the concrete comes to life: the Barbican Centre is home
to the London Symphony Orchestra, the Royal Shakespeare Company's 2 theaters in the **Barbican Theatre,** a cinema, a gallery, conference halls, a roof
garden, cafeterias and restaurants, and periodic lobby
concerts and exhibitions. Here, too, is the superbly
designed **Museum of London** (see p. 142).

HMS *Belfast*

Morgan's Lane, Tooley St., SE1. ☎ 0171/407-6434. Open daily late
Mar–Oct 10am–6pm; Nov–late Mar 10am–5pm; last admission 45
minutes before closing. Admission charged. Tube: London Bridge.

This World War II warship, a Southampton–class cruiser,
saw action in the Battle of North Cape in 1943, when
the *Scharnhorst* was sunk, in the Normandy landings,
and even in the Korean War. Now it's a floating tribute
to all that, and to wartime naval life in general. Condi-
tions on board were cramped; you'll have to weave and
duck through hatches and up ladders (very tricky with
young children), but the imagination can run riot on
the navigation bridge or next to the massive main guns.

Bethnal Green Museum of Childhood

Cambridge Heath Rd., E2. ☎ 0181/980-4315. Open Mon–Thurs, Sat
10am–5:50pm; Sun 2:30–5:50pm. Free admission. Tube: Bethnal
Green.

This museum is in the heart of the authentic East End,
off the usual tourist track. There are old toys to study
from many periods; the Tate Baby House, a fully furnished Georgian mansion in miniature dating from
about 1760, stands out. The galleries upstairs showcase
wonderful collections of children's clothes, books, edu-
cational toys, and furniture.

★★ British Museum and Library

Great Russell St., WC1. ☎ 0171/636-1555. Open Mon, Fri, Sat
9am–5pm; Tues, Wed, Thurs, 10am–9pm; Sun 2:30–6pm. Guided
tours of museum at 10:45am, 11:15am, 1:45pm, and 2:15pm; guided

tours of reading room Mon–Fri at 2:15 and 4:15pm. The Reading Room can only be viewed by guided tour or through the presentation of a reading-room pass, which requires a letter of recommendation. Free Admission. Tube: Russell Sq., Tottenham Court Rd.

The British Museum is one of the most adventurous of the world's great museums—despite its age and venerable traditions, it's constantly changing. It was founded in 1753 around the 80,000 items collected by Sir Hans Sloane, a successful physician. Sloane's will allowed the nation to purchase his collection for £20,000, well below its value, thus beginning a sequence of generous bequests. Natural history was initially best represented, but in time the museum became oriented more toward archaeology. Over the years, the museum also became a depository for the spoils of the empire.

In 1823, George III's huge library was given to the nation by his heir, and the decision was made to build a new and grand edifice to display the nation's collected treasures. With the young Robert Smirke as architect, the intention was to create a neoclassical structure around a quadrangle, which was completed by 1838 and later became the famous Reading Room.

The collections quickly outgrew its confines, but the move of the natural history exhibits to the **Natural History Museum** in the 1880s and the ethnographic exhibits to the **Museum of Mankind** in 1970 has solved much of the space problem. The British Library will be moving to a new site at St. Pancras, and the courtyard of the museum will be transformed by a stunning, covered public square; the Museum of Mankind will then be transferred back to this site. When the renovation is complete, the Reading Room will be accessible to the public for the first time.

A comprehensive catalog would fill a bookcase. However, a selective visit should include the following:

Greece & Rome   These rooms are the best place to start. Turn left in the entrance hall and, for now, pass through the temporary exhibition galleries. This leads to one of the best laid out sections, with an excellent chronological survey and some of the world's finest examples of Greek art.

Room 8 is home to the world-famous Elgin Marbles, which once adorned the Parthenon. Dating from around 440 BC, the Marbles are now the subject of controversy: The Greek government is making strenuous appeals for them to be returned to Athens. Also among the innumerable treasures are fragments of the great Nereid Monument (5thC BC), from a Greek colony at Lycia in Asia Minor, reconstructed into a facade in Room 7; and, in Room 12, a frieze of the Battle of the Greeks and Amazons from the Mausoleum of Halicarnassus, one of the Seven Wonders of the Ancient World.

The smaller collection of Roman art begins in Room 15 and continues upstairs in Room 70 with the famous Portland Vase (c. 1stC BC). Room 70 also contains "freedmen reliefs," stone portraits of freed slaves that were set into tomb walls; wall paintings from Pompeii; and a remarkable crocodile-skin suit of armor from Egypt. Fascinating insights into daily Roman life are revealed by poll tax receipts and invitations.

Rooms 71–73 cover the art of the 7th–6thC BC Etruscan and Italian people, including 2 sarcophagi; Cypriot antiquities; and artifacts from the Greek colonies in Southern Italy and Sicily.

Ancient Mesopotamia   The collections from the ancient cities of Assyria rival those of Greece. The best details among the Assyrian sculptures are in the animals, particularly the lions depicted in the relief series from Nineveh (7thC BC) in Room 17. The Nimrud Gallery (Room 19) has huge 9thC reliefs showing highly ritualized hunting and military scenes.

Ancient Egypt   The nucleus of this collection of 70,000 objects fell into British hands after Napoleon's defeat at the Battle of the Nile in 1798. The large Egyptian Sculpture Gallery (Room 25) gives an impressive indication of the overpowering scale and stern quality of Egyptian art, with its ranks of massive, shiny, hard-edged statues, seemingly ageless.

At the south end is the famous Rosetta Stone, discovered in 1797; its text, in Greek as well as in Egyptian hieroglyphs, provided the key to a previously unreadable script. Among the huge statues are a pair of 3rdC BC granite lions found at Gebel Barkal, a colossus of Rameses II (c.1250 BC); and a giant scarab beetle (c. 200 BC), an image of the sun god.

The mummies and mummy cases (there are even mummies of animals) have a macabre fascination. From the Roman period are mummy cases with unnervingly realistic portraits of the dead occupants.

Asian Art   Room 33's superb collection of Asian art includes the world's finest assembly of ancient Chinese ceramics, from flawless Ming plates to dramatic, expressive horses and camels. A display of Buddhist material from all of Asia, including finds from the Silk

Route, occupies the center of the gallery. There are also a number of good Indian sculptures, some with the characteristic eroticism of Hindu art and some truly magnificent 2nd and 3rdC sculptures from the Indian monument of Amaravati.

Books & Manuscripts Leaving Room 33 at the east end, pass through to the British Library Galleries (Rooms 29–32), due to move to the new British Library Building at St. Pancras in the late 1990s. These galleries are devoted to regularly changing thematic selections from the library's vast store of literary treasures. The medieval manuscripts, in particular, are breathtaking, with their perfect miniature paintings and the unbelievably skillful calligraphy.

The collection of holographs and annotated typescripts is supplemented by other treasures: da Vinci's and Durer's sketchbooks; 2 of the 4 originals of the Magna Carta; the last dying scribblings of Lord Nelson and Captain Scott of the Antarctic; and the 2 5thC manuscripts central to the compilation of the gospels. Among the printed books are Caxton's pioneering production of *Canterbury Tales,* the famous Gutenberg Bible and the Authorized Version of 1603, and the First Folio edition of Shakespeare's plays (1623).

Prehistory & Early Britain Upstairs are the rooms devoted to prehistoric and Romano-British objects (Rooms 36–40). Stone Age products include carvings on mammoth and walrus tusks from France and a rich collection of early metalwork. Lindow Man, the 2,000-year-old remains of a Celt discovered in 1984, is on display.

Medieval Times & Beyond Rooms 41–47 are devoted to medieval (post-Roman) and later treasures, and Room 48 to European and American decorative arts (1840–1940). In Room 41 is the famous Sutton Hoo Treasure, a 7thC Angle burial ship unearthed in Suffolk in 1939. In Room 42 is a Flemish parade shield of the 15thC showing a knight kneeling before a fairytale damsel; a skeleton looks over the knight's shoulder, and the inscription, representing the knight's words, can be translated as "You or death."

A periodically changing display of works by the Great Masters—Michelangelo, Botticelli, and others—is in Room 90.

★ **Brompton Oratory**
Brompton Rd., SW3. ☎ 0171/589-4811. Open daily 6:30am–8pm. Free admission. Tube: South Kensington.

Converts are supposedly the most zealous adherents of any faith. The Oxford Movement, a group of Victorian intellectuals turned Catholic, certainly didn't go halfway when they created this church in 1884. All the drama of the Italian baroque is here. And some of the atmosphere is original: The huge marble Apostles (1680) by Mazzuoli come from Siena Cathedral.

★ Buckingham Palace

SW1. ☎ 0171/839-1377; recorded information ☎ 0171/799 2331.
Open early Aug–Sept 9:30am–5:30pm, last admission 4:30pm.
Tickets available the day of viewing from 9am at the Green Park ticket office. Admission charged. Tube: Victoria, Hyde Park Corner.

In response to the "annus horibilis" of 1992, and in an attempt to elevate public perception of the Royal Family, the Queen has allowed the public to view the State Rooms at Buckingham Palace for 8 weeks each summer. This is the first time visitors have been allowed into the Palace, and it's a big success. The funds generated from the ticket sales are being used to restore Windsor Castle, which suffered massive damage in a fire in 1992.

The Exterior   When the royal standard is flying (signifying that the monarch is in residence), many an eye scans the windows of the palace, hoping to catch a glimpse of a Royal Family member. But visitors usually have to be content with the splendors of the palace itself—and most are.

Its familiarity, setting, and pageantry (for information on the Changing of the Guard, see "Calendar of Events," p. 268) give it a certain grandeur, but in reality Buckingham Palace is an undistinguished example of early 20thC official architecture—if you didn't know what it was you might think it a rather large town hall. Behind the facade, however, is John Nash's older palace. In 1762, George III bought Buckingham House from the Duke of Buckingham, and Queen Charlotte moved in. In 1825 his son, the Regent, commissioned Nash to rebuild on a larger scale. The **Marble Arch** was built as the entrance (and later moved), but by 1850 the project was still incomplete, and Nash was sacked under suspicion of having squandered huge amounts of money. But the best parts of the palace are still his. The clearest part of his work visible from outside is a large arch leading to the gardens to the right of the palace.

When Queen Victoria came to the throne in 1837, the palace became the official residence, and it has been so ever since. It was her need for additional accommodation that led to the large side wings and front section

Queen's Life Guard

being built, although it was more humble until the facade was added in 1913.

The Interior   The tour takes in 18 of the Palace's 661 rooms. You can't help but notice that things look a bit spare—much is covered in thick plastic, the original carpets have been removed, and the knickknacks have evidently been stowed away. In general, however, the tone is ostentatious (but can the Royal Family really be accused of ostentation?)—lots of gold gilt, elaborate plaster work, and chandeliers. Highlights include the Throne Room, with matching thrones in pink and yellow, each initialed: EIIR for Elizabeth and PIIR for Philip. This is the place where the lucky few get knighted. The dining table has been removed from the State Dining Room, but note the handsome French clocks. The Picture Gallery has some gems, including Van Dyck's portrait of Charles I and Rembrandt's *Lady with a Fan.* After a quick stop in the garden, you'll be herded into the souvenir shop, where you can purchase Palace Fine Mint Chocolates or a gold carriage clock for £595; each year 100 of these clocks are produced, and, so I'm told, they're a big seller.

The Queen's Gallery & the Royal Mews   To the left of the palace is **Buckingham Gate** and **The Queen's Gallery** (open during exhibitions only, daily 9:30am–4:30pm, last admission 4pm), where exhibitions of treasures from the fabulous royal art collections are mounted. Farther along, when the road becomes Buckingham Palace Road, is Nash's attractive **Royal Mews** (open Jan–Mar, Wed noon–4pm; Apr–early Aug, Tues–Thurs noon–4pm; early Aug–Sept, Mon–Thurs noon–4pm; and Oct–Dec, Wed 2–4pm; last admission

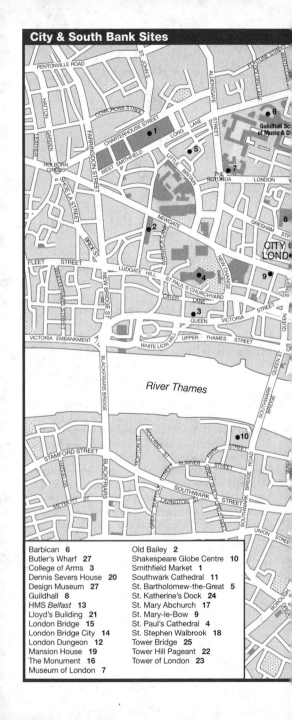

City & South Bank Sites

Barbican **6**
Butler's Wharf **27**
College of Arms **3**
Dennis Severs House **20**
Design Museum **27**
Guildhall **8**
HMS *Belfast* **13**
Lloyd's Building **21**
London Bridge **15**
London Bridge City **14**
Mansion House **19**
The Monument **16**
Museum of London **7**

Old Bailey **2**
Shakespeare Globe Centre **10**
Smithfield Market **1**
Southwark Cathedral **11**
St. Bartholomew-the-Great **5**
St. Katherine's Dock **24**
St. Mary Abchurch **17**
St. Mary-le-Bow **9**
St. Paul's Cathedral **4**
St. Stephen Walbrook **18**
Tower Bridge **25**
Tower Hill Pageant **22**
Tower of London **23**

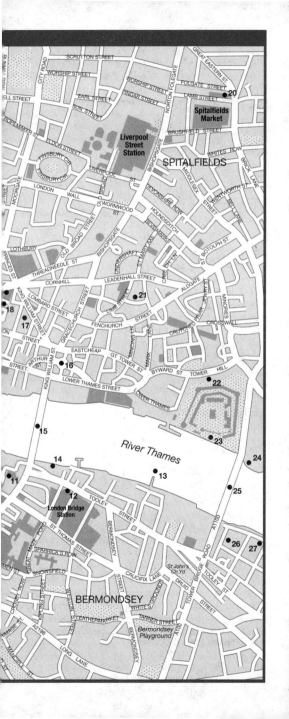

on all days at 3:30pm). On display are the Queen's beautiful carriages and harnesses; the star is the gilded and painted Gold State Coach (1762).

Cabinet War Rooms
Clive Steps, King Charles St., SW1. ☎ 0171/930-6961. Open daily 9:30am–6pm, Oct–Mar 10am–6pm; last admission 5:15pm. Admission charged. Tube: Westminster.

This was the British Government's wartime bunker in Whitehall during World War II. It must have been a grim existence, judging from the 21 tiny, spartan rooms (note the chamber pots), which have been left exactly as they were vacated after the war. The highlight is the Map Room, where Churchill charted the lines held by the Allies. Heaven for World War II aficionados.

Carlyle's House
24 Cheyne Row, SW3. ☎ 0171/352-7087. Open Apr–Oct, Wed–Sun, bank holiday Mon, 11am–5pm; last admission 4:30pm. Admission charged. Tube: Sloane Sq.

The houses in Cheyne Row were built in 1708, making them some of the oldest surviving residences in Chelsea. Thomas Carlyle (1795–1881) lived at no. 24 from 1834 until his death. You can see the house much as it was then, crammed with the memorabilia and manuscripts of the famous (although now little-read) Scottish essayist and historian. It's a perfect example of what was considered a comfortable Victorian home, despite the lack of electricity and running water on upper floors.

Charing Cross
Tube: Charing Cross.

At the south end of **Trafalgar Square,** a statue of Charles I looks down **Whitehall** to the place of his execution and occupies the site of the original Charing Cross, from where all distances to London are measured. This was the last of the Eleanor Crosses erected by Edward I in 1291 to mark the resting places of his queen's funeral cortege on its way to Westminster Abbey; Charing is a corruption of *chere reine* (dear queen). The original was destroyed in the Civil War in 1647, but when E. M. Barry designed Charing Cross Station Hotel nearby in 1863–64, he added a Victorian gothic Eleanor Cross to the forecourt, where it still stands.

★★ Chelsea Physic Garden
Royal Hospital Rd., SW3. ☎ 0171/352-5646. Open Apr–Oct, Wed–Sun 2–5pm. Admission charged. Tube: Sloane Sq.

This is one of Europe's oldest botanic gardens, founded in 1673 by the Apothecaries' Company for the collection, study, and dissemination of plants with medicinal value. Developed under the direction of physician Sir Hans Sloane, the garden still maintains its role as a research and education facility. The 4 acres are sheltered by high brick walls that provide protection for some of the more fragile species. A lovely tea is served.

★ Chiswick House

Burlington Lane, W4. ☎ 0181/995-0508. Open mid-Mar–Oct, daily 10am–1pm, 2–6pm; Oct–mid-Mar, Wed–Sun 10am–1pm, 2–4pm. Admission charged. Tube: Turnham Green, Chiswick Park.

The Palladian architecture so favored by the 18thC English gentleman, with its forms reduced to simple geometrical shapes and all detail ruthlessly contained, reached near perfection in this ravishingly beautiful mansion. Set in its own park, it retains the feel of a country house. A 1725–29 villa's octagonal dome rises from a simple square block; a portico and stairs form the entrance. The link building and summer parlor survive at the east side, where the villa was joined to the older (17thC) house. Through a low-ceilinged and severely classical octagonal room, you'll enter the 3 rooms that served as a library. An interesting exhibition of engravings, plans, and documents relating to the villa occupies these rooms. The upper reception rooms are reached by a spiral staircase, and immediately the style changes: designed by William Kent, they're brighter in color and more richly decorated. The garden has grown to the modern, wilder taste.

Cleopatra's Needle

Victoria Embankment, WC2. Tube: Embankment.

Now appropriately sited beside another symbol of timelessness, the Thames, this pink granite obelisk was made in Heliopolis in Egypt in 1500 BC, actually predating Cleopatra by centuries. Presented to Britain by Egypt in 1819, it was finally towed by sea to its present site and erected in 1878. In that year, a little time capsule containing everyday Victorian objects like hairpins and a railway timetable was buried beneath the obelisk, to be dug up and wondered at sometime in the far-off future. New York has a similar obelisk in Central Park, and there is one in Paris as well as Istanbul.

College of Arms

Queen Victoria St., EC4. ☎ 0171/248-2762. Open Mon–Fri 10am–4pm. Free admission. Tube: Mansion House, Blackfriars.

This is the official body controlling the heraldry of the United Kingdom. As a professional body, the College of Arms will investigate queries relating to genealogy and heraldry—nobody knows more about argent chevrons, batons sinister, or griffins rampant. Only the Earl Marshall's Court, also known as the Court of Chivalry, is open to the public.

★★ Courtauld Institute Galleries

Somerset House, Strand, WC2. ☎ 0171/873-2526. Open Mon–Sat 10am–6pm, Sun 2–6pm. Admission charged. Tube: Temple, Covent Garden.

When the textile industrialist Samuel Courtauld helped found London University's main art history department, the Courtauld Institute, in 1931, he provided the nucleus of an important art collection. Swelled by several subsequent bequests, this has grown into an exceptional, broad-ranging group of pictures.

The galleries on the 1st floor begin with 15th and 16thC Renaissance art and continue through the centuries to the Post-Impressionists and Modigliani. Highlights include the Morelli-Nerli *cassoni* (marriage chests) of 1472; Palma Vecchio's poetic and sensuous *Venus;* Rubens's incomparable *Landscape by Moonlight,* famous for its eerie beauty; and an important group of altarpiece *modelli* by Tiepolo. The Impressionist and Post-Impressionist paintings amount to one of the best publicly accessible collections: Impressionist works include examples by Monet, Sisley, and Renoir, including the superbly colored *La Loge.* Two large sketches by Degas reveal his extraordinary ability to fix an ordinary moment in time. As for the Post-Impressionists, you'll find an exceptional collection of Cezannes, a Van Gogh self-portrait (with bandaged ear), and two of Gauguin's haunting studies of Tahitian women.

The galleries on the 2nd floor contain the Courtauld's silver collection; riveting thematic exhibitions on subjects as diverse as Stuart Portraiture, Woman and Modernity, and Roger Fry and the Omega Workshops; and 20thC British art, including works by Sickert, Duncan Grant, and Ben Nicholson. Among the gems of 14th–16thC Italian and Netherlandish paintings are Quinten Massys's brilliant, jewel-like *Madonna* and Pieter Bruegel the Elder's rare, beautiful *Landscape with the Flight into Egypt.*

Design Museum

Butlers Wharf, Shad Thames, SE1. ☎ 0171/403-6933. Open Mon–Fri 11:30am–6pm, Sat–Sun 12–6pm. Admission charged. Tube: Tower Hill, London Bridge.

Housed in a strikingly reconstructed 1950s warehouse, the quintessentially 1980s style-obsessed museum is the first of its kind in Britain. The brainchild of Sir

Terence Conran and Stephen Bayley, it aims to show how and why objects that we take for granted, from spoons to kettles to cars, are designed the way they are. It also makes clear that, when well designed, these objects can be very beautiful.

The theme of good design begins with the building itself, with its clean, clear, all-white interior. The museum is divided into 3 sections that interact well. The permanent study collection may at first glance look like Conran's without the price tags, but it does, in fact, do much to explain and evaluate mass-market design. The Review Galleries of Contemporary Design are a fast-changing spotlight on current happenings in design, both new and speculative.

This is an agreeable place to visit, not so much a museum as a resource center (with library and lecture theater), aided by its waterfront coffee shop and more serious Blue Print Cafe (see p. 38), a restaurant serving 1st-rate Mediterranean food; both have wonderful views of the river.

Dickens's House

48 Doughty St., WC1. ☎ 0171/405-2127. Open Mon–Sat 10am–5pm, last admission 4:30pm. Admission charged. Tube: Russell Sq., Chancery Lane.

While Charles Dickens lived here between 1837 and 1839, he experienced his first taste of success. *The Pickwick Papers,* which brought him sudden prosperity, was still being published, and he worked on his first

Dickens's House

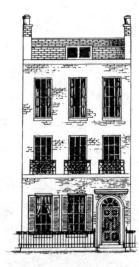

novels in the house: *Oliver Twist, Barnaby Rudge,* and *Nicholas Nickleby.*

In Dickens' time, Doughty Street had gates at either end, tended by liveried porters. His is still a handsome house; inside, there's an extensive museum of Dickens memorabilia that includes furnishings from later houses, letters and manuscripts, portraits of the writer and his family, and contemporary illustrations of his famous characters. Only the drawing room has been reconstructed to look as it might have in Dickens's day.

Downing Street
SW1. Tube: Westminster. Charing Cross.

Although physicallly dominated by the massive buildings of Whitehall, the Prime Minister's residence at Downing Street is really the powerhouse of the government. In fact, the interior of **No. 10** is more elegant and spacious than the unassuming facade might suggest, and the country has been run from its Cabinet Room since Sir Robert Walpole accepted the house ex officio from George II in 1735. **No. 11,** home of the Chancellor of the Exchequer, is the only other survivor of Sir George Downing's original terrace of 1683–86. Steps at the end of the street lead to **St. James's Park.** At the Whitehall end, a simple barrier once kept the public out of Downing Street; now ceremonial gates have been erected.

★ Dulwich College and Picture Gallery
College Rd., SE21. ☎ 0181/693-5254. Open Tues–Fri 10am–5pm, Sat 11am–5pm, Sun 2–5pm. Admission charged. Train to West Dulwich from Victoria.

In 1619, Edward Alleyn, a successful actor and colleague of Shakespeare, founded the "College of God's Gift" at Dulwich. The large almshouses that were part of the original bequest have been added to Dulwich College, making it one of London's greatest schools. Of particular interest is the remarkable Picture Gallery, in a severe neoclassical building designed by Sir John Soane in 1811–4, which incorporates a mausoleum for its founders. The 17thC Dutch school is especially well represented. Look for the majestic *Landscape with Sportsmen* by Pynacker and important works by Poussin. You'll also find Rubens sketches and English portraiture, including works by Gainsborough and Reynolds's amusing portrait of his era's great actress, *Mrs. Siddons as the Tragic Muse.* But pride of place goes to the awe-inspiring Rembrandts, including *Titus,* a moving portrait of his sick son.

★ Fenton House

Windmill Hill, Hampstead, NW3. ☎ 0171/435-3471. Open Mar, Sat–Sun 11am–5:30pm. Apr–Oct Mon, Tues, Wed 2–5:30; Sat, Sun, bank holiday Mon 11–5:30pm. Closed Nov–Feb. Last admissions 5pm. Admission charged. Tube: Hampstead.

Although Hampstead is rich in fine houses, this one is its jewel. Dating from 1693, Fenton House is a brick mansion of disarmingly simple design, hardly changed except for the benign addition of a classical portico to the east front soon after 1800. The luxurious Regency decor of the interior reflects the changes made by James Fenton in about 1810. Among the older items of furniture, look for the charming "grandmother" clock of about 1695 on the stair landing. Meissen and Nymphenburg ware as well as English pieces are among a fine porcelain collection. Also kept in the house, and perhaps its crowning glory, is the Benton Fletcher Collection of Musical Instruments, comprised of mainly early keyboard instruments. There's a lovely walled garden with hidden nooks and crannies that I've found to be generally deserted—a nice place for a break.

Concerts are performed on the keyboard instruments in summer. Call 0171/372-3206 for times and dates.

Fleet Street

EC4. Tube: Temple, Blackfriars, St. Paul's.

Fleet Street (named for the small river that now flows unseen beneath its sidewalks) is still famous as the home of British journalism, even though all the major newspapers now have abandoned the "street of shame" for Docklands and elsewhere. It begins at **Temple Bar,** the western limit of the City. Walking eastward, you'll see **Prince Henry's Room,** opposite Chancery Lane, which predates the Great Fire of 1666. The gateways to the **Temple** on the right date from the 17thC. On the left, **St. Dunstan's in the West** is a fine example of an early Victorian church in the Gothic style; it incorporates an extraordinary clock with giant striking bells (1671) and a statue of Elizabeth (1586). **El Vino's** wine bar, on the right, is famous for providing newspapermen with liquid inspiration. Farther along on the left (in Wine Office Court) is **Ye Olde Cheshire Cheese,** an ancient pub frequented by Dr. Johnson and Dickens. Soon after comes the unusually ugly ex–**Daily Telegraph building** of 1928, followed by the aggressively modern ex–**Daily Express building** of 1931, with a superb art deco entrance hall. Toward the end of Fleet Street, the wonderful wedding-cake spire of **St. Bride's** is visible on the right. Built to Wren's design in

1701–3, it's the tallest and one of the most elaborate of his spires.

Florence Nightingale Museum

2 Lambeth Palace Rd., SE1. ☎ 0171/620-0374. Open Tues–Sun 10am–4pm. Admission charged. Tube: Waterloo, Westminster.

This museum (beneath the Nightingale School, on the site of St. Thomas's hospital) celebrates the life and work of Britain's most famous nurse, "the Lady with the Lamp," and is designed very much in the modern idiom. It displays her prized possessions as well as artifacts from the Crimea War and the early days of nursing. There's also an audiovisual program, a slightly pointless recreation of a ward at Scutari as well as one of Nightingale's living room, and a resource center, where you can review her books and other archive material.

★ Gray's Inn

High Holborn, WC1. ☎ 0171/405-8164. Grounds open to public Mon–Fri. For access to chapels and halls, call first. Tube: Chancery Lane.

This ancient society of lawyers, 1 of the 4 Inns of Court, has occupied this site since the 14thC. **South Square,** the 1st quadrangle, has 1 old set of chambers (no. 1), dating from 1685. Opposite is the hall, badly burned but accurately restored. The fine late–16thC screen may have formed a backdrop to the first performance of Shakespeare's *Comedy of Errors* here in 1594. In the center of the square is a modern **statue of Francis Bacon** (1561–1626), Elizabethan statesman and scholar, one of the Inn's most distinguished former members.

Beyond the hall is **Gray's Inn Square,** full of the calm grandeur of legal London; at the south end is the frequently restored and curiously characterless chapel. More appealing is **Field Court,** dignified wrought-iron gates (1723) that lead to the gardens. Designed in formal style by Francis Bacon himself, the gardens are the best of the Inns of Court.

Guildhall

King St., EC2. ☎ 0171/606-3030. Open Mon–Sat 9am–5pm. Free admission. Tube: Bank, St. Paul's, Mansion House.

Although hidden away in its own yard in the City, the Guildhall has been the nerve center of the "Corporation of the City of London" for almost 1,000 years. The present facade is not the one that would have greeted the powerful medieval Lord Mayors such as Dick Whittington; constructed in 1788–89, it's an attractive but bizarre mélange of 18thC Gothic ideas. But the entrance porch dates from the 15thC building, as do parts of the Great Hall. The most entertaining of the statues inside are the giants Gog and Magog, new versions of old mythical figures.

The **Guildhall Library,** in an unremarkable new building on the west side, houses a sumptuous collection of books, leaflets, and manuscripts that give an absorbing and unparalleled view of London. This building also houses the oldest **Clock Museum** in the world. A French watch allegedly owned by Mary Queen of Scots, with a large silver case in the shape of a skull, and an astronomical clock said to have belonged to Sir Isaac Newton are among the collection.

★ Ham House

Ham St., Richmond. ☎ 0181/940-1950. Open Apr–Oct, Mon–Wed 1–5pm, Sat–Sun 11:30am–5:30pm; Nov–Dec, Sat–Sun 1–4pm. Last admission half an hour before closing. Garden open Sat–Thurs, 10:30am–6pm (or dusk if earlier). Admission charged for house; garden free. Tube (or train from Waterloo) to Richmond.

One of several great mansions bordering the Thames to the west of London near Hampton Court, this one is unique in that it preserves, virtually intact, a grand 17thC baroque interior. The house was built in 1610 in conventional Jacobean style, but its present appearance is mainly the result of the occupancy of Elizabeth Dysart, wife of the Duke of Lauderdale, a minister of Charles II. In the 1670s she remodeled the house in the grandest style of the period, and it was recently restored to that splendor. In addition to the spectacular interior (the Long Gallery is the most superb), there's a good collection of miniatures on display, including works by the masters of the genre, Hilliard, Oliver, and Cooper. The 17thC formal gardens alone are worth a visit. During the summer months, a ferry service operates across the Thames between Ham House and Marble Hill House.

Hampstead Heath

NW3. Sports and Entertainment Office ☎ 0181/348-9930. 24 hours. Tube: Hampstead, Belsize Park.

One of London's most famous open spaces, Hampstead Heath comprises 750 acres of meadows, hills, ponds, untamed woods, and seemingly endless secluded walkways and corners. From the kite-flyers' domain of **Parliament Hill** (where you'll have splendid views of London) to the murky bathing ponds, the Heath is a wonderful respite from the hectic rhythm of the city; on a sunny day, all of London can be found happily cohabiting here, just as New Yorkers fill Central Park. For the athlete, there are cycling tracks, cricket pitches, tennis courts, and bowling greens.

The Heath has been popular with literary London over the years; you'll find **Keats's House** perched on the southern boundary of the park. During the summer months, pack a picnic and park yourself on the grounds of **Kenwood House** for an open-air classical concert (see p. 240 for details).

★★ Hampton Court Palace

East Molesey, Surrey. ☎ 0181/781-9500. Mid-Mar–mid-Oct, Tues–Sun 9:30am–6pm, Mon 10:15am–6pm; mid-Oct–mid-Mar, Tues–Sun 9:30am–4:30pm, Mon 10:15am–4:30pm. Last admission 45 minutes before closing. Admission charged. Train from Waterloo.

This riverside palace to the west of London is not only the apotheosis of the great English Tudor style of architecture, but also incorporates a grand baroque palace designed by Wren. This dual character is clear and unsullied, since only 3 patrons played significant roles: Henry VIII's Chancellor Cardinal Wolsey, the man who personified the zenith of Church and State power; Henry himself; and, over a century later, the joint monarchs William and Mary. Queen Victoria, who preferred Windsor Castle as a Thameside home, opened Hampton Court to the public in 1838. A tragic fire in 1986 devastated some rooms, but all are now beautifully restored and reopened to the public.

The main entrance to the palace is through the mid-18thC **Trophy Gates** and along a walk that runs parallel to the river. Inset in the walls of the balancing projecting wings of Wolsey's magnificent **gatehouse** are roundels with relief busts of Roman emperors, bought as a set by him in 1521 from the Italian artist Giovanni da Maiano. Through the gate is **Base Court,** the first of Wolsey's quadrangles. At the far end is **Anne Boleyn's Gateway** (1540), built in Tudor red brick by Wolsey and later named after Henry's 2nd queen (whose introduction, at the expense of Catherine of Aragon, Wolsey had to arrange with Rome). The arch leads to **Clock Court,** with a fabulously complex astronomical clock (1540).

To enter the **State Apartments** is to move into a different age. The walls and ceilings of the **King's Staircase** are decorated with exuberant frescoes depicting gods and heroes of the ancient world. A door leads from the Grand Chamber into rooms of Wolsey's palace, with its 16thC linen-fold paneling.

The **Cumberland Suite** shows a different taste, one of the 18thC, when regal pomp gave way to elegant comfort. An important collection of paintings, largely from the Italian High Renaissance, includes works by Titian, Tintoretto, Correggio, Raphael, and Duccio. You'll also see works by Holbein, who was closely associated with the Tudors.

Before you leave the palace, be sure to seek out 3 rooms of special interest, all dating from the Tudor period: The small **Wolsey's Closet,** probably the cardinal's study, with paneled walls, a finely wrought ceiling, and recently discovered 16thC paintings; the **chapel,** also built by Wolsey, with an elaborate ceiling added by Henry VIII, pendants carved in the form of angels, a reredos designed by Wren, and marvelously carved plant forms that are the work of Grinling Gibbons; and, as a suitable climax, Henry VIII's **Great Hall** of 1531–6, hung with contemporary Flemish tapestries and boasting a superb hammerbeam roof. Smaller rooms that help make the place come alive are the newly restored and authentically equipped **kitchens** and Henry VIII's **wine cellar.** In the **Great Kitchen** is a vividly realistic re-creation of the lavish feast of St. John the Baptist, thrown by Henry VIII for his court on Midsummer's Day 1542—complete with burning fireplace and delicacies such as red deer pastis.

Last year, the spectacular gardens were restored to their former grandeur. Note the 200-year-old vine in its special greenhouse (its stem is 78 inches thick), which produces 600 bunches of grapes yearly; and the famous maze, dating in its present form from 1714. The **Chestnut Avenue,** more than a mile long, flowers spectacularly in May.

★ Highgate Cemetery

Swain's Lane, N6. ☎ 0181/340-1834. West side open by tour only, Mon–Fri noon, 2pm, and 4pm; Sat–Sun hourly 11am–4pm; east side open Mon–Fri 10am–5pm, Sat–Sun 11am–5pm. Admission charged. Tube: Archway.

Highgate Cemetery is one of the most extraordinary relics of Victorian London gone to seed, a romantic wilderness that pays tribute to nature's power to reclaim its own. A tour of the west side takes you to Christina Rossetti's grave, a weird Gothic Chapel, and the Egyptian catacombs. The most famous grave on the newer east side is the grave of Karl Marx, now surmounted by an ugly monument erected in the 1950s. Many other well-known people are buried here, including George Eliot.

Hogarth's House

Hogarth Lane, W4. ☎ 0181/994-6757. Open Apr–Sept, Mon and Wed–Sat 11am–6pm, Sun 2–6pm; Oct–Mar Mon and Wed–Sat 11am–4pm, Sun 2–4pm. Closed 2 weeks Sept, 3 weeks Dec. Free admission, donations encouraged. Tube: Chiswick Park, Turnham Green.

William Hogarth (1697–1764) was an urban artist, and only lived in the delightful riverside village of Chiswick in the summer. The house that he occupied from 1749–64 is now stranded between industrial buildings on the noisy Great West Road. Inside, however, a quieter atmosphere prevails, providing an ironic background to the fine selection of Hogarth's bustling, sarcastic, and sometimes scurrilous engravings. The artist himself is buried in the nearby village churchyard.

★ Holland House and Park

☎ 0171/602-9483. Open daily 7:30am–dusk. Tube: Holland Park.
Although Holland House has barely survived, its park retains the elegance of its prime: Narrow paths wind through mature woods; peacocks and other ornamental birds roam a large enclosure; a formal flower garden with a traditional pattern of box hedges and statuary; music drifts from the Orangery in summer; and the soothing sound of a waterfall heralds the park's most recent addition—a tranquil, well designed Japanese Garden. The bombs of 1941 destroyed most of the house; now only the east wing, with its attractive Dutch gabled roof line, stands complete. The classical gateway (1629) was designed by Inigo Jones. Open-air opera is staged during the summer months; call 0171/602-7856 for details.

Horse Guards Parade

SW1. Tube: Westminster.
This is a curiously jumbled mid-18thC classical building—all arches, pediments, and separate wings. You'll see troopers of the Household Cavalry in resplendent uniforms astride their equally well-groomed horses (see p. 268 in "The Basics" for details on the Changing of the Guard). The parade ground beyond the central arch sees the great Trooping the Colour ceremony in June (see p. 264).

★ Hyde Park

Tube: Marble Arch, Hyde Park Corner, Lancaster Gate.
From the middle of the largest open space in London, formed by Hyde Park and Kensington Gardens, you'll see nothing but wooded, rolling grassland, punctuated only by the lake known as the **Serpentine** (made in 1730). **Rotten Row,** along the southern edge, was the place to parade in the 18th and 19th centuries; it's still used by horseback riders, but has sadly lost its trees to Dutch Elm disease. A little to the north of Hyde Park

Corner is an absurd **statue of Achilles,** made in 1822 from captured French cannons. Much better is **Jacob Epstein's** *Rima* (1922), near the **Hudson Bird Sanctuary** in the center of the park.

On the northeast side is **Speakers' Corner,** which offers the dubious spectacle of wild-eyed eccentrics haranguing small groups of spectators on everything from hellfire to Utopia. Established as late as 1872 as a place where such speechmaking could be tolerated without arrest, it has in recent years begun to attract more serious attention, thanks to exiles from countries without freedom of speech. It's at its busiest on Sunday.

Imperial War Museum
Lambeth Rd., SE11. ☎ 0171/416-5000. Open daily 10am–6pm. Admission charged. Tube: Lambeth North.

"Lest we forget," the Imperial War Museum was established soon after the end of World War I to preserve the relics and memory of that terrible conflict. Today, it's essentially the museum of 20thC British warfare (pre-1914 warfare is covered by the **Army Museum**). If you're into big guns of destruction, this is your place. Suspended in the atrium are 6 famous aircraft, most notably a Sopwith Camel and a Battle of Britain Spitfire. Galleries are devoted to the museum's important collection of 20thC war art, including John Singer Sargent's harrowing *Gassed*. There's also a new permanent exhibition on the clandestine world of espionage. But the crux of this revitalized museum is the collection of 20thC warfare—one can't help but feel somewhat conflicted over the glorification of such instruments of terror.

Inns of Court
See Gray's Inn, Lincoln's Inn, and Temple.

All barristers must belong to one of these institutions, and many work from their dignified ancient buildings: **Gray's Inn, Lincoln's Inn** (the best preserved of the 3), and the Middle and Inner **Temple.**

Jewish Museum
Raymond Burton House, 129–131 Albert St., NW1. ☎ 0171/284-1997. Open Sun–Thurs 10am–4pm. Admission charged. Tube: Camden Town.

The Jewish Museum has recently moved to this elegant listed building in Camden. Jews lived in England from the time of the Norman Conquest in 1066 until Edward I expelled them in 1290. No Jews officially lived in Britain again until 1656, but under Queen Elizabeth I a small community was able to observe its

rites without interference; during the Protectorate of
Oliver Cromwell, Jews were officially readmitted.

The History Gallery includes medieval notched
wooden tax receipts; the most dramatic exhibit in the
Ceremonial Gallery is the 16thC walnut synagogue Ark
thought to be from Northern Italy, discovered at an
auction sale in Northumberland, where it had been
used as a servant's wardrobe. The museum also organizes walking tours of Jewish London (see p.103).

Dr. Johnson's House

17 Gough Sq., EC4. ☎ 0171/353-3745). May–Sept, Mon–Sat
11am–5:30pm; Oct–Apr 11am–5pm. Admission charged. Tube:
Blackfriars, Temple, Chancery Lane.

Dr. Samuel Johnson lived in this substantial terraced
house from 1748 to 1759. This man of letters par ex-
cellence was the center of a whole literary world that
flocked to see him here and in the nearby **Ye Olde
Cheshire Cheese** pub in Fleet Street. He and his 6
assistants worked on the celebrated Dictionary in the
large gabled attic. Sadly, little of the house's original
contents is left, but a few chairs and tables do lend a bit
of historic atmosphere, and pictures and memorabilia
help recreate 18thC literary life in London. Look for a
1st-edition of the Dictionary and Johnson's will.

Keats's House

Keats Grove, NW3. ☎ 0171/435-2062. Apr–Oct, Mon–Fri 10am–
1pm and 2–6pm, Sat to 5pm, Sun 2–5pm; Nov–Mar Mon–Fri 1–5pm,
Sat 10am–1pm and 2–5pm, Sun 2–5pm. Free admission. Tube:
Hampstead, Belsize Park.

The Romantic poet John Keats (1795–1821) was already in the grip of tuberculosis when, in 1820, he left
this house in Hampstead, where he had spent his 2 most
productive years, for Italy, where he died 10 months
later. The house is a monument to his earlier happiness
and the rural seclusion that inspired "Ode to a
Nightingale" and other poems. It was split into 2 cottage homes sharing a garden; in the other lived Fanny
Brawne, with whom Keats fell famously and poetically
in love. The engagement ring she wore until her own
death is part of the memorial collection, as are Keats's
manuscripts and annotated books, and letters to and
from such friends as Shelley.

Kensington Palace and Kensington Gardens

Kensington Gardens, W8. ☎ 0171/937-9561. Open summer only,
Mon–Sat 9am–5pm, Sun 10am–5pm. Last admission 4:15pm.
Admission charged. Tube: High Street Kensington, Queensway. *Note:*
Kensington Palace is about to go through a massive renovation and

there is talk of restricting entrance to only those taking the guided tour; check opening hours and restrictions before visiting.

Kensington Palace was first made a royal residence when it was bought by William and Mary in 1689. Sir Christopher Wren was instructed to enlarge the palace and, apart from further work in the 1720s, most of what you see was built under his supervision. It's a simple structure built around 3 courts, surprisingly unpretentious for a royal palace. Perhaps the most striking part is the **Orangery** (1704), a separate building a little to the northeast, probably designed by Nicholas Hawksmoor. During the warmer months, tea in the Orangery is a wonderful pit stop.

The interior is mostly private, but you can visit the State Apartments. Some of the rooms are largely as Wren left them; others were made grander by William Kent in the 1720s. One of the most attractive rooms is the sumptuous but intimate Queen's Bedroom, whose fine 17thC furnishings include the bed made for James II's queen. Look for the fine carving by Grinling Gibbons over the fireplace in the Presence Chamber. The Council Chamber holds an interesting display of paintings and exhibits from the Great Exhibition of 1851.

The house's large grounds now form **Kensington Gardens.** Just across the road from Hyde Park, the Gardens have a very different atmosphere, with formal avenues and gardens radiating out from the palace. In Queen Victoria's time, a strict dress code was in place, but these days you're more likely to find visitors clad in Lycra, as the lane just outside the palace is a favorite Rollerblading locale. There are wonderful nooks and crannies for kids to explore: The **statue of Peter Pan** is near the Italian fountains; the **Elfin Oak,** carved with wooden gnomes and little animals, is to the north; and the **Round Pond,** in the center of the park, is ideal for sailing model boats. For grownups, there's **Henry**

Kensington Palace

Moore's Arch, which spans the Serpentine, and the **Serpentine Gallery** (see p. 170).

★ Kenwood House

Hampstead Lane, NW3. ☎ 0181/348-1286. Open daily mid-Apr–Oct 10am–6pm; Nov–mid-Mar 10am–4pm. Free admission. Tube: Finsbury Park, Golders Green.

After a short walk through some well-established woods on Hampstead Heath, this exquisite 18thC mansion comes into view. Robert Adam's superb classical facade is harmoniously flanked by wings containing the orangery and library; it's some of the Scottish architect's finest work. Kenwood was saved from the hands of speculative builders in 1925 when the 1st Earl of Iveagh (Edward Cecil Guinness, of brewing fame) bought the house. He died only 2 years later, leaving it and an art collection to the people of London.

Except for the outstanding library, the entire house is now laid out as an art gallery. Eighteenth-century English painting is best represented, with excellent examples from Gainsborough and Reynolds. Kenwood's real stars, however, are Dutch paintings, with fine examples by Cuyp and Van de Velde. Other notable artists represented include Van Dyck, Guardi, Boucher, and Turner.

Concerts are given by the lake in summer (see p. 240). To reserve tickets, call 0171/413-1443.

Lambeth Palace

SE1. ☎ 0171/928-8282. Open only to organized groups reserving in advance; apply in writing to the Bursar. Also open as part of the National Gardens Scheme; call 01483/211535 for information. Tube: Lambeth North.

In the possession of the Archbishops of Canterbury since 1197, Lambeth Palace grew into prominence as the Primate's residence in the later Middle Ages. In 1547, Thomas Cranmer wrote the *Book of Common Prayer* here, but caused great controversy by eating meat during Lent in the Great Hall. The superb red-brick gatehouse dates from 1495; next to it stands the 15thC tower of the now deconsecrated church of St. Mary-at-Lambeth, which has been taken over by the **Museum of Garden History;** a replica of a 17thC knot garden has been laid out in the former churchyard (☎ 0171/633-9701; open Mon–Fri 11am–3pm, Sun 10:30am–5pm; free admission).

★ Leighton House

12 Holland Park Rd., W14. ☎ 0171/602-3316. Open Mon–Sat 11am–5:30pm. Free admission. Tube: High Street Kensington.

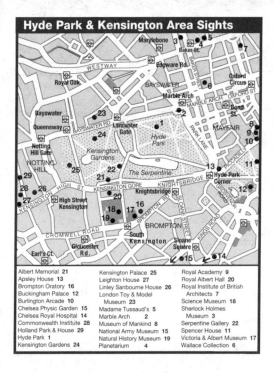

Hyde Park & Kensington Area Sights

In a street once favored by successful artists, Leighton House is actually a remarkable surprise. Lord Leighton was the most famous of Victorian artists; building his house from 1865, he gave vent to his taste for the exotic, creating a rich, fantasy-like Moorish interior—London, harem style. The highlight is the Arab Hall, with its 2 stories culminating in a dome and its walls covered with rich 13th–17thC Islamic tiles. Interesting Victorian paintings on display include works by Leighton himself and Edward Burne-Jones.

★★ Lincoln's Inn

WC2. ☎ 0171/405-1393. Courtyards open Mon–Fri 8am–7pm; chapel and gardens open Mon–Fri 12:30–2:30pm; groups can apply to see Old Hall and Great Hall by writing to the Treasury. Free admission. Tube: Holborn, Chancery Lane.

The most unspoiled of the Inns of Court was founded in the 14thC. The best way in is from Chancery Lane, through a 1518 **gatehouse** (with the original gates) and the red-brick Tudor **Old Buildings** (before 1520). Opposite the gate is the **Old Hall** (1490–2), which contains an uncharacteristically serious painting by

Hogarth and a fine wooden roof. On the north side of the court is the **chapel** (ca. 1619–23), standing on an open undercroft of Gothic vaulting with rich ribbing.

To the southwest is **New Square,** a large and remarkably well preserved square of about 1685–97. To the south is a **gateway** (1697) leading to Carey Street. The northern part of the Inn includes the great bulk of **Stone Buildings** (1774–80), with a severe classical facade on the west side; the large sundial on this wall is dated 1794. Opposite are the Inn's attractive private gardens, along with the impressive brick Victorian Gothic **library** and **New Hall.** Beyond these lie the open spaces of **Lincoln's Inn Fields,** one of London's largest public squares.

London Bridge
Free admission. Tube: Monument, London Bridge.

One might call this bridge London's *raison d'etre*—the Romans discovered that this was the farthest downstream they could easily cross the river, and built their town accordingly. Their wooden bridge survived with periodic reconstructions until the medieval stone bridge appeared in 1176–1209. It stood for more than 500 years, encrusted with houses, shops, chapels, and the famous iron spikes where traitors' heads were displayed. Eventually, all the buildings were removed and the bridge was modernized around 1749, the same time the 2nd bridge was built at Westminster. A new bridge (now in Lake Havasu, Arizona) was built 1825–31. The present structure dates from 1967–73. Many people confuse this bridge with the oft-pictured Tower Bridge. Ignorance about this will immediately set you apart as a tourist—be cool.

London Bridge City
London Bridge, SE1. Tube: Monument, London Bridge.

It's a good idea to arrive at this group of tourist attractions near London Bridge by tube, visit whichever sights you want, eat and shop in **Hay's Galleria,** and depart by pleasure craft from London Bridge Pier. Sights grouped in this area between London Bridge and Tower Bridge include **HMS *Belfast*,** the **London Dungeon,** and **Southwark Cathedral.** Just across Tower Bridge is **Butler's Wharf** and the **Design Museum.**

London Dungeon
34 Tooley St., SE1. ☎ 0171/403-0606. Open daily Apr–Sept 10am–5:30pm; Oct–Mar 10am–4:30pm. Admission charged. Tube: London Bridge.

Enjoying the London Dungeon requires a macabre sense of humor—and a strong stomach. Its location in a series of dark, damp vaults under railway arches has been carefully chosen to foster discomfort, and is ideally suited to exhibits on the "darker side of British history." The vaults echo to the recorded sounds of screams and moans (and the rumble of the occasional passing train). The ancient British heroine Boadicea, for example, is shown thrusting a blood-smeared spear into the throat of a gurgling victim. Robespierre sentences the nobility to death and heads roll in the newest exhibition, a recreation of the French Revolution known as "The Theatre of the Guillotine." Not for the fainthearted.

London Toy and Model Museum

21/23 Craven Hill, W2. ☎ 0171/402-5222. Open Mon–Sat 10am–5:30pm, Sun 11am–5:30pm; last admission 4:30pm. Admission charged. Tube: Paddington, Queensway, Bayswater, Lancaster Gate.

Reopened last year after a £4-million refurbishment, this remarkable museum appeals as much to adults as to children. It's made up of themed galleries incorporating state-of-the-art technology and interactive displays. The Model Railway gallery, with 6 different train lines, is awesome. Everything in the collection either moves, beeps, or lights up. And there's a conservatory garden cafe, where less interested mummies and daddies can pass the time away.

London Transport Museum

The Piazza, Covent Garden. ☎ 0171/379-6344. Open Sat–Thurs 10am–6pm, Fri 11am–6pm. Admission charged. Tube: Covent Garden.

As part of the renovation of Covent Garden, the former Flower Market (1871–72) now houses a large number of historic public transport vehicles in its spacious galleries. This hands-on museum chronicles the history of the capital's transport with illustrations, photographs, audiovisual displays, memorabilia such as tickets and posters, and fine models of everything from the "wherries" that plied the river to electric trams. Kids can sit in the driver's seat of a tram and a bus and work the deadman's handle in a tube train. You'll find tube engines and carriages from the 19thC and a simulation of the Circle Line from the driver's point of view.

Madame Tussaud's

Marylebone Rd., NW1. ☎ 0171/935-6861. Open daily 9am–5:30pm. Admission charged; call 0171/465-0077 to purchase advance tickets. Tube: Baker St.

The redoubtable Madame Tussaud, who lived to be 89, began her career by wax modeling the aristocracy and royalty of France's ancien régime. She came to England in 1802 and opened her waxwork museum in London in 1835. It's now linked to the **Planetarium.**

Today's museum combines the old and the new. A section at the start of the exhibition displays the famous Sleeping Beauty; it was cast from one of Madame Tussaud's oldest molds, thought to have been made of Madame du Barry, Louis XV's mistress, with a mechanism that simulates breathing. To illustrate the technology of the 1990s, there's a small display showing how the animated figures now used in **Rock Circus,** Madame Tussaud's rock-and-pop outpost, are made.

Recent celebrities, ranging from Luciano Pavarotti to Kylie Minogue, appear in the next room. (I'm told that Hugh Grant is about to be unveiled.) The following section features supposedly less ephemeral "superstars" such as Marilyn Monroe, Joan Collins(!), and Michael Jackson. Downstairs, the Grand Hall features a range of historical figures, from Henry VIII and his wives to Madame Tussaud herself. Contemporary figures include the present-day Royal Family and many international leaders, lined up with the more notable of their predecessors. Watch out for the occasional waxwork practical joke, such as the tourist asleep on a bench.

The greatest draw of all, though, is the Chamber of Horrors. Among its terrors is a reconstruction of the dark streets of Whitechapel that Jack the Ripper stalked. "The Spirit Of London" is the new, £10 million ride depicting over 400 years of London's history; for the first time, audio-animatronic figures move and speak. There's even an olfactory aspect to the journey.

The Mall

SW1. Tube: Charing Cross, Green Park.

Whenever pomp and circumstance are on hand, the Mall is where the crowds gather. Originally laid out by Charles II in 1660–2 as a formal avenue through St. James's Park, it's now a triumphal processional leading from Trafalgar Square to Buckingham Palace.

The current Mall, laid out between 1900 and 1911 and majestically lined with plane trees, slopes gently but impressively down along the side of the park to the **Victoria Memorial** and **Buckingham Palace.** Looking from Admiralty Arch, the first building on the right is **Carlton House Terrace,** built by John Nash in 1827–9 on the site of his earlier Carlton House, the great palace built for the Regent. Its 2 massive stucco facades are separated by the **Duke of York Steps.** The view is best from St. James's Park—the balancing ranges, with their Corinthian colonnades, raised broad terraces, and supporting Doric columns, are one of London's most exciting architectural views. On the south side of The Mall is the **Admiralty** of 1722–6, with the aggressively concrete **Citadel** next to it, a bold bomb-proof structure from World War II.

The rest of The Mall is surrounded by the park, with the palaces scattered along its north side visible on the right. **Marlborough House,** of stone-dressed red brick, is followed by the complex making up **St. James's Palace** and the white stucco **Clarence House,** and now the home of the Queen Mother. **Lancaster House** follows in more solemn yellow Bath stone.

The huge **Victoria Memorial,** covered with elaborate sculpture in the florid Edwardian style, occupies a circus at the end of the avenue. Queen Victoria's likeness faces up The Mall toward **Admiralty Arch.**

Mansion House

Walbrook, EC4. ☎ 0171/626-2500. Open by appointment only Tues–Thurs; apply in writing. Tube: Bank.

As if in reference to the ancient city-states, the residence of the Lord Mayor of London—symbol of the independence of the City—is classical in character. It owes its Palladian simplicity to George Dance the Younger, who designed it in 1739–53. Its 6 giant columns support the only decoration, a pediment with sculptures representing the City's dignity and opulence. But the interior is extremely ornate, with a series of state rooms leading from the portico to the grand Egyptian Hall (which is Roman in style, despite its name).

During the year, you can see the liverymen, aldermen, and sheriffs who choose the Lord Mayor parading at various antiquated ceremonies. Despite all the pomp, their power is real—this is the only private residence in the kingdom with its own court and prison cells.

Marble Arch

W1. Tube: Marble Arch.

Now in the center of a major traffic island, the Marble Arch retains only part of its original grandeur. John Nash built it in 1828 as the entrance to Buckingham Palace; it was moved to its present site in 1851 when Queen Victoria enlarged the palace. The traffic island had been the site of Tyburn Tree, London's traditional place of execution from the Middle Ages until 1783. A plaque marks the site of the permanent large triangular gallows where regular hangings, drawings, and quarterings attracted big crowds.

Marble Hill House

Richmond Rd., Twickenham. ☎ 0181/892-5115. For tickets to outdoor concerts call 0171/413-1443. Open 10am–1pm, 2–6pm Easter–Sept; Wed–Sun 10am–1pm, 2–4pm Sept–Easter. Admission charged. Tube: Richmond, or train to St. Margaret's from Waterloo.

This fine riverside mansion, a house of elegant Palladian regularity, began life with some "irregular" occupants: it was built for George II's mistress, the Countess of Suffolk, in 1723–9, and was occupied by Mrs. Fitzherbert, George IV's secret wife, in the 1790s.

The interior is quite beautiful, with a series of lovely rooms culminating in the splendid bedroom of the Countess of Suffolk, with Corinthian columns framing the alcove intended for the bed. Some attractive furniture has been restored to the house, together with a number of interesting paintings, including good copies of Van Dyck portraits. The Lazenby Collection, displayed on the 2nd floor, includes Chinese paintings on mirrors, furniture, and pottery.

The house stands in a fine open park. In the summer months, you can bring a picnic and listen to outdoor performances ranging from swing to opera. A ferry service operates across the Thames between Ham House and here.

The Monument

Monument St., EC3. ☎ 0171/626-2717. Open Apr–Sept, Mon–Fri 9am–5:40pm, Sat–Sun 2–5:40pm; Oct–Mar, Mon–Sat 9am–3:40pm. Admission charged. Tube: Monument.

Deprived of its commanding appearance by the modern buildings surrounding it, the Monument nevertheless retains the baroque drama of its conception. Designed by Wren and built in 1671 on a little hill close to the river, it commemorates the Great Fire of London, which began on September 2, 1666 in a bakery in nearby Pudding Lane. A relief on the base plinth shows Charles II in Roman dress protecting the citizens of London; the original inscription unjustly blamed the disaster on a Catholic plot. The 202-foot-high Doric column contains 311 steps up to a balcony and gilded urn. It's a stiff climb, but worth it for the view.

Museum of London

150 London Wall, EC2. ☎ 0171/600-3699. Open Tues–Sat and bank holidays 10am–5:50pm; Sun noon–5:50pm. Admission charged. Tube: Barbican, Moorgate, St. Paul's.

This museum, in a contemporary building on the corner of the Barbican, traces the social history of London from prehistory to the present day. It holds a substantial portion of important archaeological finds made in London, and is chronologically arranged so visitors follow a single winding course. Exhibits range from archaeological finds from the Stone, Bronze, and Iron ages and well-preserved artifacts from Roman London to reconstructed shop fronts and interiors, including a superb 18thC barber shop, a 19thC pub, and an early broadcasting studio; there's even an art-deco elevator from Selfridges. But grandeur steals the show: the elaborate Lord Mayor's Ceremonial Coach (1757), removed once a year for the Lord Mayor's Show, stands resplendent.

Museum of Mankind

6 Burlington Gardens, W1. ☎ 0171/437-2224. Open Mon–Sat 10am–5pm; Sun 2:30–6pm. Free admission. Tube: Piccadilly Circus, Green Park.

This museum is largely organized as a series of temporary exhibits on non-European cultures or themes, but they achieve considerable depth of coverage. The ethnographic collection is outstanding in African textiles, pottery, and sculpture; the art of Plains and northwest Native Americans; and pre-Columbian Central and South American art. There are objects brought back from the Pacific islands by Captain Cook, and from Indonesia by Sir Stamford Raffles in the 19thC. Room 7 permanently houses the museum's greatest treasures, including a life-sized skull carved from a solid piece of crystal from Mexico—a hauntingly beautiful object.

The collection will be moving back to the British Museum when space is freed up by the relocation of the British Library.

★ Museum of the Moving Image (MOMI)

South Bank, Waterloo, SE1. ☎ 0171/928-3535. Open daily 10am–6pm; last admission at 5pm. Admission charged. Tube: Waterloo, Embankment.

In a striking glass and steel building adjoining the National Film Theatre, MOMI traces the history of film, television, and video from early Japanese shadow theater to the sophisticated techniques and special effects of today. Expect lots of hands-on exhibits ranging from operating a praxinoscope to reading the television news, a section devoted to animation, and a horde of fascinating memorabilia, including Charlie Chaplin's hat and cane, Fred Astaire's tailed jacket, and a towering model of Frankenstein's monster. The Little Children's Project, which is comprised of exhibits identified by an Oscar the Grouch icon, is geared towards those under 3 feet tall.

National Army Museum

Royal Hospital Rd., SW3. ☎ 0171/730-0717. Open daily 10am–5:30pm. Free admission. Tube: Sloane Sq.

Opened in 1971 in a new building close to the Royal Hospital in Chelsea, the National Army Museum brings together objects from several older collections. A new permanent exhibition, "The Road to Waterloo," includes the skeleton of Napoleon's horse, Wellington's battlefield telescope, the saw used to amputate the Earl of Uxbridge's leg, and a huge model of the Battle of Waterloo (made shortly afterwards and never before displayed). "Flanders to Falklands" tells the story from 1914 to the Falklands War with life-size displays, audiovisuals, and dioramas. There is a fine uniform gallery, a picture gallery, a reading room, a display on the Gulf War ("The Aftermath of Battle"), and one highlighting the role of women in the army. An exciting new exhibition on Burma features a life-like reconstruction of a POW camp with a walk-on booby-trap bridge.

★★ National Gallery

Trafalgar Sq., WC2. ☎ 0171/839-3321. Open Mon–Sat 10am–6pm, Wed to 8pm during summer months; Sun 2–6pm. Free admission. Tube: Charing Cross, Leicester Sq.

The National Gallery is one of the world's finest collections of Western art. The way it's displayed is a model for other great collections: Each work is clean (the gallery's conservation department has been a leader in the science of restoration), clearly labeled, well-lit, and given adequate space.

This freshness of approach accords with the National Gallery's relative youth. In 1823, when most other European capitals already boasted public collections, the threat of the sale of John Julius Angerstein's great collection to William of Orange forced a tight-fisted Parliament to produce £57,000 to fund their own. The collection has continued to expand steadily, changing character in accordance with the taste of the different periods of acquisition. After some exploratory Italian forays in the 1840s, the pioneering director, Sir Charles Eastlake, purchased many (then) little-known early Italian works; now, the gallery's Italian collection is unequaled outside Italy. In 1861, Queen Victoria gave 20 German and Flemish pictures in Albert's memory; this inspired a new round of acquisitions, resulting in a magnificent group of Dutch and Flemish works.

National Gallery

Attempts have been made in this century to strengthen the French collection, and there are some outstanding Spanish works. British and modern art are the specialties of the **Tate Gallery,** but the National Gallery does have some fine 18thC British masterpieces.

The collection is exhibited chronologically, starting in the **Sainsbury Wing,** where the first rooms contain Leonardo's famous, beautiful black-chalk *Cartoon,* restored after gunfire damage in 1987 and now beautifully displayed, as well as his mysterious *Virgin of the Rocks.* Also here is the museum's newest acquisition, *St. Michael Triumphant Over the Devil with the Donor Antonio Juan* by Bartolome Bermejo, thought to be one of the most important 15thC Spanish works.

The other glowing medieval icons are further testimony to faith as well as artistic genius; Duccio's *Maesta* altarpiece panels from Siena Cathedral are outstanding. Then comes the transition to a more realistic style: Masaccio's innovative *Virgin and Child* has the spiritual gravity and solid forms of the Renaissance. The Renaissance can also be seen emerging in Botticelli's early *Adoration of the Magi* and his *Venus and Mars,* admired for the purity of its line.

But the Renaissance was not such an Italian monopoly as is sometimes supposed. The carefully observed naturalism of northern painters greatly influenced their Italian counterparts; the Dutch and Flemish collection here illustrates this better than any other in the world. The most famous work here is Jan Van Eyck's *Arnolfini Marriage,* full of realistic but symbolic detail.

In the **West Wing** of the main building, the superb collection of the 16thC Italian Renaissance unfolds. All the greatest masters are here. Among too many highlights to list are Michelangelo's unfinished *Entombment;* Raphael's *Pope Julius,* only recently discovered to be the original among several versions around the world; and Titian's breathtaking *Bacchus and Ariadne,* ablaze with color and movement.

Holbein's *Ambassadors* was probably the most important picture painted in England in the Tudor period; as a reminder of frailty, the oblique shape in the bottom left corner shows itself to be a skull when viewed from the right angle. It hangs with the arresting and well-preserved *A Lady with a Squirrel and a Starling;* Holbein's skill is evident in the wicked gleam in the squirrel's eye and in the folds of the sitter's shawl.

The Dutch 17thC—the golden age of painting in the Netherlands—is strongly represented: There are several terrific Rembrandts, 2 Vermeers, many fine landscapes and scenes of everyday life done in the restrained, precise style of the Dutch school, and major works by Rubens and Van Dyck, done in the grander Flanders style.

The 17thC French collection emphasizes Poussin and Claude. A small number of Spanish pictures of extraordinary quality includes El Greco's *Christ Driving the Traders from the Temple;* Velazquez's sensual tour-de-force, *The Rokeby Venus;* and Zurbaran's *St. Francis,* showing the dark religious passion so characteristic of Spanish art. The 17thC Italian works include Caravaggio's *Supper at Emmaus,* which demonstrates the artist's revolutionary use of naturalism in religious art; the disciples are seen as real working people with coarse clothes—look at the drama, even in the hands.

The **East Wing** is home to paintings from 1700 to 1920. The French 18thC is poorly represented by National Gallery standards; even so, it offers Watteau's *La Gamme d'Amour,* Chardin's acute *Young Schoolmistress,* Boucher's *Landscape with a Watermill,* and David's *Portrait of Jacobus Blauw.* A popular acquisition, found on the ceiling of a London house, is Tiepolo's *Allegory with Venus and Time,* full of light and air.

The 18th–19thC is the gallery's strongest English period. Outstanding works include Hogarth's satirical *Mariage à la Mode* paintings, and magnificent examples of that period's 2 best genres, Gainsborough's portrait of *Mr. and Mrs. Andrews* and Constable's landscape *The*

Hay Wain. Turner opened new vistas with his magical *Rain, Steam and Speed* and *The Fighting Temeraire.*

The last rooms chart the emergence of modern art. There's an impressive collection of Impressionist works, including Renoir's *Les Parapluies* (periodically moved to Dublin), Monet's stunning *Water-lilies*, and Degas's *Beach Scene*. Van Gogh's intense, dynamic *Sunflowers* introduces a Postimpressionist collection that also includes works by Seurat, Gauguin, and Klimt.

Don't miss the **Micro Gallery** on the 1st floor, a room devoted to computers, where you can look up any school of painting, individual work, or artist you choose. And a wonderful CD-ROM Gallery Guide Soundtrack, which covers over 1,000 works in the collection, is now available.

★ **National Maritime Museum and Queen's House**
Romney Rd., Greenwich. ☎ 0181/293-9618. Open Mon–Sat 10am–5pm; Sun 12–5pm. Admission charged. British Rail from Charing Cross to Maze Hill.

The Queen's House is a building of extreme classical simplicity done in the Palladian style. Henry VIII was born here, as were his 2 daughters, Mary I and Elizabeth I. James I gave the palace to his queen, Anne of Denmark, in 1613, and it was completely rebuilt to the designs of Inigo Jones between 1616 and 1635. Most interesting are the entrance hall, a perfect cube, and the graceful circular stairwell. To the sides are 2 wings added in 1807–16. The royal apartments have been carefully re-created to look as they might have while Henrietta Maria, widow of Charles I, lived here.

It's now home to the National Maritime Museum, the greatest seafaring museum in the world. Its extensive collections range from marine archaeology finds to an entire paddle tug. Exciting displays include 2 17thC decorated royal riverboats and a hands-on exhibit that juxtaposes interactive features with objects from Viking times to the present. A gallery entitled "Discovery and Seapower, 1450–1700," charts England's transition from economic obscurity to one of Europe's great naval and commercial powers. A new gallery displays the 20thC collections.

National Portrait Gallery
2 St. Martin's Place, WC2. ☎ 0171/306-0055. Open Mon–Sat 10am–6pm; Sun 12–6pm. Free admission (admission charged for selected special exhibitions). Tube: Charing Cross.

This museum was opened in 1859 as a kind of national pantheon. From the start, its emphasis was on the subjects of the pictures rather than on the art itself; as a result, artistically speaking, the collection contains some real duds. But the effort to obtain the best portraits also means that you'll find many fine paintings and drawings. (Since 1968, photographs have been systematically included, and caricatures are now accepted.) In fact, the emphasis on history gives great coherence to the exhibition, which is arranged chronologically with relevant background material. The collection begins at the top (you'll have to climb several flights of stairs), where a room is devoted to **medieval portraits.** Portraits in a modern sense were not produced in the Middle Ages, so the images are few in number; a copy of the fine representation of Richard II in Westminster Abbey dominates.

Portraits became common from the **Tudor period.** The most interesting works of the collection may be here. Perhaps the finest work is Holbein's magnificent cartoon for a lost fresco at Whitehall Palace showing *Henry VIII with his Father Henry VII.* There's an exquisite full-length image of Lady Jane Grey, the 17-year-old queen who was executed in 1554 after a 4-day reign. Several portraits of Elizabeth I are done in the incredibly detailed and elaborate style of her age. A likeness of Shakespeare from about 1610 is the only one with any claim to authenticity.

The gallery continues through the **Jacobean and Stuart periods,** with the increasing formality of the court painters giving way to the more lively 18thC images. Figures from the arts and sciences increase gradually in proportion to the political and military leaders. Sir William Beechey's fine unfinished portrait of Nelson and a romantic Byron in Greek costume are great examples of the increasing concentration on the individual that came into vogue in the 19thC. Royalty, however, is still represented in highly idealized fashion: Victoria and Albert sculpted in the costume of ancient Saxons is the most amusing example.

The portraits from the last years of the 19thC and later are varied in style. The **20thC galleries** are organized on 2 levels: the 2nd covers the years 1914–45 and is divided into areas such as politics, science, and the theater; it includes portraits of the Bloomsbury Group, James Joyce, and superb studies of Edith Sitwell by Wyndham Lewis. Royalty, however, is still idealized with due deference. Post-1945 works are displayed on the 1st level. Among them are *Elizabeth Taylor* by Andy Warhol; *Richard Rogers* by Sir Eduardo Paolozzi; a double portrait, *Sir David and Sir Richard Attenborough,* by Ivy Smith; Humphrey Ocean's *Paul McCartney;* and a new photograph of John Major.

Natural History Museum

Cromwell Rd., SW7. ☎ 0171/938-9123. Open Mon–Sat 10am–5:50pm; Sun 11–5:50pm. Tube: South Kensington. Admission charged; free after 4:30pm Mon–Fri and after 5pm Sat, Sun and bank Holidays. Tube: South Kensington.

When the British Museum was formed in 1753, much of its collection consisted of plant, animal, and geological specimens. These categories grew at enormous speed (they still do), spliting off into a separate natural history collection in 1860. In the 1970s, the museum created a series of self-contained exhibits rather than continuing to show all of its millions of specimens in old-fashioned cabinets. As part of a recent reorientation, these exhibits were collectively named the **Life Galleries.** Since 1989, the former Geological Museum's collections have been housed here in the **Earth Galleries.** There's lots to touch and see—it's all very interactive.

The Life Galleries   At the main entrance, a huge dinosaur skeleton towers over you in the giant Central Hall—absurd, terrifying, and in marked contrast to the stunning new dinosaur exhibit to the left of the entrance. The first scene—and the centerpiece— is a grisly, lifelike episode in which 3 deinonychus tear at the flesh of a huge tenontosaurus, which twitches in its death throes. All are computerized robotic dinosaurs, brilliant examples of Japanese technology. You can touch fossil skeletons and eggs, serrated dinosaur teeth, and bones, and computer graphics and videos breathe life into the extinct creatures and show their relationship to living animals.

To the right side of the Central Hall is another of the museum's most recent displays, "Creepy Crawlies." Arachnophobes beware: This exhibition contains a full-size house crawling with spiders, termites, carpet beetles, and other insects. Nearby is an ambitious new exhibit on global ecology, a display of British birds arranged by habitat, and an exceptionally lively presentation on human biology. One of the museum's most effective sections, "Discovering Mammals," traces the life-cycle of whales and other mammals with fascinating dioramas, interactive models, and vast skeletons.

A monumental staircase leads from the Central Hall to the upper floor, where an exhibition traces the evolution of man. Another, on the origin of the species, covers Darwin's work with admirable thoroughness. The traditional hall, devoted to minerals, rocks, and gems, serves as an effective contrast to the newer exhibition techniques, and is notable for the incredible diversity and beauty of its specimens. There's an exciting Discovery Centre in the basement, where children can stroke a rock python's skin or try their hand at beachcombing.

The Earth Galleries   The collection of gemstones here includes some beautiful specimens, both crude and cut. You'll also find 2 adventurous exhibitions, "The Story of the Earth" and "Treasures of the Earth," and 2 smaller exhibitions, "Britain before Man" and "British Fossils." On the 1st floor, displayed on a structure resembling a real offshore platform, "Britain's Offshore Oil and Gas" tells the full story of hydrocarbons, from both geological and operational viewpoints.

Old Bailey (Central Criminal Court)

Old Bailey, EC4. ☎ 0171/248-3277. Open Mon–Fri 10:30am–1pm, 2–4:30pm. Free admission. Tube: St. Paul's.

The Old Bailey's famous gilt figure of Justice, complete with scales and sword, looks down on a site with a grim history: The Central Criminal Court replaced the medieval Newgate Gaol, a longtime execution site and the ultimate symbol of penal squalor for 19thC reformers. Inside the heavy baroque frame of the current building (1900–7), you can watch justice being meted out from the public galleries, but you'll have to line up early when a major criminal case is being heard, as the crowds of the Newgate gallows have their modern counterparts.

Osterley Park

Isleworth, Middlesex. ☎ 0181/560-3918. Open Apr–Oct, Wed–Sat 1–5pm; Sun, bank holidays 11am–5pm (closed Good Friday). Admission charged. Tube: Osterley.

Even before Osterley was completely refurbished (1761–82) by the great Scottish architect Robert Adam, it was already one of the finest country houses in the area. It's set in a large area of parkland, with lakes, woods, and an attractive brick stable block to one side, and still contains much of the furniture Adam designed for it.

At the end of the courtyard, the main door leads into the hall, the centerpiece to the whole design, beautifully done in Adam's classical style, with white stucco reliefs on a gray background. Beyond the hall is the great gallery, a plainer room probably designed earlier by Sir William Chambers. The remaining rooms open to the public are by Adam, who even designed the door handles and friezes. The Drawing Room has a ceiling of extraordinary richness and contains fine original commodes. The Tapestry Room is hung with works from the French royal Gobelins workshop. The State Bedchamber has an absurdly elaborate 4-poster bed. Plainer, but just as effective with its delicately painted walls, is the Etruscan Dressing Room.

★ Palace of Westminster (Houses of Parliament)

Parliament Sq., SW1. House of Commons: ☎ 0171/219-4272; House of Lords: ☎ 0171/219-3107. To listen to debates, U.K. residents should apply to an MP or Peer, U.K. visitors to their Embassy or High Commission, both well in advance; or come at off-peak times (a wait of least 1 hour is common). Tours are conducted when the House is not sitting (usually Fri after 3:30pm) and during summer recesses. For a tour, U.K. residents should apply to an MP or Peer, U.K. visitors in writing to the Commons Public Information Office (House of Commons, 1 Derby Gate, London SW1A 2DG), both well in advance. During parliamentary sittings, admittance to public galleries is from St. Stephen's entrance. Free admission. Tube: Westminster.

This riverside complex of buildings, known as the Houses of Parliament, is the "new" home of the mother of parliaments. It's a high Victorian exercise in medievalism, and the effect is stunning: Sheer size combines with inventive detail to create an architectural triumph so instantly recognizable that it has come to symbolize the very system of government, representative democracy, housed within.

A royal palace was established on this site around 1000. Medieval kings would call their councils of noblemen to meet at Westminster, a forerunner of the House of Lords. In 1265, additional councils of knights and burghers was called to represent the shires and towns, which became the House of Commons. However unpalatable it was to medieval monarchs, they couldn't govern the country without the consent of lords and commons; in theory, they advised him, but in practice, he needed their assistance in raising taxes.

When Henry VIII moved his residence to the nearby Whitehall Palace, the Palace of Westminster became the permanent and exclusive base of Parliament. The 17thC saw the long struggle that would eventually lead to its constitutional preeminence. Charles I attempted to assert the royal power and crush the Commons, losing both crown and head in the process. Since his last desperate entry in 1642 to arrest parliamentary opponents, no monarch has entered the Commons. When Charles II was recalled to the throne, the struggle between

King and Parliament was renewed. In the 18thC, the monarchy lost ground steadily and parliamentary government became a reality, with a prime minister appointed by the monarch according to the electoral wishes of the country.

In constitutional terms, Parliament consists of Monarch, Lords, and Commons, all of whom have to assent to the laws by which the country is governed. But members of the Commons have acquired the dominant role: The Lords can now only delay legislation by 1 year, and royal assent is never refused; but the Lords is still the highest Court of Appeal in the land. A much criticized anachronism is that the Lords is still largely composed of hereditary peers, although increasingly they're now created for life only. The British system has developed slowly, through reforms and bitter struggles, and uniquely combines traditional ritual with democratic practice: In the Commons, for example, the hatless must take opera hats provided for them.

Tightened security limits public access to the interior of the palace. The medieval royal palace was largely destroyed by fire in 1834. In 1840, rebuilding began, with only the old cloister, Westminster Hall, and the crypt of St. Stephen's Chapel being preserved. The architect, Sir Charles Barry, was a classicist forced to work in the Gothic idiom; his assistant A.W.N. Pugin, on the other hand, was a passionate medievalist. The House of Lords was complete by 1847, the Commons by 1850; the overall work wasn't completed until 1860.

You can tell that Parliament is in session when you see the groups of reporters with their cameras hanging out on the small triangle of green in front; this is where MPs will comment to the press on current debates.

The Exterior   The most splendid views of the palace are from Westminster Bridge or across the river, taking in Barry's great regular facade, with huge, square **Victoria Tower** to the south and the more slender and original **Clock Tower** to the north. This tower is known as **Big Ben,** but that name actually applies to the huge bell inside the clock, Britain's most authoritative timepiece.

Of the few remaining medieval elements of the palace, **Westminster Hall** is outstanding. The lower walls date from the 11thC. In 1394–9, Richard II replaced the upper walls and roof with the remarkable structure that you see today. It's one of the world's greatest timber constructions and the very height of English Gothic. The other medieval survivor is the 1365 **Jewel Tower** (☎ 0171/222-2219; open daily Apr–Sept 10am–1pm, 2–6pm; Oct–Mar 10am–1pm, 2–4pm; admission charged) across Abingdon Street. It now houses an exhibition on the history of Parliament, with a video about Parliament today, useful if you're unable to go inside the Palace of Westminster itself.

The Interior   There are 2 public entrances to the Victorian parts of the palace. Britons wishing to "lobby" their MPs (a practice whereby constituents can ask their representative to come to the lobby to discuss a particular issue) head for **St. Stephen's Porch** beside the hall, which will take you above the medieval crypt (now the Parliament chapel) and to the great lobby. It also leads to the public galleries of the 2 debating chambers. Tours of the palace are sometimes given; for those, enter by the **Norman Porch** next to the Victoria Tower. The gate beneath the tower is used by the Queen only, for official ceremonies. The porch leads through to the **Robing Room,** a spectacular paneled chamber that amply demonstrates Pugin's effective use of Gothic and Tudor motifs. The **Royal Gallery,** with statues of the monarchs, is even more spectacular.

Through the **Prince's Chamber** is the **House of Lords,** a stunning chamber surrounded by sumptuous red leather benches. It feels like a monumental club lounge, an analogy not inappropriate for the more detached deliberations of the upper house. The Lord Chancellor, who chairs the debates, sits on a red-covered woolsack; behind him is the royal throne (the State Opening takes place in this chamber) beneath Pugin's masterpiece, an extraordinary gilded canopy.

Beyond the **Peers' Lobby, Central Lobby,** and **Commons' Lobby** is the **House of Commons.** It was burned during an air raid in 1941 and the entrance arch has been rebuilt, using some of the damaged stones, between statues of Winston Churchill and Lloyd George. The chamber itself was built in 1945–50 in plainer style. The governing party occupies the benches on one side, the opposition the other. Neither side is supposed to cross the red lines in the carpet, traditionally the length of 2 drawn swords.

The rest of the Houses of Parliament, consisting of more than 1,000 rooms and 2 miles of corridors, isn't open to the public. It's a place of work—committees struggling over the details of legislation and MPs handling constituency business.

Pall Mall

Tube: Charing Cross; Green Park.

When St. James's Palace became the main royal residence in the 17thC, this avenue quickly became the primary route into London, as well as the playing field for the favorite Stuart game of *palle-maille,* which resembles modern croquet. The street, now the most important in St. James's, is famous for the traditional gentlemen's clubs that line its south side, a sequence of stern classical buildings reflecting the importance of tradition in this most conservative of areas.

From the Trafalgar Square end, beyond the soaring glass slab of **New Zealand House** (1957–63), Pall Mall becomes interesting. Just past New Zealand House is the delightful little **Opera House Arcade,** the first in London, built by John Nash in 1816–8; the wrought-iron lamps are splendid. At Waterloo Place, you'll see the **Duke of York's Column** (1831–4), in front of the steps of **Carlton House Terrace.**

Back on Pall Mall, the gentlemen's clubs begin, running from Waterloo Place to the lower brick buildings of **St. James's Palace,** past **Marlborough House.** Designed to provide the English gentleman with a "country house" haven to which he can retire in the city, this uniquely English and very exclusive institution thrives virtually unchanged, still offering various mixes of schmoozing, business, witty conversation, and hallowed peace.

For more on this upright area, see "St. James's Hidden Passageways and Gentlemen's Clubs" in "City Walks," below.

The Percival David Foundation of Chinese Art

53 Gordon Sq., WC1. ☎ 0171/387-3909. Open Mon–Fri 10:30am–5pm. Free admission. Tube: Euston, Russell Sq.

This remarkably rich collection of 10th–19thC Chinese ceramics was gathered with scholarly precision by Sir Percival David, who gave it to the University in 1951. Unfortunately, the presentation of the collection is rather too scholarly—the vast numbers of bowls, jars, vases, and figurines, grouped in display cabinets by classification, tend to cancel each other out by their profusion. But the pieces themselves are very beautiful, glazed in rich and subtle colors.

Piccadilly Circus

W1. Tube: Piccadilly Circus, Green Park.

The famous "hub of Empire" put on a pretty poor show
a few years back, with a motley collection of buildings
covered in illuminated signs. But some recent developments have breathed new life into the circus. Teenagers
might enjoy the tourist trap that is the **Trocadero,** with
its blaring music, high-tech simulators, and high street
chain stores; the **Guinness World of Records**
(☎ 0171/439-7331; open daily 10am–10pm) is also
here. The recently reopened **Criterion Brasserie**
(see "Dining") and the **London Pavilion,** a shopping
and restaurant complex that includes the **Rock Circus,** have also helped bring Piccadilly back to life.

The focus of Piccadilly Circus is the **Shaftesbury
Monument** (1893), a statue and fountain of Eros
around which young people like to get together to tem-
porarily drop out. Everyone thinks that the statue is a
monument to Love; in fact, it's a memorial to the great
19thC philanthropist Lord Shaftesbury.

Piccadilly itself, stretching west to Hyde Park Corner, is lined with imposing commercial buildings and
famous shops: **Hatchard's** for books, **Fortnum and
Mason** for anything expensive, and arcades of smart
little shops, with the **Piccadilly Arcade** (1909–10)
to the south and the attractive ***Burlington Arcade**
(1815–9) to the north. Wren's **St. James's,** the **Ritz**
(see "Accommodations"), and hilly **Green Park** are
on the south side, **Burlington House** on the north.
Near Hyde Park Corner is **Apsley House** and
London's smallest police station: One officer is housed
in the **Constitution Arch** in the center of the traffic
circle.

Planetarium

Marylebone Rd., NW1. ☎ 0171/486-1121. Star shows every 40
minutes 9:40am–4:40pm weekdays, 9:40am–5:40pm weekends.
Admission charged. Tube: Baker St.

Attached to Madame Tussaud's, the Planetarium's green
copper dome is a striking landmark. Within you'll find
astronomical displays and star shows; the highlight is
the moment you tip your head back to gaze at the heav-
ens projected on the dome above by the most advanced
star projector in the world. There are 3 levels of interactive exhibits to keep the crowds happy while they
wait for the next show to start, including an interactive
display that gives you the chance to see what shape or

weight you'd be on other planets. You'll even hear Stephen Hawking talk about black holes. But it's the star show called "Cosmic Perceptions," with an awesome soundtrack, that everybody really comes for.

Public Record Office Museum
Chancery Lane, WC2. ☎ 0181/876-3444. Open Mon–Fri 9:30am–5pm. Free admission. Tube: Chancery Lane, Temple.

Most of the public records are now kept at Kew, but 1 room and a hallway in this successful example of Victorian Gothic official architecture now houses a museum that boasts some real treasures, including 2 volumes of the Domesday Book, the great survey of England carried out for William the Conqueror in 1086. Among later documents are a pipe roll of 1210–1 showing the accounts of the Sheriff of Nottingham, and patents assigned to William Penn.

The Public Record Office also maintains a complete set of microfilms of census records from 1841–81 here. If you're trying to trace your roots back to England, this is a good place to begin a genealogical search. Another office that can help you to trace your English or Welsh heritage is the **Registry of Births, Deaths, and Marriages** (St. Catherine's House, 10 Kingsway, WC2; ☎ 0171/242-0262; Tube: Temple).

★★ Regent's Park
NW1 Tube: Regent's Park, Baker St.

Regency London was certainly sophisticated; its legacy is one of England's most impressive examples of town planning. In 1809, John Nash was put in charge of an ambitious scheme that would link this former royal hunting field with Carlton House to the south via the new Regent Street. Carlton House is now gone, but the park retains much of the original plan.

It's best approached from **Portland Place,** leading into the elegant terraces of **Park Crescent** and **Park Square.** Magnificent classical terraces, mostly built in the 1820s, stretch around the flanks of the park: To the west is amazing **York Terrace** and the imaginative, almost Asian-looking **Sussex Place.** On the east are **Chester Terrace** and **Cumberland Terrace,** with vast decorated porticos making them ostentatiously grand.

The park itself is attractively landscaped, with the massive straight **Broad Walk** continuing the line of Portland Place through the center. Two circular roads (the **Inner** and **Outer Circles**) carry road traffic; on the Inner Circle, **St. John's Lodge** incorporates parts of a villa of about 1818. Here, too, is the marvelous open-air theater where you can see superb Shakespearean productions in summer (see "The Arts"). There's a small lake in **Queen Mary's Gardens** within the Inner Circle, and a larger one with islands to the west. Across the north side is a branch of the **Grand Union Canal,** and the **Zoo.**

Rock Circus

London Pavilion, Piccadilly Circus, W1. ☎ 0171/734-7203. Open Sun, Mon, Wed, Thurs 10am–9pm; Tues 11am–9pm; Fri, Sat 10am–10pm. Admission charged. Tube: Piccadilly.

Don a headset and prepare yourself for an onslaught of nostalgia at this outpost of Madame Tussaud's. Rock Circus presents the history of rock and pop music from Bill Haley to Michael Jackson through wax and "audio animatronic" figures, which move and perform golden oldies and more recent chart-toppers in an eerily lifelike way. The giants are all featured here, from Elvis and the Beatles to Springsteen and Madonna—and many, many more.

★ Royal Academy of Arts

Burlington House, Piccadilly, W1. ☎ 0171/439-7438. Open daily 10am–6pm, last admission 5:30pm. Admission charged. Tube: Piccadilly Circus, Green Park.

Built for the 1st Earl of Burlington in the newly developed Piccadilly area in about 1665, Burlington House was remodeled in 1717–20 in the elegant Palladian style. The 3rd earl made this a celebrated forum for the artists he patronized: Pope, Arbuthnot, Gay—all were often on hand. Unfortunately, the Georgian profile was obliterated by the rebuilding that marked its adoption by the Royal Academy of Arts; this new building is in the Victorian Renaissance style, with a statue of Sir Joshua Reynolds in the forecourt.

The Royal Academy was founded in 1768, with Reynolds as its 1st—and greatest—president, to foster the arts in Britain. After its first few decades, however, the most interesting developments in British art have consistently taken place outside of, and even in opposition to, the Royal Academy's dictates. Even now, the Academy's free-for-all Summer Exhibition (see p. 264) may be popular and enjoyable, but no one would claim that it does much to further British art.

The modern academy consists of 70 academicians, the country's most successful establishment artists. It hosts major loan exhibitions that are always worth watching out for. The academy also has an important collection, with many works by academicians who have always been obliged to donate to the academy. Paintings by the likes of Benjamin West, Angelica Kauffmann, and Marco Ricci are regularly on display in the grand interior. The outstanding treasure is Michelangelo's beautiful relief tondo, *Madonna and Child*.

★★ Royal Botanic Gardens (Kew Gardens)

Kew, Surrey. ☎ 0181/940-1171. Main entrance at Kew Green; entrance from tube station at Victoria Gate on Kew Road; entrance from riverside towpath at Brentford Gate. Gardens open daily from 9:30am. Closing times vary from 4pm to 6pm on weekdays and from 4pm to 7pm on weekends and public holidays, depending on the time of sunset. Last admission half an hour before closing. Greenhouses and galleries close earlier. Admission charged. Introductory tours of the Gardens are available on most days from the Victoria Gate Visitor Centre. Tube: Kew Gardens. Train to Kew Bridge from Waterloo. Exit through Victoria Gate for tube; through Victoria Gate, Main Gate, or Brentford Gate for British Rail; through Brentford Gate or Main Gate for Kew Pier; through Brentford Gate for car park. 1-mile walk from Main Gate to Pagoda.

The full name of Kew Gardens, the Royal Botanic Gardens, comes as a salutary reminder to those of us who, in the face of such supreme natural beauty, are likely to forget that this is a scientific institution—one unequaled in the studying, classifying, and cultivating of plants from around the world. For those of us less scientifically inclined, however, Kew boasts superb walks and dreamlike views. In springtime, it is sublime. In summer, it's delightful to approach the gardens via the river, on a boat from Westminster Pier.

The gardens were formed from the grounds of 2 royal residences by George III in 1759. From 1771 to 1820, Sir Joseph Banks, who had accompanied Captain Cook to the South Seas, extended the existing botanic garden by sending young botanists all over the world in search of specimens. In 1840, the gardens were handed over to the State; land grants by the Crown took the total to more than 300 acres. In 1990 a major exhibition area, using an innovative design incorporating energy-saving features, opened in the **Sir Joseph Banks Building,** and expansion continues.

Begin at the main gates by **Kew Green,** and take a sharp left to the vast **Princess of Wales Conservatory,** home to 10 different habitats, from Namib Desert and mangrove swamp to cloud forest and tropical pools. Or proceed up the **Broad Walk,** which turns left at the refurbished 18thC **Orangery** (containing a restaurant, cafeteria, and shop) and leads to the **pond** and **Palm House,** returning by smaller paths through flower-filled woodland and other gardens. Not far from the main gates is the gabled red-brick **Dutch House,** or Kew Palace. To the rear is the **Queen's Garden,** a 17thC-style garden, with tightly-clipped hedges and aromatic herbs.

Now bear right, away from the Broad Walk. The long **Riverside Avenue** passes through cedar, plane, and oak-planted woods. A detour left takes you through the **rhododendron dell** (it's almost a crime to miss it in late spring) and the **bamboo and azalea gardens,** with the beautiful lake to the south. Walk around the riverside for a fine view across the Thames to **Syon House.**

Farther southwest is **Queen Charlotte's Cottage,** thatched in rustic style and built in the 1770s as a focal point for elaborate garden parties. It's now sur-rounded by an area left wild for native British plants and wildlife. To the east is the **Evolution House,** which takes you through 3,500 million years of plant-life development, and the **Japanese Gateway,** sur-rounded by pines and flowering azaleas. Farther east is the 163-foot **Pagoda,** built in a more fanciful 18thC Asian style.

Pagoda Vista takes you back toward the entrance. On the way, take in the **Temperate House,** a large 19thC complex of greenhouses with many fine speci-mens, and the **Marianne North Gallery** to the east, home of an extraordinary collection of botanical paintings. A little farther north, mock temples and ru-ins survive from the 18thC garden. The **Palm House,** a magnificent and graceful iron-and-glass construction of 1844–8 then comes into view; it holds a fabulous collection of tropical rain forest plants and a fascinating display of seaweeds from around the world. The recently refurbished **Waterlily House** is to the left as you leave Palm House.

A series of open-air jazz concerts are hosted here in the summer. Bring a picnic and park yourself under the blue sky.

Royal Courts of Justice
Strand, WC2. ☎ 0171/936-6000. Open Mon–Fri 10am–2:30pm. Free admission. Tube: Temple, Chancery Lane.

Better known as the Law Courts, this extravagant com-plex houses the courts where important civil (not criminal) cases are heard. Long despised as an example of Victorian plagiarism, the Early English Gothic build-ings (1874–82) are now largely admired. The buildings have a dignity that's suited to their purpose, and their complex irregularity and inventive detail are a feast for the eye. Within, the sheer scale of the great hall is equally impressive.

Royal Hospital, Chelsea

Royal Hospital Rd., SW3 4SR. ☎ 0171/730-0161. Mon–Sat 10am–12pm and 2–4pm; Sun 2–4pm. Chapel and dining hall open Mon–Sat 10am–12pm, 2–4pm; Sun 2–4pm. Free admission. Tube: Sloane Sq.

Amply surrounded by parkland and retaining all the dignity of its riverside setting, Wren's stately Royal Hospital (1682–92) is a majestic sanctuary of calm in the swirl that is Chelsea. It was founded by Charles II in 1682 as a refuge for aged and disabled soldiers, on the model of Louis XIV's Les Invalides in Paris. It now houses some 400 pensioners.

The best view is from the south, where an open courtyard, with Wren's master carver Grinling Gibbons's statue of Charles II as a Roman emperor, looks down the extensive gardens toward the river. Enter the domed vestibule, lit by the lantern above, through the courtyard portico. To the right is the **chapel,** little altered since Wren's time. The **Great Hall** is on the other side of the vestibule. It's more solemn, with paneled walls and military standards. A small museum in an eastern wing covers the hospital's history.

The **Royal Hospital Burial Ground,** sandwiched between Royal Hospital and Chelsea Bridge roads, is an undiscovered treasure; for admission, ask at London Gate. Among those buried here are William Hiseland, who lived to the ripe old age of 112, and 2 women who fought in the Crimean War and whose gender was only discovered when they were wounded.

For a guided tour led by one of the charming and knowledgeable pensioners, write to the Adjutant at the address above. In May, the hospital hosts the Chelsea Flower Show (see p. 263).

★ Royal Institute of British Architects

66 Portland Place, W1. ☎ 0171/580-5533. Open Mon, Wed, Fri 10am–6pm; Tues, Thurs 8am–9pm; Sat 9am–5pm. Free admission; charges for tours and lectures. Tube: Regents Park, Great Portland St.

This monumental edifice, commissioned by architects for architects, is a classic example of an early 1930s building. It was, at the time, the perfect compromise between classicism and the prevailing art deco–style modernism. Inside you'll find a fabulous architecture bookstore, gallery spaces, and a wonderful cafe that opens onto a terrace. RIBA also organizes monthly lectures and events, occurring on the 3rd Thursday of each month. Subjects include issues of general interest and the work of Britain's most eminent architects. Saturday is neighborhood-tour day; call for details.

Royal National Theatre
Upper Ground, South Bank SE1. General inquiries: ☎ 0171/633-0880; box office: ☎ 0171/928-2252. Backstage tours up to 5 times a day. Admission charged. Tube: Waterloo.

It's a blessing that the institutionalization of London theater hasn't led to any stultifying subservience. The drama remains as true to its subversive nature as when it was banished to the South Bank in the Middle Ages. This component of the South Bank Arts Center created its own furor. The building itself (1970–5), a lumpy abstract sculpture in concrete designed by Sir Denys Lasdun, is a prime example of the Brutal style. The interior, a superb intersection of horizontal and vertical planes creating a honeycomb of useful and interesting spaces, is much more universally admired.

★ Royal Observatory
Flamsteed House, Greenwich. ☎ 0181/858-4422. Open Mon–Sat 10am–5pm; Sun 12–5pm. Admission charged. British Rail from Charing Cross to Maze Hill.

The Royal Observatory was established in 1675–6, when Wren was commissioned by Charles II to build a house for the 1st Astronomer Royal, John Flamsteed. Flamsteed House commands extensive views down over Greenwich and the river. On top of one of the towers is a large red ball erected in 1833; each day the ball falls at exactly 1pm to enable ships in the river to set their clocks accurately. At the rear of the house is a huge bulbous dome of 1894, which houses a 28-inch refracting telescope, one of the largest in the world. The astronomers have moved to more modern equipment, so Flamsteed House is now a museum, with exhibits that include clocks and telescopes used by Halley, Herschel, and other royal astronomers.

Next door is the mid-18thC **Meridian Building,** housing a display about time. This is the site of the meridian on which all the world's clock time is based via Greenwich Mean Time; you can stand with a foot in each hemisphere here.

★ Saatchi Gallery
98a Boundary Rd., NW8. ☎ 0171/624-8299. Open Thurs–Sun 12pm–6pm. Admission charged (free on Thurs). Tube: St. John's Wood.

Sibling admen Charles and Maurice Saatchi created the most powerful and influential advertising agency of the

1980s. Not surprisingly, Charles is a master of self-promotion, and he ranks as London's most influential—and controversial—name in contemporary art. In the 1980s, his collection focused on the international big names, but Charles has since abruptly changed course, selling off millions of dollars of work and devoting himself to the acquisition of new British talent. He has been known to buy out entire exhibitions if the work strikes his fancy; he has the ability to make or break the career of an aspiring artist. The gallery, a stunning 27,000-foot warehouse space in North London, regularly stages exhibitions of Saatchi's newest acquisitions. A must for any follower of the contemporary art scene.

St. Bartholomew-the-Great

Little Britain, EC1. Free admission. Tube: Barbican.

The churchyard here, through the 15thC gateway with a charming Tudor house on top, used to be the nave of one of the oldest churches in London, founded in 1123. Now only the chancel and transepts, with their 19thC refacing of flint and Portland stone, remain.

Inside, many original features survive. Huge columns in the nave support a Romanesque triforium, surmounted by a clerestory built in 1405 in Perpendicular Gothic style. Beyond the altar is the much rebuilt **Lady Chapel** (1335), where Ben Franklin worked in 1725. At the west entrance, you can see the massive crossing that once supported a huge stone tower. The present **brick tower** (1628) is above the south isle; 5 medieval bells are housed there, making it one of the oldest peals in the country. There's also a number of fine monuments. As a result of condensation, the **monument to Edward Cooke** (d. 1652) actually weeps in damp weather—a phenomenon referred to in the inscription.

St. George's, Bloomsbury

Bloomsbury Way, WC1. Free admission. Tube: Holborn.

This splendid church compares well with the near contemporary but much more famous St. Martin-in-the-Fields. Built by Nicholas Hawksmoor in 1720–31, with its huge portico of Corinthian columns and layer-cake spire topped with a statue of George I as St. George (a typical piece of baroque overstatement), this is in some ways an even more dramatic design than Gibbs's St. Martin's. With simple shapes, plenty of light, and more giant columns, the interior continues the boldness of the exterior.

St. James's Palace

St. James's Palace

Pall Mall, SW1. Not open to the public. Tube: Green Park.

This royal palace, unique in surviving the Great
Fire and plague of 1665–6 intact, offers a rare glimpse
of Tudor London. There it sits, sandwiched between
its larger offspring of St. James's Park and The
Mall, yet, for all their grandeur and boldness, dwarfing
them by its very antiquity and history. The official
royal residence from 1698 until Buckingham Palace
took over in 1837, its seniority is still recognized; the
Queen's court is "the Court of St. James" and new
monarchs are still proclaimed from here. Today, it
provides "Grace and Favour" quarters for yeomen-
at-arms, lords and ladies-in-waiting, and the Lord
Chamberlain.

Henry VIII built this palace entirely in brick with
battlements and diapering (diagonal patterning in the
brickwork). Even the 17thC State Rooms added by
Wren maintain his low, informal approach, echoing the
domesticity of Tudor architecture.

The **Queen's Chapel** (1623–7), across Marlborough Road but originally within the palace, is in an
entirely different style. It was designed by Inigo Jones
in the classical manner, with rendered white walls and
Portland stone dressings. The beautiful interior boasts
ornate baroque work from the 1660s, including fine
carving by Gibbons. To the west, attached to the

palace, is Nash's **Clarence House** (1825–7), now the Queen Mother's home; a piper plays the bagpipes in the garden at 9am when she's in residence. The palace is flanked by 2 grand mansions from later periods: **Marlborough House** to the east and **Lancaster House** to the west, with **St. James's Park** to the south.

★ St. James's Park

SW1. Tube: St. James's Park.

London's first royal park was always more art than nature. In 1536, Henry VIII drained a marsh to make a park between St. James's and Whitehall palaces filled with deer (for ornament, not hunting). In 1662, Charles II made it a public garden, laid out in the formal style of the period with avenues of trees, **The Mall** as a carriageway, and a long straight canal. In 1828, it was remodeled on the present pattern by John Nash, who created the lovely complex of trees, flowerbeds, and views across the natural-looking lake that we see today. The waterfowl, some of which breed on Duck Island at the east end, have always continued the contrivance—there are even pelicans. The view from the bridge across the lake back toward Whitehall is one of the most beautiful in London.

St. James's, Piccadilly

197 Piccadilly, W1. General inquiries: ☎ 0171/734-4511; box office: ☎ 0171/437-5053. Crafts market and antiques Thurs–Sat 10am–6pm. Free admission; tickets required for evening concerts. Tube: Piccadilly Circus, Green Park.

When St. James's was developed as a residential area after 1662, Sir Christopher Wren was commissioned to build its new church, completing it in 1674. It's basically 1 great room with plain galleries and a vaulted ceiling with plaster moldings. Damaged by bombs in 1940, the church has been well restored. The 17thC organ is topped by gilded figures carved by Grinling Gibbons, who also produced the marvelous marble font and the rich floral arrangements carved on the wooden reredos. Wonderful free lunchtime concerts are staged here at 1:10pm weekdays.

★★ St. Martin-in-the-Fields

Trafalgar Sq., WC2. ☎ 0171/930-1862; concert information: ☎ 0171/260-1456. Free admission. Tube: Charing Cross.

The first buildings in a new architectural style often seem like oddities; this church has maintained its nonconformity. Today it's a venue for concerts and a shelter for vagrants and drug addicts as well as a church.

The broad views allowed by Trafalgar Square's open spaces make it possible to enjoy this magnificent church's proportions, and it's now recognized for the seminal building it was. Designed in 1722–26 by James Gibbs (the foundation goes back to 1222) in a solemnly classical style, it is very close to a Roman temple, except for the novel placing of a tower and spire above the Corinthian portico. The interior is similar to Wren's churches of a few decades earlier: spacious and light, with galleries to the sides and a splendidly molded ceiling. The crypt contains several interesting relics, including an 18thC whipping post.

Concerts are held every weekday at 1:05pm—a perfect break from the hectic bustle of Trafalgar Square. The church also houses the **London Brass Rubbing Centre** (☎ 0171/930-9306; open Mon–Sat 10am–6pm, Sun noon–6pm), where you can make rubbings from replicas of medieval monumental brasses. The staff on hand will gladly teach you the technique. The clothing, jewelry, and souvenir market is open daily, as is the excellent **Cafe in the Crypt** for self-service meals under the arches.

St. Mary Abchurch

Abchurch Lane, EC4. Free admission. Tube: Cannon St.

After its small cobbled churchyard, simple brick exterior, and lead spire, you'll be surprised by the glories of St. Mary Abchurch's interior. Built by Wren in 1681–6, it consists of little more than 1 huge dome atop a square room, with details kept to a minimum. Although damaged in World War II, the church has been expertly restored. Note the richly carved pulpit, the paneling, some original pews, and William Snow's dome, painted in the baroque style (1708–14).

St. Mary-le-Bow

Bow Lane, Cheapside, EC2. Free admission. Tube: Bank, St. Paul's.

When Wren rebuilt London's churches after the Great Fire of 1666, he put particular emphasis on their steeples; this is his most magnificent. This great tower is still prominent among the larger modern buildings around it. The church was built in 1670–80, with the tower separated from the body of the church by a vestibule. The large, simple interior was restored after gutting during the war. The crypt retains elements from the original Norman church. The crypt's small restaurant, **The Place Below** (☎ 0171/329-0789), is a good spot for vegetarians.

St. Mary's bells are of sentimental importance to Londoners: Being born within range of their sound is the traditional qualification for being a Cockney. The bells were destroyed in the Great Fire of 1666 and again in the Blitz; the current ones include remnants that were salvaged in 1941.

★ St. Mary-le-Strand

Strand, WC2. Free admission. Tube: Temple.

It's hard to imagine a more ironic fate for a jewel of the baroque: This island in the middle of the Strand is so small that continuous traffic passes within inches of its walls (which over the years have needed drastic renovation). James Gibbs, fresh from the joys of Rome, built this church in 1714–8. The facade is a particular delight: Your eyes sweep from the portico, with its ornate capitals, up to the triangular pediment and the bold layered spire. The interior has a richly coffered ceiling with 2 tiers of columns and a pediment dramatically framing the apse. Notice the fine carving of the pulpit, originally on a taller base with a scallop-shell sounding-board behind—all part of the grand theatrical effect.

St. Pancras Station

Euston Rd. NW1. Free admission. Tube: King's Cross, St. Pancras.

That the Victorians would build a railway station as a Gothic fortress says a lot about their confidence level. St. Pancras was the glory of Victorian London. Built in 1868–74, Sir George Gilbert Scott freely used northern Italian and French Gothic styles in its design. It was also a tremendous feat of engineering, with the great train-shed covered by a single span of iron and glass.

The station's former goods yard is the site of the controversial new **British Library** building, opening in 2 phases by the year 2000. London's deepest basement has been carved out of the ground to house the Library's collection of every book published in Britain, moving here from the British Museum.

★ St. Paul's, Covent Garden

The Piazza, WC2. Free admission. Tube: Covent Garden.

Money was tight as the Duke of Bedford neared completion of his Covent Garden development, so he instructed Inigo Jones to build an economical church, suggesting as a model something like a barn. Jones declared that he would build "the handsomest barn in Europe." Today, London's first entirely classical parish church, completed in 1638, stands as the sole surviving element of the piazza. In fact, it cost a small fortune, but the barn analogy isn't entirely inappropriate. Now it's the "actors' church," so every grand theaterland funeral adds another monument to the collection here.

★★ St. Paul's Cathedral

EC4. ☎ 0171/248-2705. Open Mon–Sat 8:30am–4pm, galleries from 10am, crypt from 8:45am. Admission charged except Sun and for worshippers. Entrance and movement restricted during services. Tube: St. Paul's.

There are very few great churches in the world that strike all visitors, whatever their religious convictions, as a sublime testament to man's ability to reach toward the infinite. St. Paul's was built as both a religious and secular statement of London's faith and self-confidence after the devastating Great Fire of 1666. Nearly 300 years later, it stood alone amid the rubble of the surrounding buildings in the Blitz, preserved miraculously to breathe fresh hope into the beleaguered Londoners.

And no building so clearly demonstrates Sir Christopher Wren's prodigious skill and energetic inventiveness. In this, his greatest work, detail is used with characteristic baroque exuberance, but it's always subordinated to the highly controlled overall scheme. Even today, the great dome still dominates the encroaching modern buildings.

Wren started fresh when the Great Fire reduced the original church to ruins. He began with daringly modern designs, but the ecclesiastical authorities forced him to return to the basic Gothic cathedral plan, forming a Latin cross. But the crossing was to be covered by a dome rather than a tower or spire—the first of its kind in England—following the example of Italy's great Renaissance churches. Wren also won the right to control the cathedral's ornamentation, which, in effect, gave him the freedom to design the building's appearance as he went along.

Although the surrounding area has been spoiled by modern developments, plans are now afoot to redevelop the Paternoster Square area more sympathetically. But original elements remain. In front of the portico stands a **statue of Queen Anne,** made in 1866 to replace the original of 1709–11 (did the original look just like Queen Victoria, too?). In the churchyard gardens to the northeast is **St. Paul's Cross** (1910). Two of Wren's old cathedral buildings survive: to the south is the little **Deanery** (1670), to the north the larger red-brick **Chapter House** (1712–4). To the east, still inside the road, is the tower and elongated onion spire of Wren's ruined Church of **St. Augustine,** now attached to the celebrated St. Paul's Choir School.

The interior gives an impression of the great bulk of the structure, but it's offset by the nave's height and the vast open space beneath the dome. The emphasis is on the sweeping drama of the baroque. There seems to be a calculated attempt to create vistas with a sense of distance, focusing on the open space but leading ultimately toward the long chancel beyond the crossing. Light streams in from the nave's clerestory windows, which are invisible from the outside because of the false upper story of the external wall.

Walk to the left from the main west entrance. The small **All Soul's Chapel** contains a cluster of memorials to national heroes introduced since about 1790. Then comes **St. Dunstan's Chapel.** Outstanding monuments memorialize Victorian painter Lord Leighton and General Gordon of the Sudan. The Duke of Wellington monument, erected in the mid-19thC, is the most elaborate.

This is a good spot from which to examine the crossing, the focal point of the entire design. It's a huge space; the dome's circle is supported on 8 massive arches. The breathtaking dome itself actually consists of 3 layers: an outer skin, a cone supporting the masonry of the lantern, and a shallow domed ceiling painted with illusionistic architectural frescoes depicting scenes from the life of St. Paul (1716–9), by Sir James Thornhill. Monuments here include those to Dr. Johnson (in an unlikely toga) and Sir Joshua Reynolds, 1st president of the Royal Academy.

The chancel, stretching off toward the high altar, makes a sumptuous display, although it's not at all as Wren left it: The gaudy, fussy ceiling mosaics date from the 1890s and are really not in keeping. The modern baldachino, attempting to follow Wren's original scheme for a high altar canopy as a focal point, is in an unhappy marriage with the ceiling decorations. However, the choir stalls and organ case are magnificent, with exquisite carving by Grinling Gibbons. Behind the altar is the **Jesus Chapel,** now a memorial to Americans who perished in World War II.

Returning along the south chancel aisle, John Donne's monument shows the poet, who was Dean of St. Paul's (1620–31), wrapped in his shroud; it's the only monument to survive from the medieval cathedral. In the south aisle is a striking example of high Victorian religiosity, a late version of Holman Hunt's *Light of the World*.

The Crypt (Entrance from south transept)   The piers and columns support a crypt the size of the whole cathedral, a quiet and dignified place crammed with monuments. A few battered remains survived from before the Great Fire, but the majority are from the 19th and 20th centuries. By far, the most impressive are the tombs of Wellington and Nelson, an elegant black sarcophagus made for Cardinal Wolsey in 1524–9 but denied him after his fall from royal favor. In **Painter's Corner** you'll find the tombs of Turner and Reynolds and monuments to Van Dyck and William Blake. Wren is buried nearby. The **Treasury of the Diocese of London** also has an exhibit here, displaying elaborate vestments, illuminated medieval manuscripts, and some fine plates from 16th–20thC London churches.

Whispering Gallery and Dome (Stairs in south transept)   After the stiff climb to the gallery inside the dome, you're repaid with stupendous views of the concourse below and the painted inner dome. The acoustics that give it its name enable the slightest sounds to be heard across the span; the traditional trick is to whisper against the wall and wait for the sound to travel around to the next auditor. The next section of the ascent is not for the fainthearted: 542 steps wind up throughout the struts supporting the outer dome. The stunning views from the Golden Gallery at the lantern's base make the climb worthwhile.

★ St. Stephen Walbrook
Walbrook, EC4. Free admission. Tube: Bank.

Although a parish church, its position behind the Mansion House also makes it the Lord Mayor's church. It's appropriately grand. Wren built the church in 1672–9; it's thought that he was trying out some ideas for St. Paul's. The contrast with his St. Mary Abchurch is illuminating, for here the dome is not used to create a simple, large space but to contribute to a series of constantly changing views as you move through the columns. The crypt survives from the 15thC.

Science Museum
Exhibition Rd., SW7. ☎ 0171/938-8008. Open daily 10am–6pm. Admission charged. Tube: South Kensington.

This collection was separated from the art treasures now housed in the Victoria and Albert Museum in 1909, and moved to this solemn and functional home in 1913.

The **East Hall** is devoted to the development of industrial power. Vast and now seemingly crude machinery illustrates the development of steam power in the 18thC, as well as its continuing use into the 20thC. The transport exhibit, with an outstanding collection of famous steam locomotives, is a favorite; you'll also find carriages, cars, and fire engines. "Food for Thought" explores how we buy, prepare, and eat food.

On the next level, kids head straight for the **Launch Pad,** a marvelous hands-on exhibit where they can get down to working the machines themselves. Above that, exhibits range in subject from chemistry to nuclear physics to computers, and there are superb models of ships. More theoretical topics are well represented, such as biochemistry: Attractive models comprehensibly explain the structure of molecules. Fascinating exhibits on the top floor cover photography, cinematography, and optics. Here too is the **Aeronautics Gallery,** and a hands-on flight lab where you can test the principles of flight yourself. The excellent **Wellcome Medical Museum** has spirited dioramas that illustrate the history of medicine and its most up-to-date accomplishments.

The Science Museum succeeds in balancing the interests of both children and adults; it's a favorite destination for families, particularly on rainy weekends.

Serpentine Gallery

Kensington Gardens, W2. ☎ 0171/402-6075. Open daily 10am–6pm. Admission free. Tube: South Kensington.

This former tea pavilion in Kensington Gardens now stages an active exhibition schedule of modern and contemporary art. Helen Chadwick's famous chocolate fountain was shown here, as were some of the more controversial of Damian Hirst's pickled sheep works. Princess Di is a highly visible patron, often photographed making stunning entrances in low cut evening gowns. The small bookshop has a remarkable stock of art books.

★ Shakespeare Globe Centre

1 Bear Gardens, Bankside, SE1. ☎ 0171/928-6406. Open Mon–Sun 10am–5pm. Admission charged. Tube: London Bridge.

The original Globe Theatre was constructed on this site at the end of the 16thC. Many of Shakespeare's plays, including *Othello* and *Romeo and Juliet,* were first performed on its famous O-shaped stage. This was the perfect setting for his work; at the time, Southwark was

London's pleasure center, an area of taverns, brothels, and theaters. The Globe burned down in 1613 during a performance of *Henry VIII;* it was immediately reconstructed, but the Puritans closed it down in 1642 and demolished it in 1644.

In 1949, when American actor and director Sam Wanamaker came to London for the first time, he expected to find a Globe Theatre on Bankside. For more than 2 decades, he campaigned ceaselessly to raise funds to rebuild it; at the time of his death in 1993, 12 of the 15 auditorium bays were done. The center is scheduled to be completed by 1999; it will comprise the Globe Theatre, an indoor theater designed by Inigo Jones in 1617, and a museum. The Globe staged its first season of plays in May, under the first thatched roof in London since the Great Fire of 1666.

Sherlock Holmes Museum

221b Baker St., NW1. ☎ 0171/935-8866. Open daily 9:30am–6pm. Admission charged. Tube: Baker St.

Devotees of Sir Arthur Conan Doyle's famous sleuth and his puzzled partner, Dr. Watson, can visit their fictional address, 221b Baker St. In a case of fiction becoming fact, it has been realized in the style of their Victorian apartment, complete with personal letters and trophies from their adventures.

★★ Sir John Soane Museum

13 Lincoln's Inn Fields, WC2. ☎ 0171/405-2107; recorded information ☎ 0171/430-0175. Open Tues–Sat 10am–5pm; 1st Tues of the month 6–9pm. Tours Sat 2:30pm; tickets available at 2pm. Admission free. Tube: Holborn.

This place is a real treat. You'll find no modern ideas of museum display here, as the great architect left his house as a museum upon his death in 1837 on the condition that nothing be changed. Soane's enormous collection of pictures, architectural fragments, books, sculptures, and miscellaneous antiquities is crammed into every available space (a recent visitor was overheard commenting that the great collector was in sore need of a good editor).

Born in 1753, Soane lived at no. 12 Lincoln's Inn Fields from 1792, in a plain Georgian house he designed himself. In 1812–4 he added the much more grand and elaborate no. 13, rebuilding no. 14 to complete a balanced design in 1824. The joined interior is the most ingeniously complex layout, offering numerous vistas, both laterally and vertically, as several of the rooms and yards extend through 2 or more stories. Mirrors create additional illusory space. Most exciting are the paired Dining Room and Library, and the lovely domed Breakfast Room, which was recently restored to its original splendor.

The capricious—even humorous—way in which the multitude of objects on display, from fossils to furniture, is jumbled together is fascinating. Among the collection are several important works of art, as well as Soane's own architectural models. You'll find Hogarth's original paintings—12 in all—for 2 series, *The Rake's Progress* and *The Election,* as well as 3 Canalettos and 3 Turners. The hieroglyphic-covered alabaster sarcophagus of Seti I, a pharaoh who died in 1290 BC, is outstanding; Soane paid the princely sum of £2,000 for it.

South Bank Arts Centre
SE1. Tube: Waterloo.

The plans for a national arts center were formulated in the years after World War II, and crystallized when this derelict South Bank site was developed for the Festival of Britain in 1951.

The **Festival Hall,** one of Britain's most controversial postwar buildings, was completed in 1956. Its impressive glass facade makes full use of its panoramic riverside location. Like later South Bank buildings, however, the exterior is more massive and monumental than appealing. It's the interior that's most successful: a complex arrangement of spaces efficiently and attractively laid out, with public areas offering views across the river, bars, restaurants, and the great concert hall itself, seating almost 3,000 and with near-perfect acoustics. Smaller concerts are held in the adjacent **Queen Elizabeth Hall** and **Purcell Room,** seating 1,100 and 372 respectively.

The **National Film Theatre** (1951), under Waterloo Bridge, always shows an interesting program of historic and contemporary movies in its 2 cinemas. The **Hayward Gallery** (1968), next to the bridge, presents a program of major art exhibitions organized by the Arts Council of Great Britain. Its design, however, has been much criticized, and it has little natural light. The **Royal National Theatre** (see p. 161) continues the Brutalist theme. The newest addition is the **Museum of the Moving Image** (see p. 143) in a striking glass and steel building adjoining the Film Theatre.

Although some elements of the complex are architecturally praiseworthy and its arts output second to none, many Londoners see it as a hostile, unfriendly place isolated from the rest of the capital. It should be captivating; instead, with its windy, threatening walkways and harsh concrete walls, it alienates. But major plans, masterminded by architect Richard Rogers, are underway to improve the site. See also "The Arts."

★ Southwark Cathedral

Montague Close, SE1. Free admission. Tube: London Bridge.

This Gothic church is under siege from the encroaching railway viaducts, covered market, and approaches to London Bridge that crowd against its walls, but it's still one of the most important medieval buildings in London.

The 14th–15thC tower (with 17thC pinnacles) is its best feature. Other interesting features include the 15thC ceiling bosses opposite the present main entrance, graphically carved with heraldic devices or grotesque figures. The rebuilt chancel illustrates the beauty and purity of early Gothic architecture, with its layers of perfectly proportioned arches. Behind the high altar is a superbly rich reredos (1520).

The monuments are really worth a look, although several have been crudely painted in restoration. Look out for John Gower (d. 1408), a medieval poet and friend of Chaucer's; a knight's wooden effigy about 1275; and Richard Humber (d. 1616) with his fashionably dressed wives. Next to the north transept is a chapel devoted to John Harvard, founder of the university, who was baptized here in 1607. In the south aisle is a 1912 memorial to Shakespeare.

A short organ recital is given every Monday at 1:10pm.

★ Spencer House

27 St. James's Place, SW1. ☎ 0171/409-0526; 0171/499-8620 for advance reservations. Tours compulsory, every 15 minutes; minimum 20 visitors. No children under age 10. Open Sun 11:30am–4:45pm. Closed Jan, Aug. Admission charged. Tube: Green Park.

A 5-year restoration has returned Spencer House to its full 18thC splendor. Built for Earl Spencer, ancestor of Princess Di, the magnificent neoclassical interiors were designed by John Vardy and James "Athenian" Stuart. Vardy's Palm Room, with its spectacular screen of gilded palms, is a unique Palladian set piece, while the elegant murals of Stuart's Painted Room reflect the 18thC passion for all things classical. Stuart's original gilded furniture has been returned to the house from the Victoria and Albert Museum, and the Queen has lent 5 paintings by Benjamin West.

Staple Inn

Staple Inn
Holborn, WC1. Tube: Chancery Lane.

Close to the entrance to Gray's Inn is a remarkable survivor of Elizabethan London: a pair of timber houses
dating from 1586, forming the facade to Staple Inn, a
former Inn of Chancery. Together, they look like a
quaint jumble of haphazardly placed beams and gables,
with charming overhanging stories and oriel windows.
You can enter the courtyards of the Inn (now housing
the Society of Actuaries) through the gateway on the
left. Dr. Johnson lived at no. 2 in 1759–60, where he
supposedly wrote *Rasselas* in a week in a bid to pay for
his mother's funeral.

Strand
WC2. Tube: Charing Cross.

"Strand" means river bank; that's exactly what this street
was until the embankment was built in 1864–70 (the
old watergate still stands in Victoria Embankment Gardens). Once the main route from Westminster to the
City, it was lined with great houses; today its a motley
collection of theaters, shops, and hotels.

It begins at Temple Bar, continuing in the direction
of **Fleet Street.** On the north side are the splendid
Victorian Gothic **Royal Courts of Justice,** with an
attractive tangle of buildings opposite. The church of
St. Clement Danes, built by Wren in 1680–2 and
with a stone tower by James Gibbs (1719) occupies an
island in the middle of the road. Bombed in 1941, the
church has been exceptionally restored and is now the

church of the Royal Air Force. Behind is a **monument to Samuel Johnson** (1910), and to the front the more pompous **monument to Gladstone** (1905).

The Aldwych, an ambitious planning scheme begun in 1900, follows on the north side of the street. Its crescent shape is made up of somber buildings in heavy Edwardian style. The exquisite **St. Mary-le-Strand** occupies another island in the middle of the road, with the 1971 concrete facade of **King's College** almost opposite. **Somerset House** (now home to the Courtauld Institute Galleries; see p. 124) is just a little farther along on the south side. Two large hotels are farther west: the art deco–ish **Strand Palace** (ultratraditional **Simpson's** is opposite; see "Dining") and the famous **Savoy** (see "Accommodations"). Several theaters are along the north side, in a section largely given over to bustling shoppers. The west end, opening onto **Trafalgar Square** is marked by **Charing Cross.**

Syon House

Brentford, Middlesex. ☎ 0181/560-0881. Open Apr–Sept Wed, Sat, Sun 11am–5pm; Sept–Mar Sun only; gardens daily 10am–6pm, or until sunset if earlier. Admission charged. Tube: Gunnersbury Park.

Syon House was originally a convent. After the Reformation, it was taken over by the Lord Protector, the Duke of Somerset, who transformed it into a large mansion on the pattern of a hollow square. He went to the scaffold in 1552, as did his successor, John Dudley, and Lady Jane Grey, who set out from here to be Queen in 1553 (she lasted 4 days). The Percy family, Dukes of Northumberland, have held the house since 1594.

In 1762, Robert Adam was brought in to modernize the Tudor house, thus creating the extraordinary contrast between the plain, square exterior and the incomparable interior. The centerpiece of Adam's planning is the Great Hall, a cool, elegant room with restrained classical decoration in stucco, including Doric columns that create a dramatic entrance. Genuine Roman statues and copies of famous antique models complete the scholarly effect.

Adam's intention was to create a sequence of pleasurable contrasts: The next room, the Ante Room, is altogether more lavish and bright. The suite of state rooms continues the contrast; they're all in different, variously elaborate styles. Paintings in the house include works by Van Dyck, Lely, and Gainsborough.

The gardens, remodeled in the late 18thC by the great Capability Brown, have many rare specimens and carefully planned vistas. The Great Conservatory, with its large, almost Asian, glass dome, was added in 1830, and now holds an aquarium. There's also a huge garden center, a Koi center, and a butterfly house where you can see British and tropical specimens flying free.

★ Tate Gallery

Millbank, SW1. ☎ 0171/887-8000. Open Mon–Sat 10am–5:50pm; Sun 2–5:50pm. Admission free (tickets must be purchased for special exhibitions). Tube: Pimlico.

The Tate was founded in 1892 by businessman Sir Henry Tate, when he gave his collection of British paintings to the nation, together with funds to build a special gallery—an appropriate beginning for a gallery famous for modern art.

Under the visionary direction of Nicholas Serota, the exhibits (with the exception of the Turner galleries) now change annually to explore the wealth and variety of the collection. Each display traces the development of British art from the mid-16thC to the present, linking it with foreign art in the 20thC. Regular special displays from the permanent collection are based on common themes linking successive generations of art as well as the works of individual artists. **The Art Now Room** shows contemporary art by cutting-edge (and often controversial) contemporary artists. Throughout the year the Tate may rehang individual rooms, so works of art mentioned below may not always be on view.

New displays start at the rear of the building on the left. The first room covers the **16th–17th centuries,** when foreign artists working in England ruled the roost. In the 18thC, a truly national school appeared, led by William Hogarth, whose eye for contemporary life was unrivaled. With Reynolds and Gainsborough, 2 contradictory approaches to portraiture emerged: Reynolds favored a grand, classicizing manner (as in *Three Ladies Adorning a Term of Hymen*); Gainsborough concentrated on charm and prettiness with his extraordinarily fluent technique. In the end, though, both artists concentrated on pleasing their sitters. You'll find good examples of the development of landscape painting in the 18thC. In contrast, the eccentric mysticism of William Blake and his followers is effectively shown in a dimly lit room.

The **Pre-Raphaelites** are well represented: Millais's *Ophelia* and Rossetti's *Beata Beatrix* are among the most famous examples. There's a remarkable selection of Victorian painting. From the later 19thC, Whistler (an American painter working in England) stands out.

Next come the **French and British Impressionists** and **Postimpressionists,** with all the major figures represented with works of varying quality. Degas' bronze *Little Dancer* and Gaugin's *Faa Iheihe* are notable. An important masterpiece by Matisse, the pioneering artist of the Fauves, is the late collage *The Snail.* Cubism is demonstrated with a few high-quality pieces by Picasso and Braque. Stanley Spencer and his circle are also well represented. Works by Kandinsky and Mondrian illustrate the move to complete abstraction. Other important works by Picasso, the giant of modern art, include the *Tree Dancers,* in his unique version of the surrealist style. The surrealists themselves—Miro, Ernst, Magritte, Dali—are well represented, as are the American abstract expressionists.

A room is devoted to Henry Moore, as well as one to Francis Bacon, Lucian Freud, Kossoff, Auerbach, and Hodgkin. A high point of the gallery is the room devoted to Mark Rothko's powerful murals for the Seagram Building in New York, a potent reminder of the achievements of modern art. The 3 central Duveen Sculpture Galleries display the work of Rodin, Matisse, Epstein, and minimal artists.

The **Clore Gallery for the Turner Collection** (beautifully proportioned and lit, thanks to architect James Stirling) houses Turner's bequest of his works to the nation. They're a dazzling display of light and color, revealing an unmatched understanding of nature in all its moods and prefiguring the impressionists' innovations by several decades. The late works, such as the studies of *Norham Castle,* are outstanding.

★ Temple
WC2. Tube: Temple.

It's easy to miss the gateway to the Inner and Middle Temples amid the bustle of Fleet Street, but behind them lies a large, peaceful enclave of historic buildings and gardens. The Temple is named after the Knights Templar, a medieval religious order founded to further the Crusades, who came to this site (then outside the City walls) in about 1160. They constructed a great complex of monastic buildings; the chapel survives. In the 14thC, lawyers took over the buildings; they now comprise 2 of the 4 Inns of Court.

The red-brick **Middle Temple Gateway** was built in 1684 to a design using classical motifs; it leads to **Middle Temple Lane,** lined with chambers and courtyards. Much was destroyed by wartime bombing,

although some buildings date back to the 17thC and
earlier. Outstanding is the expertly restored **Middle
Temple Hall** of 1562–70 (open Mon–Fri 10–11:30am
and 3–4pm); it's likely that Shakespeare himself appeared
in the performance of *Twelfth Night* given here in 1602.

To the east, narrow alleys lead through to the **Inner
Temple.** Here, the most important building is the
Templar church, a fascinating medieval structure that's
1 of 5 circular churches in England based on the Church
of the Holy Sepulcher in Jerusalem. The round nave
(c. 1160–85) is one of the earliest Gothic structures in
England. On the floor of the nave are 9 13thC effigies
of knights in Purbeck marble.

The **Inner Temple Gateway,** leading back to Fleet
Street, is an attractive half-timbered house of 1610–1.
Upstairs is Prince Henry's Room. The Prince of Wales
Feathers and the initials "PH" suggest the link with
James I's son.

Theatre Museum

Russell St., WC2. ☎ 0171/836-2330. Open Tues–Sun 11am–7pm.
Admission charged. Tube: Covent Garden.

This outpost of the **Victoria and Albert Museum** is
in Covent Garden, close to West End theater and the
Royal Opera House. It's rich in theatrical history and
memorabilia, including costumes, playbills, posters,
props, and original models for the opera by master
designer Oliver Messel. There's also a box office for all
London shows and concerts, and a theatrical reference
library. Special attractions include very cool make-up
demos and costume workshops.

Tower Bridge

SE1. ☎ 0171/403-3761. Open Apr–Oct 10am–5:15pm; Nov–Mar
10am–4pm. Admission charged. Tube: Tower Hill.

With its towers and drawbridges, this landmark (the
one that everyone confuses with nearby London Bridge)
adjacent to the Tower of London has become a symbol
for the city. Built in 1886–94, it's the most easterly bridge
across the Thames. Designed so that large ships can pass
beneath its easily raised roadway, it's deceptively graceful from a distance. And, superbly lit at night, it's one of
London's most memorable sights after dark.

Enter by the north tower to reach the glass-enclosed
walkway, which offers splendid views: Butler's Wharf
downstream, HMS *Belfast* to the west, and St. Kath-
arine's Dock on the north bank. The **Tower Bridge
Museum,** to the south of the bridge, contains the original steam-driven machinery used to lift the bridge.

Recently modernized, the museum has an impressive,
hands-on display with animatronic figures who recount
the bridge's history and interactive technology showing changing views of the river through the ages.

Tower Hill Pageant
Tower Hill Terrace, Tower Hill, EC3. ☎ 0171/709-0081. Open Apr–
Oct 9:30am–5:30pm; Nov–Mar 9:30am–4:30pm. Admission charged.
Tube: Tower Hill.

This is a "dark ride" museum where computer-
controlled cars (one of them is specially adapted for
wheelchairs) take visitors past dioramas depicting scenes
of waterfront London from Roman times to the Blitz.
There is also an archaeological museum inspired by the
Museum of London's work along the waterfront, where
finds from that long-running project are displayed.

★ Tower of London
EC3 ☎ 0171/709-0765. 1-hour tours leave from Middle Tower every
half hour: last tour 3pm summer, 2:30pm winter. Open Mar–Oct
Mon–Sat 9am–6pm, Sun 10am–6pm; Nov–Feb Mon–Sat 9am–5pm,
Sun 10am–5pm. Admission charged. Tube: Tower Hill.

Spending a day within these massive walls is a real thrill.
Walking the paths of this great royal fortress, exploring
its towers, examining its superb collection of arms and
armor, getting a peek at the priceless Crown Jewels—
nothing brings England's romantic, bloody history to
life like a visit to the Tower. Consequently, London's
most substantial medieval monument is a prime tourist
attraction; head over early to avoid the crowds.

William the Conqueror founded the Tower just inside the Roman wall following his arrival in 1066, to
encourage the loyalty of the townspeople as much as to
defend them. The great stone White Tower, first of the
square Norman keeps, was completed by 1097. The
White Tower stood alone until Richard the Lion Heart
began to build a curtain wall. Edward I completed the
transformation of the Norman stronghold into a fully-
fledged medieval castle, basically what we see today.

Until James I (1603–25), the Tower was a leading
royal residence. It was also a principal armory and house
for royal treasure. The Tower's security also made it a
good prison. Monarchs have kept many of their most
notable enemies within its walls: Anne Boleyn, Sir
Thomas More, Elizabeth I (while a princess), Sir Walter
Raleigh, and, most recently, Rudolf Hess.

The Tower's longstanding traditions have cloaked it
in rich ceremony. It's still guarded by the **Yeomen Warders,** known as "Beefeaters," a company founded by

Henry VII in 1485. They still wear Tudor costume, with blue tunics carrying the sovereign's monogram on their chests, and broad, flat caps. With guardsmen from the Regular Army, Yeomen Warders participate in the **Ceremony of the Keys** at 9:30pm daily, formally locking up the Tower for the night (see p. 268). Another tradition has grown up around the 6 **ravens** that live inside the Tower's walls. They're jealously guarded and kept with a meat allowance, because legend says that the Tower will fall when the ravens leave. Look for the plaque in the moat commemorating their service. (Recently, Charlie, who had been on duty for more than 20 years, passed away. The Queen, we were told, was very upset.)

The easiest way to see the inner walls and grasp the layout is by following the **Wall Walk,** a 500-yard stroll along the elevated battlements starting at Wakefield Tower and ending at Martin Tower. Children under 16 must be accompanied by an adult.

You can enter the Tower's inner precincts through the gate in the **Bloody Tower,** overlooked by the heavily fortified round **Wakefield Tower** to the side. The Bloody Tower is legendary as the site of the 1485 murder of the young princes, sons of Edward IV, by their uncle, Richard III, who allegedly hoped to secure the throne for himself. Modern historians, however, are less certain about the event, and Richard's role in it, than Shakespeare was. Inside the tower, 2 rooms are furnished as they might have been when Sir Walter Raleigh was imprisoned here.

On the right of the great open space enclosed by fortification is a portion of 12thC wall, surviving from the Norman bailey, only exposed in 1940 when a bomb destroyed a 19thC building. When you reach the top of the steps ahead, you'll see the **Queen's House** (not open to the public), a pretty half-timbered structure begun in about 1540, on the left; Guy Fawkes was tortured there following the 1605 Gunpowder Plot.

To the north is the entrance to **Beauchamp Tower,** used as a prison. The interior is covered with carved graffiti, giving witness to the suffering of centuries of prisoners. Nearby is the **Chapel of St. Peter and Vincula,** built in the early 16thC on a 12thC foundation in Perpendicular Gothic style; some late medieval monuments remain. Beyond the chapel, **Bowyer Tower** contains a display of torture instruments.

The Crown Jewels   The Crown Jewels, recently installed in the Wellington Barracks and all sparkly and glittery behind bulletproof glass, are the Tower's greatest single attraction. Otherwise commendable attempts at crowd control don't allow you more than a brief look, but it's worth the wait. Almost all the royal regalia was melted down or sold off by Cromwell, so most of what's left dates from after the Restoration. Two exceptions are an exquisite spoon probably made for King John's coronation in 1199, and a much restored early 15thC ampulla in the form of an eagle (from which the anointing oil is poured). The **Royal Sceptre** contains the largest diamond ever cut (530 carats). The **Imperial State Crown,** originally made in 1838, incorporates an immense and beautiful ruby, worn by Henry V at the Battle of Agincourt. The oldest crown is "King Edward's," actually made for Charles II's coronation in 1660; the 5-pound crown is worn by the sovereign at coronations. The **Queen Mother's Crown,** made for her coronation in 1937, holds the famous 109-carat Kohinoor diamond, bought by the British Crown in 1849.

The White Tower and Armories   The dominant White Tower is the oldest and largest of the Tower's buildings. Its massive walls, built of Caen stone, are up to 15 feet thick. The medieval facade used to be even starker than it is now—the decorative cones were added later, and Wren enlarged the windows.

Inside are superb collections of arms and armor. On the 1st floor, the **Sporting and Tournament Galleries** contain crossbows, muskets, lances, swords, and the specialized armor made for jousting (already in the late Middle Ages a leisurely exercise in archaism). On the 2nd floor, the **Chapel of St. John** is the finest example of early Norman architecture in England—massive and severe, almost totally without ornament. More medieval armor is displayed in 2 more rooms; notice the awesome bulk of a suit made for a giant almost 7 feet tall. The 3rd-floor rooms contain outstanding examples of Tudor and later armor, with several suits beloning to Henry VIII (growing progressively larger as he grew older and fatter).

Trafalgar Square
WC2. Tube: Charing Cross.

Trafalgar Square is known as a rallying point for political demonstrations and New Year's Eve revelries—and even as a sanctuary for pigeons. When Nash began its redevelopment in the 1820s, it already had the fine **equestrian statue of Charles I** on the site of Charing

Nelson's Column, Trafalgar Square

Cross, and the superb church of **St. Martin-in-the-Fields.** Since then, the surrounding architecture has rather let down Nash's vision: the **National Gallery** (1832–8) is too small in scale to make the triumphant statement that its site demands; **Admiralty Arch** (1911), a monument to Queen Victoria that saves its best face for The Mall, is equally uninspired. All this, however, does allow **Nelson's Column,** an 170-foot granite column erected in 1842, to steal the show, as Nash intended. Its base is decorated by spirited reliefs made from the guns of ships captured at Trafalgar and other battles, and the deservedly famous lions were added by Landseer (1858–67).

Two recent changes to the vista at Trafalgar Square caused a stir: The controversial **Sainsbury Wing** of the National Gallery, by Robert Venturi and Denise Scott-Brown, has been received with mixed reactions; but **Grand Buildings,** at Northumberland Avenue, was reconstructed as an exact replica of the former structure and have helped to smarten up Trafalgar Square.

★★ Victoria and Albert Museum

Cromwell Rd., SW7. ☎ 0171/938-8500. Tours start from information desk at main entrance and run Tues–Sun at 11am, 12pm, 2pm, and 3pm; Mon 12:15pm, 2pm, 3pm. Open Tues–Sun 10am–5:50pm; Mon 12pm–5:50pm. Free admission (contributions are invited; tickets must be purchased for selected special exhibitions). Tube: South Kensington.

This is probably the world's greatest museum of the decorative arts. An outgrowth of the Great Exhibition of 1851, the "V&A" is a lively, informal place filled with a variety of extraordinary treasures; it's one of London's most popular museums. Where else is the quintessential "little black dress" part of the permanent collection? The overwhelming range of the exhibits includes everything from entire furnished rooms from the great houses of Britain and the Continent to individual spoons, shoes, and locks. One of the largest museums in the world, it's a labyrinth of galleries and passages where it's easy to get lost, and almost impossible to plan a coherent or comprehensive tour. But this drawback also contributes to the museum's appeal, for even regular visitors know that no matter how often they come, there are still new treasures to be discovered.

Finding Your Way   It's not possible to suggest a complete route through the 7 miles of galleries; the result would be both difficult to follow and exhausting. Instead, I've recommended 2 particularly well-displayed but contrasting areas as the starting and ending points—the Jones Collection and Constable Collection—and suggested some possibilities for visiting the sections in between. Along your journey, stay alert for the countless minor surprises that the museum has to offer. Note that the collection is arranged into "art and design" collections, cutting across the arts of a given culture or period, and "study collections," grouped by material and techniques. Good large plans for the galleries are available at the main entrance.

The Suggested Route   At the main entrance, turn left and follow the signs for the splendid **Jones Collection,** a dazzling display of French interior design (including some elaborate pieces that belonged to Marie-Antoinette) and decorative arts. The rich, aristocratic mood is complemented by paintings such as Boucher's *Portrait of Madame de Pompadour.* German, Dutch, and Italian decorative arts on display echo the 18thC French rococo style. The 17thC, just as elaborate but more solemn in mood, follows.

Steps lead to a series of less organized rooms devoted to the **Renaissance.** Some superb works stand out, such as Giovanni Bologna's *Samson and a Philistine;* the famous, elegantly gilded Antico miniature bronze of *Meleanger;* and several important reliefs by Donatello. Rooms on the side opposite the garden, including one done in William Morris's workshops and another with tiles by Minton and stained glass by James Goble, have been restored to their original glory.

At the end of the gallery of Gothic art is a vast and gruesome early 15thC Spanish altarpiece, showing scenes from the life of St. George, which, according to this account, consisted almost entirely of hideous torture. Be sure to study the Syon Cope closely: This early 14thC work is one of the finest embroidered pieces ever.

Also on the ground floor is the large and stunning **Dress Collection,** one of the world's great collections of everyday garments and high fashion. Check out the corsetry section. Above is the collection of **musical instruments.**

The large galleries devoted to Asian arts allow room for only a small part of the V&A's great holdings. In the **Nehru Gallery of Indian Art** and the **Gallery of Indian Sculpture** are several beautiful temple sculptures. The **Islamic Gallery** is dominated by the vast Ardabil Carpet of 1540 from a Persian mosque, and some superb lacquered pottery. Outstanding in the new **Tsui Gallery of Chinese Art** is an incredibly elaborate mid-18thC lacquer throne, 1,000-year-old ceramic and jade horses, and finely embroidered court costumes. The **Toshiba Gallery of Japanese Art** contains exquisite collections of netsuke, kimonos, armor, and ceramics.

The important **British Collection** stretches through sizable galleries on 2 upper floors to the left of the main entrance. The furniture is particularly beautiful but generally simpler than its Continental equivalents, often relying more on shape and wood quality than on elaborate decoration. Several complete rooms include Norfolk House's baroque gold-and-white Music Room (mid-18thC) and Robert Adam's much more delicate Glass Drawing Room from Northumberland House (1773–4). British decorative arts are brought up to 1960, and there are several important examples of the work of William Morris and the Arts and Crafts movement that had so much influence on modern British design.

Before leaving, be sure to visit the **Henry Cole Wing,** at the rear of the museum to the west. On the 2nd floor is the **Frank Lloyd Wright Gallery,** a collection dedicated to the 20thC American architect and father of the modern movement. There's a fabulous mock-up of one of Wright's interiors from the Kaufmann department store in Pittsburgh. This wing also houses the **Ionides Bequest,** consisting largely of 19thC paintings; outstanding are a Degas ballet scene, Millet's *Burne-Jones's Day Dream,* Gainsborough's portrait of his 2 young daughters, and works by Turner. The **Constable Collection,** the finest anywhere of the work of the most English of painters, is also here, providing a refreshing, open-air view for even the most jaded visitor: Clouds rush over Hampstead Heath, rainbows hover over Salisbury Cathedral, and the trees of Suffolk rustle in gentle breezes.

The Henry Cole Wing also houses the new **Gallery of European Ornament,** a study in design, decoration, and style in Europe from 1450 to the present. Objects as diverse as a customized leather jacket, a 1960s op-art tie, 16thC tableware, and William Morris wallpapers are brought together to illustrate the development of design, geometry, and figurative patterns over a variety of materials, functions, and geographical regions.

★ Wallace Collection

Hertford House, Manchester Sq., W1. ☎ 0171/935-0687. Open Mon–Sat 10am–5pm; Sun 2–5pm. Free admission. Tube: Bond St.

Flying in the face of the renowned English insularity, this magnificent monument to Francophilia is arguably the finest selection of French art outside of France. Together, with many other paintings and objets d'art of exceptional quality, it's a great 19thC private art collection "frozen" in a grand house equipped to contain it.

The finest objects are on the 1st floor. Large paintings by Boucher, full of the frivolous eroticism of the rococo court style, are on the walls of the top landing, as well as several scenes of Venice by Guardi and Canaletto. First-floor rooms are devoted to Flemish and Dutch art, including fine studies by Rubens. Look out for Potter's animal scenes; even the cows have personality. The large picture gallery contains many outstanding works, including pieces by Titian, Rembrandt, and Reynolds. Among the superb rococo furniture is a chest of drawers made for Louis XV's bedroom at Versailles. There's also an exquisite display of Sevres porcelain. The rest of the ground floor is an Aladdin's cave of miscellaneous treasures, including a splendid collection of terra-cotta statuettes, mostly from the Italian Renaissance, and a unique cabinet of wax portraits.

Furniture, including works attributed to the great A. C. Boulle, and more Sevres porcelain continue the French bias upstairs. Italian majolica pottery and Renaissance-era Limoges enamels are as well represented here as anywhere in the world. The remarkable collection of elaborately wrought and decorated arms and armor stands out.

★★ Westminster Abbey

Broad Sanctuary, SW1. ☎ 0171/222-5152. Nave and Cloisters open daily 8am–7pm; royal chapels open Mon–Fri 9am–4:45pm, Sat 9am–2:45pm and 3:45–5:45pm; Chapter House and museum open daily 10:30am–4pm; Abbey Garden open Tues and Thurs Apr–Sept 10am–6pm, Oct–Mar 10am–4pm; July and Aug band plays Thurs 12:30–2pm. Last admissions 45 minutes before closing. Admission charged to royal chapels. Tube: Westminster, St. James's.

Since William the Conqueror chose the new, incomplete Westminster Abbey for his coronation on Christmas Day, 1066, it has been the scene of the coronations, marriages, and burials of monarchs, a place of tribute to Britain's heroes, and in every way Britain's mother church. St. Paul's Cathedral is London's church, but Westminster Abbey belongs to the nation. It's also one of Britain's finest Gothic buildings, a soaring and graceful offering to God with a strikingly unified interior.

The abbey's royal connection preserved it from destruction during the Reformation at the dissolution of the monasteries and, in 1540, Henry VIII made it a cathedral, with its own bishop. The permanent establishment of the Protestant Church of England came under Elizabeth I, who, in 1560, gave the abbey the status of a collegiate church independent of both the Bishop of London and the Archbishop of Canterbury. It thus became a Royal Peculiar, a great church serving Crown and State.

The best times to visit are when the **Abbey Garden** is open. For some reason, nobody uses it; you'll have it all to yourself. Bring a book and a sandwich, and enjoy this hidden jewel. Jazz bands play during lunchtime in July and August.

The Exterior   After 22 years and £25 million, the restoration work on the exterior of the Abbey—the most extensive work since Wren's time—was completed last year. Cleaning has uncovered the beauty of the abbey's soft Reigate stone (where replacement is necessary, Portland stone is being used, which will better stand the test of time).

The west facade, with the main entrance, is perhaps the most dramatic approach, although Hawksmoor's towers are insubstantial—just too narrow and too high to suit the medieval facade. The abbey looks best from the north; the north transept forms a tremendous centerpiece, with its great triple porch and huge rose window framed by a superb series of flying buttresses. To the east lies the far more elaborate exterior of Henry VII's chapel, entirely covered with dense late Gothic tracery. The outer walls have turrets capped by "pepperpots" and connected to the chapel's nave by delicately pierced flying buttresses. The nave is topped by a pierced balustrade and narrow pinnacles. The whole effect is wonderfully decorative.

The Interior   Enter the abbey from the west, which will immediately present you with a stunning view along the nave. The interior is very much like a French Gothic cathedral, much higher and narrower than other English churches. Clerestory windows beneath the gracefully vaulted ceiling complete the majesty.

Set in the floor ahead of the entrance is a memorial to Winston Churchill, with the **Tomb of the Unknown Warrior** beyond; the brass lettering is made from cartridges brought back with the body from the World War I trenches. On the first pier of the nave hangs a famous and rare medieval **portrait of Richard II,** probably painted in 1398. Both aisles are filled with monuments. Among the many buried in the nave is explorer David Livingstone. On the left, in one of its arches, is a fine monument to Isaac Newton (1731). Memorials to scientists cluster near Newton's tomb: Lister, Darwin, Faraday, Rutherford; musicians including Elgar, Vaughan-Williams, and Benjamin Britten are commemorated by plaques in the floor near Purcell's monument. In the north transept the monuments come thick and heavy, and include those to 19thC statesmen.

East of the transept, among several older monuments, is one of the most impressively carved and imaginatively conceived of all—that to Mrs. J. G. Nightingale, made by Roubiliac in 1761. It shows a grim figure of Death pointing a lance at the unfortunate lady, who died after being struck by lightning.

At this point, notice the crossing, where Wren intended that a spire should rise (it was never built). To the east is the **Sanctuary.** To its right are rare and important early 14thC wall hangings, together with an early Renaissance Italian altarpiece and a collection of medieval monuments.

Before approaching the centerpiece of the whole abbey—the chapel and shrine to Edward the Confessor—visit the superb **Henry VII's chapel** at the east end of the abbey. Completed in 1512 by Henry VIII in richly elaborate Gothic style, it's a mature, sophisticated farewell flourish. For the monument within, the Italian Pietro Torrigiano produced the first Renaissance sculpture in England; the heads of the corner angels are especially beautiful. The chapel has its own subsidiary chapels and aisles. In the north aisle is the **joint tomb of Elizabeth I,** completed in 1606 with a suitably stern effigy, and her hated rival, **Mary Queen of Scots.**

Edward the Confessor's shrine is just behind the main altar of the abbey. Only the base remains from the magnificent tomb built by Henry III to contain the remains of the Confessor, but enough of the gold mosaic is there to indicate its former splendor.

Also in the chapel is the **coronation throne of 1300–1,** where almost every monarch since William I has been crowned. The graffiti on it, now part of history, was carved by 17thC schoolboys from nearby Westminster School who were allowed to roam unchecked around the abbey. Under the seat is the Stone of Scone, the mystical coronation stone of the Scottish kings, captured by Edward I in 1297. Legends identify it with Jacob's pillow when he dreamed at Bethel; it was certainly in use as a coronation stone for Macbeth and other Scottish kings from the 9thC. Its symbolic value persists: In 1950 it was stolen by Scottish nationalists, but was recovered a year later. All around are the tombs of the medieval monarchs, some of the finest sculpture surviving from this period in England.

The south transept has 2 beautiful carved angels from the mid-13thC in the the main arch, but is more famous as **Poet's Corner.** Many of the greatest writers in the English language are buried or commemorated here. The best monument, to Geoffrey Chaucer, was placed here in 1555. Also commemorated are Ben Jonson, Milton, Blake, Longfellow, and Shakespeare (a most undistinguished statue). Browning, Byron, Tennyson, Henry James, and Dylan Thomas have plaques in the floor. Artists other than writers, such as Noël Coward, are also commemorated; the last ashes to be interred here were those of Sir Laurence Olivier, who died in 1990.

In the south choir aisle a doorway leads through to the **cloister,** as dignified as a monastic cloister should be. The earliest part, dating from the 13thC, is to the east and north. It now contains a **brass-rubbing center** (open Mon–Sat 9am–6pm; in summer, Wed to 8pm), where you can rub your own copies from replicas of medieval brass monuments. On the east side, a passageway leads through to the well-restored **chapter**

house, built around 1250; it was used throughout the Middle Ages for the occasional meetings of Parliament.

Beyond the chapter house, the **Westminster Abbey Museum** houses a display of the abbey's history, including a number of royal funeral effigies.

★ Westminster Cathedral

Ashley Place, SW1. ☎ 0171/798-9055. Open daily 7am–8pm; Tower open daily Apr–Sept. Free admission; admission charged to tower 9am–5pm. Tube: Westminster, Victoria.

When designs were being considered in the late 19thC for the Roman Catholic Cathedral of Westminster, intended to be London's most important Catholic church, a neo-Gothic structure at first seemed the inevitable choice. In the end, however, an early Christian approach was courageously adopted, against all the prevalent dictates of the era. The result of this far-sighted decision is a building of great originality, a strange Byzantine basilica unique in London and cleverly avoiding a false comparison with nearby Westminster Abbey.

The cathedral was built between 1895 and 1903, using Santa Sophia in Istanbul as a model, along with some Italian Renaissance ideas, the most striking of which is the huge campanile, similar to that of Siena Cathedral. The top of the tower, (273 feet high) offers marvelous views; an elevator will take you to the top in summer.

The interior is very impressive, with a massive open space created by the great nave, supporting a roof of 4 shallow domes—purely Byzantine in inspiration. The decoration—still incomplete, with rough brick exposed above the lower levels—contributes to the solemn effect. The piers of the nave are giant columns of dark-green marble, supposedly from the same quarry as those in Santa Sophia. Other dramatic marble patterns cover the walls. The whole interior should eventually be covered with mosaics; however, those parts completed so far fail to reflect the grandeur of the overall conception.

★ Whitechapel Art Gallery

80 Whitechapel High St., E1. ☎ 0171/522-7888. Open Tues–Sun 11am–5pm (to 8pm on Wed). Free admission, except for special exhibitions. Tube: Aldgate East.

A scruffy row of shops in the East End is an unlikely place to find one of England's most celebrated Art Nouveau buildings—but there it is, with a large arched doorway in a plain facade topped by a delightful foliage relief. The gallery enjoys a high reputation for staging important temporary modern and contemporary art exhibitions. There's also a great cafe, which fills up with the more cultured members of the City community during lunchtime.

Whitehall

SW1. Tube: Charing Cross, Westminster.

The word "Whitehall" is so firmly embedded in the English frame of reference that it's applied to people, institutions, and buildings whether they belong to the street or not. Nevertheless, Whitehall itself hasn't changed; it's still lined with large government offices, and it's still Britain's administrative center. Running south from Trafalgar Square toward Westminster, it took on this character in the late 17thC, as government departments began building around the Royal Palace of Whitehall.

The northern end of Whitehall resembles any other commercial street in Central London until the you reach the **Admiralty** on the west side. In front is a handsome screen designed by Robert Adam in 1759–61. Government buildings from about 1900 are followed by the **Banqueting House,** with the attractive **Welsh Office,** occupying a private residence from 1772, soon after.

On the west side, opposite, is the **Horse Guards Parade,** built in 1750–60 to William Kent's designs. Next is **Dover House** (the Scottish Office), with an elegant facade of 1787. Whitehall is dominated here by the great bulk of the **Ministry of Defense,** a Portland stone monster finished in 1959. The modern statues in front depict Sir Walter Raleigh and Field-Marshal Montgomery. Somewhere beneath are Henry VIII's wine cellars, surviving from the old palace. Opposite is **Downing Street.**

From here, Whitehall becomes **Parliament Street,** with massive 19thC government buildings in Italian Renaissance style. At **no.79,** William Whitfield's bold new government office complex is a stunning example of modern architecture that blends beautifully with its surroundings. **The Cenotaph** (1919), the national monument to Britain's war dead, is opposite. Beneath the offices, with a public entrance in King Charles Street, are the fascinating **Cabinet War Rooms.**

William Morris Gallery

Lloyd Park, Forest Rd., E17. ☎ 0181/527-3782. Open Tues–Sat 10am–1pm, 2–5pm; 1st Sun each month 10am–1pm and 2–5pm. Free admission. Tube: Walthamstow Central.

This East London gallery is well worth a visit for anyone interested in William Morris's design ideas. It's housed in the lovely 18thC Water House, Morris's home during his school and student days. The house, set on attractive grounds, has been beautifully preserved, and contains Morris wallpapers, printed and woven textiles, embroideries, carpets, printing blocks, furniture, stained glass, and ceramics. The collection of works by Morris is complemented by Pre-Raphaelite paintings, a Rodin sculpture, decorative and applied work by Sir Frank Brangwyn, and furniture by important designers of the period, such as Walter Crane, Ernest Gimson, and William De Morgan. Highlights include the "medieval" helmet and sword designed by Morris in the 1850s as props for the Oxford Union murals, his *Woodpecker* tapestry, and his masterpiece in fine printing, the *Kelmscott Chaucer.*

The Zoo

Regent's Park, NW1. ☎ 0171/722-3333. Open daily 10am–5:30pm, until 4pm in winter. Admission charged. Tube: Regent's Park, Mornington Crescent, Camden Town.

The gardens of the Zoological Society of London occupy an attractive part of Regent's Park bisected by the Grand Union Canal. Founded in 1826, this is the oldest zoo in the world, and one of the most important. London Zoo has more than 600 species and more than 12,000 animals, and enjoys a worldwide reputation in the conservation and animal medicine.

Innovation has changed the methods of showing animals, and bold architectural experiments have displaced the old iron cage approach. The animals are mostly in larger compounds, designed to reflect their natural habitats and separated from the public by moats rather than bars, like on the **Cotton Terraces,** where you can see giraffes, camels, and okapi only a moat's width away. The **African Aviary,** a revolutionary design of nearly invisible "piano wires," keeps vultures, eagles, and spoonbills separated from visitors physically but not visually. Similarly, you can see the big cats at close range in their dens through glass, or watch as they roam paddocks stocked with suitable vegetation. These animals don't have that bored, lethargic appearance that can make zoos so depressing. Because they're so active, the monkeys and apes in the **Michael Sobell Pavilion** are perhaps the most enjoyable of the zoo's creatures. More morbidly alluring is one of the world's most extensive collections of reptiles, insects, poisonous snakes, and giant spiders.

Two special features are the newly refurbished **Moonlight World,** where you can watch nocturnal animals behaving as if it were the dead of night, and the new **Ambika Paul Children's Zoo and Farm,** with a petting zoo and pet care center. (Come at lunchtime to watch the pigs pig out.) The **Penguin Pool,** built in the 1930s, pioneered the use of prestressed concrete, and still looks contemporary. The **Snowdon Aviary,** opened in 1965, containing a variety of birds in a large open space, is superbly functional—even if it looks like a collapsed radio mast.

City Walks

The following walks aim to give you a taste of a Londoner's London: You'll discover hidden corners (Walk 3) and get to know the city's cultural—in particular its literary—heart (Walk 2).

Walk 1: An Introduction to London

This convenient orientation tour will introduce the first-time visitor to this historic city, or refresh the memory of an old friend after a long absence. A stroll through the streets of the City of Westminster—center of government and tradition and the cornerstone of the West End—links many of London's most famous landmarks. Allow 2–3 hours. Tube: Westminster.

Begin by walking along Bridge Street, past the statue of Queen Boadicea, symbol of patriotism and female warrior extraordinaire, onto Westminster Bridge itself for the best view of the **Palace of Westminster** and **Big Ben.** Look also to your right along the Victoria Embankment to see the fine government buildings. Let your gaze move around full circle to cross the river with Hungerford railway bridge; beyond it is the **South Bank Arts Centre** and, on this side, **County Hall,** former headquarters of the now defunct Greater London Council and currently owned by a Japanese consortium that is threatening to transform it into a deluxe hotel. The panorama continues past the huge stone lion at the east end of Westminster Bridge to the modern St. Thomas' Hospital, and crosses the river again by Lambeth Bridge.

From the foot of Big Ben, walk back around the west side of the Palace of Westminster past Westminster Hall. Then cross over the road to St. Margaret's Church to arrive at **Westminster Abbey.**

Walk 1: An Introduction to London

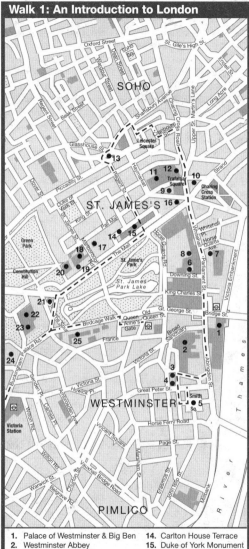

1. Palace of Westminster & Big Ben
2. Westminster Abbey
3. Westminster School
4. Watt's of Westminster
5. St. John's
6. 10 Downing Street
7. Banqueting House
8. Horse Guards Parade
9. Nelson's Column
10. St. Martin-in-the-Fields
11. National Gallery
12. National Portrait Gallery
13. Piccadilly Circus
14. Carlton House Terrace
15. Duke of York Monument
16. Admiralty Arch
17. Marlborough House
18. St. James's Palace
19. Clarence House
20. Lancaster House
21. Victoria Memorial
22. Buckingham Palace
23. Queen's Picture Gallery
24. Royal Mews
25. Wellington Barracks

For a bit of atmosphere, take a short detour to explore some of the small streets surrounding the Abbey. Continue south past the Abbey along Abingdon Street, with the Thames to your left. Turn right into Great College Street; at the end of the road, before it hooks left, look to the right—this is a back entrance to the **Westminster School,** one of England's great public schools. Follow the road to the left and continue along Tufton Street. At no. 7, pop into **Watt's of Westminster,** a shop featuring ecclesiastical textiles and accessories. Continuing south on Tufton Street, turn left at Dean Trench Street into Smith Square. The church in the center is **St. John's,** which hosts lunchtime concerts and has a nice basement cafe, a good lunch spot.

To retrace your steps back to the Abbey, pass along the north side of the church and turn left into Lord North, which will become Cowley Street before turning into Barton Street. Barton Street will bring you back to Great College Street; turn right and head toward the river, where it's a left to the Abbey.

At the Abbey, turn left into Parliament Square, following it around almost to Bridge Street again before turning left into Parliament Street, which leads to **Whitehall.** The 2nd street on the left, past the Cenotaph, is **Downing Street,** where the policeman at the door identifies "Number 10"—the residence of the Prime Minister. Going north along Whitehall, the **Banqueting House** (1622) is on the right, nearly opposite the Whitehall entrance to **Horse Guards Parade.** At the north of Whitehall is **Trafalgar Square,** a crowded area of constant activity dominated by Nelson's Column.

As you cross the square toward the **National Gallery,** with its controversial new Sainsbury Wing extension, notice also James Gibbs's beautiful church of **St. Martin-in-the-Fields** (1726). St. Martin's Place, in front and to the right of the church, has the **central Post Office** on its right; to the north, up St. Martin's Lane, is the globe-topped spire of the **London Coliseum,** home of the English National Opera. Leading around to the left, past the entrance to the **National Portrait Gallery,** is Charing Cross Road. Follow this road as far as Leicester Square tube station, then turn left along Cranbourn Street into Leicester Square itself.

Continue along the north side of Leicester Square as far as the Swiss Centre, where a right turn up Wardour

Street takes you past Lisle and Gerrard streets, the 2 main arteries of Chinatown, to Shaftesbury Avenue, the heart of theaterland and the southern boundary of **Soho.** Turn left on Shaftesbury Avenue and walk down to **Piccadilly Circus.**

Arriving at Piccadilly Circus, pause a moment to orient yourself between Shaftesbury Avenue; Regent Street, curving majestically to the west and north; and Picadilly itself, leading west toward Mayfair, Belgravia, and Knightsbridge. It's the 4th major street that you must follow: Go down Lower Regent Street to the south (which borders St. James's on the right), crossing Pall Mall. The street now becomes Waterloo Place and ends at the Duke of York Monument after passing the elegant and imposing Carlton House Terrace. Take the steps fronting the monument to **The Mall.**

At the foot of the steps look left toward **Admiralty Arch,** and Trafalgar Square beyond it. Notice also the ivy-clad wartime extension to the Admiralty, the Citadel, beyond which you can see the expanse of Horse Guards Parade. Then walk west along The Mall, with **St. James's Park** on your left, toward the gilded Victoria Memorial and **Buckingham Palace,** passing **Marlborough House, St. James's Palace, Clarence House,** and **Lancaster House** on the way. Walk around the south side of Buckingham Palace to Buckingham Gate and Buckingham Palace Road, where you'll find the entrances to the Queen's Picture Gallery and the Royal Mews.

To complete the walk, either continue along Buckingham Palace Road to Victoria Station, or retrace your steps to follow Birdcage Walk along the south side of St. James's Park in front of the recently restored Wellington Barracks. The 1st street on the right, Queen Anne's Gate, leads to St. James's Park tube station. Or continue along Birdcage Walk into Great George Street, which takes you back where you began, to Parliament Square and the Westminster tube station.

Walk 2: Bloomsbury & Covent Garden, London's Cultural Heart

Covent Garden and **Bloomsbury** have always been nurseries of artistic endeavor and achievement. Take time to notice the elegant squares around Bloomsbury. Allow 1–2 hours. Tube: Temple.

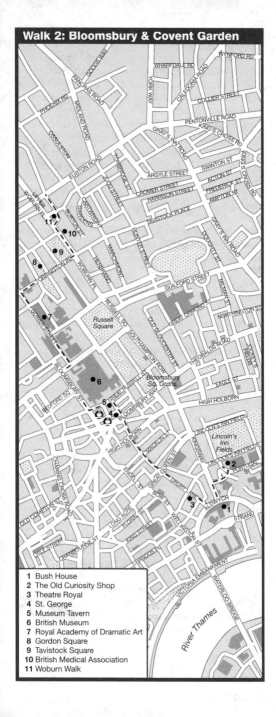

Walk 2: Bloomsbury & Covent Garden

1 Bush House
2 The Old Curiosity Shop
3 Theatre Royal
4 St. George
5 Museum Tavern
6 British Museum
7 Royal Academy of Dramatic Art
8 Gordon Square
9 Tavistock Square
10 British Medical Association
11 Woburn Walk

Begin by walking up Kingsway, which is directly opposite **Bush House;** it's from this appropriate symbol of British cultural prestige that the BBC runs its foreign radio services. The first right off Kingsway is Portugal Street, where you'll find **The Old Curiosity Shop** a little way up on the left. It's not certain whether or not Dickens based his novel on this antique store, but he knew it well.

Head back down Kingsway. Back on the Aldwych, turn up Drury Lane. **The Theatre Royal,** down Russell Street to the left and on the corner of Catherine Street, was founded in 1663. Also in Russell Street were the famous coffeehouses of the 18thC, and Dr. Johnson and Boswell first met in a bookstore at no. 8 in 1763. Proceed up Drury Lane, which continues until it turns into Museum Street. No. 47, **The Museum Street Cafe,** is a good spot for lunch; for cheaper fare, make a quick detour to **Wagamama,** 4 Streatham St. (off Coptic St.). On your way up Museum Street to more elegant **Bloomsbury,** you'll pass on the right, in Bloomsbury Way, the **church of St. George,** which Dickens used as the setting for his Bloomsbury christening in *Sketches by Boz*.

Return to Museum Street and turn right. At the far end is the **Museum Tavern,** at different times favored by Karl Marx and Dylan Thomas. Turn left here, past the **British Museum,** and then right into Bloomsbury Street, passing the peaceful and unspoiled Bedford Square, at one time or another home to many distinguished people—and therefore to a crop of blue plaques. Continue down Gower Street, pausing to see the statues of tragedy and comedy outside the **Royal Academy of Dramatic Art.**

A right turn into Torrington Place will take you past Dillon's University Bookshop and Woburn Square on the right. **Gordon Square,** on the left, was a stomping ground of the Bloomsbury Group. Torrington Place leads on to **Tavistock Square;** the garden in the square has as its focal point a statue of Mahatma Gandhi and a tree planted by Pandit Nehru.

Turn left along the far side of the square to Upper Woburn Place. On the right, a blue plaque marks the site where Dickens lived from 1851–60; it's now the headquarters of the British Medical Association. Farther down on the right, turn into **Woburn Walk,** with its bow-front shops and brass plaque in memory of the poet W. B. Yeats, who lived here at the turn of the century.

A left turn leads you back to Euston Road, where you can pick up a bus or the tube.

Walk 3: St. James's Hidden Passageways & Gentlemen's Clubs

St. James's is home to London's most exclusive men's clubs and the peculiar species that frequents them—the English Gentleman. Exclusivity is the operative word here—visitors are denied admission—but you can take a peek from the outside and imagine the well-shod passing through the portals. In the process, you'll explore some of London's secret passageways and courtyards. Allow 1–2 hours. Tube: Piccadilly Circus.

On exiting the Piccadilly tube station, continue west along the south side of Piccadilly, away from the tube station. You'll shortly come upon **St. James's Church** (1684), designed by Sir Christopher Wren. The church has been famous for its fashionable congregations, and literary allusions to it are frequent, notably in the works of Evelyn and Defoe. Turn left into the churchyard and continue into the church. Note the font, sculpted in white marble, and the carved altar; both are by Grinling Gibbons, Wren's master carver. Go through the church, past the St. James's Cafe in the courtyard; stop for refreshments if you have time.

Out on Jermyn Street, take a right and continue past the entrance to the Prince's Arcade. As you go forth, you'll pass some of London's most established men's clothiers, including **Turnbull and Asser** (no. 71–72), **Harvie & Hudson** (no. 77), and **Taylor's** (no. 74; toiletries for the "Gentleman"). On the northwest corner of Jermyn and Duke streets is **Dunhill;** stop in and head upstairs, where a quirky collection of historic pipes is on view. Continue along Jermyn Street passing the Piccadilly Arcade; stop in to nos. 19–21, where **Favourbrook** produces sumptuous waistcoats and dinner jackets from rich brocades—the ultimate "Four Weddings and a Funeral" attire.

Jermyn Street ends when it reaches St. James's Street. On the south corner you might be tempted by **Davidoff's,** purveyor of fine cigars. Before crossing to the opposite side of St. James's Street, turn right and note no. 37. It doesn't look like much on the outside, but behind the facade is **White's,** the oldest Gentlemen's club in London. This is where Charles reportedly had his bachelor party before he tied the knot with Di back in 1981; the list of members reads like a page out of *Burke's Peerage.*

Back at Jermyn Street, cross St. James's Street and continue heading west to Bennet Street. At the pub on the corner, turn left, past my favorite restaurant in London, Le Caprice, on the right (see p. 00). At the far end of the street you'll find some steps leading down to Park Place. Note the 2 historic houses to the right at the bottom of the steps; these buildings make up the residence of the **Over-Seas League,** founded in 1910 to further global understanding and comradeship during the heyday of the British Empire. Back at the bottom of the steps on Park Place, turn left; as you approach St. James's Street, you'll pass 2 more exclusive clubs, **Brooks's** on the left at the corner (it's so exclusive it doesn't even have a number) and **Pratt's** on the right, at no. 14.

Back at St. James's, turn right and take the 1st right again into **Blue Ball Yard.** The cottages and garages here were originally used as coach houses, with large wine cellars underneath. Today, they form an annex to the Stafford Hotel—the coach houses have been transformed into deluxe suites (the ground-floor rooms even have Jacuzzis), and the subterranean caves have been transformed into one of the most beautiful wine cellars in London.

Back out onto St. James's Street, turn right and right again into St. James's Place. As you continue along this street, look to the left down the gaslit courtyard; the newly restored **Duke's Hotel** is hidden down this alley, with Silvestro still manning the bar famous for it's wide choice of vintage cognacs and Cuban cigars. At the end of St. James's Place, where the road turns to the right, is **Spencer House.** The former town house of the Princess of Wales's family it now leased to Lord Rothchild, who has spent millions restoring the building. The main rooms are open to the public only on Sundays.

Follow the road to the right, passing the front entrance to the **Stafford Hotel** (inside is a cozy bar, nice for a casual lunch). Between nos. 23 and 22 on the left is a passageway that leads to **Queen's Walk** in Green Park.

At the park, turn left and pass in front of **Spencer House** and its gardens, noting the classical architectural ornament as you stroll by. To the left is another grand house worth a look, with urns along the balustrade at top. At the corner, turn left into the next path (don't worry about the sign that warns of sudden closings—this is only for legal reasons; besides, you'll see the path is only about 20 feet long, so there's no danger of being locked in). The path lets you out into Cleveland Row, which passes **St. James's Palace.** As you approach the palace, look down the police-guarded road to the right—that's **Clarence House,** home of the Queen Mother, 95 and still kicking. Continue along past the palace; the cobbled mews on the left, Russell Court, is worth a quick look as you pass by.

Back on St. James's Street, cross at the zebra crossing to the far side. At no. 3 is the well-established wine merchant **Berry Bros. and Rudd.** The creators of Cutty Sark whisky, the firm may not look like much from the outside, but it's what's underneath that has earned it its reputation: Inside, the trap door on the right-hand side of the shop is the entrance to a cellar without peer in London. These subterranean caves can store up to 18,000 cases of wine. Out the door of Berry Bros., just to the right, is the entrance to **Pickering Place,** a lovely courtyard under which extend the cellars of Berry Bros. Out again onto St. James's Street, turn right and continue along. You'll pass **Lock's the hatters,** here since 1764, and **Lobb's the bootmakers.** Mecca for the noble and terribly rich since 1849, John Lobb (great-grandson of the founder) stores the lasts of over 30,000 past and present clients in their basement (there's also a new ready-to-wear shop near Turnbull and Asser at 90 Jermyn St.).

At King Street, turn right and at Crown Passage turn right again. There's much happening down this narrow road lined with small shops and restaurants. The passage will end at **Pall Mall;** take a left and another left into the totally unnoteworthy Angel Court (this is only to get you back onto King St.). Note **Christie's** auction house on the north side of the street; you might want to peruse the viewing room if you have time. Turn right, proceeding along King Street to Duke Street, where you'll turn left. At no. 44, on the 1st floor, is the controversial **White Cube Gallery,** run by dealer Jay Jopling. Here you might see the most recent work of the *enfant terrible* of the art world, Damien Hirst; he has been moving away from the animal-in-formaldehyde motif and has recently been exploring spin art.

Between nos. 12 and 13, on the right side, is the archway for Mason's Yard. Turn into this former stableyard and note the small silver shop, **J.H. Bourdon-Smith Ltd.,** on the right. The collection of antique silver here, which extends over 2 floors, is worth a look. In the center of the yard is a very unattractive electricity substation; proceed to the end of the yard, keeping the substation to your left. A glance to the right will reveal the back of the exclusive members-only **London Library.**

The corner of the yard, diagonally opposite the yard entrance, is marked "No. 9"; take this passage into Ormond Yard. Exit the yard onto Duke of York Street (here there's a gem of a pub, the Red Lion, nice for a refreshment break) and proceed to the end. Now you're back on Jermyn Street, where a turn right and then left into Eagle Place brings you back to Piccadilly.

London for Kids

To find out what's on for children, get the pamphlet *Where to Take Children* at any of the London Tourist Board centers. For answers to specific questions, call **Kidsline** (☎ 0171/222-8070) Monday through Friday 4–6pm, during school vacations and "half term" 9am–4pm.

London Transport   Children under 5 travel free and those between the ages of 5 and 15 travel for a reduced fare on public transport, although children ages 14 and 15 need a photocard (available from any tube station; proof of age and a photograph is required).

Best Bets

An ideal introduction to London for children of all ages is the **Original London Sightseeing Tour,** which will take you around the city in a double-decker bus. A cheaper alternative is take any of the no. 11 public buses (top deck, front seat for the best view). River trips to **Hampton Court** and **Greenwich** are also popular among the kids (they especially love Hampton Court's hedge maze).

Many museums, such as the **Bethnal Green Museum of Childhood** and the **London Toy and Model Museum,** have always been directly aimed at a young audience. But many of the major museums have adopted a child-friendly, "hands-on" approach. The **Science Museum,** for instance, devotes an entire section to children: They're encouraged to play with the exhibits in the Launch Pad, which illustrate the basics of science on a simple level that parents can understand, too. **The Museum of the Moving Image (MOMI)** has a special exhibition, "The Little Children's Project," which is geared to those under 3 feet tall. Most muse-ums are also reasonably accessible to baby buggies.

Sights that appeal to adults as well kids include the Royal Mews at **Buckingham Palace,** where you can see horses up close, and the Whispering Gallery at **St. Paul's Cathedral**—kids have fun playing with the echo.

With all its open spaces, London is great for kids. **Hyde Park** and **Kensington Gardens** (separated only by a road) are the most central and well-known of London's parks. As well as having wide open spaces that are great for large-scale game-playing, the parks are home to many special attractions. Boats and paddle craft can be rented on the **Serpentine,** part of which is cordoned off and used as a swimming area in the summer. Kensington Gardens also has unique Sunday entertainments: Enthusiasts sail their model boats on the **Round Pond,** and a rainbow of kites fills the sky. Nearby is the playground donated by J. M. Barrie, with its statue of **Peter Pan.** Look out, too, for the beauti-fully carved **Elfin Oak,** near Bayswater Road, restored by the fairies (with a little help from Spike Milligan). Puppet shows are staged here on August afternoons.

Regent's Park also has rowboats to rent, but the main attraction there is the **Zoo,** which has a special Children's Zoo and farm with a touch paddock and a pet care center. Though not particularly central, **Hamp-stead Heath** also offers wide open spaces as well as an animal enclosure with deer, a pond for model boats, an outdoor swimming pool, and a playground. **Coram Fields** (40 Brunswick Sq., WC1; ☎ 0171/278-2424) in Bloomsbury was donated to the children of London by Sir Thomas Coram; adults are only allowed in if they are accompanied by a child. **Holland Park** boasts a wildlife enclosure with peacocks, Muscovy ducks, and Polish bantams, an exciting adventure playground for older children, and a toddlers' playground. **Battersea** has even more going on: a boating lake, a small zoo (open in summer), a deer enclosure, an adventure play-ground, and theater events and pony rides in summer. **Syon Park** has a wonderful butterfly house, where you can see specimens all year-round.

Other Activities About Town
Brass Rubbing
This can be a fascinating way to pass a wet afternoon. **The London Brass Rubbing Centre** in St. Martin-in-the-Fields (Trafalgar Sq., WC2; ☎ 0171/437-6023; open Mon–Sat 10am–6pm, Sun noon–6pm) has a large

collection. **Westminster Abbey** (SW1; ☎ 0171/ 222-2085; open Mon–Sat 9am–6pm) also has brass-rubbing facilities. Admission is free, but you have to pay for your materials.

Farms

There are a surprising number of city farms in the Inner London area. The most interesting are: **Freightliners** (Paradise Park, Sheringham Rd., N7; ☎ 0171/609-0467); **Kentish Town City Farm** (1 Cressfield Close, NW5; ☎ 0171/916-5420); **Mudchute Park and Farm** (Pier St., E14; ☎ 0171/ 515-5901); and **Stepping Stones Farm** (Stepney Way and High St., E1; ☎ 0171/790-8204). Some are closed on Mondays; call before you go.

Playgroups

London has many supervised adventure playgrounds that have imaginative materials and equipment created by the children themselves. To find one near you, contact **Playlink** (279 Whitechapel Rd., E1; ☎ 0171/ 820-3800).

Younger children can go to the council-run **One O'Clock Clubs.** These are not baby-sitting services; under-5s must be accompanied by an adult. Information on these clubs is available from local borough councils; the British Tourist Authority can point you in the right direction.

Pony Rides

In Richmond Park on Saturdays, **Stag Lodge Stables** (Robin Hood Gate, Richmond Park, SW15; ☎ 0181/ 974-6066) runs The Red Riders, a pony club for kids.

Attractions Within Easy Reach of London

Bekonscot Model Village (Warwick Rd., Beaconsfield, Buckinghamshire; ☎ 01494/672 919; open daily late Feb–early Nov 10am–5pm) is a beautifully landscaped miniature village and model railway only 40 minutes west of London, off the M40. You can wander around in the village and peer into the buildings (which are waist-high to an adult), exploring an idealized version of a 1930s English village, done in fascinating detail.

Chessington World of Adventures (Leatherhead Rd., Chessington, Surrey, just off the A3; ☎ 013727/ 27227; open Apr–late Oct 10am–3:30pm) guarantees an entertaining day out with a host of rides, from Dragon River via the Runaway Mine Train to Britain's first hanging roller coaster, The Vampire, and its own zoo (open all year).

Thorpe Park (Staines Rd., Chertsey, Surrey; ☎ 01932/569 393; open daily Apr–late Oct 10am–5pm, high season to 6pm), approximately 40 minutes from London to the west off the M25 motorway, is a popular family attraction. Rides range from Thunder River and The Flying Fish Mini-Roller coaster to the Fantasy Reef, which incorporates a 4-lane waterslide. Less terrifying features include pedalos, a farm, and a traditional fairground carousel.

Water Palace (619 Purley Way, Croydon; ☎ 0181/688-2090; open daily 10am–9pm), south of London on the A23 to Purley Way (or British Rail to East Croydon, then take the no. 194 bus), is a south London mecca for water-loving kids. It boasts 6 flumes, a wave pool, a fun pool, and an 180-meter lazy river ride where the current takes you around in inflatable things.

During the summer, the **National Trust** stages a series of events that cater to children. Teddy Bears' Picnics, Family Fun Days, and Living History Days are organized specifically for kids. The Fetes Champetres are open-air evening concerts always organized around a theme; they demand "fancy dress" (that's costume to us). Kids get to dress up, grownups get to listen to music, and there's fireworks at the end. Call the National Trust (☎ 0181/315-1111) for details.

Eating Out

Most restaurants tolerate children (Italian ones are often the most friendly) and some less expensive restaurants will supply children's portions. Some restaurants especially cater to children, like **Chiaroscuro** (24 Coptic St., WC1; ☎ 0171/636-2731; Tube: Tottenham Court Rd.), where, on Sundays, the upstairs dining room is turned into a toy and fun room, and kids under 10 accompanied by an adult eat free from a menu of such yummy fare as grilled chicken, sweet endives with a bowl of chips, and homemade desserts.

Masseralla's, within the famous toystore Hamleys (188 Regent St., W1; ☎ 0171/734-3161; Tube: Oxford Circus), is, as you would expect, geared to the younger set.

Smollensky's Balloon (1 Dover St., W1; ☎ 0171/491-1199; Tube: Green Park) and **Smollensky's on the Strand** (105 Strand, WC2; ☎ 0171/497-2101; Tube: Charing Cross) serve up cocktails for the kids (alcohol-free, of course), such as the Power Ranger (a cranberry- and orange-juice float), the Gladiator (fresh banana, ice cream, coconut, pineapple juice), and the

Crystal Maze (piña colada without the rum). There's live entertainment at both branches between noon and 3pm on weekends.

Hamburger and other fast-food joints are also plentiful; **Pizza Express** and **Tootsies** (for great burgers) have branches all over London. For a familiar sit-down meal, try **TGI Friday's** (6 Bedford St., WC2; ☎ 0171/379-0585; Tube: Covent Garden, Charing Cross).

Theaters & Cinemas

Some London theaters have special performances for children. **The Little Angel Marionette Theatre** in Islington (14 Dagmar Passage, Cross St., N1; ☎ 0171 226-1787) regularly shows puppet plays on weekend afternoons and also on some weekdays during school vacations; performances for small children take place on Saturday and Sunday mornings. **The Lyric Theatre,** in Hammersmith (King St., W6; ☎ 0181/741-2311) shows productions for children Saturdays at 11am and 1pm. **Polka Theatre for Children** (240 The Broadway, SW19; ☎ 0181/543-4888) stages regular plays for children, and has exhibitions linked to past productions. **The Unicorn Theatre** (6–7 Great Newport St., WC2; ☎ 0171/836-3334) also stages plays suitable for children between the ages of 4 and 12 on weekend afternoons and some weekdays during school holidays and "half term," but not in the summer.

During school vacations in particular, major cinemas show a wide selection of children's movies. **The National Film Theatre** (Southbank Arts Centre, SE1; ☎ 0171/928-3232), in particular, shows children's movies on weekend afternoons.

STAYING ACTIVE

FOR UP-TO-DATE INFORMATION ON ALL SPORTS EVENTS and access to public sports centers, contact **Sportsline** (☎ 0171/222-8000) Monday to Friday 10am–6pm.

Biking

When I first arrived in London, I spent a day biking along the **towpath from Putney Bridge to Kew.** Even on weekends, the path isn't crowded, and it's a wonderful way to see the city from a different angle. It's a bit tricky at the start, navigating across the bridge and onto the towpath, but once there, it's a lovely ride along the river. You can reward your hard work with a stroll (or a nap) in the Royal Botanic Gardens at Kew. If you're feeling fit, you can continue on to Hampton Court, but then you have to cycle back (or return on British Rail).

The central London section of the canal towpath used to be a biking zone, but now you have to get off of your bike between Maida Vale and the East End, so don't bother, as you'll be stopped if you're caught cycling within "no cycling" zones. I've yet to be ticketed, but I've gotten a stern warning.

There are also bike paths in **Hyde Park** (but not Kensington Gardens, which is most annoying), **Hampstead Heath** (there are 3 specially laid-out cycle routes), and **Richmond Park.**

If you plan on cycling in London, get yourself a *Cyclist's Route Map* from the **London Cycling Campaign** (3 Stamford St., SE1; ☎ 0171/928-7220), which outlines the best and most scenic routes.

There are a number of bike rental shops in London: **The Mountain Bike and Ski Co.** (18 Gillingham

St., SW1; ☎ 0171/834-8933) offers insurance and a
sturdy U-lock with rental; **On Your Bike** (52–53 Tooley
St., SE1; ☎ 0171/378-6669) has tandem bikes.

Boating

On a clear day, it doesn't get much better than cruising
along **Hyde Park's Serpentine** in a paddleboat. You
can rent one, or a rowboat, from the boathouse on the
north side of the Serpentine from March to October
(☎ 0171/262-3751).

You can also rent rowboats and sailing dinghies in
Regent's Park (☎ 0171/486-4759) as well as on some
stretches of the Thames and in Docklands through the
Royal Victoria Dock Project (Royal Victoria Dock,
Tidal Basin Rd., E16; ☎ 0171/511-2326).

Golf

Many of London's finest golf clubs welcome visitors
who have a handicap certificate from a recognized club.
For more information, contact the **English Golf Union**
(☎ 01116/255-3042). ·

The best access from the City is the **Royal
Blackheath Golf Club** (Court Rd., Eltham, SE9;
☎ 0181/850-1795; contact club pro Ian MacGregor
with a handicap certificate to arrange for a day visit).
The oldest golf club in England, it's only 8 miles from
London Bridge. The 18-hole, par 70 course is set in
parkland. The tricky 18th hole requires a pitch to the
green over a thick clipped hedge.

Famous pros head to the **Royal Mid-Surrey Golf
Club** (Old Deer Park, Richmond-on-Thames, Surrey; ☎ 0181/940-1894; contact club pro David Talbot
with a handicap certificate to arrange for a day visit).
Flanked by Kew Gardens and the River Thames, and
only 8 miles from Hyde Park Corner, these 2 18-hole
courses (pars 70 and 67) are London's most popular.
Many major championships have been played here.

For horticulturists, the **Coombe Hill Gold Club**
(Golf Club Dr., off Coombe Lane W., Kingston, Surrey; ☎ 0181/942-228; contact club in advance with
handicap certificate), is one of the most beautiful. In
early summer, every hole of the 18 hole, par 71 course
is highlighted with rhododendrons.

Springfield Park Golf Club (Burntwood Lane,
SW17; ☎ 0181/871-2468) is a new course, but it has
already become popular. Lessons are available.

Health Clubs

Hotels that don't have their own gym facilities usually either have a relationship with a nearby club or can arrange for you to use a local gym. Below are a few clubs that have a wide range of facilities and offer 1-day memberships.

The Sanctuary (12 Floral St., WC2; ☎ 0171/240-9635), is an exclusive women-only club, with stunning swimming pools and a wide range of treatments available. The therapy pool is accented by arches, a swing, and lush greenery; it's purportedly the most photographed pool in the country. There's also a small restaurant.

Lambton Place Health Club (Lambton Place, Westbourne Grove, W11; ☎ 0171/229-2291) has a nice-size pool and a fully equipped gym with steam room, sauna, aerobics studio, sunbeds, and treatment rooms. This is a low-key club where patrons sport old T-shirts and shorts—you'll find few lycra addicts here. There's also a small restaurant.

The Peak, Hyatt Carlton Tower (2 Cadogan Place, SW1; ☎ 0171/824-7008), has awesome views over Knightsbridge and all the facilities you'd expect, including a Clarins beauty studio, therapy rooms, and steam room. The saunas are even equipped with televisions! There's no swimming pool yet, though one is in the works.

The Savoy Fitness Gallery (The Savoy, The Strand, WC2; ☎ 0171/836-4343) has recently opened up its facilities to nonmembers. With all the amenities of a top-notch club and a stunning rooftop swimming pool, it's ideal for the serious fitness addict as well for those looking for some serious indulgence. Pricey, but a good choice on a rainy day.

With its Roman Bath motif, the **Aquilla Health Club** (11 Thurloe Place, SW7; ☎ 0171/225-0225) is a nice gym offering all the basics, plus aerobics classes and treatments.

Horseback Riding

There are several attractive locations in the royal parks where you can take lessons or saddle up for an accompanied ride. **Ross Nye's Hyde Park Riding Club** (8 Bathurst Mews, W2; ☎ 0171/262-3791) will take you out on Hyde Park's 6 miles of horse trails, including Rotten Row (a corruption of the original name, Route de Roi). Hard hats and riding boots are provided for those without gear. For a more bucolic atmosphere, try **Stag Lodge Stables** (Robin Hood Gate, Richmond Park, SW15; ☎ 0181/974-6066). Their Saturday pony club, the Red Riders, is great for kids.

In-Line Skating

It took awhile to catch on, but they're doing the New York–L.A. thing in London now, with most of the action congregating around Kensington Palace in Kensington Gardens. Lots of lycra and groovy music. You can rent skates at **Road Runner** (Unit 002, Lancaster Road, 253 Portobello Rd., W11; ☎ 0171/792-0584) and **The London Blade Skate Centre** (229 Brompton Rd., SW3; ☎ 0171/581-2039), which is conveniently located near the park.

Jogging

London is a very green city, and, as such, there are quite a few nice jogging routes. One of the best stretches is from Westminster to Notting Hill, taking in the **Royal Parks.** Start at St. James's Park, pass the lovely duck pond and work your way through to Green Park (where you'll get a glimpse of Buckingham Palace), pass under the Hyde Park Corner roundabout via the "subway" (underground walkway), and then zip through Hyde Park along the Serpentine through to Kensington Gardens.

Another green route is the outer circle of **Regent's Park,** which doesn't see too much traffic. Along the way you'll pass some of the grandest residences in London.

My favorite route is along the towpath that borders the **Grand Union Canal.** It's a lot easier to navigate now that it's closed to bicycles. The best stretch is that between Regent's Park and Little Venice. Pick it up at various places along the north side of the park and then follow it south through St. John's Wood to Little Venice. If you're feeling lazy, take one of the canal boat trips, with termini on Blomfield Road for the return trip. The drop-off point is Camden Lock, which has a great market on the weekends.

Swimming

Pools   Major indoor pools with all facilities include **Chelsea Sports Centre** (Chelsea Manor St., SW3; ☎ 0171/352-6985); **Golden Lane Pool** (Golden Lane, EC1; ☎ 0171/250-1464); **Fulham Pools** (Normand

Park, Lillie Rd., SW6; ☎ 0171/385-7628); and **Marshall Street Baths** (14–15 Marshall St., W1; ☎0171/287-1022).

Swimming Holes   The **Serpentine Lido** (Hyde Park, W2; ☎ 0171/298-2110; open May–Sept) on the south side of the pond, is about as close to a beach as you can get in central London. There are changing facilities, and the swimming section is chlorinated. It was closed for renovation at press time, but should have reopened by the time you read this.

Other centrally located swimming holes are the **Hampstead Ponds** (☎ 0171/435-2366; open daily May–Sept 10am–dusk). There are 3 bathing ponds on the heath: 1 mixed (at East Heath Rd., NW3), 1 for men only and 1 for women only (both at Millfield Lane, N6); swimming at all 3 is free. There's a small changing hut with shower for the women. The pools are all hidden by trees—you can almost imagine that you're in the country—and nudity has been known to occur. All the ponds are somewhat murky, but authorities claim they're sanitary.

Tennis

Two nice venues which open to the public are: **Regent's Park Tennis** (Outer Circle, Regent's Park, NW1; ☎ 0171/724-0643), which has outdoor courts (1 floodlit) open every day of the year except Christmas; and **Holland Park** (Holland Park, W8; ☎ 0171/602-2226), with 6 outdoor courts (priority is given to local residents; day visitors must book in person).

Yoga, Aerobics & Dance

Yoga is big in London, and the place where it's all happening is **The Life Centre** (15 Edge St., W8; ☎ 0171/221-4602). All levels of classes are offered, including the 2-hour Power Yoga class, from which participants are known to walk out in tears. You can take daily dance classes, from American Funk to classical ballet, at the **Pineapple Dance Studio** (7 Langley St., WC2; ☎0171/836-4004). In west London is **Pineapple Kensington** (38–42 Harrington Rd., SW7; ☎ 0171/581-0466). A small membership fee is required at both locations, in addition to class fees.

Another well-respected studio is **Danceworks** (16 Balderton St., W1; ☎ 0171/629-6183). In addition to dance classes, a wide range of fitness classes, from "butt attack" to "boxercise," are offered.

Beauty Treatments

For a shave and cut and more, including facial, massage, waxing (for the hairy shoulder syndrome), men should check out the **Barber Shop,** an art-deco delight in the basement of Harrods (SW1; ☎ 0171/589-1564). The **Dorchester Spa** (Dorchester Hotel, Park Lane, W1; ☎ 0171/495-7335) offers a half-day of male beauty treatments, including a fitness assessment, massage, facial, manicure, and Panthermal bath.

For women, the art form of pampering is elevated to great heights at the **Sanctuary** (see "Health Clubs," above), where no fewer than 9 different types of facials are available. If you just can't bear the thought of skipping the weekly manicure, relief can be had at the super-expensive **SuperNail,** (101 Crawford St., W1; ☎ 0171/723-1163), where Joan Collins is said to be a client. For a cheaper deal, pop into **Beauty Secrets** (110–112 King's Road, SW3; ☎ 0171/823-6276).

The best hair colorist in town is, without a doubt, **Jo Hansford** (19 Mount St., W1; ☎0171/495-7774). Color so subtle, your own mother wouldn't know it.

The stylist everyone's talking about is **Nicky Clarke** (130 Mount St., W1; ☎ 0171/491-4700). His A-list of clients makes booking an appointment weeks in advance a necessity.

Spectator Sports

Cricket   This is the most baffling sport to the newcomer, but it's an integral part of the English summer; from April to September, club matches are played all over London, in parks and on greens, mainly on Saturday and Sunday afternoons. First-class professional matches are played at the Middlesex club at **Lord's** (St. John's Wood Rd., NW8; ☎ 0171/289-1611) and at the Surrey club at **The Oval** (Kennington, SE11; ☎ 0171/735-4911). Both stage a yearly international test match (Lords in June, The Oval in Aug or Sept).

Football (Soccer)   Football matches are generally played on Saturday afternoons from August through April, with some matches on Sunday afternoons and weekday evenings. The **FA Cup Final,** the most important single match of the football season, is played in April or May at **Wembley Stadium,** which is also the scene of England's international matches, usually played on Wednesday evenings. Consult listings magazines such as *Time Out* for details and locations of club matches.

Cricket Player in Action

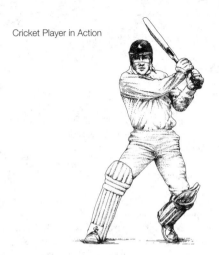

Horse Racing   There are many large racecourses within easy reach of London: to the west are **Ascot** and **Newbury;** to the southwest, **Sandown, Epsom,** and **Kempton Park.** There are long overlaps between the summer (flat) and the winter (jumping) seasons. No races are held on Sunday.

The best-known annual races, which grip the nation, are the **Grand National,** held at Aintree near Liverpool in late March, and the **Derby** at Epsom, Surrey, in early June. All races are well covered in the daily newspapers, and it's possible to bet from off-track betting shops.

Rowing   For rowing events, see "Calendar of Events" in "Basics," or contact the **Amateur Rowing Association** (6 Lower Mall, W6; ☎ 0181/748-3632).

Rugby   **Rugby Union,** a 15-a-side sport with certain affinities to American football, restricts its players to amateur status in the same way that track-and-field does. Matches are played on Saturday afternoons from September to April. International and major games take place at the sport's headquarters at Twickenham. Consult listings magazines such as *Time Out* for details and locations of club matches.

SHOPPING

S HOPPING IN LONDON IS A WONDERFUL PROCESS OF DIS-
covery. Like any cosmopolitan city, it has all the
major designer names and a bevy of glittering department stores. But it's the small boutiques or the bargains
picked up while strolling the street markets that the
serious shopper will find most satisfying. For the first-
time visitor, Harrod's is a must, but don't get stuck there;
it's expensive, filled with tourists, and a bit dowdy in
the fashion department. Go if you must, but then move on.

You'll find that certain types of stores tend to cluster together: books in the Charing Cross area, hi-tech
around Tottenham Court Road, big designer names on
Bond and Sloane streets. Shops don't stay open as late
as in some other countries: Most shops are open Monday to Saturday 9am–5:30pm, with "late-night" shopping once a week. The Chelsea and Knightsbridge
areas stay open until 7pm on Wednesday, and Oxford
Street until 8pm on Thursday. Some shops in Bond
Street and a few others in the West End close on Saturday. In response to the new Sunday Trading laws passed
in 1995, stores have been expanding their hours to include Sundays; it's slowly beginning to take hold, but
check before you go.

Prices are not generally negotiable, although bar-
gaining is acceptable in some street markets. In most
shops, all major credit and charge cards are accepted.
VAT The Value Added Tax (VAT) is a hefty $17^1/2$% levied on most goods and services, so do take the time
(and the hassle) to go through the refund process. For
purchases over £75, you can request a VAT refund form
at all the major department stores and at many of the
established smaller shops and boutiques. It's pretty simple
once you get the hang of it.

At purchase, ask for a VAT form; you'll be required
to show your passport. Make sure they include the

Size Conversion Chart

Women's Clothing

American	8	10	12	14	16	18
Continental	38	40	42	44	46	48
British	10	12	14	16	18	20

Women's Shoes

American	5	6	7	8	9	10
Continental	36	37	38	39	40	41
British	4	5	6	7	8	9

Children's Clothing

American	3	4	5	6	6X
Continental	98	104	110	116	122
British	18	20	22	24	26

Children's Shoes

American	8	9	10	11	12	13	1	2	3
Continental	24	25	27	28	29	30	32	33	34
British	7	8	9	10	11	12	13	1	2

Men's Suits

American	34	36	38	40	42	44	46	48
Continental	44	46	48	50	52	54	56	58
British	34	36	38	40	42	44	46	48

Men's Shirts

American	14½	15	15½	16	16½	17	17½	18
Continental	37	38	39	41	42	43	44	45
British	14½	15	15½	16	16½	17	17½	18

Men's Shoes

American	7	8	9	10	11	12	13
Continental	39½	41	42	43	44½	46	47
British	6	7	8	9	10	11	12

pre-addressed envelope. Fill out the customer information on the form and hold onto it until you pass through customs at the airport. Just past customs, there's a VAT refund counter; there will be long lines, so do allow some extra time. Oftentimes, customs will request to see the items, so if possible, pack such items in your carry-on. The form will then be forwarded on to the store, which will then refund you the VAT. You can specify how you want to receive the refund; the most convenient method is to have it credited to your charge card. This can be a lengthy process—have patience. Alternatively, the store can ship the goods directly to your home, but you'll still have to wait for the refund. You'll need to have your form certified at customs when you get home, after which you mail it to the store, which then refunds your money.

Shopping Districts & Streets

These neighborhoods form a jigsaw stretching 5 or 6 miles across the center of London, from Barnes in the west to Petticoat Lane in the east. Each of them is worth half a day of your time, and every one leads to another.

Oxford Street, W1

This is the main shopping thoroughfare, and the most democratic. Oxford Street runs from west to east (assuming that you see the most traditional end first); the tone continues down Regent Street. It feels like a giant version of the main street of every town in Britain. The stretch from **Marble Arch** to **Oxford Circus** is the most interesting, lined with department stores, including **Selfridges** and the flagship **Marks and Spencer.** For more fashionable goods, don't miss the upmarket enclaves of **South Molton Street** just to the south, and **St. Christopher's Place,** (entered through a tiny alleyway just past James St. on the north side). Both of these streets are dominated by the stylish "high street" outlets, such as **Jigsaw, Whistles,** and **Hobbs.**

Notting Hill Gate, W11

Most famous for the Saturday antique market that stretches along **Portobello Road,** the Notting Hill Gate area caters to a very trendy and discerning crowd. During the week, Portobello Road is taken over by a green market, where locals haggle over fruit and vegetables. Along Westbourne Grove and Ledbury Road are antique and funky designer shops like **Nick Ashley,** for urban motorcycle wear, and **Dinny Hall,** for jewelry. There are also quite a few specialty bookshops, such as **Books for Cooks** and the **Traveller's Bookshop,** as well as two of the best prepared food shops in town. And lots of cafes provide sustenance for the serious shopper. Suddenly trendy Goldborne Road, with a few antique shops and boutiques, is home to a small Portuguese community.

Knightsbridge, SW1

Most of the big designer names have stores along Sloane Street and Beauchamp Place, including **Prada, Giorgio Armani, Joseph,** and **Valentino.** And, of course, there's **Harrod's,** a London institution. Expect high prices and lots of snooty attitude.

South Kensington, SW3

Great for fashion, accessories, and housewares, the best shopping in this neighborhood is along the north bit of Fulham Road leading to Brompton Road and the boutique enclave of Walton Street. The hub of this area is Sir Terence Conran's flagship store, **Conran's.** The younger designer names, once they've made it, tend to set up shop here.

Chelsea, SW3

The spine of this shopping area is the King's Road; start from Sloane Square and work your way down. You'll pass most of the high street chains, boutiques, and quite a few antique shops. Along the way there'll be plenty of cafes and restaurants. Chelsea Green, centered around Cale Street and Jubilee Place just north of the King's Road, is a quaint cluster of small boutiques that's certainly worth a stop.

Victoria, Belgravia, Pimlico, SW1

Recently, a spate of clothing and accessory shops have opened along Elisabeth Street. You'll find milliner extraordinaire **Philip Treacy** here, as well as some very fine jewelry shops. Pimlico Road is known for high quality antiques.

Mayfair, W1

Last year, Bond Street went through an extraordinary transformation. It has always been one of the blue-chip areas for shopping, but it was looking a bit dowdy in recent years. Look again—not only have designers such as **Donna Karan, Giorgio Armani,** and **Joan and David** opened up grand retail spaces here, but some of the smaller, classic English names have also moved in: **Sotheby's** and the art galleries are here, as is **Charbonnel et Walker** for great chocolate truffles. The area is also known for custom tailoring along Savile Row and classic English country attire.

St. James's, W1

For the well-dressed man, a shopping spree in St. James's is de rigueur. He'll be able to fulfill all his needs along

Jermyn Street, whether he's a "Master of the Universe" type (**Turnbull and Asser**) or a young Turk hoping to make a good impression (**Hackett's**). To finish off the look, there's a branch of **Davidoff's,** where he can pick up some Cuban cigars (not for import into the U.S., of course).

Farther Afield

Hampstead and **Primrose Hill** both offer a wide variety of shops, from fashion to housewares. Wander along the villagey "high streets" lined with trendy boutiques. **Islington** is also good for unique boutiques; Upper Street is the spine of the community, but the interesting shops, such as **The Old Tool Chest** and **Plasterworks,** are on Cross Street. You can combine a shopping trip here with a visit to the famous **Camden Passage.**

For antiques, the charming village of **Barnes,** situated along the Thames, is a nice diversion. The streets are brimming with inspiration.

Street Markets

London has 50 or 60 street markets, and it's here that the town best demonstrates its wit, wisdom, and elusive code. If you demonstrate your own, you might knock prices down. The famous ones are still fun, but see some of the others, too. No credit cards are accepted, only English checks, so take cash.

Portobello Road

W11. Mon–Sat.

The Saturday antique market is especially well known for its silver. It's easy to find and to explore, since it's basically 1 street, but it stretches for more than a mile. Start by taking the underground to Notting Hill Gate, and walk via Pembridge Road, following the crowd. Antiques and junk come first, then freaky shops, and finally food, at the north end. If you venture a bit further, you'll come to Goldborne Road; on Saturdays, it becomes an extension of Portobello, filled with stalls selling everything from junk to furniture. Try **Jimmy Beez** for lunch.

Petticoat Lane

Middlesex Street and Brick Lane, E1. Sun.

This East End junk market is only one part of a maze of street trade where the patois embraces Cockney slang, Yiddish, and Bengali. Serious bargain-hunters start at the improbable hour of 4am with the **Cheshire Street**

(E2) and **Brick Lane** (E1) areas, where the action subsides well before 9am. The more touristy **Petticoat Lane** itself (it's real name is actually Middlesex St.) is in full swing by then, and impossibly crowded by 11am. Take your lunch on the road, grabbing a bagel at the **Brick Lane Beigel Bake.** The nearest underground stations are Liverpool Street and Aldgate East.

Camden Passage
N1. Wed, Thurs, Sat.
Art deco is something of a theme here, especially in the Athenai Arcade. Come Wednesday and Saturday for good-quality antiques; Thursday for books, prints, and drawings. **Granita** is nice for lunch, or try the **Slug and Lettuce** for pub fare. Take the tube to Angel and walk up Islington High Street.

Bermondsey
New Caledonian, Long Lane and Tower Bridge Road, SE1. Fri.
This is the insiders' antique market, where the cognoscenti hunt by flashlight at 5am, grab their purchases by 8:30am (at the latest), then retire for breakfast at **Rose's Diner** on Bermondsey Street. As if that weren't a sufficiently daunting venture, the market is also hard to find; thus it is that Bermondsey has remained a market for the seriously interested. Go by underground to London Bridge, and walk down Bermondsey Street.

Camden Lock
Camden High Street/Chalk Farm Road, NW1. Sat–Sun.
This weekend market has an entertaining mix of junk and attractions, including books, musical instruments, crafts, clothing, jewelry, and snacks. It stretches for a mile from the Chalk Farm tube station. The main market is by Regent's Canal.

Columbia Road Market
E2. Sun (until 12:30pm).
This is a gardener's paradise. Take the tube to Old Street Station and walk along Old Street until you hit Columbia Road. From here, work your way through the hordes, all drawn by the well-priced stalls of cut flowers and trays of plants. There's a small cafe on Ezra Street that serves coffee and pastries.

Greenwich Antique Market,
Greenwich High Road, SE10. Summer weekends.
The Greenwich market, devoted to antiques, books, and bric-a-brac, has yet to develop the jaded atmosphere

of Camden or Portobello. **Greenwich Covered Crafts Market** is in nearby College Approach on Saturday and Sunday.

Auctions

Sotheby's
34–35 New Bond St., W1. ☎ 0171/493-8080. Tube: Bond St.

This is the big one. Regular sales of Edwardian, Victorian, and modern 20thC furniture, rugs, carpets, porcelain, glass, prints, and works of art. The art sales take place in late June and late November. Regular viewings.

Christie's
8 King St., London SW1. ☎ 0171/839-9060. Tube: Green Park.
Also at 85 Old Brompton Rd., SW7. ☎ 0171/581-7611. Tube: South Kensington.

Both outlets of the renowned auction house hold regular sales of antique furniture, jewelry, and works of art. The South Kensington Branch tends to concentrate on textiles and ceramics. Regular viewings.

Bonham's
Montpelier St., SW7. ☎ 0171/584-9161. Tube: Knightsbridge. Also at 65–69 Lot's Rd., SW10. Tube: Sloane Sq.

Regular sales feature silver, carpets, furniture, and works of art. Lot's Road auctions take place on Tuesday, with viewings on Sunday and Monday.

Lots Road Galleries
71 Lots Rd., SW10. ☎ 0171/351-7771. Tube: Sloane Sq.

Two sales every Monday of contemporary and antique household effects. Viewings held Friday and Sunday prior to sale.

Department Stores

Many of the bigger and middle-range department stores are centered around Oxford Street. I've outlined below those that offer something special.

Harrod's
Knightsbridge, SW1. ☎ 0171/730-1234. Tube: Knightsbridge.

This is the granddaddy of British retail, boasting 25 acres of selling space. Harrod's excels in home accessories; the china and glassware departments are still cutting edge, and the food hall is a wonderful sensory experience. Kids—and grownups, too—go gaga in the toy department, and there's a great magazine department. The dress code is a bit off-putting: Ripped jeans are frowned upon, and you'll be stopped at the

Harrod's

door if you're sporting a knapsack (it must be carried in the hand, even if it's a Prada). Every July, Harrod's stages its famous sale, an event that attracts more than 300,000 shopaholics on the 1st day. When you're shopped out, you can't do better than to stop for a glass of champagne and a half-dozen oysters at the raw bar.

Harvey Nichols

109–125 Knightsbridge, SW1. ☎ 0171/235-5000. Tube: Knightsbridge.

Harvey Nicks (as it's often called) has quickly made a name for itself for its list of trendy designers; it does especially well in the young European designer section, where some of the hottest names in British fashion make their debut. One of my favorite sections is the Nathalie Hambro collection of household ornament and tableware, on the 5th floor. In 1993, an awesome designer food hall was established; this is where trendy Knightsbridgers do their local grocery shopping, and then stop for a bite at the cappuccino bar—or, if they're lucky, a windowside seat in the brasserie.

Liberty

Regent St., W1. ☎ 0171/734-1234. Tube: Oxford Circus.

Something's been happening at Liberty, and you need only wander up to the women's fashion floor to notice. The store is still the sprawling Tudor emporium known for its famous Liberty prints, but there's a younger, trendier feeling in the air. Last year, Liberty launched a new line of bed linens and scarves that are to die for—

devore silks, blue and white cottons. The houseware department is a must for tableware addicts.

Marks & Spencer
458 Oxford St., W1. ☎ 0171/935-7954. Tube: Marble Arch.

While this establishment has long been known as the place where the British shop for their underwear (or knickers, as they say), take another look: M&S has recently hired an impressive list of consultants, and the fashion department, while not exciting, is now offering good design at good value. Many Londoners are now buying their basics here, which are well-made and unfussy, especially the knitwear. Increasingly, M&S is becoming known for its food department, where tired workers can pick up fabulous curries and puddings—just heat and serve.

Fortnum & Mason
181 Piccadilly, W1. ☎ 0171/734-8040. Tube: Piccadilly Circus.

The ground-floor food hall is geared toward the tourist, with teas, jams, shortbread, and condiments all beautifully packaged and great for gifts. The fashion is not very exciting, and the atmosphere is very stuffy—terribly, terribly British. Tea here is a classic London experience.

Browns
23–27 S. Molton St., W1. ☎ 0171/491-7833. Tube: Bond St.

Very high fashion at equally high prices. All the big designer names are here, as well as up-and-coming talents. Beautiful handbags by Bill Amberg and a nice collection of jewelry are on display.

Goods A to Z
Antiques

London is an antique maven's dream. Whether you're furnishing a mansion or a studio, there's plenty to choose from. The better antique shops are centered around Pimlico, Kensington Church Street, King's Road, and Barnes, but if you trust your eye and enjoy seeking out finds, don't neglect the markets at Bermondsey or Portobello Road. There are also the "malls" on King's Road: The 2 best ones are **Antiquarius** (131–141 King's Rd., SW3; Tube: Sloane Sq.), an antiques arcade with over 150 stalls selling everything from secondhand antiques to books; and **Chelsea Antiques Market** (245A–253 King's Rd., SW3; Tube: Sloane Sq.), but don't expect to find too many bargains.

Mallet and Son (140 New Bond St., W1; Tube: Bond St.) is the best for the finest English furniture, but the high quality is matched by the prices. **Chandor and Edwards** (493B King's Rd., SW6; entrance around the corner; Tube: Sloane Sq.) makes weekly trips to the Continent, filling up their truck with finds from French flea markets. Antique dealers and collectors alike tend to gather around the shop on Mondays hoping to find fresh goods. Further down the road is **Guinevere** (574–580 Kings Rd., SW6; Tube: Fulham Broadway), a maze of rooms chock full of well-picked antiques and decorative bits, all beautifully displayed.

For Biedermeier and Empire furniture, check out **Rupert Cavendish Antiques** (610 King's Rd., SW6; Tube: Fulham Broadway). **George Sherlock** (588 King's Rd., SW6; Tube: Fulham Broadway) sells sofas and armchairs made "in the old Victorian fashion." **The Old Tool Chest** (41 Cross St., N1; Tube: Angel) stocks "ancient tools for all trades." **Jones** (194 Westbourne Grove, W11; Tube: Notting Hill Gate) has beautiful original and decorative lighting all in good working order; sconces and gilt chandeliers hang from every inch of space. For both antique and modern silver, it's fascinating to explore the **London Silver Vaults** (53 Chancery Lane, WC2; Tube: Chancery Lane).

Farther afield is the double-fronted **Tobias and the Angel** (68 White Hart Lane, SW13; British Rail: Barnes) in Barnes. This is the stuff of stylists' dreams: bundles of wooden spoons tied with ribbon; baskets edged with rosebuds; Victorian nightshirts; cut-glass cheese-domes. Angel has quite an eye.

Art

London has no real gallery center. There's a cluster of galleries around the Cork Street area, but many of the more cutting edge dealers are a bit farther afield. Check out *Time Out, Galleries* (a guide available at most exhibition spaces), or *Art Monthly* for current listings.

Old Masters Galleries

London's Old Masters paintings galleries are some of the best in the world. Clustered around Bond Street (Tube: Green Park), they can be somewhat forbidding; the casual gallery-goer might be a bit put-off. Don't be—if an exhibition is on view, you're free to enter. The best shows tend to be around auction time (see "Calendar of Events" in "Basics"), when the Big Cheese collectors and dealers come to town. Long-established names with good reputations include **Wildenstein & Co.** (147 New Bond St., W1); **Agnew's** (43 Old Bond St. and 3 Albemarle St., W1); **Colnaghi** (14 Old Bond St., W1); **Richard L. Feigen & Co**. (6 Ryder St., SW1); **Harari & Johns** (12 Duke St., SW1).

Contemporary Galleries

There's no real contemporary-arts enclave in London, but artists' studios tend to be clustered around Bermondsey and the Oval, particularly the smaller galleries and cooperative studios.

Many people criticize **Anthony d'Offay** (Dering St., W1; Tube: Oxford St.) for merely recycling New York exhibitions, but his massive space is an impressive place to see the big names, from Richard Hamilton to Kiki Smith. **Marlborough** (Albemarle St., W1; Tube: Green Park) is a big-name contemporary dealer showing, among others, Lucien Freud. Other established dealers in the area include **Annely Juda Fine Art** (23 Dering St., W1; Tube: Bond St.); **Bernard Jacobson Gallery** (14a Clifford St., W1; Tube: Green Park); **Gimpel Fils** (30 Davies St., W1; Tube: Bond St.); **Waddington Galleries** (11 Cork St., W1; Tube: Green Park); **Victoria Miro** (21 Cork St., W1; Tube: Green Park); and, off the beaten track but 1st-rate, is **Lisson Gallery** (52–54 Bell St., NW1; Tube: Edgware Rd.).

Of the smaller independent dealers, look for **Flowers East** (199 Richmond Rd., E8; Tube: Bethnal Green); **Frith Street Gallery** (60 Frith St., W1; Tube: Tottenham Court Rd.); **Jibby Beane** (Flat 6, 143–145 Gloucester Terrace, W2; by appointment only, ☎ 0171/723-5531; Tube: Lancaster Gate), who has turned her reception room into one of the best spaces for recent graduates to show their work; **Karsten Schubert** (41–42 Foley St., W1; Tube: Oxford Circus); a few doors down, **Laure Genillard** (38A Foley St., W1; Tube: Oxford Circus); and the infamous Jay Jopling's space, **White Cube** (44 Duke St., W1; Tube: Green Park), where Damien Hirst makes trouble.

Photography

The premier space for photography is the **Photographer's Gallery** (5 and 8 Great Newport St., WC2; Tube: Leicester Square), a well-established multistory gallery with exhibition spaces, a cafe, and a bookstore. The best section is the viewing room, where potential buyers can sort through the vast collection.

Another blue-chip photography gallery is **Hamilton's Gallery** (13 Carlos Place, W1; Tube:

Bond St.), where the more established names exhibit; monthly shows feature such artists as Avedon and Snowdon.

A smaller, but, to my mind, more interesting gallery is **Michael Hoppen Photography** (3 Jubilee Place, SW3; Tube: Sloane Sq.). Hoppen stocks not only the big contemporary names, but a wide range of images from the early days of the medium to the present, all beautifully mounted in unique frames.

Books

The street for the bibliophile is Charing Cross Road, WC2 (Tube: Tottenham Court Rd.), where the numerous shops include **Foyle's** (one of the world's biggest bookstores) at no. 119, **Waterstone's** next door, and **Books Etc.,** with its bargain basement, across the street. Hours pass quickly in the secondhand bookstores of fascinating alleys like Cecil Court; of particular interest is **Zwemmer** at no. 80 (Tube: Leicester Sq.) for art, architecture, and cinema reading. Recently opened is London's first music bookshop, **Helter Skelter** (4 Denmark St., WC2; Tube: Tottenham Court Rd.), where, over coffee, music buffs can browse through the recent music papers.

Away from Charing Cross Road, the most comprehensive selection is found at **Dillon's** (82 Gower St.; Tube: Euston Sq.). **Hatchards** (187 Piccadilly, W1; Tube: Piccadilly Circus) is a pleasant, well-stocked general bookstore. The **Pan Bookshop** (158 Fulham Rd., SW3; Tube: South Kensington) is useful for hardbacks as well as paperbacks, and stays open until the late hour of 9:30pm daily. **John Sandoe** (10 Blacklands Terrace, SW3; Tube: Sloane Sq.) is my idea of a perfect bookshop; the browsing is sublime, and the staff regularly comes up with intelligent recommendations.

Among travel bookstores, **Daunt Books** (83 Marylebone High St., W1l; Tube: Baker St.) sells literary works about each destination alongside the guidebooks; **Stanfords Map and Travel Bookshop** (12 Long Acre, WC2; Tube: Covent Garden) is excellent for maps and travel guides; and the **Travel Bookshop** (13 Blenheim Crescent, W11; Tube: Notting Hill Gate) also specializes in far-flung places.

For foodies, there's **Books for Cooks** (4 Blenheim Crescent, W11; Tube: Notting Hill Gate). The excellent and well-laid-out **Economists' Bookshop** (Clare Market, Portugal St., W1; Tube: Holborn) specializes in economics and the social sciences. For the long flight ahead, **The Talking Book Shop** (11 Wigmore St., W1; Tube: Bond St.) is devoted to books on tape, which you can pop into the Walkman.

China

For generations, **Thomas Goode** (19 South Audley St., W1; Tube: Green Park) has been the china stockist to European royal families. You can choose from one of their own designs or commission a special service inspired by designs in their massive archive. Another royal stockist is **Asprey** (165 New Bond St., W1; Tube: Green Park); with three royal warrants, they have to be good.

If you make it to Barnes, **The Dining Room** (62–64 White Hart Lane; British Rail: Barnes) has really quirky and beautiful old china.

Clothing
Men's Fashions
In Savile Row, W1 (Tube: Piccadilly Circus), the appositively named **H. Huntsman and Sons** (no. 11), famous for its riding clothes, have been tailors to royalty for more than a hundred years and are very expensive. Other renowned names include **Gieves & Hawkes** (no. 1), and **Anderson & Sheppard** (no. 30). **James & James** (11 Old Burlington St., W1; Tube: Oxford Circus) has gone hi-tech, using computers to design suits and lasers to cut cloth. At half the price of the custom tailoring service they offer, these come with hand-sewn custom-style James & James labels. If you always dreamed of owning a handmade suit, but always bought off-the-rack, this could be the next best thing.

On Jermyn Street, W1, you'll find traditional menswear at **Hackett's** (no. 87; Tube: Piccadilly), which sells everything the gentleman needs. Top-quality custom-made shirts are available from **Turnbull and Asser** (nos. 69, 71, and 72; Tube: Green Park). Remember the "Master of the Universe" in *Bonfire of the Vanities?* He got his shirts here. Or try **Harvie and Hudson** (nos. 77 and 97; Tube: Green Park). For exquisite off-the-rack suits and a nice range of woven silk ties, head to **Thomas Pink** (no. 86; Tube: Green Park).

Since 1750, **Swaine Adeney Brigg** (10 Old Bond St., W1; Tube: Green Park) has been providing Londoners with the best walking sticks, leather goods, and "essential accessories." Whether you're searching for a classic hip flask or a hand-stitched ostrich-handled umbrella, you'll find it here. For outerwear, the plaid-lined raincoats and fine cashmere coats that are the hallmarks of **Burberrys** (18–22 Haymarket, SW1; Tube: Piccadilly Circus), will always be classics.

The much publicized new wave of British tailoring is being practiced by people such as **Timothy Everest** (32 Elder St., E1; Tube: Liverpool St.) and **Richard James** (37a Savile Row, W1; Tube: Green Park). Floral Street would be more aptly named **Paul Smith** Street; known for his quirky men's clothing, Smith has 3 shops here. Or check out his discount shop, the end of the line for his fashions (23 Avery Row, W1; Tube: Bond St.). **The Library** (268 Brompton Rd., SW3; Tube: South Kensington) combines art and fashion; names such as Nigel Curtiss (ex-çomme des Garcons) and Antonio Miro share space with a wonderful collection of art tomes. **Nick Ashley** (son of the late Laura Ashley) is doing a serious rebellion act: His shop (57 Ledbury Rd., W11; Tube: Notting Hill Gate) sells rugged action wear for the urban biker (or biker-ish).

For street fashions, the club set hang out in **Ad Hoc/ Boy** (10–1 Moor St., W1; Tube: Tottenham Court Rd.), with lots of spandex and a piercing parlor downstairs. For instant attitude, try the **Duffer of St. George** (27 D'Arblay St., W1; Tube: Oxford St.), where you can fit yourself out in the latest trends.

For the complete *Four Weddings and a Funeral* look, head to **Favourbrook** (19–21 Piccadilly Arcade, SW1; Tube: Piccadilly Circus), where jackets, frockcoats, and waistcoats are created from imaginative and rich fabrics. There's a beautiful line of womenswear as well.

Women's Fashions

Homegrown talent has recently been getting much attention from the fashion press. Besides the well-established names like **Vivienne Westwood** (6 Davies St., W1; Tube: Bond St.), **Katherine Hamnett** (20 Sloane St., SW1; Tube: Knightsbridge), **Rifat Ozbek** (available at Brown's), and **John Galliano** (Liberty, Harvey Nichols), young upstarts such as **Alexander McQueen** and **Pearce Fionda** are suddenly hot; you can find their styles at Harvey Nichols, Liberty, **Pellicano** (63 South Molton St., W1; Tube: Bond St.), and Brown's. **World's End** (430 King's Rd., SW10; Tube: Sloane Sq.) is **Vivienne Westwood's** outlet for the younger set; expect lots of corsets and platform shoes. Westwood also has a sale shop (40–41 Conduit St., W1; Tube: Oxford Circus).

The budding talents of tomorrow often set up stalls in the fashion malls around town such as **Hyper Hyper**

(26–40 Kensington High St., W8; Tube: High Street Kensington). Streetwear is available at **Ad Hoc** (38a Kensington High St., W8; Tube: High Street Kensington); the cramped premises specialize in kinky fabrics like rubber and lycra.

Of the "high street" shops, one of the best is **Jigsaw** (main branch: 124–126 King's Rd., SW3; Tube: Sloane Sq.), carrying classic designs with a contemporary edge. **Whistle's** (27 Sloane Sq., SW1; Tube: Sloane Sq.) is a notch upscale, featuring many of the up-and-coming young designers, such as **Sonja Nuttal.**

Joseph Ettedgui's **Joseph** (main branch: 130 Draycott Ave., SW3; Tube: South Kensington) has many outlets around town; you'll find cutting-edge clothes in well-designed spaces. Ditto for **Space NK** (Thomas Neal's Centre, Earlham St., WC2; Tube: Covent Garden).

Egg (36 Kinnerton St., SW1; Tube: Hyde Park Corner) is a perfect shop for the aesthete. Clothing and textiles are handmade in a workshop in India; the clothes tend toward an Issey Miyake–ish style. Three young London-based designers have teamed up to open one of the hottest shops in London. **Selina Blow** does elegant Nehru jackets, **Harriet Anstruther** does diaphanous scarves, and **Lulu Guinness** is in charge of handbags (42 Elizabeth St., SW1; Tube: Sloane Sq.).

Of the small Notting Hill boutiques, **Graham & Green** (4, 7, and 10 Elgin Crescent, W11) stands out. While nos. 4 and 7 are filled with beautiful ethnic furnishings, no. 10 sells frocks and accessories by young designers like Lolita Lempicka, Betty Jackson, and John Rocha. Velvet cutwork scarves and sumptuous silk dressing gowns are the trademark of designer **Georgina von Etzdorf** (50 Burlington Arcade, W1; Tube: Green Park).

For classic English style, **Margaret Howell** (24 Brook St., W1; Tube: Bond St.) is my favorite. Trained as a menswear designer, Howell's trousers cut from beautiful cloth are just so right. **Droopy & Browns** (99 St. Martins Lane, W1; Tube: Leicester Sq.) is where a certain type of artsy woman who fancies herself a misplaced member of the Bloomsbury circle might shop. The clothes are exquisitely tailored with a distinctly Edwardian angle, from Thai silks, wool jersey, and quality tweeds. Velvet-collar fitted jackets and Princess-lined frocks are the predominant models.

Other homegrown talents that deserve any fashion aficionado's attention are: **Tomasz Starzewski** (15–17 Pont St., SW1; Tube: Sloane Sq.); **Caroline Charles** (170 New Bond St., W1; Tube: Green Park);

Amanda Wakely (80 Fulham Rd., SW3; Tube: South Kensington); **Katherine Hamnett**, once the bad girl of British fashion, now part of the establishment (20 Sloane St., SW1; Tube: Knightsbridge); **Jasper Conran,** Sir Terence's son, known for his subtly elegant designs (Harvey Nichols, Harrod's, and Space NK), recently sported by the Queen's niece at her wedding; and **Nicole Fahri** (158 New Bond St., W1; Tube: Green Park).

Lingerie seekers will not want to miss **Agent Provacateur** (6 Broadwick St., W1; Tube: Oxford Circus); you'll find designer knickers by such names as Chantal Thomas and Vivienne Westwood in this funky Soho shop. **Janet Reger** (2 Beauchamp Place, SW3; Tube: Knightsbridge) specializes in the best for the boudoir—pure silk camisoles and glamorous, wildly expensive pajamas.

London is a great shopping source for weddings. The budget minded will be glad to find **The Wedding Shop** (171 Fulham Rd., SW3; Tube: South Kensington), where once-worn designer dresses by the likes of Anouska Hempel and Catherine Walker are offered at a fraction of the original price.

Eyeglasses
Naomi and Christy wear them; so does Princess Di. **Cutler & Gross** (16 Knightsbridge Green, SW1; Tube: Knightsbridge) shades and specs are the trendiest eyewear in town.

Food & Wine
Any of these specialty food shops have the makings for an inspired picnic, perfect for any of the outdoor concerts that take place throughout the summer:

Part of the tradition of Soho, **Lina Stores** (18 Brewer St., W1; Tube: Piccadilly Circus) is packed with the best Italian food; there's a good choice of salamis, cheeses, and gossip. Not far away is **Neal's Yard Dairy** (17 Shorts Gardens, WC2; Tube: Covent Garden), where cheese is serious business and the odors are heavenly. **Carluccio Food Shop** (28 Neal St., WC2; Tube: Covent Garden) is another olfactory treat: The kitchen downstairs produces delicious Italian dishes that go mighty well with the fresh baked breads.

Berry Brothers & Rudd (3 St. James's St., W1; Tube: Green Park) might not look like much from the outside, but underneath the small shop are famously vast cellars that extend beneath St. James's Street.

Notting Hill Gate area residents are privileged to have two of the best food shops in London. Portobello Road punters line up at **Mr. Christian's** (11 Elgin Crescent, W11; Tube: Notting Hill Gate) every Saturday; he's famous for his fresh bread, 35 different salamis, and 160 cheeses. Otherwise, it's got to be **Tom's** (226 Westbourne Grove, W11; Tube: Notting Hill Gate), which does a brisk business in focaccia sandwiches.

And while Butler's Wharf residents might not have a convenient basic supermarket, they're not deprived of the finer things in life. **Conran's Gastrodome** (Butler's Wharf Building, Shad Thames, SE1; Tube: London Bridge) has an oil-and-spice shop, a dapper delicatessen, and a smoked fish and crustacea outlet.

Finally, to finish off the meal, my vote for best chocolates goes to **Charbonnel et Walker** (28 Old Bond St., W1; Tube: Green Park). Truffels and more in a beautiful shop.

Hats

The name to know is **Philip Treacy.** His fantasy designs verge on sculpture. You can place an order at the showroom (69 Elizabeth St., SW1; Tube: Sloane Sq.). **Herbert Johnson** (30 New Bond St., W1; Tube: Bond St.) is an institution with the Ascot crowd. For more affordable headgear, the **Hat Shop** in Covent Garden (58 Neal St., WC2; Tube: Covent Garden) stocks all manner of hats, including men's silk and hessian caps, traditional boaters, and glamorous-occasion hats.

Health & Beauty

These boutiques with their own potions and lotions are some of my favorites for olfactory pleasure:

Don't even bother trying to get an appointment with **Jo Malone** (154 Walton St., SW3; Tube: South Kensington) herself for her luxurious facial and body treatments; the Tattler crowd is well booked, and Malone is not taking any new clients. For mere mortals, she's opened a wonderful fragrance and lotion shop, stocked with her secret recipes. Across the street, you'll find the famous continental scents of the Florentine firm **Santa Maria Novella** (117 Walton St., SW3; Tube: South Kensington), where the recipes, developed by Dominican Friars, date from the 13thC.

For men, **Taylor's** (74 Jermyn St., SW1; Tube: Green Park) has developed a variety of personal products, including soaps and skin toners, shaving creams and badger shaving brushes, a variety of cologne scents, and hair and scalp treatments. The shop, established during Queen Victoria's reign, has a long list of serious devotees—including some women who adore the fresh scents. Saturdays, a traditional shave is offered; reservations are advised.

L'Artisan Parfumeur (12 Cale St., SW3; Tube: South Kensington) is decorated to look like a 19thC perfumer's cabinet. A bit new-agey is **Neal's Yard Remedies** (15 Neal's Yard, WC2; Tube: Covent Garden; also at 9 Elgin Crescent, W11; Tube: Notting Hill Gate). Herbal and Chinese tinctures, skincare products, and aromatherapy oils are packaged in old-fashioned cobalt blue bottles; many of the potions are organic. For English flower perfumes, visit the **Floris** (89 Jermyn St., SW1; Tube: Green Park) or the fashionably traditional **Penhaligon's** (41 Wellington St., WC2; Tube: Covent Garden).

Housewares, Furniture & Decorative Arts

Any student of contemporary design will want to stop into **Habitat** (206 King's Rd., SW3; Tube: Sloane Sq.) or the more upscale **Conran's** (81 Fulham Rd., SW3; Tube: South Kensington) to check out Sir Terence's current line of simple, well-designed furnishings and accessories.

Pay your respects at Tricia Guild's temple of color. Opened in 1994, **Designer's Guild** (267 King's Rd., SW3; Tube: Sloane Sq.) is a world onto itself—a chintz-free zone of eye-popping fabrics, bed linens, furnishings, tableware, and accessories. The list of hues—persimmon, saffron, lime, pimento—reads like the ingredients for a Mediterranean stew.

Cross the street to a very different state of mind. **William Yeoward** (336 King's Rd., SW3; Tube: Sloane Sq.) avers slavish reproduction; while his furniture and accessories are very much at home among Regency mahogany, they converse just as well with contemporary furnishings. Graceful proportions are often matched with 18th- and 19thC gothic fantasies; finishes range from mahogany to faux tortoise.

The Study (26 Old Church St., SW3; Tube: Sloane Sq.) is the place to see the recent furniture designs of young British talents such as Christopher Nevile and Mark Brazier-Jones. More contemporary design is also on view at **Jinan Furniture Gallery** (17 Golden Sq., W1; Tube: Piccadilly Circus). Featuring the work of British designers, Jinan also operates as a talent broker between young artisans and clientele.

Knobs are the thing at **Haute Deco** (556 King's Rd., SW6; Tube: Fulham Broadway). Best known for their brightly colored molded resin pulls and handles, they also do a line of bronze casts. **Cath Kidston** (Clarendon Cross,W11;Tube: Holland Park) sells 1940s- and 1950s-inspired objects as well as a funky collection of wall coverings and fabrics.

Among the vast grounds of **Clifton Little Venice** (3 Warwick Place, W9; Tube: Warwick Ave.), a well-known nursery and gardening center, is a house packed to the rafters with decorative garden and architectural ornaments. Cast from original Coade stone pieces, the ornaments are based on owner Peter Hone's collection. More architectural ornament is available at **McKinney & Co**. (1 Wandon Rd., SW6;Tube: Fulham Broadway), specializing in finials, rosettes, pelmets, and tie-backs; or try **Plasterworks** (38 Cross St., N1;Tube: Highbury, Islington) for architectural cornices and moldings. If you fancy a replica of the nose from Michelangelo's **David,** you can order it—as well as many other casts—from **The British Museum** cast service (☎ 0171/323-1234, ext. 119).

For the ultimate humidor, don't miss **David Linley Furniture** (60 Pimlico Rd., SW1; Tube: Sloane Sq.). Linley, the Queen's nephew, is well-known for his fine furniture and accessories, produced using traditional marquetry techniques. The humidors, to-scale models of historic houses, are exquisite.

For kitchenware, you can't do better than **David Mellor** (4 Sloane Sq., SW1; Tube: Sloane Sq.). The shop stocks everything you need—and lots of things you don't. In leafy Holland Park, **Summerill & Bishop** (100 Portland Rd., W11; Tube: Holland Park) sells Provençal-inspired kitchen goods, including hefty ceramic plates and mugs, oversized wood bowls, and enamel pots and pans perfect for the country house. I'm coveting their pearwood cheese grater.

Jewelry

There are plenty of jewelers in London, with the big names clustered around Bond Street. The royal jeweler is **Garrard** (112 Regent St.,W1;Tube: Piccadilly Circus). Anything from a jewel box to a gold-plated toothbrush can be had at **Asprey** (165 New Bond St.,W1; Tube: Green Park).

For modern jewels, **Theo Fennell** (177 Fulham Rd., SW3; Tube: South Kensington) and **Elizabeth Gage** (20 Albermarle St., W1; Tube: Green Park) are good names to know. Both produce contemporary styles inspired by antique designs.

On Elizabeth Street, look for **Erickson Beamon** (no. 38; Tube: Sloane Sq.), whose creations are sought out by big-name designers for their catwalk shows; and former New Yorker **Reema Pachachi** (no. 79; Tube: Sloane Sq.), known for her wide range of quirky designs. **Van Peterson** (194–196 Walton St., SW3; Tube: South Kensington) has just opened a new shop selling the work of other inspired designers as well as Peterson's famous baroque pearls and jet chokers.

For fashionable costume jewelry, visit **Butler and Wilson** (189 Fulham Rd., SW3; Tube: South Kensington). For funky, cheaper gems, check out **Detail** (4A Symons St., SW3; Tube: Sloane Sq.); and **Dinny Hall** (200 Westbourne Grove, W11; Tube: Notting Hill Gate), who creates lovely, subtle designs in metal.

Kids' Stuff

Princess Di has been spotted at the **Early Learning Center** (36–42 King's Rd., SW3; Tube: Sloane Sq.), where you'll find lots of indestructible toys for early learners. **The Children's Book Centre** (237 Kensington High St., W8; Tube: High Street Kensington) has an impressive stock of books for children up to age 14, and helpful assistants. The biggest toy store in the world is **Hamleys** (188 Regent St., W1; Tube: Oxford Circus). Parents who believe play should be educative favor **Galt Toys,** in Liberty. For the discerning small home owner, **The Singing Tree** (69 New King's Rd., SW6; Tube: Fulham Broadway) sells dollhouse miniware like Aga stoves and tiny silver toast racks.

More functional furniture is available at **Dragons** (23 Walton St., SW3; Tube: Knightsbridge), a shop specializing in hand-painted furniture and exclusive fabrics and wall coverings. A Dragons' nursery is a must when off-the-shelf just won't do. Choose from among precious designs featuring fluffy bears and cottontail rabbits, or work with shop designers to create a one-of-a-kind environment for your little one.

Besides being a children's clothing store, **Trotters** (34 King's Rd., SW3; Tube: Sloane Sq.), has a small haircutting station where little ones are distracted from the task at hand by colorful fish tanks. **The White House** (51 New Bond St., W1; Tube: Oxford Circus) sells absolutely exquisite children's wear and layettes—perfect for the baby that never spits up. **Anthea Moore**

Ede (16 Victoria Grove, W8; Tube: High Street Kensington) has lovely smocked dresses and velvet-collar jackets.

Your teenagers will be mighty pleased if you bring them back something from the **Dr. Martens Department Store** (1–4 King St., WC2; Tube: Covent Garden). In addition to the big clumpy boots, there are floors of Dr. Martens merchandise, including T-shirts and jeans.

Leather

At **Connolly Leather** (32 Grosvenor Crescent Mews, SW1; Tube: Hyde Park Corner), you'll feel as if you are touching and smelling leather for the very first time. This world-renowned firm that started out providing leather interiors for royal coaches and expensive cars has now ventured into luxury leather goods. Lots of bags and accessories that are too delicious for words. **J&M Davidson** (62 Ledbury Rd., W11; Tube: Notting Hill Gate) stocks a tempting range of faux-croc and suede handbags and luggage as well as a perfectly chosen house-line of women's clothing—all pieces are destined to become classics in your wardrobe.

Traditional English style can be had at **Mulberry** (11–12 Gees Court, W1; Tube: Bond St.), England's Ralph Lauren. The handbag designer of the moment is the very young and talented **Anya Hindmarch** (91 Walton St., SW3; Tube: South Kensington). Details like pockets for cradling fob watches and carved ram's head handles are her trademark.

Linens

The White House (51–52 New Bond St., W1; Tube: Bond St.) has simply the most luxurious Irish, English, and French linens and towels in London. At the far end of King's Road in Parson's Green is **Lunn Antiques** (86 New King's Rd., SW6; Tube: Parson's Green); their gorgeous antique linens and cutwork will make any bed inviting.

Music

The biggest record stores are **HMV** (363 and 150 Oxford St., W1; Tube: Oxford Circus); **Virgin Megastore** (14–30 Oxford St., W1; Tube: Tottenham Court Rd.); and **Tower Records** (1 Piccadilly Circus, W1; Tube: Piccadilly Circus). Specialty shops include **Rough Trade** (130 Talbot Rd., W11; Tube: Ladbroke Grove), a holdover from the days of punk specializing in indie and rock; and **Stern's** (116 Whitfield St., W1; Tube: Covent Garden) for African music. Jazz buffs will want to seek out **Ray's Jazz Shop** (180 Shaftesbury Ave., WC2; Tube: Leicester Sq.). Classical music is available from **Caruso & Co.** (10 Charlotte Place, W1; Tube: Goodge St.) and **Harold Moore's** (2 Great Marlborough St., W1; Tube: Oxford Circus).

Shoes

Johnny Moke (396 King's Rd., SW10; Tube: Sloane Sq.) has men's brogues and dandy shoes with giant buckles, and super-high heels for women. The most famous name in British footwear these days is **Patrick Cox** (8 Symons St., SW1; Tube: Sloane Sq.), whose "Wannabe" loafer is a favorite with models.

For men's and women's custom shoes, **John Lobb** (9 St. James's St., SW1; Tube: Green Park) is the traditionalist's choice; it's been a mecca for nobles and the terribly rich since 1849. Thousands of lasts fill the basement. Lobb's also has a new ready-to-wear shop near Turnbull and Asser at 90 Jermyn St.

More stylish and affordable is **Henrietta Park** (40 North St., SW4; Tube: Clapham Common), who has shod both film and rock stars; **Claire Norwood** (The Basement Studio, North Wing, 398 St. John St., EC1; Tube: Angel) specializes in classic styles with a twist that's different, "but not so different that it screams at you."

Of the high street shops, I like **Hobbs** (47 South Molton St.; Tube: Bond St.) and **Pied à Terre** (19 South Molton St., W1; Tube: Bond St.); both have other branches throughout London. For wedding shoes, **Emma Hope** (33 Amwell St., EC1; Tube: Angel) creates handmade romantic pumps of duchesse satin, brocade, and dupion silk. She also has a pretty fine line of nonbridal wear.

Stationery

The flagship branch of **Paperchase** (213 Tottenham Court Rd., W1; Tube: Goodge St.) has 2 floors of well-designed stationery, cards, and office supplies. **Smythson's of Bond Street** (44 New Bond St., W1; Tube: Bond St.) supplies the rich and famous; stop in to ogle the gilt-edged cards and leather-bound albums.

Textiles & Trimmings

Watts & Co. (7 Tufton St., SW1; Tube: St. James's Park) is a survivor from the 19thC Gothic Revival.

Originally providing textiles and wall coverings to the clerical trade, the shop also caters to a retail market that's hungry for its rich damask silks, pure silk brocades, and silk velvets. **Warris Vianni** (85 Goldborne Rd., W10; Tube: Ladbroke Grove) commissions hand-woven paisleys and divine dupion silks from India and Thailand. All the trimmings, braids, tassels, and ribbons you could possibly want are at **VV Rouleaux** (10 Symons St., SW3; Tube: Sloane Sq.). **Celia Birtwell** (71 Westbourne Park Rd., W2; Tube: Royal Oak) is a brilliant colorist whose bold star prints (much copied) provide a welcome alternative to florals. There's chintz galore at **Osborne and Little** (304-308 King's Rd., SW3; Tube: Sloane Sq.).

For Indian sari fabric, make the trip out to **Southall,** out by Heathrow. The Broadway is lined with eye-popping shops filled with embroidered, chiffon, and raw silks; **Partap Fashion Fabrics** (51-53 The Broadway, Middlesex; Tube: Ealing Broadway) and the basement of **New Rainbow Textiles** (98 The Broadway, Middlesex; Tube: Ealing Broadway) are good for a start.

For antique fabrics, try the **Gallery of Antique Costume and Textiles** (2 Church St., NW8; Tube: Marylebone); you might just find a perfect silk Edwardian housecoat. One of the most well-known specialists in the field is **Marilyn Garrow** (6 The Broadway, SW13; British Rail: Barnes). Designers and collectors alike roam the shelves of her shop seeking inspiration. Pieces date from 6thC Coptic to 19thC French toile.

Woolens

Visit **Peal & Co.** (Burlington Arcade, W1; Tube: Green Park) for achingly soft cashmere, the ultimate luxury. The slippers are divine; your feet will thank you. The **Scotch House** (2 Brompton Rd., SW3; Tube: Knightsbridge; also at 84 Regent St., W1; Tube: Piccadilly Circus) is the shop for Fair Isle, Shetland, Pringle, Ballantyne, and tartans.

THE ARTS

THERE'S TOO MUCH CHOICE AMONG LONDON'S riches—you could go to a different play, concert, ballet, or opera every day for a year without seeing the same show twice, or even returning to the same venue very often. If your time is more limited, venues such as the Royal Opera House or one of the West End theaters are obvious destinations. But don't neglect to check out the alternatives dotting the town; cutting-edge performance spaces like the Almeida and The Bush are garnering lots of attention these days. For entertainment in a bucolic setting, check out the Holland Park Opera or Regent's Park outdoor theater. If the weather behaves, you're in for a treat.

How to Find Out What's Going On

If you want to take advantage of London's arts scene, the best advice I can give you is to invest a little time in advance, ideally about 2 months before you leave home. To get a good idea of what's going on, log onto the Internet and check out *Time Out*'s **World Wide Web page** at **http://www.timeout.co.uk.** All the venues, from mainstream to fringe, are listed, along with their upcoming schedules. If you're not on-line, you can usually pick up a hard copy of *Time Out* at international newsstands throughout the states. Once you're in London, it's available everywhere.

If you're really serious, it might be a good idea to get in touch with the **Society of London Theatre** (Bedford Chambers, The Piazza, Covent Garden, WC2E 8HQ; ☎ 0171/836-0971). Their monthly newsletter gives details about every theater performance, including dance and opera, in a gossipy format. SoLT also produces a disabled access guide and *The Complete Guide to the West End,* which has seating plans for all of London's 50 West End theaters.

You can also get the programs for the major theaters, concert halls, galleries, and many other venues from the stateside **British Tourist Authority** offices (see "The Basics").

The Principal Arts Centers

There are 3 main centers for the performing arts. Most of London's commercial theaters and the 2 opera houses are in the **West End.** The **South Bank Arts Centre,** across the river near Waterloo Bridge, contains the Royal National Theatre, the Royal Festival Hall, and the National Film Theatre. The **Barbican Centre,** home of the Royal Shakespeare Company and the London Symphony Orchestra, is to the north of the City. Other important venues, such as **Sadler's Wells,** the **Royal Court Theatre,** and the **Old Vic,** are farther afield.

Getting to the South Bank can be fun if you walk across the bridge; you'll have great views of London. The route from the tube to the Barbican can be a bit confusing; follow the signs. After late shows, taxis can be scarce at either complex.

Getting Tickets

You can usually reserve tickets with a credit card before you leave home—absolutely necessary for the big shows, such as *Phantom of the Opera* and *Sunset Boulevard*—through the New York offices of **Edwards and Edwards** (1 Times Square Plaza, New York, NY 10036; ☎ 212/944-0290 or 800/223-6108; in London at the Palace Theatre, Shaftesbury Ave., W11; ☎ 0171/734-4555, and 12 Lower Regent St., SW1; ☎ 0171/839-3952) or **Keith Prowse** (234 W. 44th St., New York, NY 10036; ☎ 212/398-1430 or 800/669-8687; at various locations in London, ☎ 0171/836-9001), through your travel agent, or directly with the venues themselves. The concierge at the hotel where you'll be staying might also be willing to do this for you. British Airlines and many of the U.S. carriers offer airfare/theater ticket packages, as does British Rail (see "Basics").

Don't worry if your travel plans are too fluid to allow you to make plans before you get to London. There's so much going on that a few inquiries once you're here, even on the day you want to attend a performance, will probably turn up the very show to fit your mood. The **ticket booth on the west side of Leicester Square** has half-price seats (cash only) for same-day West End shows. There's a small service charge, you can buy no more than 4 seats at a time, and there can be a long line. As these are basically remainder tickets, you'll rarely find the tickets for the show you want, especially if it's a new or hot production. That's why scalpers (who you know are ripping you off), and "touts" (who deceptively rip you off by adding a commission that can often be 6 times the ticket price) prowl the area, knowing that you'll be disappointed. It's a risk buying from these sources; not only are the tickets usually overpriced, but they might be phony. The best bet for tickets is to go directly to the box office, either in person or by phone. If booking by phone and using a credit card, a small service charge will be levied, but nothing in comparison to what some of the ticket agents charge. Some box offices will have tickets available on the day of performance; otherwise, you can try lining up for returns.

You may find it more convenient to buy tickets through your concierge or a ticket agency, but be aware that the agent's commission can really elevate the price of the ticket. **First Call** (☎ 0171/497-9977), **Ticketmaster** (☎ 0171/420-1000), and **Stoll Moss** (booking for Stoll Moss theaters only; ☎ 0171/494-5080) are efficient credit-card telephone reservations agencies that can usually provide tickets for the major shows, but will charge a fee, sometimes up to 20%. Avoid ticket scalpers and touts at all costs.

Concert Halls

The 2 most important concert venues are the **Royal Albert Hall** and the **Festival Hall** (in the **South Bank Arts Centre**). Each belongs to a different era of optimism and grandeur.

Royal Festival Hall, Queen Elizabeth Hall, Purcell Room
South Bank, SE1. ☎ 0171/960-4242. Tube: Waterloo, Embankment.
The Festival Hall, built for the Festival of Britain in 1951, is part of the South Bank Arts Centre, along with the Queen Elizabeth Hall and the Purcell Room. Said by Toscanini to have the finest acoustics in the world, the 3,000-seat Festival Hall presents concerts by the leading British and international symphony orchestras. The 970-seat Queen Elizabeth Hall stages chamber music, string quartets, and other small ensembles. The 372-seat Purcell Room presents solo performances and other smaller events. All 3 halls offer not only classical music but also jazz and pop concerts. You can see and

Royal Albert Hall

hear perfectly from all the seats, so the cheaper ones are often a good buy. Early-evening conversations with music celebrities are occasionally held in the Queen Elizabeth Hall's Chelfield Room.

Royal Albert Hall

Kensington Gore, SW7. ☎ 0171/589-3203. Tube: South Kensington.
The Albert Hall, named after Queen Victoria's Prince Consort, is a spectacular example of Victorian architecture, facing Kensington Gardens and the Albert Memorial. It is self-financing, operating independently under Royal Charter.

The hall's best-known annual event is the "Proms" (promenade concerts), founded in 1912 to bring the classics to a wider audience by recapturing the spirit of informal performances in London pleasure gardens. The center of the circular hall is cleared of seats for the Proms season, which runs from mid-July to early September; a cheap ticket allows you to stand and wander at your leisure while you enjoy the music. Tickets are available at the door on the evening of the performance, except on the Last Night of the Proms, a social event booked long in advance.

Although a wide range of classical music is performed at the Albert Hall, its keynote is eclecticism, playing host to pop singers and wrestlers as well. In 1996, it began staging opera in the round.

Other Music & Arts Centers

The **Barbican Centre** (☎ 0171/628-2295 for information; ☎ 0171/638-8891 for reservations), the home of the London Symphony Orchestra, has also hosted such big names as Yo-Yo Ma.

A famous small concert hall almost within earshot of Oxford Street is **Wigmore Hall** (Wigmore St., W1; ☎ 0171/935-2141), where international musicians perform chamber music, particularly song and piano recitals and string quartets. This well-loved recital hall is even more so now that it's been completely refurbished. Sunday morning performances are a nice way to start the week. Performances are also staged most nights.

Kenwood Lakeside (Hampstead Heath; ☎ 0171/ 413-1443) is a wonderful venue for large-scale orchestral performances on summer weekends. By the lake near Kenwood House is an orchestra shell that has accommodated the Royal Philharmonic and the London Symphony, among others. Great music under the stars is also happening in the beautiful grounds of **Marble Hill House** in Twickenham (☎ 0171/413-1443). Two other lovely venues are **Dulwich Picture Gallery** (College Rd., SE21; ☎ 0171/693-5254) and **Leighton House** (12 Holland Park Rd., W14; ☎ 0171/ 602-3316). Concerts performed on early keyboard instruments take place at **Fenton House** (Windmill Hill, NW3; ☎ 0171/372-3206). (For more information on these venues, see "Sights & Attractions.")

There are lunchtime recitals at some of London's most attractive and interesting churches, including **St.-Martin-in-the-Fields** (☎ 0171/839-8362). On Thursdays during July and August, a band plays in the garden of **Westminster Abbey**—a special treat. Another one of my favorite concert locales is **St. John's Smith Square** (Smith Sq., SW1; ☎ 0171/222-1061); the lunchtime concerts are always well-attended, so tickets should be purchased in advance. Concerts at **St. James's, Piccadilly** take place at 1:10pm (☎ 0171/ 437-5053). The famous boys' choir of **St. Paul's** can be heard during Sunday services at the Cathedral; all-boy choirs also perform in **Westminster Abbey** and **Westminster Cathedral.** For information about other churches in the City, call 0171/332-1456. (For exact locations of the above churches, see "Sights & Attractions.")

Theater

Despite financial pressures, London remains one of the major world centers of theater, and the British stage still produces many of the world's greatest actors. The theater scene splits into 4 broad categories: companies subsidized by the state, in impressive buildings, producing serious drama to the highest standards; commercial theaters, mainly built at the turn of the century in a style of cozy splendor, mounting lighter plays and musicals; Off–West End theaters; and pub/club theaters. The major subsidized theaters usually have several plays in repertory at one time; most others present a single play as long as it's successful. Serious theatergoers shouldn't ignore either of the last 2 fringe categories.

Although the best seats for a big show are expensive, the London theater does offer its patrons a wide range of ticket prices, so usually only the most determinedly philistine visitor fails to catch at least one production. (Beware, though: Cheaper seats in some of the older theaters may allow only a partial view.) The theaters traditionally stay dark on Sundays, but there are signs of mold-breaking among the West End theaters. Many theaters also present a matinee on Saturday and 1 midweek day.

Many theater bars welcome advance reservations for intermission drinks, saving you from a crush, frustration, and thirst; call ahead.

Subsidized Theaters

For more on the following venues (except the Royal Court Theatre), including details on backstage tours, see "Sights & Attractions."

Royal National Theatre

Upper Ground, South Bank, SE1. Information ☎ 0171/633-0880; reservations ☎ 0171/928-2252. Tube: Waterloo, Embankment.

The National Theatre company, originally under the direction of Sir Laurence Olivier, began its life at the Old Vic in the Waterloo Road. Sir Peter Hall took over in 1973, ready for the opening of a new, custom-built theater, a modern architectural landmark in the South Bank Arts Centre. He was succeeded by Richard Eyre in 1988.

"The National" is actually 3 theaters in 1. The largest auditorium, the **Olivier,** has an amphitheater setting; the **Lyttelton** has a proscenium stage; and the **Cottesloe** is a more spartan studio theater. The 3 present a wide range of classical, modern British, and international works. Tom Stoppard's acclaimed play *Arcadia* began life here, as did *The Madness of George the III.*

Before performances, there's live music in the foyers and the picture galleries are open; early-evening lectures, poetry readings, and short plays are heard from 6pm; and there's a good restaurant, **Mezzanine,** which can be booked for lunch, pre-, or post-theater meals at the same time you reserve your tickets; there's also a ground-floor cafe. Although many performances are heavily booked, the National always retains some seats for sale on the day of show, and has reduced-price standby tickets.

It was long held to be an anomaly that the National Theatre, in its days under Olivier and Hall, had not been granted the "Royal" prefix since its foundation, in pointed contrast with the Royal Shakespeare Company. Although Buckingham Palace finally rectified that situation, Londoners doggedly continue to call it "the National."

Barbican Theatre

(Royal Shakespeare Company), Barbican Centre, EC2. Information ☎ 0171/628-2295; reservations ☎ 0171/638-8891. Tube: Barbican, Moorgate.

The RSC enjoys worldwide repute—theirs are the finest productions of the world's greatest dramatist, many would say. As a result, London theatergoers are up in arms about the recent decision to have the company tour for half the year. This is its London base, complementing its Stratford-upon-Avon home, where many of the theater's productions originate. Kenneth Branaugh recently performed *Hamlet* here. Besides Shakespeare, the company also performs a wide variety of standard and new plays. The RSC's studio theater, **The Pit,** stages a range of smaller-scale productions, from Jacobean to present-day drama.

Royal Court Theatre

Sloane Sq., SW1. Information ☎ 0171/730-5174; reservations ☎ 0171/730-2554. Tube: Sloane Sq.

Despite its name, this theater has a distinguished record of healthily controversial drama and promoting new writing. George Bernard Shaw's plays were presented here in the 1920s and 1930s; John Osborne, the original angry young man, and Arnold Wesker made their names here in the 1950s and 1960s; John Arden, Edward Bond, David Storey, and Caryl Churchill are more recent examples. There's also the **Theatre Upstairs,** a studio space for new writers and the location of the annual Barclays New Stages Festival, a venue for new avant-garde work.

Shakespeare Globe Centre

1 Bear Gardens, Bankside, SE1. ☎ 0171/928-6406 or 0171/344-4444.

By the time you read this, the Globe Theatre will be officially opened and the first season of plays will be staged, on the site of the 16thC theater where Shakespeare originally staged his work.

011 44 1 7/

Commercial Theaters

London's oldest theater, the **Theatre Royal, Drury Lane** (WC2; ☎ 0171 494-5060), specializes in musicals and hit shows. Most elegant is the **Theatre Royal, Haymarket** (SW1; ☎ 0171/930-8800). Ed Mirvish's **Old Vic** (Waterloo Rd., SE1; ☎ 0171/928-7616) stages quality productions by well-known directors. The 18thC **Richmond Theatre** (The Green, Richmond; ☎ 0181/940-0088) stages pre–West End plays. Other period pieces are performed at the twin **Aldwych** (WC2; ☎ 0171/416-6003) and the **Strand** (Aldwych, WC2; ☎ 0171/930-8800). Most famous is probably the **London Palladium** (Argyll St., W1; ☎ 0171/494-5037), which has a policy of light family entertainment, and plays host to a wealth of national and international stars.

    St. Martin's (West St., Cambridge Circus, WC2; ☎ 0171/836-1443) stages the world's longest-running play, Agatha Christie's *The Mousetrap.* **Regent's Park Open Air Theatre** (NW1; ☎ 0171/486-2431) presents a diet of Shakespeare throughout the summer; bring glasses and champagne and sit under the stars.

Off–West End & Pub Theaters

London's Off–West End fringe theatre is alive and kicking, with a number of important venues staging exciting work. Those mentioned here are most notable; *Time Out* lists the details on many more.

    West London has the excellent and well-established **Lyric** (King St., Hammersmith, W6; ☎ 0181/741-2311), a Victorian gem in a modern precinct, as well as the contemporary arts venue **Riverside Studios** (Crisp Rd., W6; ☎ 0181/741-2255). In North London, there's the **Almeida** (Almeida St., Islington, N1; ☎ 0171/359-4404) and the **Hampstead Theatre** (Avenue Rd., NW3; ☎ 0171/722-9301) in Swiss Cottage. In East London is the **Victorian Theatre Royal** (Gerry Raffles Sq., Stratford East, E15; ☎ 0181/534-0310); Soho is home to the **Donmar Warehouse** (Thomas Neal's, Earlham St., WC2; ☎ 0171/369-1732); in South London is the **Young Vic** (66 The Cut, Waterloo, SE1; ☎ 0171/928-6363) and the **Greenwich Theatre** (Croom's Hill, SE10; ☎ 0181/858-7755).

    Pub theater today is more than a small room above a noisy pub. Just for the experience, try the **Gate** in Notting Hill (above Prince Albert Pub, 11 Pembridge Rd., W11; ☎ 0171/229-0706); the **King's Head** in

Islington (115 Upper St., N1; ☎ 0171/226-1916); **The Bush** (Shepherd's Bush Green, W12; ☎ 0181/743-3388), which has been getting much attention and recently signed a deal with Walt Disney Productions, who wants first option on all Bush Plays; or the **Orange Tree** (1 Clarence St., Richmond; ☎ 0181/940-0141).

Early summer is the kick-off time for **LIFT,** the London International Festival of Theatre. Theater companies from around the globe stage cutting-edge work at a variety of locations. Call 0171/336-0508 for details.

Ballet & Opera

For true lovers of the opera or ballet, a first visit to the **Royal Opera House** can resemble a pilgrimage, so dense is the musical history associated with that august establishment. It belongs in the same top league—and its best seats are as expensive—as New York's Metropolitan, the Paris Opera, and La Scala in Milan. **Sadler's Wells,** nowadays a center for visiting opera and ballet companies, is more democratic. And the **English National Opera** at the glorious London Coliseum is refreshingly different: Opera is sung in English and prices are genuinely affordable (as a result, tickets are often scarce).

Royal Opera House (Royal Opera and Royal Ballet)
Bow St., WC2 (box office on Floral St.). ☎ 0171/304-4000. Closed early Aug–mid-Sept. Tube: Covent Garden.

"Covent Garden" is Londoners' shorthand for the Royal Opera House, one of the most historically interesting theaters in London. It's now one of the world's most important venues for opera and ballet; the greats appear here regularly.

Original known as the Theatre Royal, it was established from the first permissions granted by Charles II for the opening of playhouses after the Restoration. The present building was finally completed in 1858. Plans are afoot for a massive £88 million expansion and refurbishment in 1997, funds courtesy of the National Lottery. The community is up in arms and the controversy continues to rage.

The Royal Opera and Royal Ballet both perform here in seasons of alternating productions. Mail reservations open about 6 weeks before the beginning of a season, and tickets are quickly snapped up, but 65 seats up in "the gods" (the equivalent of the bleachers) are held until the day of the performance, and 1 hour before show time some cheaper standing room tickets are made available; each person can purchase only one ticket, and there can be long lines, sometimes overnight.

For cheaper aural pleasure, pray that your visit co-incides with one of the performances that are relayed live onto the big screen in **The Piazza.** This is truly opera for the people. Fans arrive early to claim a small bit of pavement for this free performance. Or you can gaze upon the peons below from the **Opera Terrace Cafe** (45 East Terrace, Central Market, Covent Garden, WC2; ☎ 0171/379-0666), which overlooks the screen and offers a fixed price buffet.

Sadler's Wells Theatre
Rosebery Ave., EC1. ☎ 0171/278-8916. Tube: Angel.

It is a strange name for a theater, and Islington is perhaps an unlikely location. The site was originally a garden in which there was a health-giving well; its owner, whose name was Sadler, opened a "musick house" there in 1683. The theater was the base for the Sadler's Wells Royal Ballet company until its recent move to Birmingham; now it functions as a venue for international opera, ballet, and music companies. Behind Sadler's Wells is the **Lilian Bayliss Theatre,** which hosts smaller productions. There's also good children's theater.

London Coliseum (English National Opera)
St. Martin's Lane, WC2. Information ☎ 0171/836-0111; Reservations ☎ 0171/632-8300. Tube: Charing Cross.

One of London's largest auditoriums is barely visible from the street, but its illuminated globe stands out in the night skyline. For many years a music hall, it now houses the English National Opera, whose prestigious, reasonably priced, large-scale productions are sung in English. In summer, the company takes a break and international visiting dance companies take over.

Almeida Opera
Almeida St., N1. ☎ 0171/359-4404. Tube: Angel.

Long known as one of London's best fringe theaters, the Almeida has forayed into opera. Launched in 1992, it's quickly becoming one of the best spots to hear contemporary and avant-garde work.

Open-Air Opera
During the summer months, outdoor opera is staged in the **Holland Park Bandshell** (W11; ☎ 0171/

602-7856), where buckets of champagne and chilled strawberries come out at intermission. If you don't want to spring for the tickets, bring a picnic and park yourself along the south side of Holland House; you won't see the action on stage, but you'll still be able to enjoy the music. More outdoor opera is performed riverside in the beautiful setting of **Marble Hill** (Richmond Rd., Twickenham; ☎ 0171/413-1443).

From mid-May through August, you can rub shoulders with high society at the **Glyndebourne Festival** (☎ 01273/813-813) in Sussex. Tickets are hard to come by, but if you succeed, you'll have the opportunity to explore the beautiful grounds. Long intermissions provide time for splendid champagne picnics.

Other Dance Venues

Other important venues for dance are the **Royal Festival Hall** in the South Bank Centre (☎ 0171/928-8800) and the **Riverside Studios,** an excellent contemporary-arts complex in West London (Crisp Rd., Hammersmith, W6; ☎ 0181/741-2255).

Contemporary Art

London is catching up to New York as a center for the visual arts. The global dealing of Old Master works has always centered around the London galleries and auctions houses, but these days, just as much print space and money is being devoted to the younger artists and their galleries.

What I find interesting about London's current art scene is the incredible polarization between the traditionalists and the conceptualists. Unlike New York, where a prominent collector's home is as likely to house a Claude Lorrain drawing as it is to display a black canvas by Ellsworth Kelly, the 2 factions in London never mingle. You either read *Modern Painters* or you read *Frieze*. Brian Sewell, the leader of the *Modern Painters* brigade, regularly rails against the travesty of conceptual art, with Damien Hirst and his pickled sheep being his pet peeve. As the debate wages on, it's not surprising that many London-trained contemporary artists find their way to New York, seeking a more sympathetic audience for their avant-garde tendencies.

But perhaps such vitriolic outbursts only serve to heighten the attention currently being focused on a contemporary art scene that's finally gaining prominence on the international stage. London's recent graduates from Goldsmith's and the Royal College of Art are regularly popping up in shows in New York's Soho. Damien Hirst and Rachel Whitehead (the 1994 Turner prize winner) are well-known on the international stage (though more often than not their names are mentioned as part of a diatribe against conceptual art). The **Serpentine Gallery,** with Princess Di its most prominent patron, regularly shows the work of London's most cutting edge artists. Last year, an exhibition of Helen Chadwick's work was held; her chocolate fountain and "piss" flowers were hotly debated in the press. Charles Saatchi can single-handedly make or break the career of a young talent; his warehouse **Saatchi Gallery** in St. John's Wood regularly stages surveys of young British Art. The **Tate,** under the direction of Nicholas Serota, is furiously bidding for a share of Lottery funds in order to proceed with plans to create a massive contemporary art space across the river in the South Bank power station. If Serota gets his way, it will be a showcase on a grand scale for an international roster of contemporary artists. Private galleries are surviving in staid London as well: **Karsten Schubert, Jay Jopling** (White Cube Gallery), and **Victoria Miro** continue to outrage Sewell with their conceptually inspired artists.

For where to go, see "Art" in "Shopping," as well as "Sights & Attractions" for on-view-only venues such as the Serpentine and Saatchi galleries.

Cinema

London has an enormous selection of cinemas, but a lesser choice of movies. Two chains, MGM and Odeon, dominate, and concentrate on box-office hits. It's advisable to reserve seats (especially on weekends); you can do it over the phone with your credit card. There's a small charge for this service, but it guarantees you a place and you avoid the long lines at the box office. In the first-run theaters, movie-goers are given assigned seats; as a result, there's not the free-for-all that often occurs the United States's bigger cinemas. All the prebooking information you need is listed in *Time Out* and the *Evening Standard*.

Art-house films are more likely to be shown by independents. When the rain just won't let up, you can sit through a Fassbinder triple-header or find yourself at the edge of your seat as the *Manchurian Candidate* reveals its twisted plot. There are a few theaters that are particularly worth checking out: In Brixton, there's the shabby but lovable **Ritzy** (Brixton Oval, Coldharbour Lane, SW2; ☎ 0171/737-2121; Tube:

Brixton), currently in the process of being restored to its original 1911 glory. **The Institute of Contemporary Arts** (Nash House, The Mall, SW1; ☎ 0171/930-3647; Tube: Piccadilly), more commonly known as the ICA, has a cinema; temporary art exhibitions are also presented at this important avant-garde center. The true celluloid freak heads for the **National Film Theatre** (South Bank Arts Centre, SE1; information ☎ 0171/633-0274, reservations ☎ 0171/928-3232; Tube: Waterloo, Embankment), where a wide range of films are presented in 2 theaters, with retrospectives on the work of individual directors and performers. The **Museum of the Moving Image** (MOMI) has cycles of classic films Tuesday and Sunday starting at 7:30pm. **The Everyman Cinema** (Holly Bush Vale, Hampstead, NW3; ☎ 0171/435-1525; Tube: Hampstead) was the world's first repertory cinema.

London also hosts the annual **London Film Festival.** For 3 weeks in the fall, over 200 international films are shown at a variety of locations. Call 0171/928-3232 for details.

NIGHTLIFE

THE CLOSING HOURS OF PUBS AND RESTAURANTS AND the paucity of late-night transport have won London a reputation for being insufficiently nocturnal that it only partly deserves. Like an aging, dignified actress, London cherishes its beauty sleep, but isn't above the occasional exploit in the wee hours.

Late-night drinking occurs in private clubs; these establishments require introduction by a member. If you're a frequent visitor to London, it might be worth your while to arrange "overseas" memberships to some of the better-known spots, such as **Annabels** (44 Berkeley Sq., W1; ☎ 0171/629-1096) and **Tramp** (40 Jermyn St., SW1; ☎ 0171/734-0565), both catering to a big City crowd; **The Groucho Club** (45 Dean St., W1; ☎ 0171/439-4685), for media trendies and "artists"; and, for grown-ups, **Morton's** (28 Berkeley Sq., W1; ☎ 0171/499-0363).

For the Londoner—and the visitor who thinks of it—a drink in a pub or a bar is a likely part of an evening at the theater, either as a rendezvous beforehand or for a nightcap afterward. Since most of the West End theaters are near Soho or Covent Garden, these neighborhoods are the most convenient, and the most lively, after dark. Don't be put off by Soho's seediness. Elegant Mayfair has a villagey enclave called Shepherd Market, with pleasant pubs, restaurants, and ladies of the night whose presence is not excessively assertive. Elsewhere, Mayfair is mostly an area of expensive restaurants, private clubs, and casinos.

Dropping into a pub is kind of like going native (see "Pubs" in "Dining" for an introduction to one of the capital's special pleasures). If it's a little too local for you, there are alternatives, like gaming clubs; getting into one, however, can take a little work. You'll have to ask your hotel concierge, or, better yet, know a

member. Somewhat more accessible are the nightclubs
and discos, many of which have a transient existence.
Finally, London is one of the world's great rock power-
houses; for some, it's a place of pilgrimage.

Bars

London has its own distinctive style when it comes to
traditional cocktail bars, most commonly found in the
city's luxury hotels. The Savoy's **American Bar** inspired the famous *Savoy Cocktail Book,* and is believed
to have been the first cocktail bar in Europe. Revamped
a few years back in art-deco style, it's sleek, chic, and
reminiscent of a 1930s Hollywood movie set. Appropriately, they mix a mean dry martini. **Blake's** has
famous Octavio behind the bar—he makes the best
Bloody Marys in town. Another inspired barman is
Gilberto Pretti at **Dukes,** where you can choose one
of a wide range of ancient cognacs to taste while puff-
ing on a stogie. The **Hilton's** rooftop bar, while a bit
uninspired in the decor department, has positively the
best views in town. The **Athenaeum** (with 54 malt
whiskies on hand), the **Four Seasons,** and **Hyde Park
Hotel,** have good cocktail bars. (For exact locations,
see "Accommodations.")

Beyond the hotels, **Cafe Royale** (68 Regent St.,
W1; ☎ 0171/437-9090) has a plush cocktail bar that
would satisfy Ivana Trump—red velvet seats, glittering
chandeliers, and an extensive list of pricey cocktails. At
Flamingo (9 Hanover St., W1; ☎ 0171/493-0689)
barman extraordinaire Dick Bradsell serves up cocktails to a sophisticated clientele in a subterranean space;
there's live salsa on the weekends. In Kensington, try
Bistro 190 (in the Gore Hotel, 190 Queen's Gate, SW7;
☎ 0171/581-8172), a comfy bar with lots of wood
paneling and tattered oriental carpets that attracts a mix
of Chelsea babes and dudes.

For Knightsbridge or Sloane Street shoppers, the
Ebury Wine Bar (139 Ebury St., SW1; ☎ 0171/
730-5447) is pleasant and well run. In Holland Park,
Julie's Bar (137 Portland Rd., W11; ☎ 0171/
727-7985) is an attractive and sophisticated relic of the
1960s, with ecclesiastical decor and barman Johnny
Ekperigin mixing a range of drinks named after
clientele-types; whether you go for the Timberland or
the Versace says a lot about who you are. **Green's**
(36 Duke St., SW1; ☎ 0171/930-4566) serves some of
the best champagne and oysters in London in an attractive wood-paneled bar, and **Kettners** (29 Romilly St.,

W1; ☎ 0171/734-6112) also has a pleasant champagne bar. **Cafe Pelican** (45 St. Martin's Lane, WC2; ☎ 0171/379-0309) has a friendly brasserie-style ambiance and is convenient to the Coliseum. New on the scene is **Foundation,** in the basement of trendy Harvey Nichols (109–25 Knightsbridge, SW1), the Barneys of London.

The young trendies hang out at **Beach Blanket Babylon** (45 Ledbury Rd., W11; ☎ 0171/229-2907). This gothic fantasy bar and restaurant is the perfect stage set for bacchanalian revelry. Darker and grungier is the **Mas Cafe** (6–8 All Saints Rd., W2), a Mediterranean-inspired restaurant with a bar scene that far outshines its food. Young studs come in search of babes at **Mwah Mwah** at The Queen's Elm (241 Fulham Rd., SW10); behind the traditional pub veneer, the meat market is open for business. **R Bar** (4 Sydney St., SW3; ☎ 0171/352-3433) is another lively hangout, catering to fast Chelsea types; park yourself at a banquette and stare down your enemies. For sports mavens, there's **Shoeless Joe's** (555 King's Rd., SW6), a sports bar with big screens broadcasting major international sporting events.

In Soho, the young and tortured can be found drinking late into the night at **Riki-Tik** (23–24 Bateman St., W1; ☎ 0171/437-1977), where you'll find a wide choice of bottled beers in addition to the colorful customers. **Freedom** (60–66 Wardour St., W1; ☎ 0171/734-0071) attracts a stylish mix of gays and straights.

Casinos

London does have casinos but, in recent years, faced with the regulatory activity of the Gaming Board, their numbers have really dwindled. Several famous names have vanished or had their licenses suspended, and the future of others is uncertain. It's the more urbane type of casino, usually found in Mayfair or Knightsbridge, which has fallen afoul of the Board; 1 or 2 brasher places still brightly proclaim their presence in Soho. Those casinos that have remained in business are not permitted to advertise, which includes mentions in guidebooks, but hotel concierges usually know where they are. To visit one, you must either join, which takes 48 hours, or be the guest of a member.

Nightclubs & Discos

It's the nature of such diversions to be affected by fashion; discos have been known to open and close with alarming swiftness, or to announce a violent shift from one trend to another. *Time Out* keeps club-seekers up-to-date; beyond that, perusing the gossip columns of *The Daily Mail* and *The Evening Standard* and the high-class glossies and trendy youth magazines should keep you tolerably well informed.

Exclusive Clubs If nightingales still sing in Berkeley Square, their songs are directed at the habitués of **Annabels** (no. 44; ☎ 0171/629-3558). "The world's best nightclub," says London's most famous gossip columnist, Nigel Dempster. It's hermetically discreet and expensive, and you must be accompanied by a member, or be one yourself.

Other smart-set nightspots, most of which offer "overseas" memberships or have membership included in the price of admission for the short-term visitor, include the music industry hang-out **Browns** (4 Great Queen St., WC2; ☎ 0171/831-0802), with a handkerchief-sized dance floor and a lavishly appointed space to relax upstairs. The **Dorchester Club** (53 Park Lane, W1; ☎ 0171/495-7344) is done up in classic Dorchester style with a rich, besuited clientele to match. A somewhat more traditional club with a strong "Sloanie" following is **Raffles** (287 King's Rd., SW3; ☎ 0171/352-1091). You'll find a similar crowd in a different environment at **Roof Gardens** (99 Kensington High St., W8; ☎ 0171/937-8923), open Thursdays and Saturdays only; as the name suggests, greenery abounds. **Tokyo Joe** (85 Piccadilly, W1; ☎ 0171/409-1832) is primarily membership only, but an open overseas guest policy results in a high proportion of the same.

A stalwart among London clubs, recently celebrating its 25th year, is **Tramp** (40 Jermyn St., SW1; ☎ 0171/734-0565), which has a glitzy mix of film and pop stars and minor aristocracy bopping to generic music.

Open Clubs Many of the best nightspots for the young (or young at heart) to meet and see and be seen have live rock bands and theme parties on different nights of the week (*Time Out* has a good listing of these events). These clubs are open to anybody:

The recently renovated and extremely popular **Camden Palace** (1A Camden High St., NW1; ☎ 0171/387-0428) offers every conceivable type of music—depending on the night. At **Cuba** (11 Kensington High St., W8; ☎ 0171/938-4137), popular with the well-heeled Kensington Eurotrash, patrons take their drinks at the bar on the ground floor and then head downstairs to the reasonably priced club, playing a mixture of South American and House music.

Open Friday and Saturday only, the gothic-themed **Electric Ballroom** (187 Camden High St., NW1; ☎ 0171/485-9006) has 2 levels of very different music. Models and fashion glitterati head for **Emporium** (62 Kingly St., W1; ☎ 0171/734-3190), a trend-setting Ibiza-influenced hangout playing a wide range of music. Top of the league at time of writing, **Hanover Grand** (6 Hanover St., W1; ☎ 0171/499-7977), wildly popular with the young club set, features 2 dance floors with 2 beats of music. **Heaven** (Under the Arches, Villiers St., WC2; ☎ 0171/839-3852) is London's top gay club, with a strict gay-only policy on Saturday.

Hippodrome (Leicester Sq., WC2; ☎ 0171/ 437-4311) has been around for awhile; it's touristy and a bit tacky. **Iceni** (11 White Horse St., W1; ☎ 0171/ 495-5333) is a theatrically draped venue spread over 3 floors, with as many choices in music, plus a game room and mini-cinema. **Kartouche** (329–331 Fulham Rd., SW10; ☎ 0171/823-3515) is the Chelsea headquarters for monied 20-somethings. A long surviving club with mixed clientele and music, **Legends** (29 Old Burlington St., W1; ☎ 0171/437-9933) is a 1980s relic with an upstairs bar that opens onto the street. Gaining recognition among clubbers again is **Limelight** (136 Shaftesbury Ave., W1; ☎ 0171/434-0572) where hip house music sounds sweeter in a converted church. There's always **Stringfellows** (16 Upper St. Martin's Lane, WC2; ☎ 0171/240-5534) for pseudo-glam. **Subterania** (12 Acklam Rd., W10; ☎ 0181/960-4590) is an affordable, informal club with a good ethnic mix in music and people.

You'll find diversity in music and design at the **Wag Club** (35 Wardour St., W1; ☎ 0171/437-5534): Celtic medieval on 1 level, fur sculptures and art on the next. Destined to be a big hit is **Venom** (13–17 Bear St., WC2; ☎ 0171/839-4188), the newest and most spectacular club in town—no expense has been spared in design and sound.

Rock

London has an ever-lively, ever-changing rock scene. Club, concert, and pub dates are all listed in *Time Out*. The major rock venues include: **Earls Court Exhibition Centre** (Warwick Rd., SW5; ☎ 0171/385-1200); the **Mean Fiddler** (24–28A Harlesden High St.,

NW10; ☎ 0181/961-5490); the **Hammersmith Odeon** (Queen Caroline St.,W6; ☎ 0181/416-6080); **Royal Albert Hall** (Kensington Gore, SW7; ☎ 0171/ 589-8212); the **Forum Club** (9–17 Highgate Rd., NW5; ☎ 0171/284-0303); and **Wembley Arena** (Empire Way, Wembley; ☎ 0181/900-1234). The legendary **Marquee** (105 Charing Cross Rd.,WC2; ☎ 0171/ 437-6601) was closed at press time, but may reopen.

Jazz

Big-name jazz is always available in London, even though the city only has a few jazz clubs. Almost every well-known name in international jazz has played at **Ronnie Scott's** (47 Frith St.,W1; ☎ 0171/439-0747). It looks and feels like a private club, but anybody can enjoy the jazz; meals and drinks are served during the show. Nearby, jazz and blues are on the bill at the **100 Club** (100 Oxford St., W1; ☎ 0171/636-0933).

Chelsea's **606 Club** (90 Lots Rd., SW10; ☎ 0171/ 352-5953) is a relaxed, informal atmosphere where up-and-coming musicians perform alongside established names. Good music is accompanied by good food until 2am. Vocals on Sunday evenings.

The popular **Jazz Cafe** (5 Parkway, NW1; 0171/ 916-6060) is a trendy venue where the music spans Latin, soul, African, and hip-hop as well as jazz. **Simpsons-in-the-Strand,** the temple of traditional English fare, has just inaugurated late-night jazz evenings. A light menu is served until 1am (see "Dining").

Leading British musicians and occasional guests from other countries perform every evening at **Pizza Express** (10 Dean St., Soho,W1; ☎ 0171/437-9595) and at **Pizza on the Park** (11 Knightsbridge, Hyde Park Corner, SW1; ☎ 0171/235-5550). The **Blue Note** (1 Hoxton Sq., NW1; ☎ 0171/729-2476) is a packed and steamy cafe with a jazz room on the ground floor.

Jazz cognoscenti have long been fond of the **Bull's Head** pub (373 Lonsdale Rd., Barnes; ☎ 0181/ 876-5241), despite its unlikely villagey setting on the river. It offers fine jazz nightly, especially at Sunday lunch (noon–3pm), and serves Young's splendid beer.

Jazz en plein air is performed every summer at the **Royal Botanic Gardens** at Kew (information ☎ 0181/332-5000; reservations ☎ 0171/344-4444). Sit under the stars and listen to swing and blues in beautiful surroundings.

Folk Music

The **English Folk Dance and Song Society** (Cecil Sharp House, 2 Regent's Park Rd., NW1; ☎ 0171/485-2206) has performances on Saturday at 7:30pm. British, Irish, and American folk music are also performed in a variety of clubs and pubs (check *Time Out*) and at the **Fleadh Festival** in June (see p. 264).

Only in London

While most Londoners go to bed early, there are some late-night revelers among the species; you'll find them at the **Brick Lane Beigel Bake** (159 Brick Lane, E1). It's a great place to soak up atmosphere and chat up the taxi drivers, who make this a regular stop on the night shift.

Insomniacs head for the **Gate,** in Notting Hill, for midnight movies (see p. xxx). Or, for a cheap thrill, get yourself on the **N11 night bus** at Trafalgar Square—upper deck, front row—and cruise the sights of London all night long. If you're looking for a more private experience, hail a **taxi** from the South Bank, say, after dining at Conran's Le Pont de la Tour. One of the best drives in London is the nighttime route over Tower Bridge and into the West End. You'll feel like an actor in a period drama as you head south towards Westminster, along The Mall, past the Palace, and around Marble Arch heading up to Park Lane. The city positively sparkles.

If you can manage to leave a nightclub (or a warm bed) sufficiently early, head to **Smithfield Market** (Long Lane and Farringdon Rd., EC1), the last wholesale market in London to remain on its original site. This is a meat market (a real one) with lots of carcasses on display (including bunnies and piggies)—not everyone's idea of fun. Lots of pubs and cafes in the immediate vicinity open early to cater to the porters who work the market. The **Hope Pub** on Cowcross Street does a great breakfast, as does the **Fox & Anchor** on Charterhouse Street. If you're still hankering for the demimonde, there's always **Bar Italia** (22 Frith St., W1), a Soho institution open 23 hours a day. Not too far away is **Harry's** (19 Kingly St., W1), providing sustenance to clubbers until 6am.

THE BASICS

Before You Go

Tourist Offices

Contact the **British Tourist Authority** for information, at 551 Fifth Ave., Suite 701, New York, NY 10176 (☎ 212/986-2200 or 800/462-2748). You can also get lots of useful information from **Time Out's World Wide Web page** at http://www.timeout.co.uk.

Documents Required

A valid national passport is often all that is needed to visit Britain, since citizens of the United States, the Commonwealth, and most European and South American countries don't need visas. The maximum allowed stay as a visitor is 6 months. Vaccination certificates aren't required, but you should check if one is needed for re-entry into your own country.

Your valid driver's license and at least 1 year's driving experience is required to drive personal or rented cars.

Travel & Health Insurance

Visitors from countries with no reciprocal health agreement are not covered for any medical help other than accidents or emergencies; even then, you'll be expected to pay if you have to stay the night in hospital. No charge is made for visitors from countries with a reciprocal arrangement, such as EC (European Community) member countries, but U.S. residents and others will have to be insured.

Check with your at-home insurance carrier to see if your coverage extends to travel abroad. If it doesn't or if coverage is inadequate, consider purchasing short-term traveler's health insurance, or a comprehensive travel policy that covers catastrophes and mishaps as well, such as lost deposits paid to hotels and emergency costs such as special tickets home. Many travel agents can sell you a health or comprehensive policy for a nominal fee. Or, you can contact the following companies: **Access America** (☎ 800/284-8300); **Healthcare Abroad (MEDEX;** ☎ 703/687-3166 or 800/237-6615); **Mutual of Omaha (Tele-Trip;** ☎ 800/228-9792); **Travel Guard International** (☎ 800/826-1300); **Travel Insured International, Inc.** (☎ 800/243-3174 within the U.S., 203/528-7663 abroad).

The **IAMAT** (International Association for Medical Assistance to Travelers) is a nonprofit organization that has a directory of English-speaking doctors who will provide services for a fixed fee. There are member hospitals and clinics throughout the world, including several clinics in London. Membership is free. For further information write to IAMAT headquarters in the United States at 417 Center St., Lewiston, NY 14092.

Money

Currency There is no exchange control in Britain, so you can carry any amount of any currency through customs, in or out of the country. The unit of currency is the pound sterling, divided into 100 pence (p). There are coins for 1p, 2p, 5p, 10p, 20p, 50p, and £1, and notes for £5, £10, £20, and £50.

Exchanging Money At press time, the exchange rate was hovering around £1 = $1.60 (U.S.). It's been holding relatively steady for a year or more; but bear in mind that rates adjust on a daily basis and can fluctuate wildly. It's always wise to exchange enough money before departure to get you from the airport to your hotel. This way, you avoid delays and the lousy rates at the airport—and you might make it to the front of the taxi "queue" before everybody who wasn't so wise. Banks generally offer the best rates of exchange; they're usually open Monday to Friday 9:30am–3:30pm. Many of the "high street" branches are now open until 5pm; a handful of Central London branches are open until noon on Saturday, such as **Barclays** (208 Kensington High St., W8). Money exchange is now also available at competitive rates at major London post offices, with a 1% service charge. Money can be exchanged during off-hours at a variety of bureaux de change throughout the city, found at small shops and in hotels, railway stations (including the international terminal at Waterloo Station), travel agencies, and airports, but their exchange rates are poorer and they charge high service fees. Examine the prices and rates carefully before handing over your dollars, as there is no consumer organization to regulate the activities of privately run bureaux de change. *Time Out* recently did a survey of various exchange facilities, and American Express came out on top, with the lowest commission charged on dollar transactions. **American Express** is at 6 Haymarket, SW1 (☎ 0171/930-4411) and other locations throughout the city. Other reputable firms are **Thomas Cook,** 45 Berkeley St., W1 (☎ 0171/499-4000 or 0171/408-4000), branches of which can also be found at Victoria Station, Marble Arch, and other city locations; and, for 24-hour foreign exchange, **Chequepoint,** at 548 Oxford St., W1 (☎ 0171-723-1005) and other locations throughout London (hours will vary).

Traveler's Checks   Traveler's checks are widely accepted in hotels and large stores, but not often in smaller shops and restaurants. The exchange rate is roughly the same as for cash. Besides the major banks, good places to exchange traveler's checks for pounds are **American Express, Thomas Cook,** and **Barclays** (see "Exchanging Money," above), all of whom will cash their own traveler's checks without charging a commission. Thomas Cook and American Express now offer checks that can be signed by either of 2 persons.

ATMs   Approximately 250,000 Automated Teller Machines (ATMs) in 100 countries are tied to international networks like Cirrus and Plus. By using your bank card to withdraw money you will debit the amount from your account. When using an ATM abroad, the money will be in local currency; the rate of exchange tends to be as good, if not better, than what you would receive at an airport money counter or a hotel. Note that international withdrawal fees will be higher than domestic—ask your bank for specifics. To use your bank card at an ATM you'll need a Personal Identification Number (PIN). Contact your bank to program your PIN for the area you'll be visiting. Most ATMs outside the U.S. require a 4-digit PIN.

For a directory of **Cirrus** ATMs, call 800/424-7787; for **Plus** locations, call 800/843-7587. You can also access the Visa/PLUS International ATM Locator Guide through Internet: http://www.visa.com/visa. London now also has a network of **Citibank** cash machines. Call 0800/005500 for locations.

Credit Cards   Major international credit and charge cards, such as American Express, MasterCard (linked in

Britain with the Access Card), Visa (linked with Barclaycard), and Diners Club are widely accepted for most goods and services.

Getting Money From Home   Located in more than 70 countries, **American Express MoneyGram** (☎ 800/543-4080 in the U.S., or ☎ 0171/930-4411 in Great Britain) can wire money around the world. Senders must go to an agent in person. Up to $1,000 can be charged on a credit card (only Discover, MasterCard, or Visa—you can't use American Express). Amounts over $1,000 must be paid in cash; the maximum amount for a single transaction is $10,000. Recipients must present a reference number (phoned in from sender) and identification to pick up the cash.

Western Union works in a similar fashion, except that they also allow customers to wire money over the phone by using their credit cards (MasterCard and Visa only). Call 800/325-6000 for worldwide locations; in London, call 0800/833-833 to find the nearest collection location.

Fees for both of the above companies range from 5% to 10%, depending on the amount sent and method of payment.

Customs & Duties

Upon Arrival in Britain   If you're visiting the United Kingdom for less than 6 months, you are entitled to bring in, free of duty and tax, all personal effects that you intend to take with you when you leave, except tobacco goods, alcoholic drinks, and perfume. Be sure to carry dated receipts for valuable items, such as cameras and watches, or you may be charged a duty.

The limits for goods bought duty-free and tax paid within the EC have been virtually abolished. The much higher thresholds, above which you must be able to prove that the goods are for your own personal use, have been set at 800 cigarettes (or 400 cigarillos or 200 cigars or 1km of tobacco); 10 liters of liquor or strong liquor (more than 22% alcohol by volume); 90 liters of wine (no more than 60 liters of sparkling wine); 20 liters of fortified wines; and 110 liters of beer.

For goods bought anywhere outside the EC, or duty- and tax-free within the EC—including purchases from a U.K. duty-free shop—the limits remain as follows: 200 cigarettes (or 100 cigarillos or 50 cigars or 250gm tobacco); 1 liter of liquor or strong liquor (more than 22% alcohol by volume), or 2 liters of alcoholic drink (less than 22% alcohol), fortified wine, or sparkling wine, plus 2 liters of still table wine; 50g/60cc/2 fluid oz. perfume and 250cc/9 fluid oz. toilet water; and 136 pounds worth of all other goods, including gifts and souvenirs.

If you have anything in excess of the duty-free allowances, pass through the channel with red "Goods to declare" notices; otherwise pass through the green "Nothing to declare" channel.

For exemption from Value-Added Tax (VAT) on goods bought in Britain for export, see "Shopping."

Note: Travelers under 17 are not entitled to the allowances on tobacco goods and alcoholic drinks. Prohibited and restricted goods include narcotics, weapons, obscene publications and videos, counterfeit and copied goods, and animals and birds (if caught, you risk serious penalties and your animal may be destroyed).

Returning Home   U.S. citizens who have been out of the country for at least 48 hours and haven't already used the exemption (or any part of it) in the past 30 days may bring home $400 worth of foreign goods duty-free. Each family member, regardless of age, may do so; your exemptions can be pooled, so one of you can bring in more if another brings in less. A flat 10% duty applies to the next $1,000 of goods; above $1,400, the rate varies with the merchandise. (If the 48-hour or 30-day limits apply, your duty-free allowance drops to $25, which may not be pooled.)

Travelers 21 or older may bring back one liter of alcohol duty-free, provided the beverage laws of the state through which they re-enter the United States allow it. In addition, 100 non-Cuban cigars and 200 cigarettes are allowed, regardless of age. Antiques and works of art more than 100 years old are duty-free.

When to Go

Unlike, say, the folks in Washington, D.C., Londoners do not all take their vacations at the same time, so the capital never "closes down." It does, on the contrary, become very crowded at the height of summer; that's when the tourists arrive in droves. Consider sidestepping this stampede; the British climate may be unpredictable, but it's rarely extreme: The average temperature in July and August is 71°F; in December and January it's 44°F. The weather changes character so often in the course of a day that it's a constant and characteristic topic of British conversation.

London, being in one of the mildest parts of the country, can be very pleasant in the spring and fall. Yes, it rains, but you'll rarely get a true downpour. It's heaviest in November ($2^1/_2$ inches on average). I'm partial to May—the window boxes all get replanted, the trees are in bloom, and leafy residential streets are fragrant with lilac.

A whole calendar of outdoor sporting (and social) events is launched every March (see "Calendar of Events," below). But even in winter, London remains alive with activity. Several of the main exhibitions take place at this time of year. And one famous winter institution that London cast aside many years ago is the pea-soup fog. It's been vanquished by clean-air legislation, which, while robbing some of London's artists of their most intriguing subjects, has made the city a much more pleasant place in the colder months— year-round.

For weather forecasts in London and around the world, call **900/WEATHER;** calls are 95¢ a minute.

Calendar of Events

Upon your arrival in London, pick up a copy of *Time Out,* the most up-to-date source for what's happening in the city. It's available at all newsstands. *Time Out* has recently joined the Net, so you can also log on for current information at **http://www.timeout.co.uk.**

For exact dates of events listed below, call the London Tourist Board and Convention Bureau's **Visitorcall** service at 0839/123456, or the **City of London Information Office** at 0171/332-1456.

January
1st of January: London Parade, from Parliament Square to Berkeley Square in Mayfair. Bands, floats, and carriages. Procession starts around 2:45pm.

1st week: January sales. Most shops offer good reductions. Many sales now start as early as late December. The most voracious shoppers camp out at Harrod's overnight to get in first.

Mid-January: London Contemporary Art Fair at the Business Design Center; call 0171/359-3535.

End of January/early February: Chinese New Year, Chinatown, around Gerrard Street, W1. Dragons, lanterns, flags, torches, and the Lion Dance.

Last Sunday: **Charles I Commemoration,** Whitehall, SW1. At 11am on the anniversary of his execution, the unofficial King's Army parades from St. James's Palace to the Banqueting House.

January through March: Rugby Union Internationals, Twickenham; for information, call 0181/892-8161.

March
March 1 (or nearest Sunday): St. David's Day. A member of the Royal Family usually presents the Welsh Guards with the principality's national emblem, a leek; call 0171/414-3291 for location and further information.

2nd Week: Ideal Home Exhibition, Earl's Court Exhibition Center, SW5. A huge exhibition of everything for in and around the home; call 01895/677-677.

Mid-March: Chelsea Antiques Fair, a twice-yearly gathering of England's best dealers (again in mid-Sept), held at Old Town Hall, King's Road SW3 (☎ 01444/482-514). **London International Book Fair,** Olympia Exhibition Center, W14; call 0181/910-7899 for information. Over 4,000 journalists and buyers fight to get the first look during **London Fashion Week;** call 0171/636-5577 for details (held again in Oct). **Open House,** a 1-day event during which members of the public have access to normally closed buildings of architectural significance; call 0181/341-1371 for schedule and further information.

Shrove Tuesday, (last day before Lent): Great Spitalfields Pancake Race. Teams of 4 run in relays, tossing their pancakes. At noon at Old Spitalfields Market, Brushfield Street, E1. To join in, call 0171/375-0441.

April
Early April: Boat Race, Putney to Mortlake. Oxford and Cambridge University eights battle upstream with awesome power. Park yourself at one of the Thames-side pubs along the route—the Dove in Hammersmith is a good choice—to see the action. Check *Time Out* for exact dates and times.

Holy Week, Tuesday: Abbey Choir performs at Westminster Abbey, SW1; call 0171/222-5152.

Easter Sunday: Hundreds of fanatics hope for a fine wind at **Blackheath,** SE3, the scene of a 2-day kite festival; call 0171/836-1666 for details.

Easter Monday: Harness Horse Parade, a morning parade of heavy working horses in superb gleaming brass harnesses and plumes, at Battersea Park, SW11;

call 01733/234-451. **Chaucer Festival,** celebrating Chaucer's *Canterbury Tales* with readings, services, concerts, and a costumed cavalcade at Suffolk Cathedral, SE5; call 01227/470-379.

Mid-April: 30,000 competitors, from very fast to very mad, run in the **London Marathon,** from Greenwich Park to Buckingham Palace (☎ 0161/703-8161).

April 21: The **Queen's Birthday** is celebrated with 21-gun salutes in Hyde Park and on Tower Hill at noon by troops in parade dress.

Late April/early May: The showpiece rugby league match, the **Rugby League Cup Final** is held at Wembley Stadium; call 0181/900-1234 for exact date and details. **National Gardens Scheme:** More than 100 private gardens in Greater London are open to the public on set days through October, and tea is sometimes served; pick up a current copy of the NGS guidebook from most bookstores for schedule information, or contact The National Gardens Scheme Charitable Trust, Hatchlands Park, East Clandon, Guildford, Surrey GU4 7RT (☎ 01483/211-535).

May

2nd Sunday: May Fayre and Puppet Festival, Covent Garden. Procession at 10am, service at St. Paul's at 11:30am, then Punch and Judy shows until 6pm at the site where Pepys watched England's first show in 1662; call 0171/375-0441.

Mid-May: England's showpiece soccer match, the **FA Cup Final,** is held at Wembley Stadium; for exact date and details, call 0181/902-8833. The **Royal Windsor Horse Show** is held at Home Park, Windsor Castle (☎ 01753/860-633); you might even spot a royal.

Ascension Day: Beating the Bounds. The boundary stones of parishes were traditionally "whacked" with a stick in defiance (even though one of the marks is in mid-river, it is still ceremonially whacked on an annual basis). The festivities start at about 4pm at All-Hallows-by-the-Tower, EC3.

Late May: Glyndebourne Festival Opera Season, Sussex, through August: Exclusive performances in a beautiful setting, with champagne picnics in between performances. Since the completion of the new theater last year, tickets are a bit easier to come by (☎ 01273/813-813). **Chelsea Flower Show,** Royal Hospital, Chelsea, SW3, a massive and superb 4-day horticultural display (☎ 0171/834-4333). **Regent's**

Park Open-Air Theatre season begins: Shakespeare tends to dominate but the program has expanded to include other genres; bring wine, glasses, and a sweater (☎ 0171/486-2431).

June

Early June: Summer Exhibition, Royal Academy, Piccadilly, W1, through August: An extensive potpourri surveying the British art scene (☎ 0171/439-4996). **Beating Retreat** at Horse Guards Parade, Whitehall, SW1: Military massed bands and marching in front of members of the Royal family (The "retreat," surprisingly, relates to the setting of the sun, not the British empire); for tickets write: Household Division, Horse Guards, Whitehall, SW1A 2AX.

1st Saturday: The Derby, Epsom Downs, Surrey. This great horse race has been taking place—and attracting huge crowds—for more than 200 years (☎ 01372/ 470-047).

Early June: The **Fleadh** (Gaelic word for a festival of music, pronounced "flah"), Finsbury Park, N4: An annual festival of Irish rock and folk music; call 0181/ 963-0940 for information. The **Greenwich Festival,** Greenwich, SE10, is 2 weeks of music, theater, and dance events, plus fireworks over the Thames on opening night (☎ 0181/305-1818).

Mid-June: Test Match, 5 days of international cricket matches, takes place at Lords Cricket Ground, NW8 (☎ 0171/289-8979). **Grosvenor House Art and Antiques Fair,** Grosvenor House Hotel, Park Lane, W1: This is the most prestigious of antique fairs, where all items are vetted for quality and authenticity (☎ 0171/ 495-6406). **Royal Ascot:** The Berkshire racecourse sees some fine racing, but the event is more important for the royals on parade as well as the society folk out to impress one other and have fun with outré headgear; for tickets, call 0344/22211. **London International Festival of Theatre:** Each year over 175 cutting-edge stage and performance artists from around the world are invited to participate; 1996 events will be geared to kids (☎ 0171/490-3965).

June 11 (or nearest Saturday): Trooping the Colour, Horse Guards Parade, SW1. The Queen leaves from Buckingham Palace in procession to receive the Colour from her Foot Guards amid full pageantry. Tickets for grandstand seats must be applied for in advance; write to: The Brigade Major (Trooping the Colour),

HQ, Household Division, Horse Guards, Whitehall, SW1A 2AX (☎ 0171/414-2497).

Mid-June: Spitalfields Festival. The architecturally splendid Christ Church, Commercial Street, E1 (☎ 0171-377-0287), designed by Hawksmoor, is the setting for a series of classical baroque and modern music. Lunchtime and evening concerts are often organized in conjunction with guided walks around the area.

Last week in June/1st week in July: The world's top tennis players battle it out at the **Wimbledon Tennis Championships.** Tickets for Centre and Number 1 courts are allotted by ballot; for application send a SASE between September 1 and December 31 to: All England Lawn Tennis Club, P.O. Box 98, Church Road, SW19 5AE. Or be prepared to wait for hours for secondary court tickets on the day of play. For recorded information, call 0181/946-2244.

June–September: Outdoor concerts in all major parks. Be sure to pack a picnic to bring to Kenwood Lakeside, Hampstead, NW3, or Marble Hill Park, Twickenham, SW7. Tickets are available through Ticketmaster (☎ 0171/413-1443). Concerts are also held at the Crystal Palace Bowl, SE20 (☎ 0181/460-6677). Throughout the summer, military and jazz bands perform in Royal Parks; call 0171/298-2100.

Late June/early July: Sotheby's (☎ 0171-493-8080) and **Christie's** (☎ 0171-839-9060) **Impressionist/ Modern, Contemporary,** and **Old Master auctions** (held again in late November–early December).

July

1st week: Henley Royal Regatta, Henley-on-Thames, Oxfordshire. Yet another sporting event—rowing—that's also part of the "season." Don't be surprised to see some serious drinking taking place on the picnic blankets alongside the river. Call 01491/572 153.

Early July: City of London Festival: classical concerts at various venues throughout the City, including St. Paul's Cathedral; for details, call 0171/332-1456. The widely acclaimed 5-day international **Hampton Court Palace Flower Show,** East Molesey, Surrey (☎ 0171/834-4333), is eclipsing its sister show in Chelsea; here, you can actually purchase the exhibits.

Mid-July: Doggett's Coat and Badge Race, a rowing contest for single sculls from London Bridge to Cadogan Pier in Chelsea— against the tide. The best viewing is from London Bridge.

Late July: Promenade Concerts (the "Proms").
One of the world's greatest classical music festivals is
held at Royal Albert Hall, SW7 (☎ 0171-589-8212),
through September.

Last week in July: Military prowess and pageantry on
display at the **Royal Tournament,** Earl's Court
Exhibition Centre, Warwick Road, SW5 (☎ 0171/
244-0244).

August
Early August: Buckingham Palace opens to the
public through September. Purchase tickets that day at
Green Park ticket office (☎ 0171/799-2331).

**Last Sunday and Monday: The Notting Hill Car-
nival,** Ladbroke Grove, W11. This West Indian street
carnival featuring music, food, and more is purported
to be the largest street festival in Europe. Occasionally
things gets rowdy, but usually the crowd is well-
behaved. Call 0181/964-0544 for information.

September
Mid-September: Chelsea Antiques Fair, Chelsea
Old Town Hall, King's Road, SW3 (see March, above,
for details).

3rd Sunday: Horsemen's Sunday, Church of St.
John and St. Michael, Hyde Park Crescent. A weird
ceremony in which the horses are gathered for a
blessing by a vicar on horseback. After, they are
paraded through the park to Kensington Paddock, where
show-jumping takes place. Call 0171/262-1732.

**During the month: Raising of the Thames Bar-
rier,** Unity Way, SE18. Once a year, a full test is done
on this miracle of modern engineering; all 10 of the
massive steel gates are raised against the high tide. Call
0181/854-1373.

October
1st Monday: Judges Service, Westminster Abbey,
SW1. The judiciary attends a service in Westminster
Abbey to mark the opening of the law term. Afterward, in full regalia—wigs and all—they form a
procession and walk to the House of Lords for their
"Annual Breakfast." You'll have a great view of the
procession from behind the Abbey.

1st Sunday: Pearly Harvest Festival, St. Martin-in-
the-Fields, WC2: at 3pm, see the Pearly Kings and
Queens, Cockney folk leaders, in full uniform. The
Punch and Judy Festival, Covent Garden Market,

WC2 (☎ 0171/836-9136), is Mecca for Punch and Judy scholars.

Early October: Top international competitors meet at the **Horse of the Year Show,** a show-jumping event held at Wembley Arena. Call 0181/900-1234 for details.

Mid-October: London Fashion Week (see March, above, for details).

Late October: Quit Rents Ceremony, Royal Courts of Justice, WC2. An official receives token rents on behalf of the Queen; the ceremony includes splitting sticks and counting horseshoes. Call 0171/936-6131 for free tickets.

November
November 5: Guy Fawkes Night. To celebrate the 1605 Gunpowder Plot to blow up Parliament, fireworks and bonfires flare up all over town, with effigies of the conspiracy's leader burned. Check *Time Out* for locations.

1st week: State Opening of Parliament. The processional route starts at 10:37am from Buckingham Palace, and then progresses via The Mall and Horse Guards Parade to the Palace of Westminster. Members of the Royal Family attend; everybody's in full regalia and ancient gilded state coaches. The north side of the mall is a good vantage point, but arrive early. Call 0171/219-4272 for exact date and more details.

2nd Saturday: Thousands line the streets during the **Lord Mayor's Show,** the City's most spectacular event. Every year, the new Lord Mayor is carried by gilded State Coach from Guildhall to the Law Courts, Strand, WC2, followed by colorful floats. Call 0171/332-1456 to confirm date and time.

Sunday nearest November 11: Remembrance Sunday honors the war dead. The Queen and State attend a 10:30am ceremony at the Cenotaph, Whitehall, SW1.

Mid-November: London Jazz Festival is a 10-day event that always attracts big jazz names; most performances at the Royal Festival Hall (☎ 0171 /928-8800). **London Film Festival,** National Film Theatre, South Bank (☎ 0171/928-3232): For 2 weeks, over 200 international films are shown at a variety of locations.

Late November: The **Christmas lights** are lit along Regent, Bond, and Oxford streets. Regent Street was voted the best in my own informal survey.

Late November/Early December: Sotheby's and **Christie's auctions** (see June for details).

December
Early December: There's caroling most evenings beneath the **Norwegian Christmas Tree** in Trafalgar Square.

December 31: Watch Night, St. Paul's Cathedral, where a rather lovely New Year's Eve service takes place at 11:30pm; call 0171/248-2705 for information. **Trafalgar Square** is the other traditional spot for high-spirited revelers; **Parliament Square** is great for watching Big Ben strike 12.

Late December: Harrods' After-Christmas Sale, Knightsbridge. Call 0171/730-1234 for exact dates and hours.

Daily Events
11am (10am Sunday): **Changing of the Guard,** Horse Guards Parade. A mounted guard leaves Hyde Park Barracks.

11:30am (only alternate days in winter, and canceled if weather is bad): **Changing of the Guard,** Buckingham Palace.

9:30pm: Ceremony of the Keys, Tower of London. Ceremonial changing of guards. Write at least 2 months in advance to: Operation Department, Ceremony of the Keys, Waterloo Block, HM Tower of London, EC3N 4AB, for free tickets. For further information, call 0171/709-0765.

Learning Vacations & Package Tours
The National Trust, which oversees the preservation and restoration of hundreds of historic properties around the country, offers a series of "Working Holiday" tours throughout Britain. In exchange for your hard work, commitment, and a small fee, the Trust will put you up and feed you. Contact the National Trust, P.O. Box 538, Melksham, Wiltshire, SN12 8SU (☎ 01225/790 290).

　　British Rail offers a series of package tours aimed at the independent traveler. The tours are organized around various themes and locations, such as the London Theater, "Scenic Britain," and now, with the opening of the Channel Tunnel, France. Rail passes and accommodations are included; many of the tours can also be booked to include airfare. Contact British Rail in the USA: 1500 Broadway, New York, NY, 10036-4015 (☎ 800/677-8585).

Mail

Post offices are usually open Monday to Friday 9am–5:30pm, Saturday 9am–12:30pm. A notable exception is the post office in William IV Street, off Trafalgar Square, which is open Monday to Saturday 8am–8pm. Post offices are marked by a black star in the *London A to Z* maps, available at bookstores throughout the city. For general information, call 0345/223 344. Stamps are available at post offices, some shops (generally news agents), and, occasionally, from machines. There are 2 classes of inland mail, but the 2nd class is sometimes a lot slower and somewhat unreliable, so spring for 1st class. You will also have to specify which rate you want for international mail, as mail traveling internationally won't automatically go via air mail. In addition to the boxes in post offices, mail can also be dropped in the red boxes placed along the main streets.

For special services, such as express, recorded, or guaranteed delivery, inquire at the post office or call the information number listed above. All of the major courier services, such as Federal Express, have offices in London.

Postal Codes & Street Signs Compass points appear in the beginning of the postal codes; they're also printed on street signs. Much of the West End is W1 (West One), addresses in the City are usually EC (East Central), and so on. The system is not as logical as it might be, however, so Londoners tend to give verbal directions in terms of the area's or the district's name.

Rates A standard letter to North America is 41p; postcards cost 35p. Letters within Britain sent 1st-class cost 25p; 2nd-class, 19p.

Electric Current

The electric current is 240V A/C. Plugs have 3 square pins and take 3-, 5-, or 13-amp fuses. Foreign visitors will need adapters for their own appliances; buy them before departure.

Tips for Travelers with Disabilities

London is not very user-friendly for disabled visitors; steps leading up to buildings are their biggest barrier. That said, compared with the rest of Europe, London is surprisingly conscientious when it comes to wheel-chair access; most sidewalks have cuts, and major sights have proper access. The transport system, cinemas, and theaters are still pretty much off-limits, but London Transport does publish a leaflet called *Access to the Underground,* which gives details of elevators and ramps at individual underground stations; call 0171/918-3312. The new Eurostar trains that ply the Channel Tunnel have been well-equipped with the wheelchair-bound in mind. Many hotels, even the smaller ones, will provide ramps and ground-floor rooms for guests who need them. And the London Black Cab is perfectly suited for the wheelchair-bound; the interiors have plenty of room for maneuvering.

The Royal Association for Disability and Rehabilitation (RADAR, 12 City Forum, 250 City Rd., London EC14 8AF; ☎ 0171/250-3222) publishes information for disabled visitors to Britain. **The Society of London Theatre** (Bedford Chambers, The Piazza, Covent Garden, WC2E 8HQ; ☎ 0171/836-0971) produces a free *Disabled Guide to the West End.*

Can-be-Done, Ltd. (7-11 Kensington High St., London W8 5NP; ☎ 0181/907-2400) arranges tours around London and England for both disabled and able-bodied visitors. **William Forrester** (☎ 01483/575 401) offers guided tours around London in an adapted mini-bus. **Stationlink,** a wheelchair-accessible "midibus" service, connects nine British Rail stations and Victoria Coach Station; contact London Transport's **Unit for Disabled Passengers** (172 Buckingham Palace Rd., SW1W 9TN; ☎ 0171/222-5600). **Artsline** (☎ 0171/388-2227) provides information on accessibility to arts events, and **Holiday Care Service** (2nd floor, Imperial Buildings, Victoria Road, Horley, Surrey RH6 7PZ; ☎ 01293/774 535) can tell you about accessible accommodations. **Tripscope** (☎ 0181/994-9294) is a hotline for disabled people touring London and the rest of Britain; they have an extensive database on wheelchair-accessible facilities.

Tips for Travelers with Children

The London Black Cab is a lifesaver for families; the roomy interior allows a stroller to be lifted right into the cab without unstrapping baby. If you're staying with friends, you can hire baby equipment from **Chelsea Baby Hire** (83 Burntwood Lane, SW17 0AJ; ☎ 0181/944-8124). If you want a night out without the kids, you're in luck: London has it's own children's hotel,

Pippa Pop-ins (430 Fulham Rd., SW6, ☎ 0171/385-2458), which accommodates children overnight in a wonderful nursery filled with lots of toys and caring minders. Other recommendable baby-sitting services are: **Baby-sitters Unlimited** (☎ 0181/892-8888); **Childminders** (☎ 0171/935-2049 or 9763); and **Universal Aunts** (☎ 0171/386-5900).

To find out what's on for children, pick up the leaflet *Where to Take Children,* published by the London Tourist Board and Convention Bureau. If you have specific questions, ring **Kidsline** (☎ 0171/222-8070) Monday to Friday 4–6pm and summer holidays 9am–4pm, or the **London Tourist Board's** special children's information line (☎ 0839/123-404).

Forte Hotel offers great deals for parents traveling with kids. Up to 2 children under 16 stay free when sharing a room with 1 or 2 adults. The **Basil Street Hotel** is child-friendly, with 2-room suites connected by a shared bathroom.

For more tips, see "London for Kids" in "Sights and Attractions."

Car Rentals

It's probably not worth your while to rent a car if you don't intend to venture outside London. Parking is difficult, and with the newly privatized parking-offense unit, ticketing is swift and fierce (or even worse, you might get clamped; see "Driving Around London" in "Getting Around," below).

If you want to rent, you must be over 21 and hold a full valid national license. Insurance is usually included in the rate, but check first. You can arrange to rent a car through a travel agent or at desks in airports, major stations, and large hotels, or you can call one of the major companies directly, such as **Avis** (☎ 0181/848-8733) or **Hertz** (☎ 0181/679-1799). All these companies can arrange for cars to be waiting if you arrive by air or train, and automatic transmissions are readily available.

Arriving by Plane

London's **Heathrow Airport,** west of the capital, is one of the busiest in the world, and there are regular flights from most countries on a wide range of international airlines. **Gatwick Airport,** to the south, is the city's other busy international airport. To the northeast, London's 3rd and most modern airport, **Stansted,** a beautiful structure designed by Norman Foster, is becoming increasingly popular as U.S. and European airlines take up spare capacity there. **Luton Airport,** to the north, is mainly an air charter destination. All 4 major airports are within an hour of the city center. **London City Airport,** which connects with many European cities from Docklands, is highly convenient for the business traveler. (Negotiations are underway concerning London City Airport's accommodation of GulfStar IV jets, bringing intercontinental travelers directly into the city. Hopefully, landing permission will be secured by 1996.)

The flying time between London and New York is $6^1/_2$ hours. Many U.S. airlines serve London nonstop, including **Continental, Delta, TWA, United, American,** and **Northwest Airlines;** the U.K. airlines with offices in the United States include **British Airways** and **Virgin Atlantic.** All airlines offer overnight flights with early morning arrivals to the capital. Competition between Virgin and British Airways is fierce; Virgin is trying to woo the frequent business traveler with such perks as complimentary chauffeur-driven Range Rovers to and from the airports, on-board massages and beauty treatments, waiting lounges with libraries, hair stylists, video-game rooms, and individual video monitors mounted at each seat.

As London is oftentimes used by various Asian and Pacific airlines as a stopping point, also consider these companies. Air fares vary enormously, so consult your travel agent.

Arriving by Train

The Chunnel, linking Dover with Calais, opened in May 1994. Despite a few well-publicized breakdowns, it's a big success. **Eurostar** now offers hourly train service between Waterloo Station in the heart of London and Gare du Nord in Paris, as well as between London and Brussels. Travel time between London and Paris is a fast 3 hours; it's 3 hours and 15 minutes to Brussels. There are 2 classes of service: Standard is perfectly comfortable, with onboard trolley snack service and buffet cars. First class pampers you all the way, with spacious reclining seats, complimentary champagne, and a selection of international newspapers.

Currently a number of "Eurostar Link" trains connect to other cities in Britain; starting in mid-1996, Eurostar will have an overnight service that will run between London and Amsterdam, Dortmund, and Frankfurt; passengers will be delivered to their

Eurostar at Waterloo

destinations in the early morning, after a night aboard deluxe sleepers served by designer-outfitted crews.

Departing London via Eurostar   The British Rail Terminal at Waterloo, a stunning masterpiece of contemporary architecture designed by Nicholas Grimshaw, is easily reached by tube from the Bakerloo, Northern, Waterloo, and City lines. Make sure to arrive at least 20 minutes before departure, or you may be refused boarding. Otherwise, it's easy-easy: check-in is automatic—just enter your ticket into the turnstile and you're through; custom controls are carried out on the train, and, before you know it, voila, Paris!

Tickets   Eurostar tickets can be booked directly from Eurostar once you're in Britain by calling 0345/881-881, or through travel agents. In the United States, you can buy tickets using your credit card by calling British Rail at 800/677-8585; they also offer a British Rail Pass/Eurostar combination package.

Arriving by Car

The completion of the Channel Tunnel also means that visitors can arrive by car. Eurotunnel operates **Le Shuttle** (☎ 0990/353 535), the train service that carries automobiles between Folkestone on the British side and Calais in France. During the week, it's a policy of "turn up and go"; weekends require reservations.

Hertz offers **Le Swap,** a service for passengers taking Le Shuttle. At Calais, you can switch cars for either a left-hand or right-hand–drive vehicle, depending on to which country you're heading. Once you arrive on the English side, the M20 takes you directly into London.

Staying in London
Getting Around
By Public Transport

London Regional Transport's network of buses and underground trains (often referred to as "the tube") is extensive and efficient. But, as in all great cities, try to avoid traveling at rush hour. Free bus and tube maps and details of services are available at the **Travel Information Centres** located at the following tube stations: Heathrow Underground at Terminal 1,2,3; Euston; King's Cross; Liverpool Street; St. James's Park; Piccadilly Circus; Oxford Circus; Waterloo; and Victoria. London Transport has a 24-hour information hotline (☎ 0171/222-1234); you may have to wait awhile for an answer, as the calls are stacked and dealt with in rotation.

For all public transport, remember to wait your turn in the queue.

Fares & Passes   The transport system is divided into 6 fare zones. Zone 1 covers the Circle Line of the underground and a small area beyond, and incorporates most of the places you're likely to visit. Currently, the fare for a one-way trip within Zone 1 is £1. The price increases as you add more zones. Children under 16 pay a reduced fare, and those under 5 travel free. Children ages 14 and 15 must have a Child Rate Photocard, available at all tube stations; proof of date of birth and a passport-size photo is needed to obtain this (most tube stations have self-service photo booths).

If you don't plan to make extensive use of the tube, you can purchase one-way and round-trip tickets from the ticket machines located in the stations. Carefully choose your destination when purchasing tickets; London Transport has been fiercely enforcing £10 on-the-spot penalties against those riders who travel outside of the zones stipulated on their purchased ticket.

If you're feeling intrepid and intend to use the system as your primary means of transport, it's worthwhile buying a special ticket. The most convenient is the **Visitor Travelcard** (only available for purchase outside London), which allows you unlimited travel on the bus (except the Airbus) and underground, as well as on British Rail services within the greater London area and the Docklands Light Railway. Visitor Travelcards are available for 2, 3, 4, and 7 days, and range in cost from $17 to $49. Cards can be purchased from **British Rail** (☎ 800/677-8585).

Once in Britain, you can purchase a **Travelcard** at underground stations, London Travel Information Centres, and from news agents displaying the "pass agent" sign. The Travelcard is good for travel after 9:30am (all times during the weekend) on the tube, Docklands Light Railway, and London Buses (but not Airbuses or Night buses). You must buy a Travelcard for all the zones through which you plan to travel, so select carefully. They are valid for 1- and 7-day and 1-month periods. If you're purchasing a ticket valid for more than 1 day (or any reduced-price ticket for a 14- or 15-year-old), you'll need a passport-sized photograph; most stations have passport photo machines adjacent to the ticket booth. To avoid the time restrictions, visitors can purchase an **LT Card,** a commuter travel card good for anywhere from 1 to 7 days.

You can buy a 1-day **Bus Pass,** valid at all times only on the buses for selected zones, in advance, at most news agents displaying the "pass agent" sign, at London Travel Information Centres, and at larger bus stations. The date of travel is scratched off on your first journey of the day on which you decide to use your pass. For a 7-day Bus Pass, you'll need a passport-sized photograph.

Navigating the Underground

The underground is the easiest and fastest way to get around the city. During rush hour the crush can be brutal, as can the lack of air-conditioning in summer (Londoners continue to believe that each successive hot summer is a unique aberration). Americans are often amused by certain tube colloquialisms—exits are marked "Way Out" and riders are continually warned to "Mind the Gap." The stations are easily recognized by the London Transport symbol, a red horizontal line through a red circle. On maps, each rail line has its own color (the Circle Line is yellow, the Central Line red, etc.), so it's easy to plan your journey and note where you have to change lines.

Buy your ticket before boarding, either from a ticket office or a machine in the station, where the fares to each destination will be on display. Show your ticket to a collector or put it in the automatic entry gate and walk through, picking it up as you go—you'll need to present it at the end of your journey. Follow the signs to the platform for the line and direction you want. Check the indicators above the platform and on the front of the train to make sure it's going to your destination; some trains don't go to the end of the line, and some lines divide into 2 or more branches. Most platforms have an electronic board posted overhead that indicates the line and destination of the next approaching train. Many of these signs also display the approximate number of minutes until the next train (London Transport must use a different clock then the rest of us; 2 minutes is very often more like 5).

Trains stop at every station, with only a few exceptions on weekends. The first tube trains run at about 5am, and they begin to close down after 11:30pm; you might have trouble with connections then. Smoking is forbidden throughout the system.

The Buses

London's red buses are usually slower than the tube, but can be a cheaper means of getting about town. They also offer good views from the upper deck. Do use them, and don't be discouraged by the complex network of routes; people waiting in the line will usually help you, and the conductor will answer your questions and tell you, if necessary, when you've reached your destination.

Each bus runs along part or all of a numbered route. Find out which route you want from the map at the bus stop, and look at the indicator on the front of the bus to check that it's going far enough along the route for you. There are 2 types of bus stops: a **normal stop,** with the red LT symbol on a white background, where all buses stop; and a **request stop,** with a white LT symbol on a red sign bearing the word "Request," where the bus will stop only if you raise your hand (or, if you're on the bus and want to get off, you must ring the bell). All bus stops become request stops at night.

On some buses, the conductor will come around and collect your fare or check your Travelcard or Bus Pass during the journey; on others, you'll have to pay as you enter. The buses run between about 5am and 11:30pm. There are a few night buses on special routes, running once an hour or so; most pass through Trafalgar Square.

In Central London, small "midi" buses have been introduced by London Transport on selected central

London routes. They're specially designed to give speedier rides to people traveling just a few stops. **Green Line Coaches** run from Central London into the country outside London Transport's area. They stop only rarely in London, and are more expensive than red buses. Ask at a Travel Information Centre about fares and routes.

Docklands Light Railway

The Docklands Light Railway links the City with the rapidly developing Docklands area. It operates Monday to Friday 5:30am–12:30am, with selected main routes now offering weekend service 6:30am–11:30pm. For information, call 0171/538-0311.

Taxis

London's distinctive black taxis (actually, most taxis now sport fanciful colorful advertisements, the Häagen Dazs motif being a favorite) are driven by some of the best drivers in the world, who have to pass an examination to prove their detailed knowledge of the city before they get a license. They can be hailed as they cruise the streets (an available cab illuminates its yellow light), but not at curbs that are adjacent to zigzag lines. You'll also find them at stands at stations, and outside hotels and large shops.

Once they have stopped for you, taxis are obliged to take you anywhere you want to go within 6 miles of the pick-up point, provided it's within the metropolitan area. The fare, always shown on the meter, consists of a basic rental charge and subsequent additions according to the length of your journey; there are additional charges for extra passengers, night or weekend journeys, and for baggage. In all cases, notices are displayed inside the taxi with details of all charges. Give the driver a 10% to 15% tip.

Private taxis (usually sedans, known as "minicabs") cannot be hailed but must be ordered by phone. You'll find the numbers by some public telephones and in the Yellow Pages directory under "Taxis and Private Hire Vehicles." Stick to the black taxis if possible; the strict regulations governing fares for black taxis do not apply to minicabs. If you have to use a minicab, try to fix the fare with the driver at the start of the journey to avoid problems when you reach your destination. Don't be tempted by a minicab driver that tries to lure you in while you're waiting on the street; not only is this illegal, but it undermines the black taxis, who have trained for years in order to procure licenses.

Driving Around London

Driving in London is not as aggressive as in most large cities, but there are a few difficulties for foreign visitors: The city has a totally unplanned road system with an abundance of one-way routes, and everyone appears to be on the wrong side of the road. If you can face all that, make sure you're carrying your license and that all your lights are working.

You must drive on the left and you must pass only on the right. The speed limit in London and all built-up areas (i.e., streets with lampposts) is 30 m.p.h. (48kph) unless otherwise indicated. Standard international road signs are generally used. Pedestrian crossings are marked by black and white zones; sometimes they're controlled by traffic lights. In either case, pedestrians have the right of way and traffic must stop to let them cross, unless there is a green traffic light showing, in which case drivers have priority. Observe lane division rules: Slower traffic keeps to the inside (left) and faster traffic passes on the outside (right). Be sure to get into the correct lane coming up to an intersection, as different lanes may be controlled by different traffic signals. "Roundabouts" (traffic circles) can be a real trip. My first time around Piccadilly Circus was a hair-raising experience. Stick to the outside lane in order to easily exit at the right street; if you feel you can't, just go around again—I've done it many times.

Horns cannot be used from 11:30pm to 7am except in emergencies. The wearing of seat belts in both front seats is compulsory, as is the wearing of rear seat belts if the car is fitted with them. There are strong penalties for driving under the influence of alcohol—don't do it.

Parking   Parking is extremely difficult on streets in Central London; it's usually possible only at meters for a maximum of 2 hours. Two yellow lines or, more rarely, a red line by the roadside means no parking at all; 1 yellow line means no parking during the work day (8am–6:30pm Mon–Sat). Always look for an explanatory sign in the restricted zones: It will give details of the maximum stay allowed, or indicate that the space is for residents only. Parking is always prohibited near pedestrian crossings and intersections.

As noted above, with the privatization of parking enforcement, ticketing is swift (and the penalties are high—£60). If you violate parking regulations, you will be fined (but not on the spot). Or worse, your car may immobilized by a wheel clamp. Detailed instructions on how to get it released will be pasted to the windshield; it involves going to the pound to pay an "unclamping" fee and then waiting several hours for the clamp to be removed. If your car is missing, don't panic—call 0171/747-4747 to check and see if it has been towed.

Off the streets, there are various parking lots and garages, often indicated by a blue sign with a large **P.** Charges for these should be displayed clearly somewhere near the entrance.

Roadside assistance is available from the **Royal Automobile Club** (for breakdowns, call 0800/828 282; for information call 0181/686-2314) and the **Automobile Association** (☎ 0990-500 600); both clubs have reciprocal arrangements with AAA. If you're driving a rental, check your rental agreement before you call one of these companies for assistance; many of the major leasing companies provide free roadside assistance.

Getting to London from the Airport
From Heathrow
Via Underground   Heathrow is the west terminus of the underground's Piccadilly Line; trains link the airport with all parts of the city between 5am (6:45am on Sun) and 11pm. It will probably take you about 40 minutes to get where you're going; the current fare is £3.10. This isn't a good option if you have lots of luggage as you'll probably have to change trains, and rush-hour crowds will be most unappreciative of your heavy luggage taking up valuable space. If you've purchased a Visitor Travelcard for all zones (see "Fares and

Passes," above), you can use it to take the tube into the city. If you arrive into Heathrow without a Travelcard and want to get into town via the tube but won't need a 6-zone card during your stay, buy a Travelcard for the zones you need and then pay for a 1-time extension to get you into town.

By Car   The M4 motorway is the other main link between Heathrow and the city proper. The trip to the center takes anywhere from 30 minutes to more than an hour, depending upon traffic. Once on the highway, follows signs for West End (not The West, which will you take you out to Windsor). If you arrive on an overnight flight, the morning rush hour will just about be in full swing—be prepared.

By Bus   This is the best alternative for those with lots of luggage. London Transport operates an **Airbus** (☎ 0181/897-3305) that runs daily every 15 to 20 minutes from 6:30am to 8:30pm via 2 routes, stopping at the major hotel areas in Central London. It can take anywhere from an hour to 90 minutes, depending on your destination and traffic flow. You can purchase Airbus vouchers in advance from British Rail's U.S. office (☎ 800/677-8585).

By Taxi   A more expensive alternative is to take a taxi. They're always readily available at the airport, but make sure you take a black metered-cab and not one of the "pirate" operators or minicabs, who may overcharge. The average fare from West London to Heathrow is £30; extra charges are levied for luggage and additional passengers.

From the Other Airports
Gatwick Airport   Gatwick, in the south, is farther out of the city. The easiest way into London is to take the **Gatwick Express,** the fast, comfortable British Rail service from the airport station. Trains depart every 15 minutes 5am–9pm and at half-hour intervals until 11:50pm, reaching Victoria Station in London in 30 minutes; you'll then be able to reach all parts of the city easily from Victoria. There's no extra charge for British Rail Pass holders.

The airport is next to the M23 motorway, an hour or more from Central London, and there are bus services around-the-clock. Because of the distance from London, a cab isn't a realistic proposition for most travelers—it will cost you dearly.

Stansted Airport Stansted, northeast of London, is
linked by the **Stansted Express** train to Liverpool Street
Station. The trains run 5:30am–11pm weekdays and
6:30am–11pm on weekends; the ride takes about 40
minutes. Stansted is about an hour's drive from London on the M11 motorway.

Luton Airport Hopefully, you won't arrive at Luton,
north of the capital and near the M1 motorway; it has
very inconvenient bus and rail links to King's Cross.

London City Airport From the inner-city London
City Airport, take the **Shuttlebus** service. The red bus
connects with Liverpool Street and takes about 30 minutes; the yellow bus connects with Canary Wharf (the
Docklands Light Railway) and takes 10 minutes. There's
also a British Rail service, which hooks up with the
Central and District tube lines.

Opening & Closing Hours

Most shops are open Monday to Saturday 9am–6pm.
Many large city-center shops and supermarkets stay open
late on Wednesday or Thursday. Banks are open 9:30am–
3:30pm, with some branches open on Saturday mornings. Museums are usually open Monday to Saturday
10am–5pm and Sunday 2pm–5pm, and they're usually
open on minor holidays.

The big news is the recent liberalization of Sunday
trading laws. London is no longer a ghost town on Sundays; you'll now actually be able to find someplace to
eat and drink outside of your hotel, and some theaters
are now offering Sunday matinees.

Pubs are now open Monday to Saturday 11am–
11pm, and Sunday noon–10:30pm. Most bars close at
11pm, except those with late licenses or classified as
private clubs.

Special Passes

If you plan on visiting the major museums and art
galleries, you might want to get yourself a **White Card,**
a new pass that's available for periods of 3 or 7 days.
The pass, validated at the first venue you visit, offers
unlimited access for families or individuals to many of
London's best museums and galleries, such as the
Courtauld, the Design Museum, the Hayward Gallery,
and the Royal Academy of Arts. The White Card is
available from the Tourist Information Centre at Victoria
Station as well as from all London Transport Information Centres (see "Tourist Offices & Other Useful

Addresses & Numbers," below); prices range from £14 for the Individual Adult 3-day card to £50 for a Family 7-day card.

Public Holidays

You'll find most establishments closed on the following holidays: New Year's Day, January 1; Good Friday; Easter Monday; May Day (1st Mon in May); Spring Bank Holiday (last Mon in May); August Bank Holiday (last Mon in Aug); Christmas Day, December 25; and Boxing Day, December 26.

Time Zones

London time is Greenwich Mean Time (GMT) in winter and changes to European Summer Time (EST), 1 hour ahead of GMT, from the end of March to late October. In winter, this puts it 5 hours ahead of Eastern Standard Time and 6 to 8 hours ahead of other U.S. time zones; in summer, add another hour's difference.

Rest Rooms

With some exceptions, the public lavatories found in main streets (often in French-style, automated "superloos," which I'm terrified to use after hearing a rumor years ago about an unfortunate victim who was sanitized to death), parks, and tube stations can often be dirty and vandalized. You'll find well-maintained lavatories that can be used by anybody in all larger public buildings, such as museums and art galleries, large department stores, and railway stations. I am obligated to say that it is not acceptable to use the lavatories in hotels, restaurants, and pubs if you're not a customer, but I can't say that I always stick to this rule. Public lavatories are usually free of charge, but you may need a small coin to get in or to use a proper washroom.

Rush Hours

During the working week (Mon–Fri), the rush hours are approximately 8–9:30am and 5–7pm. Unlike some cities, London does not become totally choked, but traffic congestion is worsening. If your last visit to London was, say, 5 years ago, allow more time now than you did then for getting around at peak times.

Smoking

While Londoners don't smoke nearly as much as residents of Paris or Rome, London is still not a particularly friendly place for the nonsmoker. Most restaurants have nonsmoking tables, but they're usually separated from the smoking section by only a little bit of space. Nonsmoking rooms are available in the bigger hotels. While some of the smaller hotels claim that they have nonsmoking rooms, I've often found that this means that the room is smoke-free only during my visit; if you're bothered by the odor, ask to be shown another room.

Smoking is not allowed throughout the London transport system and in public buildings. Like any city where smoking rules have been introduced, you'll see many Londoners crowded around doorways during work hours for their "fag" break.

Telephones

Public telephones are found in booths on main streets and in post offices, hotels, pubs, stations, and in other public places. To make things confusing, there are 2 telephone services in the UK: **British Telecom (BT)** and **Mercury** (Mercury public telephones are being phased out). Some public telephones take coins, and the minimum charge is 10p; others take phonecards, which can be bought from post offices and shops displaying the phonecard sign (mostly news agents). Follow the instructions displayed by the telephone. You will be refunded any unused coins. The ringing tone is a repeated double trill; an intermittent shrill tone means that the line is busy.

If you need a number either inside or outside London, dial **Directory Inquiries** at 192. You can reach the **Local Operator** by dialing 100.

Area codes are not necessary for local calls but must be used when telephoning from outside the area. There are 2 area codes for London, one for inner London, **0171,** and another, **0181,** for outer London. All of the United Kingdom recently changed area codes; all old numbers with an area code that started with 0 now start with 01. This does not affect mobile phone numbers, toll free numbers, or information and entertainment lines.

Most international calls can be dialed direct (IDD) from public telephones. Dial 00 and then the country code. If you experience difficulty, call 155 to reach the **International Operator,** or 153 for **International Directory Inquiries.** You can reach the **AT&T operator** by dialing 0500/89-0011, thereby avoiding nasty hotel surcharges.

For the **police, ambulance services,** or the **fire department,** dial 999; if you need the exact **time,** call 123 (within London only); for **telemessages** and **international telegrams**, call 0800/190 190; for the **greater London weather forecast,** call 0891/ 505 301; for the **national forecast,** dial 0891/ 505 300.

Taxes

The **Value Added Tax (VAT),** levied on most purchases and on restaurant and hotel bills, is a hefty 17$^1/_2$%. You can request a VAT refund for purchases over £75; see "Shopping" for refund procedure.

Tipping

Tipping is customary in a few cases. A tip of 10% to 15% is usual in hotels, restaurants, and hair salons unless a service charge is already incorporated into the bill. Take care—very often a restaurant will add a service charge to the bill and then leave the service line on the credit card slip blank. If you're unsure whether or not a service charge has already been included, ask. Taxi drivers also expect 10% or 15% of the fare. You need only give small tips—50p to £1—to porters, doormen, and bellhops.

Tourist Offices & Other Useful Addresses & Numbers

London Tourist Board & Convention Bureau Information Centers

Victoria Station Forecourt, SW1, open Easter–Oct daily 8am–7pm; Nov–Easter Mon–Sat 8am–6pm, Sun 9am–4pm.

Heathrow Terminal 1,2,3 Underground Station Concourse, open daily 8:30am–6pm.

Heathrow Terminal 3 Arrivals Concourse, open daily 6am–11pm.

Liverpool Street Underground Station, EC2, open Mon 8:15am–7pm, Tues–Sat 8:15am–6pm, Sun 8:30am–4:45pm.

Waterloo International Terminal, Arrivals Hall, SE1, open Mon–Sun 8:30am–9pm.

Selfridges (basement), Oxford Street, W1, open daily 8:30am–7pm, Thurs to 8pm.

There are also tourist centers in **Greenwich** (☎ 0181/858-6376), **Islington** (☎0171/278-8787), and **Richmond** (☎ 0181/940-9125).

Travel & Transport Centers

American Express Travel Service, 6 Haymarket, SW1 (☎ 0171/930-4411), is a valuable source of information for any traveler in need of help, advice, or emergency services.

British Rail Travel Centre at 4–12 Regent St., SW1; for information, call 0171/928-5100.

British Tourist Authority and English Tourist Board, Thames Tower, Black's Road, W6 (☎ 0171/ 846-9000).

British Travel Centre, 12 Regent St., W1 (☎ 0181 846-9000).

London Transport Information Centre, 55 Broadway, SW1; 24-hour telephone service (☎ 0171/222-1234).

Travel Information Centres are located at the following stations:

Euston, Heathrow Central, King's Cross, Oxford Circus, Piccadilly Circus, Victoria, Hammersmith, Liverpool Street, St. James's Park.

Visitor's Hot Lines

London Tourist Bureau Accommodation Booking Line: Call in advance of your arrival to book with a credit card (☎ 0171/824-8844; fax 0171/259-9056). Open Mon–Fri 9:30am–5:30pm. A small reservation charge will be made. On-the-spot hotel reservations can be made at LTB centers at Victoria Station, Heathrow, Selfridges, and Liverpool station.

City of London Information Centre, St. Paul's Churchyard, EC4 (☎ 0171/332-1456).

Kidsline (☎ 0171/222-8070), open Mon–Fri 4pm–6pm, holidays 9am–4pm.

Visitorcall (☎ 0839/123 456) is operated by the London Tourist Board. It delivers recorded messages on specific subjects, such as what's on, places to visit, entertainment, and accommodations. Calls are charged at a higher rate than normal local calls.

On-Line Information Services

Time Out **(http://www.timeout.co.uk)** is the source for what's happening in London.

London Guide **(http://www.cs.ucl.ac.uk/misc/uk/ london.html)** is run by London's University College and has practical information for the traveler looking for cheap dining and accommodations in the Bloomsbury area close to the University. There are also travelogues and tips for the theatergoer.

Embassies & Consulates

Australia: Australia House, Strand, WC2 (☎ 0171/379-4334)

Canada: 1 Grosvenor St., W1 (☎ 0171/258-6600)

Ireland: 17 Grosvenor Place, SW1 (☎ 0171/235-2171)

Japan: 101-104 Piccadilly, W1 (☎ 0171/465-6500)

New Zealand: 80 Haymarket, SW1 (☎ 0171/930-8422)

United States: 24 Grosvenor Square, W1 (☎ 0171/499-9000)

Dental Emergencies

Dental Emergency Care Service (☎ 0171/937-3951) is available 24 hours.

The Royal Hospital, Whitechapel Road, E1, (☎ 0171/377-7000) is open for dental emergencies 7pm–11pm.

Hospitals with Casualty (Emergency) Departments

Charing Cross Hospital, Fulham Palace Road, W6 (☎ 0181/846-1234).

St. Thomas's Hospital, Lambeth Palace Road, SE1 (☎ 0171/928-9292).

St. Bartholomew's (Barts), West Smithfield, EC1 (☎ 0171/601-8888).

Chelsea & Westminster, Horseferry Road, SW1 (☎ 0181/746-8080).

Medical Express, 117a Harley St., W1 (☎ 0171/499-1991), is a private casualty clinic.

Emergency Services (From any telephone)

For **Police, Ambulance,** or **Fire,** dial 999. No coins are needed. The operator will ask which service you require.

Late-Night Chemists/Pharmacies

Every pharmacy has the late-night roster for its immediate area displayed in its window. For even later requirements, go to **Bliss,** 50 Willesden Lane, NW6 (☎ 0171/624-8000), and 5 Marble Arch, W1 (☎ 0171/723-6116); both branches are open 9am–midnight daily.

All-Night Service Stations

Fountain Garage, 83 Park Lane, W1 (☎ 0171/629-4151) is a good, centrally located 24-hour gas station.

Lost Traveler's Checks

Notify the local police at once, then follow the instructions provided with your travelers checks, or contact the issuing company's nearest office. Contact your consulate or **American Express** (☎ 0171/930-4411) if you are stranded with no money.

Lost Property

Report your loss to the police immediately (many insurance companies will not recognize claims without a police report). Special lost-property offices are located at:

British Rail, at main stations (see above).

Heathrow Airport Lost Property Office (☎ 0181/745-7727).

London Transport, 200 Baker St., NW1 (☎ 0171/486-2496); you'll get a recorded message telling you how to proceed.

Metropolitan Police Lost Property Office, 15 Penton St., NW1 (☎ 0171/833-0996).

Portraits
of London

AD 43: The invading Romans under Claudius defeated the Celtic tribes of Southeast Britain and bridged the Thames close to the site of the later London Bridge. By AD 60, London was a thriving port and at the center of the Roman road network.

410: With the dissolution of their empire, the Romans withdrew; London reverted to a farming town under the Angle and Saxon warrior kings.

700–820: London was an important provincial market town in the united England. Christianity was slowly reintroduced, stimulating learning.

836: The city was sacked by the Vikings; it remained a borderland pawn in their struggle with the western Saxon kingdoms for nearly 2 centuries.

1014: London was taken by storm for the last time; Olaf, an Anglo-Saxon, tied his boats to London Bridge and sailed downstream to destroy it, and thus isolated the Viking invaders (hence "London Bridge is Falling Down").

1052: Disgusted by London's switching of support to his enemies, King Edward the Confessor started to build a new abbey and palace named Westminster. The tension between the City and the Crown was born.

1066: The Norman invasion. William the Conqueror forced London into submission.

1066–1100: London accepted and thrived under the Norman rule. William built the fortified Tower of

London. Merchants prospered, and the City became a formidable counterweight to the Crown based at Westminster.

1215: The Charter of Incorporation confirmed the authority of the Lord Mayor.

1217: The first stone bridge over the Thames, London Bridge, was built.

1269: Henry III began the construction of the new Westminster Abbey.

1338: Edward III made Westminster the regular meeting place of Parliament.

1348: The Black Death, which killed half of the city's 60,000 population.

1381: The Peasants' Revolt. Seeking an end to feudalism, a working-class "army," led by Wat Tyler, took over London for 2 days. After his capture of the Tower of London, Tyler was killed by the Lord Mayor while attempting to parley with Richard II.

1500–1600: London's population exploded from 50,000 to 220,000 during the stable, booming Tudor years. New slum areas arose outside London.

1533: The Reformation: When Henry VIII divorced his first wife, Catherine of Aragon, in defiance of the Pope, England broke with the Catholic Church. The new gentry class snapped up land vacated by the dissolution of the monasteries.

1600–70: The new gentry, now an aristocracy, began to develop their new land, moving westward, building on the edge of the countryside in Piccadilly and Leicester Square.

1642–9: London financed Parliament in the Civil War. In 1649, London was the setting for Charles I's execution.

1649–60: The Commonwealth republic. London supported the restoration of Charles II in 1660.

1665–6: The Great Plague. In this last and worst outbreak, at least 100,000 died.

1666: The Great Fire. Medieval London was destroyed by fire.

1666–1700: Reconstruction with stone buildings and wider streets. Wren built 51 churches, culminating in St. Paul's. By 1700, 300,000 Londoners were widely dispersed.

1700–50: Both the new urban poor and the elite pushed up the population to 675,000. The villages of Knightsbridge and Marylebone were incorporated, and St. James's and Mayfair were developed. To the east and south were slums, where gin consumption averaged 2 pints per person per week and only 1 child in 4 lived beyond the age of 5.

1774: The City, still self-governing, elected the radical John Wilkes as Mayor after he was expelled from Parliament 3 times; it still distrusted the cultured West End and the almost omnipotent Parliament.

1780–1820: As urban pressures increased, the middle and upper classes began moving to the suburbs in the west.

1820–38: The Prince Regent, later George IV, and architect Nash developed Regent's Park and Regent Street, Buckingham Palace, and The Mall.

1835: Local councils were installed throughout Britain, except in London; it continued to be "governed" by more than 150 parishes, encompassing 300 administrative bodies.

1839: The new Palace of Westminster (the present one) was started.

1832–66: Cholera killed thousands. An underground sewer system and the embankment along the Thames were built. The clearance of land for railways worsened citywide destitution.

1851: The Great Exhibition in Hyde Park celebrated British supremacy in trade, science, and industry. Britain's lead was consolidated by Prince Albert's development of the museums and learned institutions of South Kensington.

1863: Railways opened to the working class for the first time. The first underground line opened. Increased mobility and public health and education measures improved Londoners' quality of life.

1889: The London County Council (LCC) was formed, giving London comprehensive local government for the first time.

1897: Queen Victoria's Diamond Jubilee. London was described as the "centre of an empire on which the sun never sets."

1900–5: Four new electric underground lines rapidly expanded the city into sprawling suburbs.

1920–30: Vast new housing estates, funded in part by the "Homes for Heroes" program, quadrupled the size of London.

1940: The Blitz. London was bombed, mainly in the City and East End. St. Paul's stood alone amid the rubble. The city's staunch resistance in the face of destruction is often remembered as London's "finest hour."

1945–55: Private and local government redevelopment resulted in its fast modernization.

1951: The Festival of Britain celebrated the centennial of the Great Exhibition and gave birth to the South Bank Arts Centre.

1955–65: Boom years for property developers, who erected skyscrapers, while the LCC concentrated on suburban housing. The population of Central London stood at its lowest. Mass immigration from the Caribbean, India, Pakistan, and Hong Kong began. In 1956, the Clean Air Act marked the end of central London as an industrial area.

1960–70: "Swinging London." An economic boom, immigration, and changing values and wealth patterns made London more cosmopolitan. In 1965, the Greater London Council succeeded the LCC.

1986: The Labour GLC was abolished by the Thatcher-led Conservative government, leaving London without a central governing body.

1992: Britain joined the European Single Market. Deep recession signaled the end of the booming 1980s and the start of a more sober decade. New building slowed; house prices tumbled.

1994: The Irish Republican Army (IRA) announced a complete cessation of military operations. The Chunnel Tunnel, the 1st rail link between London and the continent, opened.

1995: The National Lottery instituted; it's a windfall for charities and the arts.

1996: The IRA breaks a 17-month cease-fire with a truck bomb at Docklands that claims 2 lives.

The Architecture of London

London wasn't the grand vision of an emperor or king; there has been no Haussmann or Olmsted. The city that is London today was conceived by various waves of building speculators at the behest of aristocratic land-owners. As such, panoramic skyline views are rare; but even the most jaded preservationist would not fail to be impressed by the pervasive grandeur that derives from the city's blending of a rich heritage of fine buildings and history into the everyday life of a bustling city.

Although the Prince of Wales' outspoken criticism of modern architecture in the capital has infuriated contemporary architects, it has succeeded in focusing attention on the subject of preservation and accelerating the trend away from the brutalism of the 1960s and 1970s. Curves have replaced hard lines, steel, glass, and brick have replaced concrete, and architects are employing classical motifs—pediments, porticoes, columns, moldings—within the context of modern architecture.

The ongoing conflict between the modernists and the traditionalists—in which the traditionalists have the lead—has forced many talented architects, such as Nigel Coates, Norman Foster, Richard Rogers, and Zaha Hadid, to search for commissions abroad. The future looks bright, though. With the conception of the Millennium project, a grand scheme of commissions to be financed in part by the National Lottery, London's brightest architects are drafting plans in anticipation of a wave of public and private construction. Designs on the drawing board include plans to reconfigure the **British Museum** with a covered public square, a renovation of the Bankside Power station on the south bank into the **Tate's** new Museum of Modern Art, a reconfiguring of the area around **Royal Albert Hall** (dubbed "Albertopolis"), a rethink of the drab **South Bank Arts Centre** (Richard Rogers has come up with plans for a "crystal palace"), and the construction of a new 500-seat auditorium adjacent to the **Royal Opera House** in Covent Garden. The controversy surrounding many of these projects is already being played out in the press. Who knows—contemporary London might finally have the chance to display some stylistic imagination.

London's Architecture Through the Ages

London is a microcosm of the succession of architectural styles that have adorned Britain since Norman times, as the original Roman settlement has been overlaid by subsequent building. It's still blessed, however, with the stones and mortar of its Roman founders in the remnants of the 2ndC city wall, particularly near the Barbican.

The Norman Period (1066–1200)   The Normans built sturdy buildings based on mass and volume. Massive round piers, round arches (often with "dog-tooth" or chevron ornament), and plain barrel vaulting were common. Defense was still the vital consideration when the huge, square **White Tower** (in the **Tower of London**), one of Europe's finest surviving examples of a Norman keep, was built in 1078.

From Gothic (1180–1540) to Tudor (1540–1603)   Gothic buildings are lighter, more dynamic structures, often with flying buttresses, crockets (carved ornaments in the form of a curled leaf), pointed arches and windows, and spires. Galleries and arcades replaced internal walls. The main periods of the Gothic age are **Early English (1180–1260),** marked by simplicity and airiness; **Decorated (1250–1370),** using more extensive surface decoration and window tracery with the advent of stained glass; and **Perpendicular (1300–1540),** with long slender columns stressing vertical lines, elaborate fan-vaulting, and paneled windows. **Westminster Abbey,** begun in 1245, is London's finest remaining medieval building, with the abbey's east arm epitomizing the elegant Early English style, and the later nave built in the Perpendicular style. Timber roofing, one of the glories of the English Gothic, survives in the hammerbeam roof of **Westminster Hall,** in the Great Hall of **Hampton Court** (1536), and also in **St. James's Palace.**

The influence of the Italian Renaissance is apparent in Tudor-age decoration, especially in plasterwork and carved gables. This is when red brick came into extensive use, often on geometrical **"E"** and **"H"** plans augmented with flat, pointed arches and large mullioned windows with leaded glass in lozenge patterns. **St. James's Palace** is a superb red-brick example of the ornate Tudor adaptations of Gothic building.

Jacobean (1603–25)   This brief period is notable for its greater extravagance in wood and plaster decoration, its dark oak-paneled interiors, and the wider use of Italian motifs—more for their manner than their meaning—in both building and furniture.

From Classical (1615–66) to English Baroque (1690–1720)   Inigo Jones, born in 1573 in Smithfield, brought to London the vigor and sophistication of Italian Renaissance styles—most notably the elegant symmetry of Andrea Palladio—with extraordinary sureness and originality. Jones' particular contribution to the building of London was the development of **Covent**

Garden, especially the **Piazza** (1631–39), and the first 2 Palladian buildings in London, the **Banqueting House** (1619–22) in Whitehall, based on a double cube, and the delightful **Queen's House** in Greenwich.

After the Great Fire of 1666, Sir Christopher Wren (1632–1723), perhaps Britain's greatest architect, and Nicholas Hawksmoor returned to classical simplicity and developed it into a dignified, sophisticated English Baroque, in which fluidity and elaboration of Continental Baroque are tempered by English moderation. Classical pediments over niches, doors, windows, and facades, with an emphasis on symmetry, as well as heroic monuments, like that of Nelson in St. Paul's, are keynotes of the style.

An Oxford-educated scientist and later Surveyor of the King's Works, Wren was entrusted with the rebuilding of the City after the fire. He designed a staggering number of London's greatest buildings. He designed church towers and steeples to lead the eye to the dome of **St. Paul's Cathedral.** In his buildings, Wren used elements of the classical Renaissance style, but was obliged to adapt its geometrical grandeur and piazzas to the framework of the medieval city's alleys and courtyards. Wren's master-carver, **Grinling Gibbons** (1648–1721), decorated many of the great architect's outstanding buildings with incomparably naturalistic flowers, leaves, fruits, and musical instruments—all sculpted in wood or stone with Baroque exuberance. The greatest profusion can be seen at **St. Paul's** or **Hampton Court.** Wren's secular buildings include the **Royal Naval Hospital** in Greenwich (1696–1702), and the **Royal Hospital** in Chelsea (1681–91). **St. James's Palace** also testifies to his genius.

Wren's assistant **Nicholas Hawksmoor** designed several churches that are increasingly appreciated; a fine example is **St. Mary Woolnoth** (1716–24). Wren also influenced **Sir James Gibbs** (1682–1754), a leader of the English Baroque. Continuing where Wren had left off, this Scottish architect introduced some of the more theatrical elements of the Italian Baroque to London church building. Excellent examples can be seen at **St. Mary-le-Strand** and **St. Martin-in-the-Fields.**

The Georgian Period (1720–1820)   Fashion swung away from Baroque and back to the rules and conventions of classical architecture, with Italianate buildings, columns, and porticoes, often quite plain, combined with the new art of landscape gardening. Classical elements persist, based on Greek orders of Doric, Ionic, and Corinthian, but on a more domestic scale. This move is typified by the Palladian **Chiswick House** (1725–29), which also has a garden landscaped by **William Kent.** The same notions of refinement and good taste were evident in the terraces built at this time. The dominant designer was **Robert Adam** (1728–92), whose terraced town-houses were unified by an elegant facade.

The Regency Years (1780–1820)   Georgian style developed into a more lighthearted style owing much to rococo, with delicate interior ornament and often panels of stucco relief. Architect **John Nash** (1752–1835) gave a sense of shape and elegance to the heart of modern London. Seen from **Piccadilly Circus,** the bold, sweeping curve of **Regent Street** echoes Nash's plan for a triumphal "Royal Mile" from the Prince Regent's residence at **Carlton House** to **Regent's Park.** At either end are 2 pristine examples of Nash's work: **Carlton House Terrace** (1827–32) and **Park Crescent** (1812–22). His original design for **Buckingham Palace** was partly concealed by later additions, and the surviving west wing, overlooking the palace garden, remains hidden from outside view. Nash's elegant terraces and crescents were mirrored in the development of Belgravia and Chelsea in the 1820s and 1830s, largely by **Thomas Cubitt.**

The Victorian Age (1830–1900)   The sterner values of the Victorian period were reflected in extravagant neo-Gothic structures, with heavily ornamented facades to public buildings. The **Houses of Parliament** (1840–50), designed by **Sir Charles Barry** and **Augustus Pugin,** are emblematic of the style. This Gothic Revival architecture had moments of fantasy, as the spires and complex details of **St. Pancras Station** (1868–74) happily demonstrate.

The railway era also brought some breathtaking examples of civil engineering; the interior of **Paddington Station** (1850–54) is the best remaining of these. Similarly inspired use of cast iron and sheet glass is seen in the magnificent conservatorium at **Kew Gardens** (1844–8).

The Edwardian Age (1905–1920)   This style—notable for the direct simplicity in its domestic buildings and honest use of brick, stone, and wood—is rather plainer than Victorian, but reflects the stability and wealth of Empire (at its height before the Great War) in its soundness. Elements of Art Nouveau were introduced from the Glasgow and Viennese schools.

Between the Wars   The 20thC has produced some of London's least attractive architecture. But the passing of time is leading to a greater appreciation of surviving industrial buildings from the 1910s to the 1930s, such as the Art Nouveau–influenced **Michelin building** (1910) on the Fulham Road, the art deco **Hoover factory** (1932) on Western Avenue, and the now sadly abandoned **Battersea Power Station** (1932–4). Bauhaus refugees founded the design group **Tecton,** which designed Highgate's **Highpoint Flats** (1936), described by Le Corbusier as "a vertical garden city."

Modernism (1930–present) and Postmodernism (1970–present)   The influence of Bauhaus, based on rationalism and function, came into play in modern building. Ornamentation gave way to airy interiors with glass facades, often on green squares, and an imaginative use of new materials, such as aluminum, stainless steel, and plastics. The postwar age also saw a rise in brutalism in concrete, with an accent on basic sculptural form—often at the expense of human considerations.

Postmodernism is more eclectic and hi-tech, with neoclassical elements as well as extensive use of reflecting-glass facades, sometimes with emphasis on engineering features. Uninhibited use of color and materials makes this a highly pictorial style. In corporate projects, the building is the message—a sort of 3-dimensional logo.

Notable postwar buildings, all of which have provoked controversy, are Oxford Street's dominant **Centrepoint** (1965), which became a symbol of profligate speculation, the **National Theatre** (1967–77), in the cold, horizontal style of the South Bank complex, and **Richard Rogers's** vast glass and tubular steel **Lloyd's Building** (1986). Rogers (b. 1933) is an innovative contemporary architect who was commissioned to do the controversial Lloyd's building after winning acclaim for his Pompidou Center in Paris. His recent work includes the restoration and conversion of the **Channel 4 Headquarters,** completed in 1994, and Billingsgate Market. In addition to Rogers's projects, recent attention has focused on the Broadgate complex of shops and offices in the City; the 800-foot tower at **Canary Wharf,** Docklands (**Cesar Pelli**); the **Sainsbury Wing** at the National Gallery, designed by American husband-and-wife team **Robert Venturi** and **Denise Scott-Brown,** of which the interior, at least, has been greeted by universal acclaim; and **Waterloo**

Terminal, a glass serpentine by **Nicholas Grimshaw** built in 1993.

Royal London

Where to begin? As it stands now, Diana and Charles are separated, and Diana has agreed to a very profitable divorce—around £18 million, provided she moves out of Kensington Palace and gives up the right to be called "Her Royal Highness." Charles has admitted adultery on national television, and, it has been reported, enjoys talking to plants. Even more bizarre, when he's not managing his network of charities, he purportedly wishes to be Camilla Parker-Bowles's tampon. Diana has admitted adultery on TV, too, but she still manages to be a much more sympathetic figure than her husband. She suffers from bulimia and depression, and, when her head is not "down the loo," makes stunning entrances in designer outfits at some of London's most fashionable cultural events. *Princess in Love,* the unauthorized account of Diana's love affair with James Hewitt, made struggling journalist Anna Pasternak a best-selling author. The heir to the throne, William, has just passed his examinations and is enrolled at Eton, preparing to follow in his father's footsteps (but not too closely, we hope).

Prince Andrew and Sarah Ferguson beat Charles and Di to divorce court. It would be too simple to blame the American tycoon, John Bryan, who was photographed sucking the Duchess's toes. To counteract the negative image, Fergie recently appeared in *Hello* looking very chaste and proper.

The Queen's only daughter, Princess Anne, has fared no better. She ditched her mate, Captain Mark Phillips, in 1992. That leaves Charles's youngest brother, Prince Edward, who is on the verge of marrying Sophie Rhys-Jones. Many liken her to a middle-class Diana. Not to worry, she's learning fast; if she does take on the Windsor name, Sophie's sure to keep the tabloids happy.

The past few years, to say the least, have not been easy ones for the Queen. She openly declared 1992—the year some of the most salacious details of the younger royals' personal lives hit the tabloids, and Windsor Castle suffered a terrible fire—an "annus horribilis." Most likely in order to salvage the last remaining shreds of public support for the monarchy, she recently opened up Buckingham Palace for 2 months of the year; it's the first time in the monarchy's history that common feet have traipsed through the royal abode. What's more, the Queen has now agreed to pay income tax.

Some might argue that this all started with Edward VIII and that nasty affair with the American divorcée Wallis Simpson, but the royal family has dodged scandal for centuries. The monarchy was replaced by the Commonwealth from 1649 to 1660, when Charles I attempted to gain control over the Puritan parliament. Not long afterward, with the arrival of the German house of Hanover, confidence waned again. The Hanovers were a particularly corrupt crowd, prone to excesses and insanity—George I spoke no English, and George III was a loon who eventually completely lost his mind. His successor, George IV, wasn't much better. His marriage to Caroline was a bad match from the beginning; they parted ways early on, and she didn't reappear until he took the throne—at which point she was keen to participate. The scandal that ensued pitted the Tory Party, who supported George (casting Caroline as woman scorned) against the Whigs, who saw her as a wronged woman whose case had merit. In the end, the issue was dropped, but not before events escalated to the brink of a full-scale constitutional crisis. Things didn't improve much with Queen Victoria, the last Hanoverian, when she withdrew from public life after the death of her husband Albert in 1861; but by this point, parliamentary democracy was well ensconced and the royals were looking for ways to occupy their days.

At the time of the Prince of Wales's wedding in 1981, *The Times* conceded that the Queen has "almost no executive function to perform," but concluded that she has "a 'presence' in the highest reaches of the political process." Before a general election can take place, the Queen must dissolve Parliament. After the contest, she appoints as Prime Minister the leader of the victorious party and invites him or her to form a government.

The kingdom is not, of course, just England—otherwise the Queen's husband and her son and heir would not be Duke of Edinburgh and Prince of Wales. The Queen is also official head of state of many countries united in the Commonwealth of Nations, including Australia and Canada. But arguably the most important job of the monarchy is to represent the family of nations that together, and by consent, compose the United Kingdom. Because they have smaller populations, Scotland and Wales are represented in Parliament in smaller numbers than England is, but they are equal in the view of the Crown. In countries of less age, national unity can be an objective in itself. But Britain, being neither young nor 1 nation, needs some means to articulate its wholeness; that unity is embodied in the Queen.

For the visitor from other parts of the realm, the rituals, pageantry, and palaces of royal London are the tangible demonstration of a heritage. The monarchy has had its low points, of course, but, despite further tremors caused by revelations, true or otherwise, about the less-than-perfect younger royals, most Britons still regard the monarchy as the keystone of the State.

Where to See the Royal Family

The daily Court Circular, which gives details of all the Royal Family's public engagements, is printed in *The Times,* the *Daily Telegraph,* and the *Independent.* The Queen also presides over certain annual events, often accompanied by other family members; call the London Tourist Board's **Information Line** (☎ 0839/123-143) for exact dates and times.

The State Opening of Parliament, at the beginning of each new session of Parliament (usually late Oct or early Nov), is the most apparently political of the Queen's regular duties, in that she announces in her speech a program of proposed legislation. In fact, the measures outlined are put forward not at the discretion of the Queen but on behalf of her government. Thousands line the route between Buckingham Palace and Westminster, but the ceremony itself is not open to the public.

Remembrance Sunday, on the Sunday nearest November 11, sees the Queen placing wreaths on the Cenotaph in Whitehall to commemorate the dead of World Wars I and II.

Imperial State Crown

Trooping the Colour takes place on the 2nd Saturday in June to honor the Queen's official birthday. Each year, a different Guards regiment presents itself for inspection; the "colour" is its regimental flag. The Queen rides in a landau to Horse Guards Parade, off Whitehall, receives the salute amid marching bands, and often makes an appearance on the balcony of Buckingham Palace upon her return. Many spectators follow the procession. Tickets are available for seats and can be obtained by writing to the Public Information Office, Household Division, Horse Guards, Whitehall, London SW1A 2AX.

Royal Residences

Buckingham Palace didn't become the principal royal residence until the time of Queen Victoria (1836–1902), even though monarchs had used it since George III bought it in 1762. The palace is in every sense the center, home, and headquarters of the British monarchy.

Before Victoria, **St. James's Palace,** built for Henry VIII (1509–47), was the sovereign's official residence. Its status is still honored in the accreditation of foreign diplomats to "the Court of St. James," and it's the headquarters of the Gentlemen at Arms, who form a personal bodyguard for the Queen, as well as the Yeomen of the Guard. These, rather than the Tower Yeomen, are the true "Beefeaters" (a word probably derived from "buffetier," meaning an attendant at royal buffets). St. James's Palace also includes **Clarence House,** home of the dowager Queen Elizabeth, the Queen Mother, one of the most dearly loved members of the Royal Family.

Kensington Palace was acquired as a home by William III, who wanted a place in the country around London. It's now the London home of the Princess of Wales, the Queen's sister Princess Margaret, and other royals including Princess Di (for now, at least). Originally the home of Edward the Confessor (1042–66), **Windsor Castle,** just outside of London, is still used extensively as a country home by the Royal Family.

Customs & Etiquette

General rules of etiquette and common courtesy will be sufficient to get you through most situations. If in doubt, err on the side of the formal. Of course, there's a special code of conduct that applies to Royalty concerning when to curtsy, correct forms of address, etc., but chances are the closest you'll come to some royal blood is a glimpse of a waving gloved hand. If you do indeed have the opportunity to rub shoulders with the Windsors, a tight skirt or jeans is obviously not a good idea.

Otherwise, London is pretty laid-back dresswise. The Glyndebourne attendee would do well to sport evening dress, but you won't need your formal wear for most occasions. Jackets and ties are only required at the stuffiest restaurants. The theater is quite a democratic place as well these days; no need to panic over proper attire.

The British can come across a bit frosty. Unlike America, a first-name basis is not encouraged amongst strangers—"Hi, I'm Bill and I'll be your waiter tonight" is not done here. If someone is introduced to you as James, do not assume they're a Jim. In business, most people will refer to you using a proper title, Mr. or Sir for men, Miss, Mrs., or Madame for women (Ms. is still very much considered an aberration—though it is achieving a slight degree of acceptance and is tolerated among Americans). The double-barreled kiss has crept over from the continent; if you've spent a boozy evening at a dinner party, you'll probably be brushing cheeks when you say your farewells (though more recently it's been reduced to a "mwah mwah" sound that avoids all physical contact). Do bring a small gift if invited to dinner, and a thank-you phone call or note is pretty much the norm—but your mother should have taught you that anyway.

The British custom of "queuing" is in marked contrast to the French mad dash. Londoners line up for everything—including the bus. It's important that you wait your turn.

Don't even try to fake the accent (the most upper upper example manifesting itself in the speech of Sir John Gielgud); chances are you'll be found out, or worse—you might be mistaken for an aspiring extra in a Noël Coward play.

In general, certain topics of conversation are considered off-limits, with money being the big no-no. Wealth, the British like to pretend, is more influential in the United States and other corrupt foreign countries. Discussions of monetary matters are considered in bad taste (unless, of course, you're a Lloyd's Name). While money is off-limits, sex is okay—hey, even Prince Charles admitted to adultery on national television. Lavatory humor gets a big laugh here—perhaps it's a holdover from "public-school" days. Lavatory subjects in general are okay; I can't tell you the number of dinner parties I have attended where the conversation has dwelled upon the benefits of colonic irrigation (Princess Di is said to be a convert). And, of course, discussions of the weather will always be welcome.

While some may have you think that Britain is moving toward a classless society, don't believe it—there's a hidden code of behavior that keeps everyone in their proper place. While certainly more fluid than it was in the past, the class system in London is very much alive and kicking. People in this country are prone to decoding their friends and acquaintances in terms of the way they speak, how they hold their knife and fork, their breed of dog, the make of their car, how they dress, and the daily paper they read (while no one admits to reading *The Sun,* they all do). Then there's the postal code—whether yours is Notting Hill's W11 or Chelsea's SW3 has much to say about you. It's a complex and unspoken map of class that takes years to learn. The well-bred say sofa, not couch; one retires to the drawing room, never the lounge.

As the English and Americans share the same language (though some might argue only barely), the opportunity for miscommunications and social gaffes is usually at a minimum. If indeed offense does occur, groveling is always a good tactic. A little humble pie will go a long way. As we all know, many prominent British public figures (Hugh Grant comes immediately to mind) have certainly found it effective.

INDEX

LONDON

1-2 Kensington/Hyde Park
3-13 London Street Atlas
14 London Environs
15 London Underground

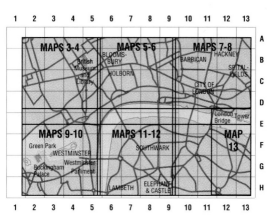

KEY TO MAP SYMBOLS

City Maps

	Major Place of Interest	P	Parking
	Park	M	Metro
	Built-up Area	—	Railroad
	Divided highway	←	One way street
	Primary road	i	Information
	Secondary road	7	Adjoining Page No.
	Other road		

Area Maps

ROADS
Freeway
Tollway
Road under construction
Other divided highway
Primary road
Secondary road
Other road

CITY
London
Other City
■ Point of Interest

0   1   2 miles
0   1   2 Kilometers

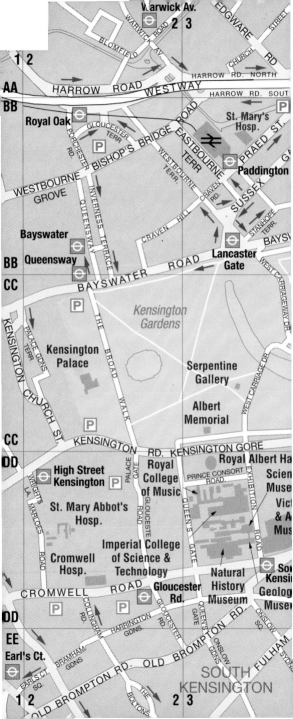

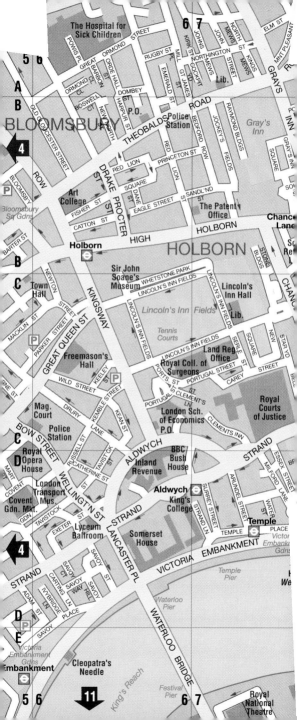

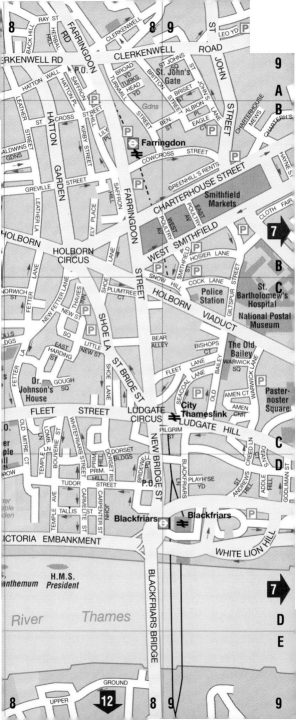

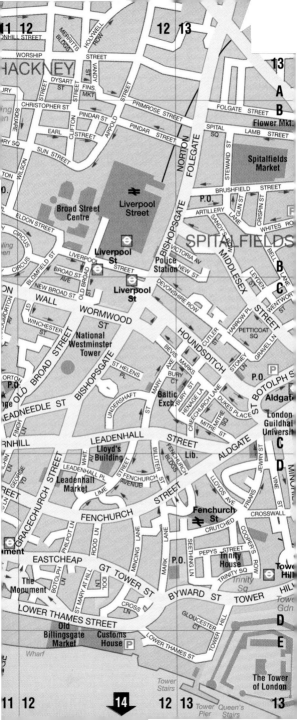

11 12

ONHILL STREET

WORSHIP

HOLWELL ROW

MERRITTS BLDGS

12 13

13

A

B

FOLGATE STREET

HACKNEY

DYSART ST

FINS. MKT.

VANDY

Flower Mkt.

CHRISTOPHER ST

PINDAR ST

APPOLD

PRIMROSE STREET

SPITAL SQ

LAMB STREET

STEWARD ST

Spitalfields Market

EARL

CLIFTON STREET

PINDAR STREET

FOLGATE

SUN STREET

WILSON

NORTON

BRUSHFIELD STREET

P.O.

ELDON STREET

CIRCUS

CIRCUS

Broad Street Centre

Liverpool Street

ARTILLERY

GUN ST

GANDY ST

CRISPIN ST

WHITES RO

F

BISHOPSGATE

SPITALFIELDS

Liverpool St

VICTORIA AV

MIDDLESEX

BELL

LANE

B

BLOMFIELD ST

BROAD ST AVE

OLD BROAD ST

LIVERPOOL STREET

Police Station

NEW ST

LEYDEN

WENTWOR

STREET

NEW BROAD ST

Liverpool St

DEVONSHIRE ROW

C

WALL

WORMWOOD ST

WINCHESTER

HOUNDSDITCH

CUTLER

HARROW PL

PETTICOAT SQ

GRAVEL LN

National Westminster Tower

BISHOPSGATE

BEVIS

MARKS

ST HELENS PL

BURY ST

STONEY

P.O.

P

MORTON

OLD BROAD STREET

UNDERSHAFT

ST

MARY

Baltic Exch

HENAGE LA

CREECHURCH LANE

DUKES PLACE

ST BOTOLPH S

Aldgat

P.O.

THREADNEEDLE ST

FINCH

Lloyd's Building

MITRE ST

MITRE SQ

ALDGATE

London Guildhal Universi

C

ORNHILL

LEADENHALL STREET

Lib.

BISHOPSGATE

LEADENHALL PL

WHIT

ST

FENCHURCH BLDGS

BILLITER

D

JEWRY ST

VINE ST

MINOR

GEORGE YD

Leadenhall Market

LIME

FENCHURCH AVENUE

STREET

LLOYDS AVE

FRIARS

STREET

GRACECHURCH STREET

FENCHURCH

STREET

Fenchurch St

CROSSWALL

PHILPOT LN

ROOD LN

MINCING LANE

MARK LANE

CRUTCHED

COOPER'S ROW

ment

EASTCHEAP

BOTOLPH LN

ST MARY AT HILL

IDOL LN

PEPYS STREET

P.O.

Trinity House

Trinity Sq

Tower Hill

The Monument

GT TOWER ST

SEETHING LN

TRINITY SQ

TOWER

HILL

LOWER THAMES STREET

BYWARD ST

CROSS LN

GLOUCESTER CT

Tower Gdn

D

Old Billingsgate Market

Customs House

P

TOWER HILL

LOWER THAMES ST

E

Wharf

Tower Stairs

The Tower of London

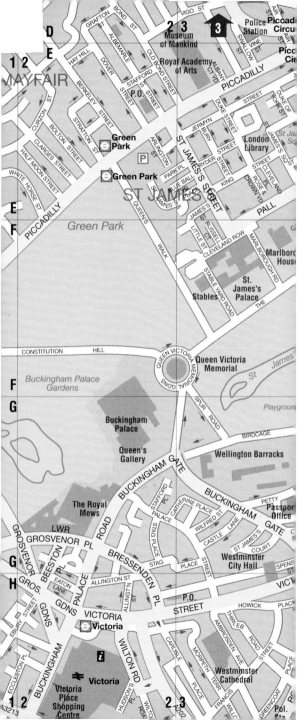

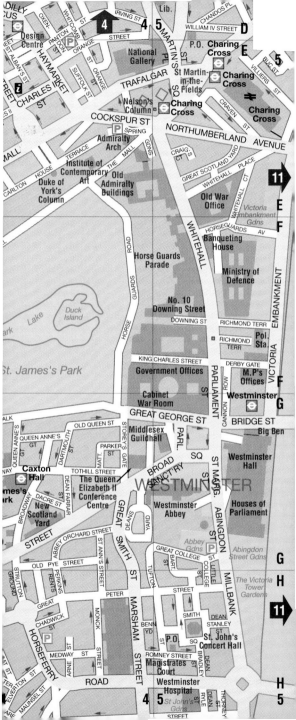

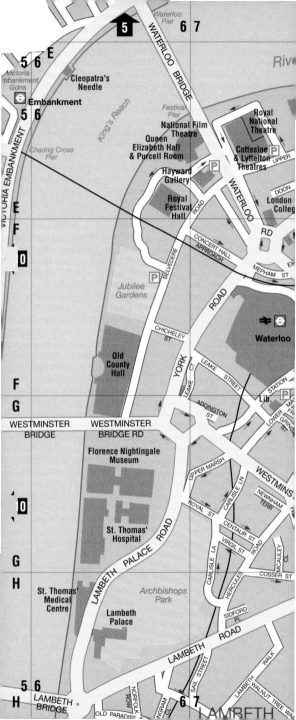

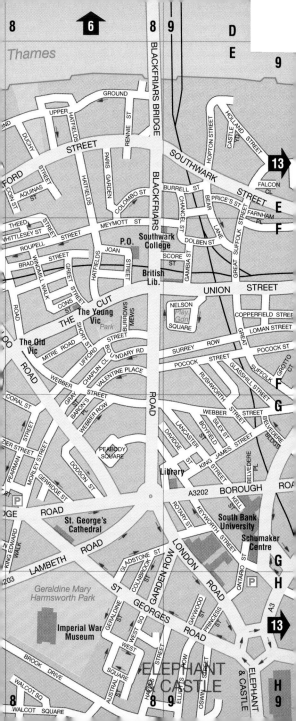

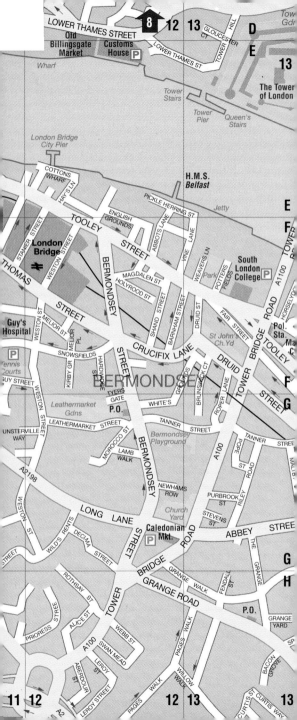

Old Billingsgate Market
Customs House P
LOWER THAMES ST
GLOUCESTER CT
TOWER HILL
Tower Gdn

Wharf

Tower Stairs
Tower Pier
Queen's Stairs

The Tower of London

London Bridge City Pier

COTTONS WHARF
HAY'S LN

H.M.S. Belfast
E
F

TOOLEY STREET
ENGLISH GROUNDS
PICKLE HERRING ST
Jetty

STAINER STREET
WESTON STREET
ABBOTS LANE
VINE LANE
WEAVERS LN

London Bridge

BERMONDSEY STREET
MAGDALEN ST
HOLYROOD ST
SHAND STREET
BARNHAM STREET
DRUID ST
PARK
POTTERS FIELDS
South London College P
TOWER BRIDGE ROAD
A1100
HORSELYD

THOMAS STREET

Guy's Hospital P
Tennis Courts
GUY STREET
WESTON ST
MELIOR ST
MELIOR PL
SNOWSFIELDS
KIRBY GR
HARDWIDGE ST
CRUCIFIX LANE
GROOMS
FAIR STREET
St John's Ch.Yd
BRUNSWICK CT
ROPER LANE
DRUID ST
TOOLEY STREET
Pol. Sta. Ma C
F
G

BERMONDSEY
TYERS GATE
P.O.
WHITE'S
TANNER STREET

UNSTERVILLE WAY
WESTON STREET
Leathermarket Gdns
LEATHERMARKET STREET
BERMONDSEY STREET
MORGANCO ST
MOROCCO ST
LAMB WALK
Bermondsey Playground
A100
POPE ST
RILEY ROAD
TANNER STREE
MALB

A2198
LONG LANE
WESTON ST
WILD'S RENTS
DECIMA STREET
NEWHAMS ROW
Church Yard
PURBROOK ST
STEVENS ST
ABBEY STREE
THE GRANGE
G
H

Caledonian Mkt. P
TOWER BRIDGE ROAD
GRANGE ROAD
GRANGE WALK
FENDALL ST
P.O.
GRANGE YARD

ROTHSAY ST
PRIORESS STREE
ALICE ST
A100
ABERDOUR ST
LEROY STREET
WEBB ST
SWAN MEAD
LEROY ST
PAGES WALK
WILLOW WALK
BACON GROVE
CURTIS ST
CURTIS WAY
SP

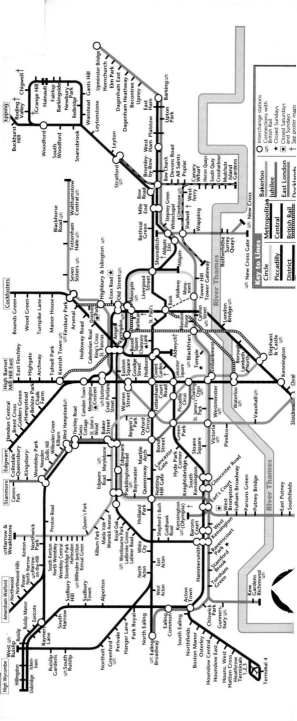